CHILDREN OF CHEMICALLY DEPENDENT PARENTS

Multiperspectives from the Cutting Edge

Edited by

Timothy M. Rivinus, M.D.

BRUNNER/MAZEL Publishers • New York

Library of Congress Cataloging-in-Publication Data
Children of chemically dependent parents : multiperspectives from the
cutting edge / edited by Timothy M. Rivinus.
        p.   cm.
    Includes bibliographical references and index.
    ISBN 0-87630-595-8 :
    1. Children of alcoholics—Mental helath.   2. Children of narcotic
addicts—Mental health.   3. Adult children of alcoholics—Mental
health.   4. Adult children of narcotic addicts—Mental health.
I. Rivinus, Timothy M.
    [DNLM: 1. Child of Impaired Parents.   2. Substance Dependence.
WM 270 C5368]
RJ507.A42C49   1990
362.29′13—dc20
DNLM/DLC
for Library of Congress   90-15181
                                                                    CIP

Published by
BRUNNER/MAZEL, Inc.
19 Union Square West
New York, New York 10003

Designed by Tere LoPrete

Manufactured in the United States of America

10   9   8   7   6   5   4   3   2   1

Contents

Contributors

Dorothy M. Bianco, Ph.D., Department of Psychology, Rhode Island College, Providence, Rhode Island

Sheila B. Blume, M.D., Medical Director, Alcoholism, Chemical Dependency and Compulsive Gambling Programs, South Oaks Hospital, Amityville, Long Island; Clinical Professor of Psychiatry, State University of New York at Stony Brook, New York

Stephanie Brown, Ph.D., Director, The Addictions Institute, Menlo Park, California; Research Associate, Mental Research Institute, Palo Alto, California

Timmen Cermak, M.D., Clinical Director, Genesis Psychotherapy and Training Center; Assistant Clinical Professor, U.C. Medical Center, Department of Psychiatry, San Francisco, California

Michele Clark, L.C.S.W., Co-Director Alcoholism Program, Women's Mental Health Collective, Somerville, Massachusetts

Robert L. DuPont, M.D., President, Institute for Behavior and Health, Inc., Rockville, Maryland; Clinical Professor of Psychiatry, Georgetown University School of Medicine, Washington, DC

Noel Jette, L.I.C.S.W., Co-Director Alcoholism Program, Women's Mental Health Collective, Somerville, Massachusetts

Jeannette L. Johnson, Ph.D., University of Maryland School of Medicine, Department of Psychiatry, Division of Alcohol and Drug Abuse, Drug Treatment Center, Baltimore, Maryland

David Levoy, M.D., Assistant Director, Child Assessment Unit, Department of Child Psychiatry, Cambridge Hospital, Massachusetts

Michael R. Liepman, M.D., Director, Project APT and Assistant Professor of

Psychiatry, University of Massachusetts Medical School; Chief, Chemical Dependency Service, Department of Psychiatry, The Med Center—Memorial, Worcester, Massachusetts

Mary Ellin Logue, Ed.D., Research Associate, RMC Research Corp., Hampton, New Hampshire

Helga M. Matzko, M.A., C.A.G.S., Private Practice, Cranston, Rhode Island

Marilyn Matzko, A.C.S.W., Clinical Social Worker, Bradley Hospital, East Providence, Rhode Island

John P. McGovern, M.D., Sc.D., LL.D., Clinical Professor of Pediatrics and Microbiology, Baylor College of Medicine, Houston, Texas; Adjunct Professor, Institute for the Medical Humanities, University of Texas Medical Branch, Galvaston, Texas

James McGuire, M.D., Clinical Assistant Professor, Department of Psychiatry and Human Behavior, Brown University Program in Medicine; Attending Psychiatrist, Children's Inpatient Unit, Bradley Hospital, East Providence, Rhode Island

Thomas W. Perrin, M.A., Alcoholism Consultant and Family Alcoholism Counselor, Rutherford, New Jersey

Timothy M. Rivinus, M.D., Director, Substance Abuse Treatment and Research, Butler Hospital, Associate Professor of Psychiatry and Human Behavior, Brown University Program in Medicine, Providence, Rhode Island

Loretta Young Silvia, Ph.D., CADAC Assistant Professor of Psychiatry and Behavioral Medicine, Bowman Gray School of Medicine, Wake Forest University, Winston-Salem, North Carolina

David C. Treadway, Ph.D., Co-Director, The Extern Family Therapy Program, Weston, Massachusetts

Susan D. Wallace, Executive Director, Caritas House, Pawtucket, Rhode Island

Migs Woodside, President, Children of Alcoholics Foundation, Inc., New York, New York

Foreword

In 1969, Toronto's Addiction Research Foundation published a book by R. Margaret Cork, a senior social worker at the foundation, which she called *The Forgotten Children*. It was a study of 116 children whose parents suffered from alcoholism, and it documented, often in the children's own words, the chaos and silent suffering that marked their lives. The title was a most appropriate one, since research on alcohol and drug abuse was still in its infancy in the 1960s, and research on the children born into these disturbed families was virtually nonexistent. Worse yet, two fallacious assumptions were made: (1) children of addicted parents could not be helped unless the parent sought treatment, and (2) the children would recover automatically once the parents had stopped drinking or using drugs. Cork's study indicated the focus on the *children as individuals* with their own characteristic constellations of problems and their own needs for help. Interest grew slowly as this concern competed for scarce treatment and research resources, although the known familial nature of alcoholism made children of alcoholics the obvious target group for prevention efforts. The founding of the Children of Alcoholics Foundation in 1982 and its initiatives to review and stimulate sound scientific research in this area have facilitated this process (Russell, Henderson & Blume, 1985; Children of Alcoholics Foundation, 1984; Blume, 1985).

Although research and academic interest grew slowly through the 1980s, public interest exploded. Psychotherapists began to work intensively with members of chemically dependent families and self-help groups proliferated. Books on the subject for the general public have become best sellers. The National Association for Children of Alcoholics assumed a leadership role in this new movement. Thousands of adults and children from chemically dependent families have profited from the attention focused on their problems. DuPont and McGovern discuss this social movement in Chapter 13.

Russell et al. (1985) estimate that approximately 28,600,000 Americans, 6,600,000 of them under the age of 18, are children of alcoholics. This is one in every eight Americans. Although precise estimates are not available for the offspring of parents addicted to other drugs, they are not uncommon in our case loads. All of us concerned with health and human services have a major responsibility to this group. We must acquaint ourselves with current knowledge in the field and learn how to apply it to those we serve. This book will help fill the professional's need for current, clinically applicable information and innovative approaches. In addition, it will provide the clinician with a broad view of related research, cultural, and public-policy issues.

If Dr. Cork were with us today, I know she would feel that the children for whom she cared so much are no longer forgotten.

Sheila B. Blume, M.D.

REFERENCES

Blume, S.B. (1985). In *Report of the Conference on Prevention Research*. New York: *Children of Alcoholics Foundation*. (May be obtained from the foundation at Box 4185, Grand Central Station, New York, NY 10163.)

Children of Alcoholics Foundation (1986). In *Report of the Conference on Research Needs and Opportunities for Children of Alcoholics*. New York: Children of Alcoholics Foundation. (May be obtained from the foundation at Box 4185, Grand Central Station, New York, NY 10163.)

Cork, R.M. (1969). *The Forgotten Children*. Toronto: Addiction Research Foundation.

Russell, M., Henderson, C., & Blume, S.B. (1985). *Children of alcoholics: A review of the literature*. New York: Children of Alcoholics Foundation. (May be obtained from the foundation at Box 4185, Grand Central Station, New York, NY 10163.)

Preface

When I first embarked on a career in the alcoholism field, 42 years after the founding of Alcoholics Anonymous (AA), I was warned by one of my parents, a counselor, that there was much more about alcohol treatment than I would find in self-help groups. When I arrived at graduate school, I was surprised to discover that my parent was more than correct. Ignorance and therapeutic xenophobia were mutual: academia was knowledgeable about theory and scholarship, but ignorant of the practicalities of dealing with incurable addictions. Our budding counselors were well versed in the therapeutics of the self-help groups from whence they came, but were ignorant of the wonders that academia had to offer. Scholarship in the indigenous alcoholism community was (and remains) nonexistent. (The first modern work on children of alcoholics was that by Charles Deutsch [1982].) The chasm that separated the academic and treatment communities was so deep that many of our blended graduates were scapegoated when they worked in treatment settings.

When it came to children of alcoholics, ignorance and xenophobia were doubled and redoubled by both communities. Traditionally trained psychotherapists remained ignorant of alcoholism dynamics at any level. Children of alcoholics were not thought a proper subject for doctoral dissertations. The National Institute on Alcohol Abuse and Alcoholism rejected the idea that a bibliography about children of alcoholics might be useful. The alcoholism treatment community paid lip service to spouses, and none at all to children. The traditional alcoholism self-help groups claimed that they provided all that adult children required, and that minor children either had no need of their services or were too young to benefit from them.

What infuriated me most was that too many therapists, including my own, did not take a good alcohol and other drug history, or if they recognized alcoholism they either ignored it or overreacted to it. It is not uncommon to find persons with *decades* of psychoanalytic treatment, with never a mention of the alcoholism that existed in their families for generations. I did not understand how therapists could choose to ignore patterns of development and response that affected half of their treatment population, to say nothing of my own emotional development.

Denial is not limited to psychotherapists. Social historians defend themselves equally well against the facts. Writes psychohistorian Lloyd de Mause (1988), "Masses of evidence are hidden, distorted, softened, or ignored. The child's early years are played down, formal educational content is endlessly examined, and emotional content is avoided by stressing child legislation and avoiding the home" (p. 5).

My own community, according to school administrators, is free from drug and alcohol problems. Strangely enough, beer bottles litter our school lawns and our adolescents die from drunk driving just as they do in communities that ignore alcohol issues. Our local AA group was founded over 47 years ago, which suggests that we have several generations of children of alcoholics growing up in our village.

That is the way it was at the beginning of this decade. This book is evidence that much has changed for the better. Children of alcoholics are beginning to be taken seriously by the academic community. Traditionally trained therapists are now screening for alcoholism in the family, and treating their dysfunctions. There exists a powerful and rapidly growing indigenous alcoholism constituency, consisting of members of thousands of self-help groups, their families, and the treatment community.

Even in this imperfect world, significant exchanges of learning between the academic world and the alcoholism constituency remain possible. I look forward to the time when self-help communities will learn from academia what academia does best: learn not to generalize so quickly; rely less on insight and intuition, and rely more on examination and measurement of the facts; leave a documentary trail so that we can examine the premises on which conclusions are based; and question every authority whose conclusions rest on a weak foundation. Academia, in turn, would learn from the self-help groups that specific coping skills are more important for survival and recovery than insight and the interpretation of transference; that the *why* of how something works is far less important than the recognition that it *does* work;* that theory may be wonderful to look at, but that it must be tested in the marketplace to prove its usefulness.

Thomas W. Perrin

REFERENCES

Deutsch, C. (1982). *Broken bottles, broken dreams.* New York: Teacher's College Press.
De Mause, L. (1988). *The history of childhood. The untold story of child abuse.* New York: Peter Bedrick.

*Medicine relies on thousands of drugs the therapeutic mechanisms of which are unknown. Neither the manufacturers of my arthritis medicine, nor I, know *why* it works. What is beneficial to both manufacturer and consumer is that it *does* work, and I am grateful that it does. AA and the other self-help groups following its principles work for hundreds of thousands of people. Similarly, *why* AA benefits its members is far less practical a subject of inquiry than is the recognition that it *works*.

Acknowledgments

Rarely noted by editors are the agonies and pleasures of editorial work. Asking colleagues to meet deadlines and to make changes in their valuable work is not easy for author or editor. All an editor has to offer is goodwill and there is little in the way of financial remuneration for those who have contributed. The quality of the chapters in this volume far outstrips our ability to repay the authors in money or praise. Many of the authors I have not met, yet they all responded to a call for papers with a willingness that allowed the editor to build a thoughtful tower using the blocks of their creative effort. Thank you, good contributors.

My parents, siblings, and relatives have struggled with alcoholism in themselves and their families. They have provided me with the pioneering spirit to question and overcome. I thank them for the will to learn from experience.

My wife, Maggie, like myself, is a child of a chemically dependent parent (COSAP). How being a COSAP can affect one's biology and psychology is something that can be learned in the company of an "other." My significant "other," in this and much more, is Maggie.

I also wish to acknowledge the special help and encouragement along the way of Mike Liepman and Steven Dashef. Without their urging and counsel—Dr. Dashef at the beginning and Dr. Liepman in the middle—I am not sure I would have had to courage to continue. I also thank Sheila Blume and Tom Perrin for timely material, support, and encouragement. My thanks also to the late Ann Alhadeff at the beginning of this work, and throughout to Natalie Gilman and Suzi Tucker, of Brunner/Mazel.

Thanks for her support with preliminary drafts and the coordination of this volume go to Marge Corvese Mascena. Without her help, it would not have come to pass. I thank, as well, Marion Johnson, Zoe Black, and Missy Tatum.

I also wish to acknowledge the encouragement of the late Dr. Norman Zinberg, who was to have contributed a chapter to this book but, at the end of his life, found himself unable to do so. His contributions to the field have inspired many of us.

Finally, I dedicate this volume to all COSAPs wherever you are. I hope this volume will be of help to you!

Introduction

Being the child of a substance-abusing parent (COSAP) has as many implications as there are children in that predicament. There are 28 million children of alcoholic parents (COAs) in the United States; with one out of every eight Americans a COA (Woodside, 1988). Sons of alcoholic fathers are between four and five times more likely to become alcoholics than are sons of nonalcoholics; daughters of alcoholic mothers are three times more likely to become alcoholics than are control daughters (Devor & Cloninger, 1989). Daughters of alcoholic parents are also more likely to marry alcoholic men and to produce offspring who are at high risk for addiction in addition to being COAs (Nici, 1979). So it goes, cascading down the generations. And, in addition to millions of COAs, there are untold numbers of children of cocaine- and other substance-abusing parents whose intergenerational troubles have just begun.

As we march forward in our search for the genetic factors that contribute to alcoholism susceptibility (Blum et al., 1990) we realize that there is a large population "at risk" for transmission of alcoholism (see also Chapter 1). Thus, alcoholism achieves the status of the number-one preventable genetically transmissible health liability faced by the United States and many other Western countries (Peterson, Kristenson, Krant, Trell, & Sternby, 1982; Robins et al., 1984).

It is also clear that alcoholism perfectly fulfills the criteria for the necessary and sufficient combination of natural and nurtural factors to generate disorder. Not only are COAs genetically susceptible, but they are frequently subjected to sufficient amounts of environmental stress which may cause them to breach the threshold of phenotypic disorder. Furthermore, the addictive potential of the numerous other substances abused by parents and their devastating physical and psychological fallout on children make moot many questions of genetic susceptibility. The substance-use disorders, particularly in a day when there is no shortage of psychoactive and addictive drugs to substitute for alcohol, already constitute a large-scale environmentally driven public-health problem.

It is well documented that physical and sexual abuse are among the serious traumatic consequences of being a COSAP (Krugman, 1987; Potter-Efron & Potter-Efron, 1985; Flanzer, 1984; Orme & Rimmer, 1981; Gelles, 1972). Not as clearly defined are the emotional traumata of a parent's addiction, such as abandonment of the family, loss of the parent through early death or divorce, or the loss of social status that often is the result of chronic addiction and its drain on a family's finances. More subtle, and less easy to study and characterize, are the psychological effects of being a COSAP.

These are among the subjects that have given birth to hundreds of popular and scientific publications (Ackerman, 1987), national conferences and conventions, and a self-help movement that has attracted hundreds of thousands of adherents (see Chapter 13). With the understanding that there are wide differences (including the existence of no problems at all or even conferred strength resulting from being a COSAP) among individuals, the first purpose of this book is to review critically the findings of others and summarize what clinicians and researchers have learned in working with COSAPs.

The volume was conceived by the editor during the quest for greater personal understanding of the experience of being the child of a substance-abusing parent. As part of this search and in a pattern ever more familiar to me, I sought intellectual explanations for the experience. I found a growing body of self-help literature by and about COSAPs paralleled by a refined body of biological and epidemiological research suggesting that many COSAPs are genetically and experientially "different," have more problems, and are more susceptible to addiction themselves (Devor & Cloninger, 1989; Earls, Reich, Jung, & Cloninger, 1988). This literature was also paralleled by a large body of psychological theory, research, and practice that rarely referenced the problems of being a COSAP.

With some exceptions (Brown, 1988), there appeared to be a wide gap between the literature of the self-healing afflicted and that of professionals and academicians. Therefore, the primary objective of this volume is to bridge this gap, to supplement and broaden the literature springing from the self-help movement by tying it to basic science theory and research efforts. Many of the chapters adapt and synthesize the work deriving from the field of addiction studies and the COSAP self-help movement into established therapies as they stand in the early 1990s (see, especially, Chapters 4–6 and 8–13). In addition, Chapters 1–3, 8, 10, and 12 review and apply basic science and clinical research strategies to the special issues of the COSAP.

A second objective of this book is to review and focus on the plight of the *younger* children of addicted parents. The oppression of many COSAPs begins biologically at conception. Surprisingly, very little has been written about the young COSAP, particularly from a developmental or treatment perspective. It is our intention here to give some much-needed attention to this population (see Chapters 1–3, 8, and 9). In Chapter 8, we consider efforts to treat young, psychiatrically hospitalized children of alcoholic parents and to diagnose and categorize them appropriately. Chapter 9 describes the treatment and follow-up of adolescent girls whose parents are chemically dependent.

A third objective of this volume is to integrate basic science, clinical and research findings with public policy and public health prevention efforts (see Chapters 15, 16, and 17). By integrating science with policy I would hope to challenge ancient, but still prevalent, and uninformed stereotypes of the addicted and their offspring (Burk and Sher, 1990).

OVERVIEW

Chapter 1, "Biological Aspects of Children of Alcoholic Parents" by Loretta Silvia and Michael Liepman, sets the tone for the volume by intergrating research with a developmental, a clinical, and a public-policy focus. It identifies COSAPs as a high-risk group, based on their biology; their early, sometimes prenatal, exposure to drugs and alcohol; and their exposure to the stress of growing up with parents who are chemically dependent. It emphasizes the power of biology, from a genetic, toxicological, and teratogenic point of view. The authors stress the interaction of biology and the environment to produce a clinical "phenotype." If a specific gene for some forms of susceptibility to alcoholism were to be identified (Blum et al., 1990), we may move specifically to identify those at specific risk. Then the question becomes: What are we prepared to do with our knowledge about those at risk?

Jeannette L. Johnson, in Chapter 2, entitled "Forgotten No Longer: An Overview of Research on Children of Chemically Dependent Parents," acknowledges that research on COSAPs is in an early stage. She notes important studies carried out in the early 20th century, and she brings together the large body of research done over the past 40 years. Dr. Johnson reviews the research on the children of parents dependent on alcohol and other chemicals and cautions us not to form premature conclusions based on current research. She also reminds us that most research focuses on risk, not on resiliency, and warns us not to label or stigmatize COSAPs.

Chapter 3, "Young Children of Substance-Abusing Parents: A Developmental View of Risk and Resiliency" by Mary Ellin Logue and the editor, represents an effort to place the study of COSAPs into the growing literature on risk and resiliency. Systematic studies, using scientific methods, of COAs date back at least to the 1940s. A substantial body of comparative data exists on COAs that focuses on school achievement, social and emotional adaptation, gender differences, the development of later substance abuse, behavior disorder, and the gender of the substance-abusing parent.

In "Children of Chemically Dependent Parents: A Theoretical Crossroads," Stephanie Brown provides a synthesis of the needs of COSAPs and the findings that have resulted from the self-help movement. She then applies these findings to major systems of developmental psychology, psychoanalytically oriented psychology, cognitive developmental theory, control mastery, and systems theory.

Dr. Brown's Chapter 4, and Chapter 5, "Psychoanalytic Theory and Children of Alcoholic Parents: Ships Passing in the Night?" by the editor, integrate the disease model of chemical dependence (with particular reference to the COSAP) and recent developments in interpersonal and intrapersonal theory and practice. Psychodynamic theory has historically struggled to understand the addictions, but its practitioners have often missed the mark by failing to recognize the power of the addictive chemicals as the *agents of disorder* in individuals and within systems.

The author of Chapter 6, "The Relationship between Codependence and Narcissism," Timmen Cermak, M.D., gave us in a previous publication a separate diagnostic category for those afflicted by the trauma of living with a chemically dependent family member (Cermak, 1986). He now introduces us to his thinking on the depth psychology of this disorder. Starting with Freud's understanding of narcissism and then proceeding to the current theories of self-psychology and trauma theory, the author reconstructs the potentially traumatic childhood of a child of a chemically dependent parent. He helps us to understand, developmentally, how a COSAP may wind up repeating the pattern of either the chemically dependent or the codependent parent. It is in childhood that the dance between the narcissicist and the "echoist" (a term coined by Dr. Cermak for this situation) may begin and, later, may continue to plague adult adaptation. He describes the bipolar aspects of the narcissistically injured codependent child and clarifies how dependent and pseudomutual personality traits can coexist in the same patient with narcissistically aggressive and apparently "selfish" traits. He then discusses the therapy of these disorders.

One of the coauthors of Chapter 7 described his experience doing long-term therapy with child and adolescent COSAPs this way: "I think they live thousands of little deaths of their parent each year." (McGuire, 1989). Not only does the young COSAP lose the parent who is every child's birthright, the idealized "good" parent (Miller, 1983; Kohut, 1977, 1984), but the COSAP repeatedly loses the good parent he or she really *sometimes* has. Alcoholic and chemically dependent parents sometimes (sober or drunk) can be wonderful, loving, and caring. To see them die "thousands of little deaths" with increasing frequency as the addiction progresses is a chronic trauma for the COSAP. It may result in a special situation that for some young children only careful and long-term corrective emotional and reparenting experiences in therapy can begin to address. "Chronic Trauma Disorder of Childhood: Children in Search of a Diagnosis" attempts to characterize, diagnostically, the results of chronic childhood trauma in a group of children (of which COSAPs represent a substantial subgroup) requiring psychiatric hospital care.

Chapter 8, "The Chemically Dependent Female Adolescent: A Treatment Challenge" by Dorothy M. Bianco and Susan D. Wallace, represents the fruit of 15 years of data collection and analysis from a treatment program for substance-abusing adolescent girls and their families. The ability of a program to examine itself, using epidemiological research methods, is a major contribution to the literature on troubled adolescent girls. The girls the authors studied, prior to intervention, were well on their way to becoming the next generation of chemically dependent mothers. Furthermore, most girls in their program were COSAPs themselves, and appeared to be suffering from chronic trauma disorder (CTD) described in Chapter 8. Dr. Bianco and Mrs. Wallace offer the components of successful programming and make a clear statement of the dedication that it takes, over generations, to intervene with these troubled youngsters and families.

In Chapter 9, "Breaking the Cycle: Treating Adult Children of Alcoholics," David Treadway provides a clinical centerpiece for this collection. Dr. Treadway is well known for his presentations and his illuminating book *Before It's Too Late: Working with Substance Abuse in the Family* (Treadway, 1989). His chapter offers many creative guidelines for the successful treatment of COSAPs and highlights the issues of COSAP parents, partners, and professionals.

The authors of Chapter 10, "Short-Term Psychoeducational Group for Adult Children of Alcoholics: Catalyst for Change," (like those of Chapter 8) provide another fine example of clinical innovation combined with follow-up research. Michelle Clark and Noel Jette describe the critical stage when a client is in crisis but is not ready for major commitment to change. While it is true that people have to be ready to change, this chapter describes how to prepare people in crisis for transition in an efficient, stepwise way.

Chapter 11, "Treatment of Children of Substance-Abusing Parents," presents the editor's personal views on treatment of COSAPs from the point of view of a hospital-based, child and family psychiatrist who also has the power (sometimes abused in the treatment of COSAPs) of the prescription pad.

Helga Matzko, in Chapter 12, entitled "The ACOA Substance-Abuse Counselor: Family-of-Origin Influences on Personal Growth and Therapeutic Effectiveness," addresses the issues of COSAPs who themselves provide service as counselors or therapists. She points to the obvious but often unaddressed fact that many COSAP therapists choose their profession as a stepping-stone in their own recovery and healing. She gives creative suggestions to treatment programs to assist these healers with support, therapy, and educational opportunity.

Chapter 13 by Robert DuPont and John McGovern, "The Growing Impact of the Children-of-Alcoholics Movement in Medicine: A Revolution in Our Midst," documents the history of a healing revolution. By reviewing their personal and academic development in the field of addiction medicine, the authors recount how their own professional growth incorporated the rapid changes in the field. Major discoveries have marked the field, discoveries coming not only from the laboratory, but also from the millions of people who have joined self-help movements. If the cycle of addiction is to be interrupted, it will have to start with the findings of the afflicted themselves.

In Chapter 14, "Policy, Issues, and Action: An Agenda for Children of Substance Abusers," Migs Woodside outlines the present needs and provides a map for future service and research for children of addicted parents that covers primary, secondary, and tertiary prevention. She does not neglect the legal "tangles" (as she calls them) of intervention and prevention for this high-risk group. She emphasizes the necessity of treating children now as a way of accessing future generations.

"The Effects of Psychoactive Substances on the Next Generation: The Epidemic View," Chapter 15, by the editor is an attempt to focus on the epidemic proportions of COSAP issues. COSAP treatment, research, and public policy consensus suggest that help for the COSAP, as for others "at risk" in our society, is "within our reach" (Schorr, 1989).

A NOTE ON ABBREVIATIONS

There are many terms used to describe children of chemically dependent parents. COA stands for child(ren) of alcoholics, or better stated, of alcoholic parents. ACOA, particularly on the East Coast, stands for adult child(ren) of alcoholics; this has been compressed into ACA (adult child of an alcoholic) on the West Coast. In a pioneering paper on the treatment of adolescent children of alcoholic parents, the further abbreviation ADCA has been introduced (Bogdaniak & Piercy, 1987). The term "codependent" has many definitions (Cermak, 1986; Mendenhall, 1989; Potter-Efron & Potter-Efron, 1989; Whitfield, 1989), many of which apply to COSAPs. However, to minimize confusion, "codependent" will not be used in this volume as a synonym for a new term we have coined—children of substance-abusing parents (COSAPs). It incorporates the term "substance abuse," which is current in diagnostic nomenclature, encompasses *all* substances abused by parents, and focuses on the status of children—young and old.

REFERENCES

Ackerman, R. J. (1987). *Children of alcoholics, A bibliography and resource guide.* Deerfield Beach, FL: Health Communications.

Blum, K., Noble, E. P., Sheridan, P. J., et al. (1990). Allelic association of human dopamine D_2 receptor gene in alcoholism. *Journal of the American Medical Association, 263,* 2055–2060.

Bogdaniak, R. C., & Piercy, P. F. (1987). Therapeutic issues of adolescent children of alcoholics (ADCA) groups. *International Journal of Psychotherapy, 37,* 569–588.

Brown, S. (1988). *Treating adult children of alcoholics, A developmental perspective.* New York: Wiley Inc.

Burk, J. P. & Sher, K. J. (1990). Labeling the child of an alcoholic: Negative stereotyping by mental health professionals and peers. *Journal of Studies on Alcohol, 51,* 156–163.

Cermak, T. (1986). *Diagnosing and treating co-dependence of alcoholics.* Minneapolis, MN: Johnson Institute Books.

Devor, E. J., & Cloninger, C. R. (1989). Genetics of alcoholism. *Annual Review of Genetics,* 23, 19–36.

Earls, F., Reich, W., Jung, K. G., & Cloninger, C. R. (1988). Psychopathology in children of alcoholic and antisocial parents. *Alcoholism: Clinical and Experimental Research,* 12(4), 481–487.

Flanzer, J. (1984). Alcohol abuse and family violence: The domestic chemical connection. *Family Focus and Chemical Dependency,* 7(4), 5–6.

Gelles, R. (1972). *The violent home: The study of aggression between husbands and wives.* Beverly Hills, CA: Sage Publications.

Kohut, H. (1977). Preface. In J. D. Blaine & D. A. Julius (Eds.), *The psychodynamics of drug dependence.* (NIDA Research Monograph no. 12) (pp. vii–ix). Washington, DC: U.S. Government Printing Office.

Kohut, H. (1984). How does analysis cure? In A. Goldberg (Ed.), *How does analysis cure?* Chicago: University of Chicago Press.

Krugman, L. (1987). Trauma in the family: Perspectives on the intergenerational transmission of violence. In B. A. van der Kolk (Ed.), *Psychological trauma* (pp. 127–152). Washington, DC: American Psychiatric Press.

McGuire, J. (1989). Personal communication.

Mendenhall, W. (1989). Co-dependency definitions and dynamics. *Alcoholism Treatment Quarterly,* 6, 3–18.

Miller, A. (1983). *For your own good: Hidden cruelty in childrearing and the roots of violence.* New York: Farrar, Strauss, Giraux.

Nici, J. (1979). Wives of alcoholics as "repeaters." *Journal of Studies on Alcohol,* 40, pp. 677–682.

Orme, T. C., & Rimmer, J. (1981). Alcoholism and child abuse: A review. *Journal of Studies on Alcohol,* 42(3), 273–287.

Petersson, B., Kristenson, H., Krant, P., Trell, E., & Sternby, W. H. (1982). Alcohol related deaths: A major contributor to mortality in urban middle-aged men. *Lancet,* 2, 1088–1090.

Potter-Efron, R. T., & Potter-Efron, P. S. (1985). Family violence as a treatment issue with chemically dependent adolescents. *Alcoholism Treatment Quarterly,* 2(2), 1–15.

Potter-Efron, R. T., & Potter-Efron, P. S. (1989). Assessment of co-dependency with individuals from alcoholic and chemically dependent families. *Alcoholism Treatment Quarterly,* 6, 37–58.

Robins, L. N., Helzer, J. E., Weissman, M. M., Orvaschel, H., Gruenberg, E., Burke, J. D., & Reiger, D. A. (1984). Lifetime prevalence of specific psychiatric disorders in three sites. *Archives of General Psychiatry,* 41, 949–958.

Schorr, L. (1989). *Within Our Reach, Breaking the Cycle and Disadvantage* (pp. 291–294). New York: Doubleday.

Treadway, D. C. (1989). *Before it's too late: Working with substance abuse in the family.* New York: Norton.

Whitfield, C. L. (1989). Co-dependence: Our most common addiction—some physical, mental, emotional and spiritual perspectives. *Alcoholism Treatment Quarterly, 6,* 19–36.

Woodside, M. (1988). Symposium paper: Research on children of alcoholics: Past and future. *British Journal of Addiction, 83,* 785–792.

PART I

ACADEMIC PERSPECTIVES

1

Biological Aspects of Children of Alcoholic Parents

Loretta Young Silvia, Ph.D.

Michael R. Liepman, M.D.

In the social sciences, the nature–nurture, or heredity–environment, controversy over the etiology of a variety of behavioral disorders, including alcoholism, has raged for many years, continuing into the 1990s with particular focus on the cause of alcoholism, as evidenced in the recent U.S. Supreme Court decision upholding the 1932 Veterans Administration's declaration that alcoholic drinking constitutes "willful misconduct." This is the most recent manifestation of a long and bitter disagreement between those who believe that the consumption of alcohol by alcoholics is simply immoral behavior and those who believe (as did Dr. Bob who cofounded Alcoholics Anonymous in 1937) that alcoholics have an inborn uncontrollable reaction to alcohol (the so-called "X-factor") that is different from that of the nonalcoholic. In 1958, Anastasi changed the question being asked from "*Which* type of factor, hereditary, and environmental, is responsible for individual differences in a given trait?" to "*How* are individual differences influenced by heredity and environment?" (p. 197) Since biology forms the framework for the human psyche, it is unreasonable fully to separate the psyche from the soma. These components are interactive in many ways, just as software interacts with hardware in computers. Even though we can distinguish between hardware and software, neither can function without the other, and incompatibilities often arise that can interfere with function. Contextual (sociocultural and family systems) factors also play a role in the expression of psychic and biological traits.

Much has been written (some even debuts in this book) about the characteristics of children of alcoholics (and other dysfunctional families). Children raised in an alcoholic family (COAs) are subjected to a variety of psychosocial stresses and some specific environmental influences that cause them to develop differently than so-called "normal" children. We realize that such influences contribute substantially to their ultimate personality and adult behavior, but in this chapter we will concentrate on the biological factors that play important roles in the development of COAs and in their eventual risk of becoming addicted themselves. We will realistically place biological factors alongside environmental factors, realizing that they interact in a variety of ways (see also Chapters 2–3).

A BRIEF REVIEW OF GENETICS

Genetic inheritance is governed by a biological process that takes place within the cells of the body. Each living cell has at its center a nucleus containing DNA organized into chromosomes. In humans, there are 46 chromosomes—one chromosome of each of 23 pairs donated by each parent. The chromosomes have regions called genes. The genes control a single structure and/or function in the body; the chromosomes serve as cellular blueprints for constructing enzymes, receptors, and structural proteins. The chromosomes in the nucleus of every cell in one's body are identical, having been copied from the original set that was assembled at conception.

DNA codes comprise combinations of four guanine-nucleotide bases represented as: G, C, A, and T. A single gene may contain thousands of these bases in a string (e.g., TGGATACCGAGCTTAC . . .), each triplet (e.g., TGG, ATA, CCG, etc.) having a particular meaning. The total sets of DNA blueprints for humans are 96–99% identical in all human beings; it is this high degree of similarity that determines humanness. The 1–4% of dissimilarities in DNA codes between individuals represent the differences that are responsible for all of the variability in traits among individuals, such as height, build, gender, complexion, facial structure, fingerprints, metabolism, temperament, risk factors for various genetic illnesses, and racial characteristics.

Transmission of Genes in Reproduction

When a sperm unites with an egg at conception, one each of the father's 23 pairs of chromosomes are combined with one each of the mother's 23 pairs for a total of 23 pairs, or 46 chromosomes. Thus, rather than reproducing one of the parents, the offspring becomes a hybrid of half of the genes of each.

Only identical twins have 100% identical copies of all chromosomes (because they both grew from a single conceptus that split into two). If a parent has two different genes (A and B) on each singlet of the pair of a particular chromosome (e.g., chromosome 9), there is a 50% chance that the first child will receive gene A, and also a 50% chance that the second child will receive gene A, thus, there is a $0.5 \times 0.5 = 25\%$ chance that both will receive gene A. There is a 25% + 25% = 50% chance that a sibling pair would both have either gene A or gene B in common.

Thus, for full-sibling pairs other than identical twins, including fraternal twins (who grow simultaneously from two different sperms that combine with two different eggs), roughly half of the chromosomes are in common between the siblings.

A person's genotype is his or her fundamental hereditary constitution as determined by the totality of the DNA codes of all its genes on all 46 chromosomes. The genotype of an individual in relation to any particular trait is determined largely by ancestors, obtaining genes exactly copied from its two biological parents, who in turn obtained their genes exactly copied from their parents and so on. Half of a person's genes come on the 23 chromosomes from each parent, and each parent transmits only half of his or her genes to each offspring (23 chromosomes are randomly chosen from each of the 23 pairs). This introduces "chance" into the process of reproduction so that siblings with the same parents can have quite different genotypes simply by the random process of selection of which chromosomes will be transmitted to the next generation in the fated sperm or egg cell (i.e., germ cells). In this manner, among traits that vary in human beings, offspring carry approximately a 50% resemblance to each parent, a 25% resemblance to each grandparent, a 12.5% resemblance to each great grandparent, and so on.

Mutations

One exception to the above is when a mutation occurs. Although quite rare (one out of 10,000 cell divisions), mutations can introduce chance changes into the genetic heritage passed down from ancestry. Because there are so many sites at risk for mutation, every person has several mutations somewhere in his or her DNA. But most of these do not make a noticeable difference because they are in silent portions of the chromosome, or they do not change the overall structure of the resulting gene product. Some combinations of genes are inviable and the embryo or fetus dies in utero. Only rarely does a mutation result in a new phenotype that has not been present in the ancestry. Exposure to mutation-producing environmental hazards such as certain chemicals or ionizing radiation or X-rays can increase the risk of mutations in the DNA of germ cells or the newly developing fetus. When mutations occur after conception, not all cells will have the altered genotype, resulting in a mosaic distribution of altered cells throughout the body.

A genetic defect can be large or small. The presence of an extra chromosome results in the massive genetic alterations of Down's syndrome (trisomy-21 is a disorder in which three versions of the 21st chromosome are inherited by the victim) whereas the tiny damage (only a single error in a DNA code) on a single gene results in phenylketonuria. In Down's syndrome, the child is impaired intellectually, has organ damage, often develops leukemia, and has facial and stature stigmata that alert the surrounding community to the syndrome; there are probably thousands of genes that are triply represented in this disorder, leading to all sorts of chemical imbalances in the body. Phenylketonuria, on the other hand, is more subtle, the defect being in one gene governing one enzyme structure that interferes with the function of processing the metabolites of phenylalanine, a component of normal human diet (including Nutrasweet ®). A child discovered to have this defect at birth through mandatory state screening of newborns can be protected lifelong from mental retardation by being fed a phenylalanine-free diet.

Genotypes and Gene Expression

Since each chromosome is represented in two versions (the father's and the mother's), each child has two sets of genes for each trait. When a particular pair of genes are identical, the child is said to be homozygous for that gene (e.g., [A/A] or [B/B]), whereas when the father's gene is different from the mother's gene (e.g., [A/B]), the child is said to be heterozygous. Some traits are expressed only when the child is homozygous for that gene (e.g., blue-eyed individuals have received two genes [bl/bl] that specify the structures of defective pigment-producing enzymes for their eyes); the heterozygotes for eye color [bl/Br] have hazel eyes because only one of their genes specifies a functioning pigment-producing enzyme. However, not as much pigment is produced by heterozygotes as by brown-eyed homozygotes [Br/Br], both of whose pigment-producing enzymes function properly. Sometimes it is more difficult to distinguish the heterozygote from one of the homozygotes (e.g., hazel to brown eyes is a more subtle difference than hazel to blue eyes). When this occurs, the homozygote/heterozygote phenotypes that cannot be distinguished are said to be dominantly inherited and the distinct homozygous phenotype is said to be recessively inherited.

The phenotype of an organism refers to the class made up of all individuals with an observable characteristic (e.g., blue-eyed individuals, or dwarfs, or albinos). The phenotype is the form in which one or more genotypes are expressed in the individual. Often, a phenotype is composed of several different genotypes; that is, the genes that are responsible for a particular trait may be found in several different configurations (i.e., alleles) on the DNA. For instance, a recent discovery of the genetic defect responsible for the cystic fibrosis phenotype showed that the delineated genotype was responsible for only 70% of cases, and there are several other genotypes of the same gene that are responsible for the other 30% of cases (Kerem et al., 1989). In some phenotypes, the genetic defects may even occur on different genes, such as in the blood disorder thalassemia. Sometimes these different genes may not even be located on the same chromosome pair.

Hidden Genes

A recessive genotype can be hidden (or not expressed) in an individual, yet it can be passed on to the next generation. The recessive gene for defective eye pigment is not apparent unless it is joined in the same individual with another similarly defective gene. In this manner, a blue-eyed individual may turn up among a mostly brown/hazel-eyed family without a clue as to where the trait came from unless someone remembers a distant relative who had blue eyes. Recessive traits are "carried" in hidden form until expressed in homozygotes. The existence of hidden genes helps explain situations in which a trait seems to skip generations.

Another way in which genotypes are hidden is when another factor is required for gene expression. This is the case for sex-limited traits (gene–gene interactions) in which only one gender expresses a trait, such as male-pattern baldness or vaginal or breast characteristics. This is also the case for gene-environment interactions when one needs to be exposed to a specific environmental condition to express the trait (e.g., cholinesterase deficiency is discovered by the inability of a surgery patient to detoxify certain anesthetic agents, or the flushing reaction is discovered after alcohol ingestion by persons with aldehyde dehydrogenase deficiency).

Interactions of Genetics and Environment

There are several ways in which heredity and environment can interact. A genetic trait can produce conditions that lead to reduced or increased vigor or success in the environment. For instance, an extremely beautiful woman may use her beauty to become a famous model or actress, or she may integrate her beauty with other assets to climb the corporate ladder or to become successful in a profession or politics; on the other hand, she may be sexually abused at a young age and become a drug addict and prostitute, or once married, her husband may become jealous when other men stare at her and he may beat her when they return home. Hereditary deafness may interfere with social interaction and thus lead to intellectual retardation unless the child is offered special services for the deaf at an early age.

Physical characteristics of the environment, such as climate or altitude, and social characteristics, such as culture, often influence the value of a genotype or phenotype. Dobzhansky (1950) once posed a hypothetical situation in which a culture determined that carriers of the AB blood type would become aristocracy, whereas those in the O blood group would become laborers. In this unusual situation, blood group would become an important hereditary determinant of behavior. It is important to recognize that the effect of heredity on behavior is usually indirect. All we can know from our observations of behavior is that a given trait shows evidence of being influenced by a genetic factor. This is not, nor should it ever be taken to be, a causative explanation. It simply defines a problem for genetic research. It is very important to note the environmental context in which a genetic trait is expressed as this may alter its meaning or importance. For instance, a dwarf born into a circus community would have great value, whereas if born into a community obsessed with basketball, it is likely that the same child would have great difficulty.

Environmental factors may selectively favor particular genetic traits over others in terms of reproduction, thus loading the population's gene pool with the favored genotypes. For example, if a tall man were culturally favored to have more wives, over many generations, the population would get taller since more children would be born with tall ancestry than with short ancestry. In Africa, the sickle-cell trait was selectively retained in the population despite the homozygous sickle phenotype being lethal. The homozygous normal phenotype was killed off by malaria infections; only the heterozygous phenotype survived because it was resistent to malaria (the red blood cells have a reduced life span that is too short for the malaria parasite to complete its reproductive life cycle). Thus, the gene pool in Africa contains about 50% sickle genotype and 50% normal.

It appears that more males than females are alcoholics. However, the prevalence of alcoholism-predisposing genotypes might be equal among males and females. The lower prevalence of alcoholism in females could be the result of different standards needed to make a diagnosis. Alternatively, sociocultural factors may differentially influence the consumption patterns of alcohol by men and women, resulting in lower consumption by women with a concomitant lower prevalence of alcoholism in women (phenotype) even though the genotype may not differ.

Gene–Gene Interactions Among Genetic Traits

A gene–gene interaction results from the interaction of one genetic factor with another. For example, a person with a genetic predisposition to alcoholism and the specific histocompatibility (HLA) type that is prone to cirrhosis of the liver will develop alcoholic cirrhosis if drinking continues long enough. Note that environment may play a role in this example: during the Prohibition era, when alcohol was less available in many parts of the country, the mortality rate from alcoholic cirrhosis dropped substantially even though the genotypes in the population did not change. Once the restrictions on alcohol ceased, the death rate from cirrhosis began to rise again. Hence the phenotypic expression of genotype may be influenced by environmental factors.

GENETIC RISK OF DEVELOPING ALCOHOLISM

There is little controversy over the commonly held view that alcoholism runs in families. The controversy is greatest when one tries to determine how alcoholism is transmitted across generations. There have been studies of sociocultural factors that contribute to risk of alcoholism that will not be reviewed here (Cahalan, Cisin, & Crossley, 1969; Wolin, Bennett, Noonan, & Teitelbaum, 1980). We will concentrate on examining the genetic studies. In humans there are three approaches to the study of hereditary factors in family illnesses. All three—twin studies, adoption studies, and genetic-marker studies—have been used in alcoholism etiology research.

Twin Studies

Twin studies are important to genetic inquiry because they allow measurement of the degree of phenotypic expression of a genetic trait. The percent of phenotypic expression equals the concordance rate between identical twins in affected twin pairs. The phenotypic concordance between fraternal twins in affected twin pairs should be about half of that found in identical twin pairs since genotypic concordance should be about 50%.

When twin pairs were compared for the presence or absence of alcoholism, Kaij (1960) found that identical twins were 71% concordant whereas fraternal twins were only 32% concordant, and the more severe the alcoholism, the greater was the discrepancy between concordance rates in identical and fraternal twins. These findings were supported by Loehlin (1972) after analyzing 850 questionnaires from same-sex twins in the United States, and by Jonsson and Nilsson (1968) in an analysis of data from 7,500 twin pairs in Sweden. Another study (Partanen et al., 1966) found that identical twins were more concordant than fraternal twins for quantity and frequency of drinking but not for adverse consequences, although younger identical twins tended to be more concordant for adverse effects.

It is noteworthy that even though the phenotypic concordance rate for alcoholism in identical twins is high (71%), there is a 29% phenotypic discordance for identical twins (despite their 100% genotypic concordance), suggesting that there must be a strong environmental influence that prevents alcoholism from being expressed in some individuals. Fingarette (1988) misinterpreted this lack of 100% concordance between twin pairs as an indication that alcoholism is not inherited. But alcoholism cannot occur in those who abstain, as do approximately 30% of people in the United States. Thus, by abstaining, 29% of identical twins of alcoholics could avoid becoming alcoholic. If one were to multiply the 71% expressivity figure derived from the identical-twin pairs of Kaij (1960) by the 50% expected genotypic concordance of fraternal twins, one would expect 35.5% phenotypic concordance of fraternal twins (observed = 32%).

Adoption Studies

Adoption studies are helpful in clarifying the factors that are transmitted across generations via genetic versus environmental (learning, sociocultural) pathways. Thus phenotypic expression can be teased apart into those characteristics that are genotypically determined and those that are learned. The seminal work in this area was done in Denmark by Goodwin and his colleagues (Goodwin, 1971; Goodwin et al., 1973). There were four subject groups, all children of alcoholic natural parents: (1) sons raised by nonalcoholic adoptive parents, (2) sons raised by alcoholic biological parents, (3) daughters raised by nonalcoholic adoptive parents, and (4) daughters raised by alcoholic biological parents. Each group was paired with a control group matched for age and for circumstances of the adoption (for groups 1 and 3 only). Sons of alcoholics were four times more likely to be alcoholic regardless of whether they were raised by alcoholic biological or nonalcoholic adoptive parents. The only other significant difference in a wide range of variables was a higher rate of divorce among the sons of alcoholics raised by adoptive parents. Findings for the daughters were inconclusive, but an unexplained higher rate of alcoholism than expected from national prevalence data was found in both the proband and control daughters. The adopted-out daughters of alcoholics and controls did not differ on such variables as depression or drug use. However, 30% of daughters raised by their alcoholic natural parents had been treated for depression before the age of 32, compared with 5% of the controls. Thus Goodwin concluded that children of alcoholic natural parents are particularly vulnerable to alcoholism regardless of who raised them, and that the genetic vulnerability is specific to alcoholism and does not involve increased risk of other psychopathology. Note that Goodwin based his study on a fairly young set of probands; the age of probands could alter study outcome if there are more than one type of alcoholism with different age of onset, different gender distribution, and different heritabilities. Goodwin's studies have also been criticized for the manner in which he determined who was alcoholic.

Goodwin's findings contradicted findings of an earlier study by Roe and Burks (1945), who obtained data from 49 foster children in the 20–40 age range. Of these, 27 had an alcoholic biological parent and 22 had nonalcoholic parents. They found no evidence of a drinking problem in either group. However, the sample was small, and in contrast to the Goodwin study, no criteria for alcoholism were used. Parents were simply described as heavy drinkers.

Bohman (1978) confirmed Goodwin's findings in a study of 2,324 Swedish adoptees. Male adoptees whose natural fathers were alcoholic manifested alcoholism at a rate of 20% compared with 6% of the control group. Although not statistically significant, it is interesting to note that the prevalence of alcoholism was 33% among male adoptees whose natural mothers were alcoholic, compared with 19% of the control group.

Fingarette (1988) misinterpreted the genetic studies by noting the high percentage of COAs who are *not* alcoholic in some of these studies. He apparently did not realize that had these studies been done on populations who had completed their entire lives, the numbers would likely be larger. But by restricting the studies to certain ages, the scientists were able to identify only a portion of the persons (with early onset) who were destined to become alcoholic during their lives.

In the last decade it has been assumed by most informed scientists that there is a hereditary influence on the development of alcoholism and the emphasis in adoption studies has expanded in an effort to assess the relative contributions of heredity and environment. The questions have sought to determine what characteristics of biological and adoptive parents influence the risk of alcohol abuse in the adoptee. In addition, the researchers have begun to look at whether a genetic predisposition to alcoholism may be manifested in other psychopathological ways depending on the environment and gender of the individual. Bohman et al. (1981, 1984), Cadoret et al. (1978, 1980, 1985, 1986, 1987), and Cloninger et al. (1978, 1981, 1984, 1985, 1987, 1988) have all worked from a nature–nurture perspective. In particular, Reich et al. (1988) presented convincing data that the environmental contribution has recently been shifting, in particular among younger females. And Tarter and Edwards (1988) reviewed the neuropsychological literature arguing that cognitive deficits, "hyperactivity," and emotional lability can predispose to the development of alcoholism.

In 1981, Cloninger, Bohman, and Sigvardsson suggested that there are two forms of alcoholism. Their sample consisted of 862 men born out of wedlock with verifiable paternity in Stockholm between 1930 and 1949 and adopted by nonrelatives before the age of three years. Thanks to the centralized Danish registry for health problems and local community temperence boards that recorded mentions of drinking-related problems among their neighbors, fairly complete data were available for the biological and adoptive parents, and for the adoptees, over time. Past research had suggested that there were differences in severity of alcoholism that might have a hereditary explanation. Various discriminant function and cross-factoring analyses resulted in the identification of two types of alcohol abuse that are under different genetic and environmental influences.

Type 1 (so-called milieu-limited alcoholism) is characterized by mild alcohol abuse and minimal criminality in one or both parents. The postnatal or adoptive environment appears to determine both the frequency and severity of alcoholism in susceptible sons. Alcohol problems are usually isolated or mild, but may be severe, and their onset is usually after the age of 25. Relative risk (the ratio of the risk of alcoholism in congenitally predisposed sons to that of others) is 2 with postnatal provocation and 1 without it. A relative risk of 1 indicates no difference for predisposed and controls. Heritability of this type among identical twins is about 20% for both males and females (Svikis et al., 1987). The temperament of Type 1 alcoholics leans toward the anxiety-ridden people-pleaser as defined in Cloninger's (1987) three-dimensional TPQ grid (high on harm avoidance, high on reward dependence, and low on thrill seeking).

Type 2 (male-limited) alcoholism is characterized by severe alcohol abuse, criminality, and extensive treatment in the biological father and a 'normal' mother. The postnatal environment has little effect on prevalence, though it may influence severity. Onset of alcohol problems usually occurs in adolescence, and drug-abuse, school, and criminal problems are frequent among this group. The relative risk in congenitally predisposed sons is 9. Heritability of this type among male identical twins is 80%, and it was not found among female identical twins (Svikis et al., 1987). Cloninger's TPQ temperament factors for Type 2 alcoholics are high on thrill seeking, low on harm avoidance, and low on reward dependence, consistent with antisocial personality disorder.

Previous studies had neglected genetic heterogeneity, making interpretations difficult. However, Cloninger et al. suggest that the Goodwin findings are similar to their high-heritability or Type 2 alcoholics while the Roe and Burks heavy-drinker results are consistent with Type 1 alcoholism. From these findings one might assume that many male and all female alcoholics are Type 1; that is, their genetic predisposition to alcoholism is strongly mediated by environmental factors. Since Type 2 alcoholism has been identified as male limited, a fairly obvious question then is, what becomes of the daughters of Type 2 alcoholics? Bohman and colleagues (Bohman et al., 1984; Sigvardsson et al., 1984) studied two clinically distinct somatoform disorders in adopted-out women testing the hypothesis that some forms of somatization, antisocial behavior, and alcohol abuse may have a common pathogenesis. They had observed that in intact families of individuals with Briquet's syndrome (mental disorder primarily seen in women characterized by multiple somatic complaints and resultant medical and surgical treatments), and in families of persons with antisocial personality (ASP), the ill women usually have somatization disorder whereas the men have ASP and/or are alcohol abusers. The alcoholics in families of women with somatization disorder have unusually high rates of fighting and arrests for criminal activities (features of Type 2 alcoholism). Alcoholics without such features (Type 1) do not have an excess of somatization disorder in their female relatives. This suggests that only one form of alcoholism is related to somatization disorder. In addition, two clinically different forms of somatization disorder had been identified earlier (Cloninger et al., 1984). High-frequency somatizers had an average of more than five sick leaves annually from the age of 16, with particularly high rates of abdominal complaints, urogenital problems, backaches, and psychiatric distress. The diversiform somatizers averaged more than two sick leaves annually with a diversified pattern of complaints and lower rates of both backaches and psychiatric problems than either the high-frequency somatizers or nonsomatizers.

Genetics of Drug Abuse

Considerably less work has been done on genetic influences on drug abuse. Cadoret et al. (1986) sampled 242 male and 201 female adoptees who had been separated at birth from their biological parents. Since ASP had been linked to both alcoholism and drug abuse, they attempted to elucidate the relationships among alcoholism, drug abuse, and ASP, and further to identify the relative contributions of genetics and environment. Their findings suggest two types of genetic influence in drug abuse. First, antisocial behavior in biological relatives is associated with ASP in the proband (the person who suffers from the disorder), which in turn is associated with drug abuse. Second, it appears that alcohol problems in the biological relatives are highly correlated with drug abuse in individuals without ASP. Thus, they suggest that there are two genetic pathways to drug abuse: (1) ASP in biological relatives and (2) alcoholism in biological relatives. Additional work is needed in this area since this sample was small and the adoption records of biological parents were considerably less complete than those used in the previously cited Danish and Swedish studies. Dramatic changes in substance-use trends have been occurring lately (Reich et al., 1988), which make genetic study more difficult. There seems to be a connection between parental substance abuse and child substance abuse, that may represent a combination of genetic and environmental factors. Biological factors are suggested by studies showing a subgroup of cocaine addicts as having hyperactivity. It will be important to watch for studies that clarify the complex interactions between other psychopathology and substance-use disorders.

Conclusions of Twin and Adoption Studies

In conclusion, it appears that the evidence of a hereditary factor in the transmission of alcoholism is well supported. We know that alcoholism runs in families. It appears that any further investigations ought to consider the type of alcoholism being examined and the environment that may mediate its manifestations. It is also important to note that there are many alcoholics without a known history of alcoholism in their families of origin and that not all children of alcoholics become alcoholic. Fingarette (1988) has used this finding to deny a genetic influence on alcoholism. However, either a recessive inheritance pattern or incomplete penetrance due to environmental influences can cause a genetic disorder to disappear for one or more generations, only to reemerge later. Our search for an understanding of alcoholism, and its prevention and treatment, requires that we stop fighting over whether heredity or environment is responsible for alcoholism, and start asking in what ways heredity and environment do influence the development of alcoholism. Work in the past decade has clearly advanced this position, with important results.

BIOLOGICAL MARKERS OF ALCOHOLISM

Observable biological traits that are associated with a particular phenotype are called biological markers because they help us to recognize the trait. Sometimes biological markers are a reflection of the trait we are examining (e.g., blue eyes are the biological marker for defective pigment genes and elevated liver enzymes reflect liver damage from drinking too much alcohol), but a biological marker also can be associated with another trait that has nothing to do with the trait's pathophysiology per se (e.g., an association between blood type and alcoholism). Biological markers are useful for scientists in teasing apart the mechanisms of disease states; to clinicians and public-health workers, they provide a tool for case finding and prevention.

Genetic research on biological markers may be undertaken from two perspectives—*association* and *linkage*. *Association* is shown when a biological marker coexists with a particular illness more often than is expected by chance in a proband as compared with a randomly selected control group. *Linkage* is demonstrated by studying individual families to determine whether the presence or absence of a particular biological marker is correlated with the presence or absence of the illness in members of that family. If linkage is demonstrated, it can be assumed that genes for the marker and genes contributing to the illness are on the same chromosome, and close enough on that chromosome that the two genes pass together from one generation to the next. (When chromosomes are being lined up in pairs to be split into two sets of 23 for packaging in a pair of eggs or sperm, the arms of the chromosomes may become entangled and sections of a chromosome may cross over, switching to the opposite pair-mate. This form of mutation of chromosome structure is rare, but the frequency of crossovers makes possible calculation of distances between the locations of two particular genes that reside on the same chromosome. In order to study linkage, large kindreds must be studied.)

The work of Bohman and Cloninger cited above has given important direction to other researchers who have been looking for biological variables that might increase our understanding of alcoholism and its transmission. These can be divided roughly into neurophysiological differences, neuropsychological differences, and biochemical differences. In 1979, Goodwin noted that more than a score of genetic-marker studies had been published and that almost invariably, efforts to replicate the findings were inconclusive and/or contradictory. Some of the early attempts to identify such markers as color blindness, blood groups, and finger-ridge counts have been pretty well dismissed at this time. However, with the important findings of Cloninger suggesting at least two types of alcoholism, new explanations of previously contradictory findings are more easily understood, and future work may be based on alcoholic type and less subject to discrepancies.

Recombinant DNA techniques are now being used to map the entire human genome. Such efforts are rapidly identifying new genotypic information about gene locations and structures, as well as different alleles (variants) of genes that can be found in various populations. It will not be long before we know a great deal about the genes that contribute to the development of alcoholism and other disorders and one such candidate gene may already have been identified (Blum et al., 1990).

Neurophysiological Markers

Interest in neurophysiological function has resulted from observations of brain damage in alcoholics and a history of childhood learning difficulties in many alcoholics. While most of the brain damage observed in aging alcoholics probably results from excessive drinking, there may be predisposing neuropsychological deficits in many children destined to become alcoholics (Tarter & Edwards, 1988). Whether the learning difficulties result from biological or stress factors is as yet uncertain. And whether the inability to excel or keep up in school and its leading to problems with self-esteem and to gravitating to deviant peer groups is the mechanism by which high-risk youth become substance abusers remains a mystery. However, it is likely that some of the learning disabilities seen in children of alcoholics may result from the fetal alcohol syndrome, in which maternal drinking affects the normal development of neural tissue in the brain. Birth injuries may also account for some of this brain pathology. And there may be genetic factors underlying some of the deficits.

Among the distinctive biological variables that have been studied in alcoholics are electroencephalographic (EEG) patterns. As early as 1941, Davis et al. noted that awake nondrinking alcoholics tended to have resting-state EEG recordings that contained excess high-frequency waves (fast EEG activity) and were deficient in alpha-, theta-, and delta-brain-wave activity. The pattern of fast EEG activity has been shown to be transmitted genetically. Alpha activity corresponds to a state of pleasant stimulation and calm alertness.

Consistent with Cloninger's Type 2 alcoholism, Gabrielli et al. (1982) proposed that these fast EEG waves might be found in the male children of alcoholics, but not in the female children. A control group of normal children were compared with children of alcoholic, schizophrenic, and character-disordered parents. As had been hypothesized, the male children of alcoholics did have a significant excess of fast EEG activity and the daughters did not. Although many of the alcoholic parents had other psychiatric problems in addition to alcoholism, the authors concluded that since most forms of psychopathology are associated with slow EEG activity, it is unlikely that the findings were indicative of an inherited biological factor associated with another psychiatric diagnosis. These studies might suggest that sober alcoholics and their male offspring are more anxious than control subjects, consistent with Cloninger's Type 1 temperament.

In an attempt to distinguish family-history-positive (FHP) from family-history-negative (FHN) subjects, Pollack et al. (1983) examined alpha-wave activity in a group of men aged 19 to 21. He assumed that the FHP subjects would show greater alpha waves after the ingestion of a low dose of alcohol. Three EEG recordings and two blood alcohol levels were measured over a period of 130 minutes. Blood alcohol levels did not distinguish the FHP from the FHN subjects. However, measurement of EEG alpha activity did. The FHP subjects showed more slow alpha energy and less fast alpha energy when compared with FHN controls at baseline, and greater slowing of in alpha frequency after alcohol administration.

This notion that alcohol might have a relaxing effect by increasing alpha waves and percent time in alpha and decreasing the variance of EEG frequency was further explored by Propping et al. (1980, 1981). Resting EEG recordings were taken on alcoholics and their first-degree relatives and compared with controls. Female alcoholics showed a predominance of beta or high-frequency activity and a paucity of alpha waves as compared with controls. No significant differences in the EEG patterns were observed between the male alcoholics and controls. Alcoholic subjects were then divided into two groups with extreme resting EEGs ("good" and "poor"). Relatives showed patterns similar to those of the alcoholics (i.e., the alcoholics with "good" alpha synchronization had relatives with "good" patterns). When these findings were examined by gender, it was found that results held up only for relatives of male alcoholics.

Important advances have been made through studies of responses to sensory stimulation. Petrie (1960), in a study of pain, demonstrated that healthy people have characteristic perceptual reactance patterns to sensory stimulation that can be classified in two distinct types: augmentors and reducers. In a research paradigm in which a stimulus is gradually increased, "augmentors" amplify their brain potentials in response to increasing stimulation, whereas "reducers" dampen what is being perceived. He demonstrated that these characteristic patterns change in the presence of alcohol. Augmentors become reducers, whereas reducers remain reducers and do not show much effect. In testing alcoholics and nonalcoholics, Petrie found that sober alcoholics tend to be augmentors on perceptual reaction tests. Essentially, this means that they are more sensitive to painful stimuli than are nonalcoholics. He suggested that alcoholics may use alcohol to reduce the sensory stimulation.

Although this augmenting tendency has been considered by many to be a personality trait, Hennecke (1984) argues that her work with children indicates that augmenting is more a neurophysiological response than a psychological one. She found the tendency to augment in both the sons and daughters of alcoholic fathers, and believes it may signal a predisposition to alcoholism in later years. Elmasian et al. (1982) supported this interpretation in a study that found that auditory evoked brain potentials are greater for nonalcoholic first-degree relatives of alcoholics when compared with controls with no family history of alcoholism. This suggests that the trait is not attributable to the acquired effects of alcohol ingestion. Buffington and colleagues (1981) investigated the similarity of responses in alcoholics and their relatives. They found that male alcoholics and a female first-degree relative (mother, sister, or daughter) had fewer similar responses than had been reported in previous studies using matched pairs (twins) but more similar responses than were found in nonrelative pairs.

Begleiter and colleagues (1984; 1988) noted that FHP sons of alcoholic fathers had different P_{300} ERPs than FHN controls. (ERPs are brain waves measured using a high-tech apparatus that induces a repetitive stimulus such as a tone, an image, or a math problem and then measures the EEG waves that follow this precisely timed stimulus. The extraneous brain activity unrelated to the stimulus and its processing cancels out, with the repetitions leaving a tracing of the specific brain response to this stimulus. ERPs are under a very high degree of genetic control. P_{300} refers to the 300-millisecond component of the ERP that is believed to represent attention, decision making, and cognitive appraisals.) Begleiter's ERP-abnormal subjects on follow-up four years later have shown a high propensity for becoming alcoholic (75% by the age of 16) in a pattern that resembles the Cloninger Type 2 alcoholic (Begleiter, personal communication). P_{300} amplitude was found by Elmasian et al. (1982) to be significantly reduced after drinking in FHPs when compared with

FHNs. Reaction time was significantly higher in FHP subjects whether they were given alcohol or placebo.

Hill and her associates (1988) have posited that variants of cognitive functioning and electrophysiological activity found in nonalcoholic relatives of alcoholics reflect traits that are antecedent to the development of alcoholism. After considering a number of factors of vulnerability, Hill chose to focus on a variant of alcoholism that is more severe, characterized by multiply affected relatives (high-density families), and having an early onset. This group of subjects seems to be similar to, if not the same as, those identified by Cloninger as Type 2. This research team carefully controlled for the presence of other psychiatric disorders. Hill chose families in which one male sibling had been treated for alcoholism and at least one male sibling over the age of 30 appeared to be unaffected by alcoholism. The unaffected siblings had shorter P_{300} latency than the proband or other family members on ERP testing.

Biochemical Markers

Researchers have sought to identify neurochemical differences between alcoholics and nonalcoholics. Monoamine oxidase (MAO), an enzyme that can also be measured in blood platelets, is involved in the metabolism of neurotransmitters in the central nervous system. As early as 1970, Brown reported low MAO levels in alcoholics when compared with nonalcoholics. Purchall et al. (1980) observed a significant correlation between MAO in a large group of college students and their parents. College students with low levels of MAO had parents with low levels of MAO, and the prevalence of alcoholism among the low-MAO parents was significantly higher than among high-MAO parents. This suggests that low MAO levels are not the result of abusive drinking. However, Schuckit (1984) reported finding no *significant* differences in MAO levels between FHP and FHN men but he did report a nonsignificant trend toward lower MAO levels in FHP males.

Once again, the useful differentiation of types of alcoholism suggested by Cloninger may be important. Von Knorring et al. (1985) studied 36 alcoholics and 34 control subjects who were FHN. The alcoholic outpatients were classified as either Type 1 (milieu-limited) or Type 2 (male-limited) according to age at onset, severity of alcoholism, social and legal problems, and family history. The Type 2 alcoholics had significantly lower platelet MAO levels than did either the Type 1 or controls, between whom there was essentially no difference. Low MAO levels have been associated with sensation seeking (Schooler et al., 1978; von Knorring, Oreland, & Winblad, 1984), hyperactivity (Wender, 1971), and stimulus augmenting (Coursey, Buchsbaum, & Murphy, 1979; Buchsbaum et al., 1973). Schuckit's family-history risk studies have largely been done on college students who are predominantly FHN or FHP Type 1, since Type 2 males tend to drop out of school because of alcoholism, thrill-seeking, and antisocial activities.

It is possible that the presumed genetic predisposition to alcoholism could be due to an individual's reaction to the effect of alcohol. This would be seen with the first few drinks and does not appear to depend on quantity. The assumption is that the acute reactions may be related to the activity of enzymes that metabolize alcohol, (i.e., ADH and ALDH) and by the circulating levels of alcohol's intermediary metabolite, acetaldehyde.

Harada and colleagues (1980, 1981) established the genetic basis of ADH and ALDH. They observed that the "flushing" response to alcohol so prevalent in Orientals at low doses of alcohol was rare in Caucasians. At first this was believed to be because of the observed low incidence of atypical ADH found in Caucasians when compared with Orientals. However, more recently Harada et al. (1982) have suggested that the absence of a high-affinity ALDH isozyme rather than the presence of atypical ADH may be the determining factor. This would imply that delayed oxidation of acetaldehyde rather than faster production would be responsible for the observed flushing response to alcohol ingestion. The flushing response, similar to the disulfiram-ethanol reaction (DER) of acetaldehyde poisoning seen in persons who drink while taking Antabuse ®, is believed to represent a genetic protective barrier to alcoholism for Orientals and others with this phenotype that makes drinking so aversive that the person will never be able to drink enough to become alcoholic. This, however, is inconsistent with the findings of Saunders and Williams (1983) that American Indians, among whom there is a high prevalence of alcoholism, are also deficient in the high-affinity ALDH isozyme. There are also reports that alcoholism is becoming a problem among Orientals in Tokyo who are incorporating Western recreational patterns into their life-styles. Since some alcoholics taking disulfiram will repeatedly drink in spite of the aversive DER, it may be more accurate to view the flushing phenotype as a barrier that may sometimes be overcome by the desire to drink. Suggestions that high acetaldehyde levels may induce production of tetrahydroisoquinolines (TIQs) that can induce uncontrolled excessive drinking in experimental animals (Blum et al., 1978; Deitrich & Collins, 1977; Deitrich & Erwin, 1980; Myers & Melchior, 1977) might explain the seemingly paradoxical findings of Saunders and Williams (1983).

Schuckit and his colleagues (1979, 1982) studied college-age men divided into FHP and FHN for alcoholism. They found that the groups did not differ on blood alcohol levels, but that the men with positive family histories had significantly elevated concentrations of blood acetaldehyde after a moderate dose of alcohol. However, a study of 11-year-olds, also divided by family history (Behar et al., 1983), did not confirm that males at risk for the development of alcoholism had higher blood acetaldehyde levels after the ingestion of alcohol. This may be so because the doses appropriate to children were too low to produce a discernible change. Truitt (1971) first showed an elevation in acetaldehyde in alcoholics after drinking. Schuckit's finding of an elevation of postdrinking acetaldehyde in only FHP nonalcoholics suggests that this is a hereditary trait, probably secondary to some anomaly in ADH/ALDH enzyme interaction. Methodological problems in the measurement of acetaldehyde have plagued this line of research. Nonetheless, if it can be shown that inherited metabolic differences in acetaldehyde metabolism predispose some drinkers to the development of alcoholism, this may shed light on a mechanism of alcoholism etiology. Acetaldehyde has been implicated as a cause of acquired biological consequences of heavy drinking (Israel et al., 1986) by its irreversible binding to various proteins in the body and resultant auto-immune activation. Although studies of acetaldehyde have not yet been conclusive, they are provocative. It is possible that methodological problems have blocked the ability to confirm the importance of acetaldehyde in alcoholism.

STUDIES OF TOLERANCE

The issue of tolerance, both genetic and acquired, has been examined in animals using measures of sleep time to test tolerance of the hypnotic effect of alcohol and the effects on motor coordination and reflex impairment (Tabakoff et al., 1980). Schuckit (1980) found that FHP men showed less impairment on almost every measure of subjective and objective intoxication. One concern of social scientists has always been the expectancy factor, that is, the influence that anticipating a reaction might have on reports of a reaction. To control for this, Schuckit and his colleagues employed a placebo condition that confirmed that the reports of perceived intoxication were really due to the actual differences in the physiological effects of alcohol and not to the expectation of an effect. FHP men not only reported feeling less intoxicated than FHN controls after ingesting the same amount of alcohol, but also made fewer errors on a pursuit rotor test and showed higher levels of reaction and movement time. These findings suggest that tolerance to the effects of alcohol may be greater in FHPs, which might lead to increased use of alcohol to obtain or maintain a desired effect. FHP drinkers also may experience fewer adverse effects during initial experimentation with alcohol because of greater tolerance to its impairing effects, thus permitting them to progress further in drinking escalation before realizing that they need to reduce or cease drinking. Combined with the aforementioned data on augmentors and reducers, the greater tolerance may in some way reflect this difference.

STRESS IN CHILDREN OF ALCOHOLICS

As a group, children of alcoholic parents are exposed to a variety of stressors and potentially harmful events. Holmes and Rahe (1967) and others (Rahe & Arthur, 1978; Rahe, Meyer, & Smith, 1964) have shown that stress can interact with the risk of physical illness. Studies have shown that stress can induce hormonal changes, alter sleep patterns, affect mood, and even induce certain illnesses (e.g., hypertension, impaired immunity, hypersecretion of stomach acid leading to ulcers) or exacerbate others (e.g., diabetes, hemophilia, arthritis). It is as yet unclear exactly how stress does all this, but it appears that social support can favorably mediate the effects of stress (Lowenthal & Haven, 1968; Nuckolls, Cassell, & Kaplan, 1972). Hence, the most harmful effects of stress are borne by those who experience it without adequate social support.

In a study of COAs using primary care and emergency services at an HMO (health maintenance organization), the frequency of utilization for accidents and childhood illnesses went up substantially more than baseline when the alcoholic parent was actively drinking as compared with when the same parent had begun sobriety (Putnam et al., in press). Likewise, when a similar comparison was made with another sample of COAs in which the alcoholic father was in either relapse or recovery, the children of the relapsing alcoholics were substantially depressed and functioning poorly in school compared with the children of either the recovering fathers or the nonalcoholic control fathers (Moos & Billings, 1982).

Studies of alcoholic families have shown that the "rule of secrecy" about the family's problems usually prevents children from seeking extrafamilial social support for their predicament. Meanwhile, within the family, the involvement of close family members in the enabling process often precludes their being helpful to these children under stress (Black, 1982; Koppel, Stimmler, & Perone, 1980; Levinson & Ashenberg-Straussner, 1978). For instance, COAs are exposed to "blackouts" in which the alcoholic parent has partial amnesia concerning certain events that occurred while drinking. Combined with lying by both parents in a defensive effort to conceal the family problems, this generates a warped sense of reality or values for the COAs. Small children whose efforts to discuss their feelings about a troubling event or act by a parent (e.g., an embarrassing behavior, violence, sexual abuse) are thwarted may lead them to question their own sanity as denials are encountered from everyone in their social network. Sometimes the family rule of secrecy prevents the COAs from even trying to discuss problems with each other, thus interfering with the important social-support function of the family. Further stressful events may be borne without social support as the child shuts down emotionally, becoming a silent victim. Such children present to health-care providers as very meek or passive children with phobias, somatization disorders (e.g., headaches, abdominal syndromes, or allergic problems with underlying psychic components), psychosomatic disorders, (e.g., ulcers, enuresis, asthma), injuries of mysterious etiology, substance-abuse disorders, depression and suicide attempts, or eating disorders. Under careful diagnostic scrutiny, they may have components of post-traumatic stress disorder (PTSD) (see also Chapters 4-8). Even if placed in therapy, they may not reveal the traumata that they are enduring unless they see their parents recovering simultaneously and can displace themselves from the "old way" in which their family functioned before recovery (see Chapters 4 and 5). They may be able to deal with these matters, despite the failure of parents, and recover as adolescents (through Alateen or residential therapeutic community treatment) or as adults (in AA, ACOA, Al-Anon, or retrospective therapies) (see also Chapters 10-13).

If the children do not get the help they need during early development, they may become enraged at their world and act this anger out by destructive juvenile-delinquent behavior. If parental denial continues to prevail, these children will come into the jurisdiction of community agencies. If the child is not provided with effective treatment at this phase, he or she will bounce from placement to placement on the road to incorrigibility and adult ASP (see also Chapters 7 and 8). Again, effective treatment may still need to include some help for the substance-abusing parent(s), however, older teens may be able to recover from their problems in spite of their parents' continuing illness (see Chapters 6 and 8-12). It is not clear to the authors whether the above scenario of environmental influences on a developing child is sufficient to cause ASP without the genetic component of Cloninger's Type 2 or of Cadoret's ASP with drug addiction. But it is important to heed Schuckit's (1973) warning that secondary ASP (a phenocopy, that is, a nongenetic mimicry of a genetic phenotype) can appear as a component of addictive disorders such as alcoholism that disappears upon recovery from alcoholism.

Stress takes many forms in alcoholic and other dysfunctional families. Substance-abusing parents may alter their behavior in a Jeckyl/Hyde manner as they switch from being sober to being intoxicated, and vice versa (Liepman, Nirenberg, & Silvia, 1989). Such parental inconsistency may interfere with a child's learning how best to behave to meet his or her needs (Liepman, White, & Nirenberg, 1987). Children raised in this fluctuating environment eventually learn to compensate for the changes by becoming quite observant of the drinking or drugging status of the affected parent and then reacting accordingly. This produces in the child more than one set of behaviors that are chosen (unconsciously or consciously) to fit the circumstances. A rather remarkable demonstration of human versatility for defensive purposes, this may later come in handy when adjusting to a spouse or child with an active substance-abuse problem, or when suffering with one's own substance-abuse disorder. Unfortunately, this superb flexibility may interfere with seeking help for the problem, thus enabling it to progress to a greater degree before recovering.

Many COAs face the chronic worry of not knowing whether or when to expect the substance-abusing parent to return home, especially when they realize that life-threatening risks are being taken by that parent (e.g., driving while intoxicated, fighting in bars, risking accidental overdoses, attempting suicide, becoming indebted to dangerous drug dealers). They may also dread the return of the affected parent because this may precede violence, sexual abuse, or verbal abuse of members in the household, especially the other parent (who is usually their main source of social support in dealing with the substance-abusing parent) (see Chapters 7, 9, & 11).

To elucidate the impact on children of interpersonal conflict between parents, Minuchin once studied a pair of sisters with juvenile-onset diabetes melitus, only one of whom repeatedly suffered from episodes of ketoacidosis requiring hospitalization (Minuchin et al., 1978). He had the sisters watch their parents through a one-way window while he instructed the parents to disagree with each other. Then he instructed them to stop fighting without resolution of the disagreement. Whereas the fatty-acid levels of both sisters rose moderately during the disagreement phase, the well sister's level returned to baseline when the parents stopped fighting while the ill sister's fatty acids continued to rise astronomically. This suggests that individual differences, perhaps genetic factors or environmental factors based on family roles, may govern biological response to stressors. We must be mindful of the complexity of these interacting factors. Since interpersonal conflict between parents in chemically dependent families is common, childhood reactions to stress should be commonplace among COAs.

Fetal Alcohol Effects

Children whose mothers drank (or used other drugs) during pregnancy are at risk of fetal toxic damage. The fetal alcohol syndrome (FAS) can affect the formation of major organs in the body, leading to facial, skeletal, and organ abnormalities, and growth, and mental retardation. Children affected by the FAS or other fetal toxic damage may be permanently handicapped in their ability to compete with their peers. Stress during pregnancy can also affect normal development in other ways. For instance, severe maternal stress has been noted during pregnancies of mothers of homosexual men. It is not clear whether this is one reason for the high rate of alcoholism among gay persons.

Neonatal withdrawal from alcohol or other drugs can alter sleep patterns and response to the social stimulation and cuddling so crucial to mother–child bonding. It has been suggested that the disruption of this process by neonatal withdrawal may increase the risk for childhood psychopathology and victimization resulting from parental child abuse and neglect.

SUMMARY

Children of alcoholic or other dysfunctional families are exposed to substantial stress during their development. While this is also the case for a number of children without substance-abusing families, the dynamics and defense patterns of chemically dependent families often block appropriate use of social support that might mediate reactions to stress. To make matters worse, COAs often inherit genotypes that make them more likely to encounter difficulties in life, such as attention-deficit disorder, ASP, or a predisposition to substance-use disorders. Thus, biological factors interact with psychosocial environmental factors to produce a complex interplay that often leads to troubling outcome for these unfortunate victims of circumstance. Such children are at high risk for medical problems, substance-use disorders, and psychopathology. Those attempting to prevent problems in children, and clinicians dedicated to helping these victims to recover, would be wise to consider the biological factors that cannot be modified with therapy as handicaps that must be accepted in recovery.

REFERENCES

Anastasi, A. (1958). Heredity, environment and the question "How?" *Psychological Review*, 65, 197–208.

Begleiter, H., & Porjesz, B. (1988). *Alcoholism: Clinical and Experimental Research*, 12, 488–493.

Begleiter, H., Porjesz, B., Behari, B., & Kissin, B. (1984). Even-related potentials in boys at risk for alcoholism. *Science (Washington, DC)*, 225, 1493–1496.

Behar, D., Berg, C. J., Rapoport, J. L., Nelson, W., Linnoila, M., Cohen, M., Bozevich, C., & Marshall, T. (1983). Behavioral and physiological effects of ethanol in high-risk and control children: A pilot study. *Alcoholism: Clinical and Experimental Research*, 7, 404–410.

Black, C. (1982). *It will never happen to me*. Denver, CO: MAC Printing & Publication Division.

Blum, K., Hamilton, M. G., Hirst, M., & Wallace, J. E. (1978). Putative role of isoquinoline alkaloids in alcoholism: A link to opiates. *Alcoholism: Clinical and Experimental Research*, 2, 113–120.

Blum, K., Noble, E. P., Sheridan, P. J., et al. (1990). Allelic association of human dopamine D_2 receptor gene in alcoholism. *JAMA*, 263, 2055–2060.

Bohman, M. (1978). Some genetic aspects of alcoholism and criminality: A population of adoptees. *Archives of General Psychiatry*, 35, 269–276.

Bohman, M., Cloninger, C. R., von Knorring, A-L., & Sigvardsson, S. (1984). An adoption study of somatoform disorders: III. Cross-fostering analysis and genetic relationship to alcoholism and criminality. *Archives of General Psychiatry*, 41, 872–878.

Bohman, M., Sigvardsson, S., & Cloninger, C. R. (1981). Maternal inheritance of alcohol abuse. *Archives of General Psychiatry*, 38, 965–969.

Brown, J. B. (1970). Platelet MAO and alcoholism. *American Journal of Psychiatry*, 134, 206–207.

Buchsbaum, M., Landau, S., Murphy, D., & Goodwin, D. (1973). Average evoked response in bipolar and unipolar affective disorders: Relationship to sex, age of onset and monoamine oxidase. *Biological Psychiatry*, 7, 199–212.

Buffington, V., Martin, D. C., & Becker, J. (1981). VER similarity between alcoholic probands and their first degree relatives. *Psychophysiology*, 18, 529–533.

Cadoret, R., & Cain, C. (1980). Sex differences in predictors of antisocial behavior in adoptees. *Archives of General Psychiatry, 37,* 1171–1175.

Cadoret, R., & Gath, A. (1978). Inheritance of alcoholism in adoptees. *British Journal of Psychiatry, 132,* 252–258.

Cadoret, R. J., O'Gorman, T. W., Troughton, E., & Heywood, E. (1985). Alcoholism and antisocial personality: Interrelationships, genetic and environmental factors. *Archives of General Psychiatry, 42,* 161–167.

Cadoret, R. J., Troughton, E., & O'Gorman, T. W. (1987). Genetic and environmental factors in alcohol abuse and antisocial personality. *Journal of Studies on Alcohol, 48,* 1–8.

Cadoret, R. J., Troughton, E., O'Gorman, T. W., & Heywood, E. (1986). An adoption study of genetic and environmental factors in drug abuse. *Archives of General Psychiatry, 43,* 1131–1136.

Cahalan, D., Cisin, I. H., & Crossley, H. M. (1969). *American drinking practices: A national study of drinking behavior and attitudes.* New Brunswick, NJ: Rutgers Center for Alcohol Studies.

Cloninger, C. R. (1987). Neurogenetic adaptive mechanisms in alcoholism. *Science (Washington, DC), 236,* 410–416.

Cloninger, C. R., Bohman, M., & Sigvardsson, S. (1981). Inheritance of alcohol abuse: Cross-fostering analysis of adopted men. *Archives of General Psychiatry, 38,* 861–868.

Cloninger, C. R., Bohman, M., Sigvardsson, S., & von Knorring, A-L. (1985). Psychopathology in adopted-out children of alcoholics: The Stockholm study. In M. Galanter (Ed.), *Recent Developments in Alcoholism, 3,* 37–51.

Cloninger, C. R., Christiansen, K. O., Reich, T., & Gottesman, I. I. (1978). Implications of sex differences in the prevalences of antisocial personality, alcoholism and criminality for familial transmission. *Archives of General Psychiatry, 35,* 941–951.

Cloninger, C. R., Sigvardsson, S., & Bohman, M. (1981). Childhood personality predicts alcohol abuse in young adults. *Alcoholism: Clinical and Experimental Research, 12,* 494–505.

Cloninger, C. R., von Knorring, A-L., & Bohman, M. (1984). An adoption study of somatoform disorders: II. Identification of two discrete somatoform disorders. *Archives of General Psychiatry, 41,* 863–871.

Coursey, R., Buchsbaum, M., & Murphy, D. (1979). Platelet MAO activity and evoked potentials in the identification of subjects biologically at risk for psychiatric disorders. *British Journal of Psychiatry, 134,* 372–381.

Davis, P. A., Gibbs, F. A., Davis, H., Jetter, W. W., & Trowbridge, L. S. (1941). The effects of alcohol upon the electroencephalogram. *Quarterly Journal of Studies on Alcohol, 1,* 626–637.

Deitrich, R. A., & Collins, A. C. (1977). Pharmacogenetics of alcoholism. In K. Blum (Ed.), *Alcohol and opiates* (pp. 109–139). New York: Academic Press.

Deitrich, R. A., & Erwin, E. (1980). Biogenic amine-aldehyde condensation products: Tetrahydroisoquinolines and tryptolines (beta-carbolines). *Annual Review of Pharmacology, 20,* 55–80.

Dobzhansky, T. (1950). The genetic nature of differences among men. In S. Persons (Ed.), *Evolutionary thought in America* (pp. 86–155). New Haven, CT: Yale University Press.

Elmasian, R., Neville, H., Woods, D., Schuckit, M., & Bloom, F. (1982). Event-related potentials are different in individuals at high risk for developing alcoholism. *Proceedings of the National Academy of Sciences USA, 70,* 7900–7903.

Fingarette, H. (1988). *Heavy drinking: The myth of alcoholism.* Los Angeles: University of California Press.

Gabrielli, W. F., Mednick, S. A., Volakva, J., Schulsinger, F., & Itil, T. M. (1982). Electroencephalograms in children of alcoholic fathers. *Psychophysiology, 19,* 404–407.

Goodwin, D. (1971). Is alcoholism hereditary? A review and critique. *Archives of General Psychiatry, 25,* 545–549.

Goodwin, D. W. (1979). Alcoholism and heredity: A review and hypothesis. *Archives of General Psychiatry, 36,* 57–61.

Goodwin, D. W., Schulsinger, F., Hermanson, L., Guze, S. B., & Winokur, G. (1973). Alcohol problems in adoptees raised apart from alcoholic biological parents. *Archives of General Psychiatry, 28,* 238–243.

Harada, S., Agarwal, D., & Goedde, H. (1980). Isoenzymes of alcohol dehydrogenase and aldehyde dehydrogenase in Japanese and their role in alcohol sensitivity. *Advances in Experimental Medicine and Biology, 132,* 31–39.

Harada, S., Agarwal, D., & Goedde, H. (1981). Aldehyde dehydrogenase deficiency as a cause of facial flushing reaction to alcohol in Japanese. *Lancet, ii(8253),* 982.

Harada, S., Agarwal, D., Goedde, H., Tagaki, S., & Ishikawa, B. (1982). Possible protective role against alcoholism for aldehyde dehydrogenase isozyme deficiency in Japan. *Lancet, ii(8302),* 827.

Hennecke, L. (1984). Stimulus augmenting and field dependence in children of alcoholic fathers. *Journal of Studies on Alcohol, 45,* 486–492.

Hill, S. Y., Aston, C., & Rabin, B. (1988). Suggestive evidence of genetic linkage between alcoholism and the MNS blood group. *Alcoholism: Clinical and Experimental Research, 12,* 811–814.

Holmes, T. H., & Rahe, R. H. (1967). The Social Readjustment Rating Scale. *Journal of Psychosomatic Research, 11,* 213–218.

Israel, Y., Hurwitz, E., Niemela, O., & Arnon, R., (1986). Monoclonal and polyclonal antibodies against acetaldehyde-containing epitopes in acetaldehyde-protein adducts. *Proceedings of the National Academy of Sciences USA 83,* 7923–7927.

Jonsson, A., & Nilsson, T. (1968). Alkohol konsumtion hos monozygota och dizygota tvillingar. *Nordisk Hygienisk Tidskrift, 49,* 21–25.

Kaij, L. (1960). *Alcoholism in twins.* Stockholm: Almquist & Wiskell.

Kerem, B-S., Rommens, J. M., Buchanan, J. A., Markiewicz, D., Cox, T. K., Chakravarti, A., Buchwald, M., & Tsui, L-C. (1989). Identification of the cystic fibrosis gene: Genetic analysis. *Science, 245.* 1073–1080.

Koppel, F., Stimmler, L., & Perone, F. (1980). The enabler: A motivational tool in treating the alcoholic. *Social Casework, 61,* 577–583.

Levinson, V. R., & Ashenberg-Straussner, S. L. (1978). Social workers as "enablers" in the treatment of alcoholics. *Social Casework, 59*, 14–20.

Liepman, M. R., Silvia, L. Y., & Nirenberg, T. D. (1989). The use of family behavior loop mapping for substance abuse. *Family Relations, 38*, 282–287.

Liepman, M. R., White, W. T., & Nirenberg, T. D. (1986). Children in alcoholic families. In D. C. Lewis & C. N. Williams (Eds.), *Providing care for children of alcoholics: Clinical and research perspectives* (pp. 39–64). Pompano Beach, FL: Health Communications, Inc.

Loehlin, J. C. (1972). An analysis of alcohol-related questionnaire items from the national merit twin study. *Annals of the New York Academy of Sciences, 197*, 117–120.

Lowenthal, M. R., & Haven, C. (1968). Interaction and adaptation: Intimacy as a critical variable. In F. Neugarten (Ed.): *Middle age and aging* (pp. 78–84). Chicago: University of Chicago Press.

Minuchin, S., Rosman, B. L., Baker, L., & Liebman, R. (1978). *Psychosomatic families: Anorexia nervosa in context.* Cambridge, MA: Harvard University Press.

Moos, R., & Billings, A. (1982). Children of alcoholics during the recovery process: Alcoholic and matched control families. *Addictive Behaviors, 7*, 155–163.

Myers, R. D., & Melchior, C. L. (1977). Alcohol drinking: Abnormal intake caused by tetrahydropapaveroline in brain. *Science, 196*, 554–556.

Nuckolls, K. B., Cassell, J., & Kaplan, B. (1972). Psychosocial assets, life crises, and the prognosis of pregnancy. *American Journal of Epidemiology, 95*, 431–442.

Partanen, J., Bruun, K., & Markkanen, T. (1966). *Inheritance of drinking behavior: A study of intelligence, personality and use of alcohol in adult twins.* The Finnish Foundation for Alcohol Studies Publication No. 14. Helsinki: Finnish Foundation for Alcohol Studies.

Petrie, A. (1960). Some psychological aspects of pain and the relief of suffering. *Annals of the New York Academy of Sciences, 86*, 13–27.

Pollack, V. E., Volakva, J., Goodwin, D. W., Mednick, S. A., Gabrielli, W. F., Knop, J., & Schulsinger, F. (1983). The EEG after alcohol administration in men at risk for alcoholism. *Archives of General Psychiatry, 40*, 857–861.

Propping, P., Kruger, J., & Janah, A. (1980). Effect of alcohol on genetically determined variants of the normal electroencephalogram. *Psychiatry Research, 2*, 85–98.

Propping, P., Kruger, J., & Mark, W. (1981). Genetic predisposition to alcoholism: An EEG study in alcoholics and their relatives. *Human Genetics, 59*, 51–59.

Puchall, L. B., Coursey, R. D., Buchsbaum, M. S., et al. (1980). Parents of high risk subjects defined by levels of monoamine oxidase activity. *Schizophrenia Bulletin, 6*, 338–346.

Putnam, S. L., Rockett, I.R.H., & Stout, R. L. (in press). Parental alcoholism and children's health: A study of pediatric illness, injury, and utilization in a health maintenance organization. *Journal of Studies on Alcohol.*

Rahe, R. H., & Arthur, R. J. (1978). Life change and illness studies: Past history and future directions. *Human Stress, 4*, 3–15.

Rahe, R. H., Meyer, M., & Smith, M. (1964). Social stress and illness onset. *Journal of Psychosomatic Research, 8*, 35–44.

Reich, T., Cloninger, C. R., Van Eerdewegh, P., Rice, J. P., & Mullaney, J. (1988). Secular trends in the familial transmission of alcoholism. *Alcoholism: Clinical and Experimental Research*, 12, 458–464.

Roe, A., & Burks, B. (1945). Adult adjustment of foster children of alcoholic and psychotic parentage and the influence of the foster home. In *Memoirs of the Section on Alcohol Studies at Yale University*, No. 3 (pp. 1–164). New Haven, CT: Yale University.

Saunders, J. & Williams, R. (1983). The genetics of alcoholism: Is there an inherited susceptibility to alcohol related problems? *Alcohol and Alcoholism*, 18, 189–217.

Schooler, C., Zahn, T., Murphy, D., & Buchsbaum, M. (1978). Psychological correlates of monoamine oxidase activity in normals. *Journal of Nervous and Mental Diseases*, 166, 177–186.

Schuckit, M. A. (1973). Alcoholism and sociopathy: Diagnostic confusion. *Quarterly Journal of Studies on Alcohol*, 34, 157–164.

Schuckit, M. A. (1980). Self-rating of alcohol intoxication by young men with and without family histories of alcoholism. *Journal of Studies on Alcohol*, 41, 242–249.

Schuckit, M. A. (1984). Genetic and biochemical factors in the etiology of alcoholism. In L. Grinspoon (Ed.), *Psychiatry Update vol. III* (pp. 320–327). Washington, D.C.: American Psychiatric Press.

Schuckit, M. A. (1988). Reactions to alcohol in sons of alcoholics and controls. *Alcoholism: Clinical and Experimental Research*, 12, 465–470.

Schuckit, M. A., & Duby, J. (1982). Alcohol-related flushing and the risk for alcoholism in sons of alcoholics. *Journal of Clinical Psychiatry*, 43, 415–418.

Schuckit, M. A., & Rayses, V. (1979). Ethanol ingestion: Differences in blood acetaldehyde concentrations in relatives of alcoholics and controls. *Science*, 203, 54–55.

Schuckit, M. A., Shaskan, E., Duby, J., Vega, R., & Moss, M. (1981). Dopamine-beta-hydroxylase activity levels in men at high risk for alcoholism and controls. *Biological Psychiatry*, 16, 1067–1075.

Schuckit, M. A., Shaskan, E., Duby, J., Vega, R., & Moss, M. (1982). Platelet monoamine oxidase activity in relatives of alcoholics. *Archives of General Psychiatry*, 39, 137–140.

Sigvardsson, S., von Knorring, A-L., Bohman, M., & Cloninger, C. R. (1984). An adoption study of somatoform disorders: I. The relationship of somatization to psychiatric disability. *Archives of General Psychiatry*, 41, 853–862.

Svikis, D. S., Pickens, R., Lykken, D., Heston, L., & Clayton, P. J. (1987). Familial influences in twin concordance for alcoholism. *Behavioral Genetics*, 17, 641.

Tabakoff, B., Ritzmann, R. D., Taju, T. S., & Deitrich, R. A. (1980). Characterization of acute and chronic tolerance in mice selected for inherent differences in sensitivity to ethanol. *Alcoholism: Clinical and Experimental Research*, 4, 70–74.

Tarter, R. E., & Edwards, K. (1988). Psychological factors associated with the risk for alcoholism. *Alcoholism: Clinical and Experimental Research*, 12, 471–480.

Truitt, E. B., Jr. (1971). Blood acetaldehyde levels after alcohol consumption by alcoholic and non-alcoholic subjects. In M. K. Roach, W. M. McIsaac, & P. J. Creaven (Eds.): *Biological aspects of alcohol: Advances in mental sciences, vol. 3,* (pp. 212–223).

Von Knorring, A-L., Bohman, M., von Knorring, L., & Oreland, L. (1985). Platelet MAO activity as a biological marker in subgroups of alcoholism. *Acta Psychiatria Scandanavia*, 71, 51–58.

Von Knorring, L., Oreland, L., & Winblad, B. (1984). Personality traits related to mono-amine oxidase (MAO) in platelets. *Psychiatric Research, 12,* 11–26.

Wender, P. (1971). *Minimal brain dysfunction in children.* New York: Wiley.

Wolin, S. J., Bennett, L. A., Noonan, D. L., & Teitelbaum, M. A. (1980). Disrupted family rituals: A factor in the intergenerational transmission of alcoholism. *Journal of Studies on Alcohol, 41,* 199–214.

2

Forgotten No Longer: An Overview of Research on Children of Chemically Dependent Parents

Jeannette L. Johnson, Ph.D.

To help understand the complex problems of chemical addiction, etiological research is turning to the study of the children of chemically dependent parents for two reasons.* First is the increase over the past two decades in the scientific evidence of vulnerability to chemical dependence. Substantial research has linked the transmission of chemical dependence, especially alcoholism, to genetic and environmental risk factors (Cloninger, Reich, & Wetzel, 1979; Goodwin, 1985; Russell, Henderson, & Blume, 1985; West & Prinz, 1987). This research shows that children of chemically dependent parents are at high risk for substance abuse and other problem behaviors (Kumpfer, 1987).

The second reason has been fostered by the dedication of grass-roots organizations. Begun in the early 1980s, these organizations have developed into national public-advocacy groups for children of alcoholics (COAs) (Gravitz & Bowden, 1985; Worden, 1984). Vigorous advocacy, special programs, workshops, and conferences promote the health and welfare of the offspring of chemically dependent parents in order to prevent and treat the many problems that they can encounter (see Foreword and Chapters 13 and 14).

Understanding the specific contributions of antecedent behaviors to the vulnerability for chemical dependence is an important research and clinical agenda. Through the early identification of biological, psychological, and environmental risk factors, we can advance our efforts toward the prevention of drug abuse. Studies determining the relative contributions of psychosocial and biological factors to chemical dependence can also aid efforts to develop specific prevention strategies

*The author gratefully acknowledges the support and encouragement of Drs. Barry Brown, Wally Pickworth, and David Newlin.

that in turn, target the specific problems of different groups of children at risk (see also Chapter 3).

Data addressing risk research should allow us to distinguish among *broad* group differences (e.g., children of chemically dependent parents versus children who have undergone crises unrelated to chemical dependence, such as chronic illness), *specific* group differences (e.g., COAs as opposed to children of other chemically addicted parents), and *within*-group differences (e.g., COAs with problems compared with COAs without problems). To encourage the understanding of the specificity of functioning in high-risk children, the following overview of the research literature separates COAs from children of other chemically dependent parents—for clarity, they are referred to as addict parents.

REVIEW OF THE LITERATURE ON CHILDREN OF ALCOHOLICS

Overarching Research Paradigms

Etiological studies of alcoholism differ from etiological studies of other chemical dependence for two reasons: there is more of it and it is organized into distinct research paradigms. Cloninger, Reich, and their many colleagues (Cloninger, Bohman, & Sigvaardsson, 1981; Reich et al., 1981, 1988; Rice, Cloninger, & Reich, 1978) propose three types of research models for analyzing data on alcoholism: (1) polygenetic, which focuses on the genetic component; (2) cultural, which focuses on the cultural component; and (3) multifactorial, which takes into account both genetic and cultural factors.

The research of COAs is replete with studies of the genetic factors in the transmission of alcoholism (NIAAA, 1985). From the genetic perspective, a biologically determined inclination toward alcoholism is considered to be the basic factor in transmission (Blum et al., 1990). Genetic hypotheses are fostered by the demonstration of a significant contribution of biological relatives' alcoholism to the determinants of alcohol use and abuse in other family members. However, because genetic factors may be highly heritable for some types of alcoholism but not for others, environmental hypotheses are employed to ascertain which environmental factors operate independently of genetic factors (see also Chapter 1). The environmental point of view emphasizes the influence of social or familial values and behaviors on alcohol use. Thus, the environment has a critical role in the development of alcoholism among the offspring of alcoholics—for example, an environment that contributes to childhood deprivation.

More recently, some researchers have recommended a multifactorial framework for understanding the transmission of alcoholism (El Guebaly & Offord, 1977, 1979; Russell, Henderson, & Blume, 1986; Sher, 1987; Windle, 1989). Here, predisposing genetic factors interact with environmental experiences, which, in turn, are viewed as precipitating factors in transmission. McCord (1988) illustrates this interaction by showing how particular types of maternal behavior, combined with paternal alcoholism, are influential in the intergenerational transmission of alcoholism.

Early Reports

Gutzke (1984) and Warner and Rosett (1975) provide historical reviews concerning the influence of maternal alcoholism on infants (see also Chapter 1). Reports appearing at the turn of the century describe such influence on infant mortality, the incidence of epilepsy, and familial alcoholism in females confined to the Liverpool Prison (Sullivan & Scholar, 1899). Not surprisingly, mothers confined during pregnancy (and so unable to obtain alcohol) gave birth to healthier babies.

Many earlier studies echo findings from contemporary research. For instance, MacNicholl suggested in 1905 that COAs were at risk for cognitive deficits. In 1910, a series of studies (Elderton & Pearson, 1910; Pearson, 1910; Pearson & Elderton, 1910) measuring mortality, physiology, and general health in the offspring of alcoholic parents found differences between the COAs and the children of nonalcoholics. These authors concluded that if mothers stopped drinking during gestation, their children would be healthier.

Despite the methodological criticisms of some of this initial work (Keynes, 1910–1911), these early authors discussed alcoholism etiology in much the same way we do today: either it is nature or nurture, or some combination of the two. More than four decades have passed since MacNicholl's study, and yet his conclusions summarize contemporary clinical and scientific positions:

> First. Alcohol at the threshold of life is a bar to success and a foe to health.
> Second. Alcohol, by destroying the integrity of nerve structures, lowering the standard of organic relations, launches hereditary influences which by continuous transmission gain momentum and potency and leave their impact upon gland and nerve until the mental faculties are demoralized, physical energies hopelessly impaired, and the moral nature becomes degenerate and dies.
> Third. If we are to make any material change in the ranks of mental deficients we must adopt methods of prevention as well as methods of cure.
> It is a momentous problem that confronts us. The spirit in which we meet it may be a possible aid or hindrance to its solution. (p. 117)

Contemporary Research

In 1969, Margaret Cork heralded much of the contemporary interest in children of alcoholics with her classic book, *The Forgotten Children*. She describes in great detail the life histories, feelings, and problems of COAs in an effort to promote an understanding of these children. By conducting informal, intimate, and unstructured interviews with 115 male and female children (aged 10–16), she could poignantly narrate the children's responses to the stressful and sometimes adversarial environments created by alcoholic parents. According to these children, parental alcoholism negatively affected their interpersonal relationships, both within and outside the family.

Contemporary research on COAs has further refined their potential problems. There is a wide range of research covering such domains as behavioral disorders (Fine et al., 1976), social conditions (Nylander & Rydelius, 1982), developmental experience (Noll & Zucker, 1983), psychopathology (Earls et al., 1988), symptomatology (Haberman, 1966), delinquency (Monnelly et al., 1983), responses to alcohol (Pollock et al., 1986), and neuropsychological mechanisms (Tarter et al., 1984). This research has been amply reviewed (Adler & Raphael, 1983; Corder, McRee, & Rohrer, 1984; el Guebaly and Offord, 1977, 1979; Russell, Henderson, & Blume, 1985; Sher, 1987; Windle, 1989).

In one review, Sher (1987) discusses the research on COAs from several perspectives: genetic, environmental, and psychosocial influences; family environmental influences and disorders associated with a family history of alcoholism; biochemical and psychological factors; neuropsychological and neurophysiological functioning; and, alcohol-related factors (e.g., responsivity, sensitivity, exposure, and expectancies). In addition, he discusses possible moderating variables, or protective factors, related to the transmission of alcoholism.

The following review of the literature on COAs is divided into four broad areas.

HERITABILITY

Issues related to heritability are not without controversy (Littrell, 1988; Peele, 1986 [see Chapter 1]). Nevertheless, many studies of related individuals (e.g., families, adopted-out siblings, twins) support a genetic theory of alcoholism transmission (Amark, 1951; Cotton, 1979; Kaij, 1960; Schuckit, Goodwin, & Winokur, 1972). Goodwin (1976, 1985), for example, reports that the prevalence of alcoholism among male relatives of alcoholics (which is approximately 25%) exceeds the estimated population prevalence for alcoholics, which is 3–5%. Similarly, the prevalence of alcoholism among female relatives of alcoholics (which is approximately 5–10%) exceeds the estimated population prevalence for alcoholics (0.1–1%).

Scandinavian adoption studies provide a convincing picture of the possible genetic influence of alcoholism (Goodwin et al., 1973, 1974, 1977; Bohman, 1978; Cloninger, Bohman, & Sigvaardson, 1981; Cadoret et al., 1980, 1987). These studies show that biology influences alcoholism more than the adoptive family's environment. For example, male adoptees with a biological paternal history positive for alcoholism are four times more likely to become alcoholic than those without

(Cadoret, Cain, & Grove, 1980). Twin studies demonstrate that the frequency of alcoholism among monozygotic twins is higher than among dizygotic twins (Hrubec & Omenn, 1981).

FETAL ALCOHOL SYNDROME

A second group of studies are those that involve infants born to alcoholic mothers and investigate the teratogenic effects of maternal alcohol use. Such studies report strong relationships between in utero alcohol use and later childhood problems, such as minor physical anomalies, hyperactivity, mental retardation, and electro-encephalographic (EEG) anomalies (Abel, 1980, 1981, 1982; Jones & Smith, 1973; Ulleland, 1972). Jones and Smith (1973) described this as the fetal alcohol syndrome (FAS). FAS is typically a cluster of four characteristics seen in the offspring of mothers who drink excessively during pregnancy: central-nervous-system dysfunction, abnormal facial features, behavioral deficits, and growth deficiency. These problems do not necessarily disappear over the course of development.

FAMILY STUDIES

In general, parental alcoholism disrupts family life and contributes to dysfunction in the offspring (Wilson & Orford, 1978). Studies of alcoholic family interaction show that the transmission of alcoholism in family members involves many different factors (Jacob & Seilhamer, 1987; Jacob et al., 1978; Steinglass, Bennett, Wolin, & Reiss, 1987). Alcoholic families report higher levels of conflict than do nonalcoholic families (Moos & Billings, 1982), with the drinking itself appearing as the primary factor in the family disruption. Furthermore, adult COAs continue to have problems even after leaving the family of origin's household (Johnson & Bennett, 1989). Bennett and her colleagues show that the degree of organization and disruption in the alcoholic family will distinguish the differential well-being of adult COAs (Bennett et al., 1987; Wolin et al., 1980; Steinglass et al., 1987).

Another area of research examines family rituals, such as dinners, holidays, and vacations (Wolin, Bennett, & Noonan, 1979; Bennett & Wolin, 1986). Family-ritual disruption is significantly associated with the differential transmission of alcoholism; maintaining family rituals during periods of heavy parental drinking results in less transmission of alcoholism than when rituals are altered. Ritual stability in alcoholic families during childhood and adolescence appears to influence later alcoholism. Thus, those alcoholic families that show more stability also evidence less alcoholism in their adult offspring.

RISK-FACTOR RESEARCH

In examining the potential biological and psychosocial risk factors in COAs, these children are considered at risk because there is a greater likelihood that they will develop alcoholism compared to a randomly selected child from the same community. Because physiological, social, and psychological changes accompany alcoholism, the high-risk paradigm overcomes the conceptual and methodological difficulties of studying the transmission of alcoholism in individuals who are already alcoholic. In the latter case, it is difficult to separate antecedent influences from the consequences of alcoholism. The following highlights two prominent areas of risk factor research which hold promise for future identification of potential risk markers for alcoholism.

Biological Markers

Biological mechanisms that differentiate COAs from children of nonalcoholics involve several different physiological systems (Cloninger, Reich, & Wetzel, 1979; Deitrich & Spuhler, 1984; Schuckit et al., 1985). Compared with children of nonalcoholics, COAs differ on the basis of EEG (Gabrielli et al., 1982), event-related potentials (Begleiter et al., 1984), and endocrine deviations (Schuckit, Parker, & Rossman, 1983). Begleiter and his colleagues (1984) showed that the P3 component of the event-related potential, an electrophysiological measure of cognitive processing, is significantly decreased in COAs as compared with children of nonalcoholics. This line of research promises to be instrumental in the future identification of biological markers for alcoholism.

Cognition

To date, research on cognitive differences in COAs has not shown that their academic or intellectual performance is consistently different from or lower than that of children of nonalcoholics. There is sufficient evidence, however, that makes this line of research worthy of pursuit. For example, lowered academic functioning in COAs has been reported by several researchers (Hughes, 1977; Knop et al., 1985; Schuckit & Chiles, 1978), but other data do not agree with these findings (Rimmer, 1982). Similarly, lowered levels of intellectual functioning in COAs has been reported by some researchers (Aronsen et al., 1985; Ervin et al., 1984; Gabrielli & Mednick, 1983; Steinhausen, Gobel, & Nestler, 1984), but not by others (Herjanic et al., 1978; Kern et al., 1981; Tarter et al., 1984).

Researchers offer different explanations for the inconsistencies found in the literature. Tarter, Jacob, and Bremer (1989) recently suggested that an anterior cerebral dysfunction was responsible for the observed cognitive deficits in COAs, implicating a possible biological basis for these differences. After examining perceptions of cognitive competence and actual cognitive performance, Johnson and Rolf (1988) suggested that the observed negative perceptions of cognitive competence in COAs may affect the motivation to perform at an optimal level. Werner's (1986) research shows that cognitive deficits may not characterize COAs as a group. Her longitudinal study on the island of Kauai compared a subgroup of COAs with problems (e.g., repeated or serious delinquencies, mental health problems requiring treatment) with COAs without problems. She showed that those with problems scored lower on verbal and quantitative cognitive measures, suggesting that, perhaps, only a subgroup of COAs is at risk for cognitive deficits.

Summary of COA Literature Review

Sher (1987) summarized his comprehensive synthesis of the research findings by stating: "However, for a number of reasons, it is difficult to evaluate our current state of knowledge" (p. 91). He cites several reasons for this. First, the spurious reliability of individual findings makes it difficult to have confidence in the research data, even if the findings appear replicable across laboratories. Second, because most studies are univariate, they prevent an integration of biological, psychological, and social perspectives. Thus, we do not have a complete picture of the strengths and weaknesses of COAs. Third, because behavior is studied at a single point in time, longitudinal data are not yet available to describe the developmental progression of the risk and protective factors influencing the transmission of alcoholism. These methodological problems are discussed in greater detail in a later section of this chapter.

Johnson and Bennett (1988) suggest that even though research on COAs is in its infancy, comparisons between these children and children of nonalcoholics that indicate significant differences in important areas of behavioral functioning should not be ignored, but interpreted with caution. They state: "Given time and an adequate number of studies, research will eventually synthesize a testable, replicable hypothesis. Until such a time that research findings advance, it would be unfair to generalize to all children who grow up in alcoholic homes" (p. 18).

REVIEW OF THE LITERATURE ON CHILDREN OF ADDICTS

In contrast to the dominant paradigms in alcoholism research, many diverse research paradigms govern etiological studies of chemical dependence other than alcoholism. Dependence on other chemicals is explained by social control theory (Hirschi, 1969), generalized social interaction of interpersonal influence (Kandel, Kessler, & Margulies, 1978), peer influence (Sutherland & Cressy, 1970), parental modeling (Stenmark et al., 1974), family systems (Klagsbrun & Davis, 1977; Steinglass, Werner, & Mendelson, 1971), deviance (Davis et al., 1974), or multivariate interactions (Kaplan, Johnson, & Bailey, 1988). Blechman (1982) discusses three dominant social-science hypotheses that account for the familial transmission of substance abuse: broken homes, overprotective mothers, and the reinforcement of substance-abuse behavior in families. She concludes that these hypotheses are not yet strongly supported by data.

The literature on children of addict parents is sparse. Little is known about the children of heroin addicts, cocaine abusers, or polydrug abusers. Researchers nonetheless suggest that the children of addict parents are at great risk for later dysfunctional behaviors, and that they, too, deserve significant attention to prevent intergenerational transmission (Carr, 1975; Coppolillo, 1975; Mondanaro, 1975; Nichtern, 1973; Singer, 1974; Kumpfer, 1987).

Family Studies/Heritability

Family-history variables are considered prime among the risk factors contributing to substance-abuse behavior (Kumpfer, 1987). Croughan (1987) summarizes the brief literature on family studies of drug abuse by concluding that family factors play a major role in substance-use habits. Parents' and adolescents' use of substances are strongly correlated; generally, if parents take drugs, sooner or later their children will also (Fawzy, Coombs, & Gerber, 1983; Annis, 1974; Stenmark et al., 1974). Adolescents who use drugs are more likely to have one or more parents who also use drugs (Skiffington & Brown, 1981; Simcha-Fagan, Gersten, & Langner, 1986).

The influence of parental attitudes on a child's drug-taking behaviors may be as important as actual drug abuse by the parents (Barnes & Windle, 1987). An adolescent who perceives that a parent is permissive about the use of drugs is more likely to use drugs (McDermott, 1984).

Some research now suggests that genetics may play a role in drug abuse. In their study of adoptees, Cadoret et al. (1986) showed that drug abuse was related to biological alcoholism in nonantisocial probands. Indeed, evidence of familial transmission in substance abuse, specific to drug abuse and not alcoholism, was recently reported (Meller, et al., 1988). In this study, Meller and his colleagues asked whether there was specific familial transmission of substance abuse, separate from alcoholism. They interviewed 301 patients admitted to a chemical-dependency treatment center about their biological parents' use of alcohol and other drugs. While the sample size of drug abusers was small (27) compared with the polydrug abusers (177) and alcoholics (97), there was a clear indication that substance abuse in first-degree relatives was related to substance abuse in the proband, independent of alcoholism. Meller and his colleagues conclude that a genetically transmitted biochemical vulnerability to alcohol dependence could exist independently of a vulnerability to other substances of abuse.

Fetal Exposure

Since most drugs cross the placenta, pregnant addicts risk passive drug dependency in their fetus (Calabrese & Gulledge, 1985). Information on drug use in childbearing women is limited, and many questions about the in utero effects of drug use on offspring remain unanswered (Carr, 1975). Prenatal drug withdrawal, caused by the pregnant woman's withdrawal, can inhibit fetal oxygen consumption, resulting in hypoxia or death. Postnatal drug withdrawal is characterized by the neonatal abstinence syndrome: hyperirritability, tremors, gastrointestinal dysfunction, respiratory distress, and amorphous autonomic system problems.

Infants of heroin addicts or methadone-maintained mothers exhibit more tension, greater activity, and poorer coordination than their age-matched peers (Bernstein et al., 1984; Marcus, Hans, & Jeremy, 1984; Jeremy & Bernstein, 1984; Marcus et al., 1984; Regan, Ehrlich, & Finnegan, 1987). Cocaine abuse during pregnancy is a significant predictor of low birthweight and gestational age (Chouteau, Namerow, & Leppert, 1988). Infants of drug addicts are also at risk for a variety of psychosocial problems, such as child abuse or neglect (Regan, Ehrlich, & Finnegan, 1987). Moreover, infants of drug-addicted women are now also at risk for HIV infection. As of December 1988 (U.S. Department of Health and Human Services), 1,002 infants had been born to HIV-infected mothers. These infants run a 50% chance of contracting AIDS themselves.

Moral arguments complicate our understanding of neonatal drug addiction. Health-care and legal systems have grappled with a justice or care perspective and have divided the problem into rights and responsibilities (Becker & Burke, 1988). These arguments play a role in determining the outcomes of the policy decisions about infants of drug-addicted mothers.

Risk-Factor Research

An indication of the scarcity of research on school-aged children of heroin-addicted parents is shown in the recent literature review by Hayford, Epps, and Dahl-Regis (1988). This review includes only 11 studies, ten of which are about infants.

Clinical reports describe psychological and social problems for the children of addict parents (Nichtern, 1973; Coppolillo, 1975). Bauman and Levine (1986) compared preschool children of methadone-maintained mothers (MM) with children of non-drug-addicted mothers (NDA). On an extensive battery that included tests of intelligence and personality, they showed that children of MM mothers were more impulsive, immature, and irresponsible. Furthermore, such children performed more poorly on the Stanford-Binet (MM mean $IQ = 92.71$, S.D. $= 15.36$; NDA mean $IQ = 100.41$, S.D. $= 18.36$). When COAs are compared with children of heroin addicts on measures of cognitive functioning and self-esteem, however, significant differences do not exist (Herjanic et al., 1978).

Studies of school-aged children of addict parents are compromised by the possibility of fetal exposure to heroin. Thus, separating environmental or genetic effects is difficult when the child may have been contaminated in utero by the mother's substance abuse. Wilson, Desmond, and Verniaud (1973) reported behavioral disturbances in heroin-exposed children aged 12–24 months. Sardemann and colleagues (1976) found delayed language development in heroin-exposed children aged 24–32 months. Learning problems and behavioral disturbances in 33 children of addict parents have also been reported (Nichtern, 1973).

Questions about differences in personality, psychosocial competence, and affect in children of addict parents remain unanswered (see also Chapter 3). The affective functioning of such children would seem an important area for further study, as mood disorders are a significant concern in the treatment of adult opiate users (Rounsaville & Kleber, 1985). Studies of first-order relatives of opiate- and cocaine-abuse clients suggest that mood and anxiety disorders appear disproportionately in the families of substance users (Rounsaville & Kleber, 1985). In a recent paper examining depression in opioid users, Maddux, Desmond, and Costello (1987) found strong relationships between substance-use status and depressed mood; depression varied according to abstinence from either alcohol, opioids, or methadone, a finding that has also been confirmed by others (Frederick, Resnik, & Wittlin, 1973; Lang, Stimmel, & Brown, 1972; Wieland & Sola, 1970).

One study, conducted by Wilson and her colleagues (1979), compared four groups of children on a comprehensive psychological assessment battery. These groups consisted of 77 children between the ages of three and six who either (1) were exposed to heroin in utero, (2) were not exposed to heroin in utero but whose mothers were involved in the drug culture, (3) were members of a high-risk comparison group (birth complications due to medical problems), or (4) were members of a socioeconomic comparison group. The extensive assessment battery included perinatal measures, a physical examination, social and environmental information, parent reports, psychometric measures (primarily measures of intelligence), sensorimotor tests, and behavioral measures. Not surprisingly, the heroin-exposed group scored lower than all other groups on physical, intellectual, sensorimotor, and behavioral measures. The children whose mothers were actively involved in the drug culture (either through marriage to an addict or through substance abuse subsequent to the birth of the child) scored slightly higher (i.e., better) than the heroin-exposed group, but significantly lower (i.e., worse) than the two comparison groups.

Summary of Children-of-Addicts Literature

Children of addict parents are at great risk for behavioral problems and physiological damage if they are exposed in utero to their mother's drug addiction. Some of these problems may last well through maturation, but the brevity of the data does not justify a consensus opinion about the developmental trajectories of such damage. If children are not exposed to chemicals in utero, they nevertheless appear at risk for behavioral problems if their parents are involved in the drug culture. Again, the lack of data does not warrant summary conclusions about these risks. It is apparent that there is a much-needed area of research that will allow refinement of the risks and protective factors operating in the lives of these children.

METHODOLOGICAL CONSIDERATIONS

In high-risk research, methodological weaknesses impair our ability to determine the specific pathways leading to chemical dependence and to distinguish true risk factors from transient factors. The methodological problems unique to research on children of chemically dependent parents include problems related to the heterogeneity of parental chemical abuse, sample selection, variable selection and measurement, and development.

Heterogeneity

Even though the most commonly studied chemically dependent family is the intact, paternal alcoholic household, there are many combinations of relationships resulting from divorce, stepparenting, cohabitation, and single parenting that combine with the varieties of individual patterns of drug use. Parents reflect not only different combinations of and types of chemical dependence, but combinations that change over time. Alcoholism may co-occur with other drug dependencies at different points during life. What effects dual-substance-abusing behavior has on offspring and the effects of variable patterns of parental chemical abuse is currently unknown. Multiple marriages, changing cohabitation arrangements, and sporadic periods of single parenting may occur. Sometimes the changing partners are chemically dependent, sometimes they are not. The heterogeneity of parental chemical dependence complicates studies attempting to isolate precursors to chemical dependence in offspring. Environmental fluctuations coupled with the biological and psychological fluctuations of normal development influence the types of variables that can be chosen for study and the types of statistical techniques available for data analysis.

Sample Selection

Describing our samples in better detail eliminates the sampling problems encountered when biased groups of children are selected for study (West & Prinz, 1987). Without evidence from nonclinical cases, we cannot determine the magnitude of risk to offspring of chemically dependent parents. Overreports of psychopathology occur when the children sampled are from parents who are in treatment or the children are in treatment themselves. Thus, there is a tendency to observe pathology in this preselected sample. More important, we are unable to determine which factors allow the child to remain unaffected by parental pathology or to overcome the stress that may be present in their familial environment. For example, many studies have examined COAs who are juvenile offenders or have been referred to guidance centers. It is difficult to generalize from children who are in treatment to nontreatment populations. Studies of large samples of children of chemically dependent parents before they act out or are diagnosed with psychological problems are necessary to discover how they reach a particular diagnostic state.

Variable Selection and Measurement

High-risk status is a complicated, multifactorial problem that is assessed best with several replicable and quantifiable procedures. Because chemical dependence is most likely determined by several influences, identification of risk and protective factors requires a broad assessment of children at different ages. Such assessments ideally include family-environment measures (such as family alcohol use and the maintenance of family traditions) and within-individual processes (such as psychological structures, temperament, and physiology).

Complex behavior such as chemical dependence is most likely determined by a number of factors. Multivariate assessment can increase predictive power and our understanding of potentially understudied and complex risk factors, especially when they interact. Recognizing that this approach also provokes methodological and statistical problems (e.g., too many measures capitalize on chance), the perfect balance appears to be between enough measures and too few.

Sources of information on children are plentiful, and include peer ratings, parental reports (both mother and father), teacher reports, self-reports, clinical observations, and experimental performance evaluations (e.g., laboratory testing). It is likely that some differences in children's behavior may depend on the person who reports it and some may not. Disagreements between informant reports of children's behavior provide important clinical information about how children respond to different environmental contexts.

Attention to Development

Developmental research shows that children are qualitatively and quantitatively distinct at different ages; they think and feel and act according to differences in cognitive and affective stages of development (see also Chapter 3). Frequently, however, developmental differences and predicted changes in children's performance are ignored in studies examining risk for chemical dependence. Thus, subjects of wide age ranges, both sexes, and differing cognitive developmental stages are combined into a single group.

Developmental changes elaborately described by Piaget (1963) suggest that newly acquired cognitive developmental skills during adolescence increase cognitive independence. Adolescence becomes a time of increased risks for significant emotional problems (e.g., episodes of serious anxiety or depression) and health-impairing behaviors (eating disorders, chemical dependence, and withdrawal from supportive relationships with family and peers). To understand better the sources and modifiers of the increased risk for maladaptation during development, research needs to address the challenging biological developmental and sociological issues of adolescence. How is it that some adolescents can stop at experimentation and others continue on to abuse and dependence?

Research Paradigms

Most studies on children of chemically dependent parents are not longitudinal; that is, they examine behavior at one point for marker status or rely on retrospective data to infer causal chains. From these studies, it is unclear whether we see true deficits, or merely developmental delay.

Cross-sectional designs are useful when they utilize statistical models that enhance their usefulness. Structural modeling techniques, for example, provide ways to analyze such cross-sectional designs. Convergence models make limited remeasurements of cross-sectional groups so that temporarily overlapping measurements can be used as a link between adjacent segments of a developmental function. However, while cross-sectional designs may initially be appropriate for the identification of potential markers, they are problematic if samples of children are so heterogeneous as to restrict generalizability to other groups. Small, heterogeneous samples, due to variations in age, sex, and family factors, diminish generalizability. Generalizing findings from cross-sectional sample groups to the larger population is enhanced by large numbers of subjects.

Longitudinal studies of the same individual allow us to predict when early disorders and behavioral deviations will be transient or when they will be precursors to chemical dependency. There are two advantages to studying young children over the course of development: (1) they will not have been placed under therapy regimens, including medication, which could confound attempts at thorough experimental controls, and (2) retrospective biographical errors of adult childhood memories are avoided when current childhood behaviors are measured.

Longitudinal research would also enable us to explain specific childhood outcomes. Outcome behaviors could be studied simultaneously to understand whether specific antecedents are required for specific outcomes, or, perhaps, whether specific antecedents are merely generalizable to a broad variety of problem-outcome behavior. Both causal modeling and design of prevention programs would be furthered by understanding the early antecedents and paths leading to alcoholism, other substance use, or psychiatric symptoms.

DIFFERENCES BETWEEN COAS AND CHILDREN OF ADDICTS

Patterns of parental chemical dependence influence both the biological and environmental heterogeneity of their offspring. There are several ways in which children of addict parents differ from COAs.

THE ACTIVITY SURROUNDING THE DRUG

Unlike alcohol, the possession of heroin or cocaine is illegal. Alcohol can be bought openly, but drugs like heroin or cocaine are obtained illegally and at risk (e.g., the possibility of arrest and imprisonment). Because of the inherent risks of illegal activity, children of addict parents are exposed to an aspect of life that COAs are not.

The activity of drug taking is central to the child's experience of the parent's drug addiction. The paraphernalia of drugs (syringes, needles, crack vials, rolling papers) differs enormously from a cocktail or a bottle of beer. Most individuals consume alcohol openly and without fear of legal reprisal (except, of course, when driving drunk). On the other hand, illicit drugs must be taken secretly. Some children are unaware of the parent's drug habit (at least while the children are young); other children actively or passively participate. Active participation can take the form of holding, buying, or giving the drugs to the parent, or, perhaps, buying the drug paraphernalia for the parent. Children passively participate when they watch a parent or a parent's friends smoke or inject drugs. In either case, the implications for the child's social, emotional, and moral development are portentous (see Chapters 7 and 8).

The difference between COAs and children of addict parents, however, lies in the legality of the activities. For this reason, the child of an addict parent must contend with the community's response to illegal drug activity. Media coverage of drug abuse often emphasizes the darker side of life. Murders, PCP-crazed individuals, HIV-positive crack addicts, and teenage prostitutes hooked on drugs are frequently the focus of news stories on television and in print. How does this type of media coverage affect the emotional and social development of young children who must live with addict parents? In fact, how does community outrage against a parent's illicit activity affect the child's response to the community?

PUBLIC SUPPORT

While there are several public-advocacy groups for COAs, there are *none* for children of addict parents. As a result of public awareness and student-assistance programs, COAs no longer remain a hidden problem (Ackerman, 1987). Two organizations responsible for changing public awareness in this respect are the National Association of Children of Alcoholics and the Children of Alcoholics Foundation, Inc. (see Chapters 13 and 14). These organizations support many publications addressing the psychological needs of COAs. Through discussion and networking, regional and national conferences provide invaluable support systems for adult COAs. Many of the participants in the grass-roots movement focus on treatment, prevention, intervention, and education for both school-aged and adult COAs.

IMPACT OF AIDS

Unlike COAs, the AIDS epidemic directly confronts the children of addict parents—especially if the parents are intravenous (IV) drug users. Loss of significant others due to AIDS-related illness may become more pronounced in the lives of the children of addict parents. Addict parents may have AIDS (or be HIV positive), their friends may have AIDS, or babies in the community may be HIV positive. As of December 1988, 21,407 cases of AIDS among IV drug abusers had been reported to the Centers for Disease Control AIDS surveillance system. Only 5,717 of these cases were homosexuals. These statistics, moreover, are for reported AIDS cases and not for individuals diagnosed as HIV positive. The long and variable incubation period of HIV infection will affect the futures of children of IV drug abusers in an unforeseeable fashion, especially since HIV-positive individuals represent approximately 20 times the number of reported AIDS cases.

The larger threat for IV-drug-abusing parents, however, is if their children begin to use IV drugs themselves. Adolescents are unlikely to protect themselves from the risk of HIV transmission. In a survey of 1,071 adolescent drug users, only 18% reported accurate knowledge about HIV protection (Reilly & Homel, 1988).

HOME ENVIRONMENT

Home environment is a critically important variable in shaping cognitive skills, academic achievement, and psychosocial adjustment (see also Chapter 3). The upsets associated with families in which there is an active substance-abusing parent doubtlessly contribute to problems for the children. Disadvantaged or deviant home environments are the source of many childhood behavioral problems (Hinde, 1980; Rutter, 1971; Rutter, Quinton, & Liddle, 1983; Rutter & Madge, 1976). Conduct disorder in childhood is associated with certain parenting styles, such as how much time the mother spends monitoring a young adolescent's behavior (Patterson & Stouthamer-Loeber, 1984). Research on the relationship between parenting practices and social competency in children shows that hostile, inconsistent parenting predicts the development of socially incompetent (aggressive) behavior in children (Baldwin, 1955; Eron, 1982; George & Main, 1979). On the other hand, warm, responsive parenting is related to socially competent behavior in children (Baumrind, 1967; Bryant & Crockenberg, 1980).

The type of chemical dependence can influence the type of childhood home environment, especially if the parent is addicted to heroin or crack. Children living with crack-addicted parents, for instance, are being seen in emergency rooms with evidence of cocaine in their bloodstream attributable to passive inhalation of crack (NIDA, 1987/1988). Parents involved with illegal activities may invite adult friends with similar proclivities into the home. The presence of adult antisocial role models is a strong possibility for children living with addict parents. Moreover, the possibility of parental imprisonment is especially problematic for such children. Children of imprisoned parents experience a special loss—their parents are gone and yet not gone. Sack, Seidler, and Thomas (1976) suggest that children of imprisoned fathers also participate in the parent's imprisonment: from the arrest and trial through prison visitation and adjustment to the community attitudes toward their parent's incarceration. School performance suffers, and in some cases, the child exhibits antisocial behavior.

The relationship of parental drinking to family violence has received considerable attention. According to Sher (1987), while clinical reports often indicate a strong connection between parental alcoholism and family violence, the empirical data give a highly inconsistent picture. Family violence cannot be conclusively related to parental alcoholism. Studies focusing first on family violence and second on the incidence of parental alcoholism, as well as those beginning with the dynamics of alcoholic families and subsequent assessment of family violence, have resulted in highly inconsistent rates of reported spouse and child abuse. Mayer and Black (1977), for example, report extremely wide-ranging rates (2–62%) of alcoholism among parents who have abused their children. Sher (1987) similarly found that the reported rate of child abuse among alcoholic parents varied between 0% and 92%. A widespread belief in the association between parental alcoholism and family violence may have preceded conclusive research.

Summary of Thoughts About the Future

With the increasing drug-abuse problems in our society and the social disorganization accompanying addiction (e.g., joblessness, crime, parental absence due to imprisonment or treatment), the children of chemically dependent parents are at great risk for many problems, which include, but are not limited to, drug abuse. This review separated research on COAs from that on children of addict parents and showed that we know comparatively little about the children of addict parents.

CHANGING PATTERNS OF CHEMICAL DEPENDENCE

The revised third edition of the *Diagnostic and Statistical Manual of Mental Disorders.* (American Psychiatric Association, 1987) defines ten classes of abusable psychoactive substances: alcohol, amphetamines, cannabis, cocaine, hallucinogens, inhalants, nicotine, opioids, phencyclidines and the sedative-hypnotic-anxiolytic group. Frequently, drugs of choice are determined by their availability, by cultural influence, or by monetary considerations. As the popularity of abusable substances changes over time (partially as a result of the growth in the synthetic drug industry), a related research issue concerning high-risk children arises that speaks to the changing patterns of parental chemical dependence.

In contemporary society, abuse or dependence is not limited to one class but may involve several different classes of substances. Polysubstance abusers constitute the major proportion of patients at chemical-dependency treatment centers (Meller,

Keafer, & Widmer, 1986). With population changes in patterns of chemical dependence, questions about the differences and similarities among high-risk children remain unanswered when etiological studies of chemical dependence focus only on children of alcoholics. Polysubstance abuse that is coupled with alcoholism complicates future etiological studies of the transmission of alcoholism. What types of childhood environmental experiences accompany parental dual dependency? Some evidence about the effects of dual dependency shows that alcoholic opiate addicts report more disruptive childhood events than do nonalcoholic addicts (Kosten, Rounsaville, & Kleber, 1985).

PREVENTION AND INTERVENTION

Intervention is a logical next step after the problems of children of chemically dependent parents have been identified. A cautionary note against overgeneralization of research is necessary, however, especially when the research is still in early stages (see also Chapters 4, 5, 13, and 14). With children, our ethical responsibility takes precedence over our research; however, overgeneralization tends to confuse rather than clarify.

Preventive intervention programs have increased exponentially within the past five years without the necessary theory-based foundations and evaluations. Because of the lack of evaluation, two important questions remain unanswered: Would a general preventive intervention designed for all types of problem behaviors provide a more cost-effective service than preventive interventions designed to target specific problems? Do COAs require unique preventive interventions, or would a prevention effort aimed at all children, regardless of family factors, be just as effective in the prevention of alcoholism or other chemical dependence?

A rapidly growing industry is responding to the issues of high-risk children with the promise of effective treatment and recovery. A variety of prevention and intervention approaches based on community, school, or family models are currently recommended (Cable, Noel, & Swanson, 1986; Morehouse & Scola, 1986; NIAAA, 1979). Without necessary program evaluations, however, in the long run they may overpromise positive results to a large and needy group of individuals. Nevertheless, it is important to clarify the course of those children's development and to accelerate efforts to develop and test early intervention strategies (see Chapters 3, 8–10).

REFERENCES

Abel, E. L. (1980). The fetal alcohol syndrome: Behavioral teratology. *Psychological Bulletin*, 88, 29–50.

Abel, E. L. (1981). Behavioral teratology of alcohol. *Psychological Bulletin*, 90, 564–581.

Abel, E. L. (1982). Consumption of alcohol during pregnancy: A review of effects on growth and development of offspring. *Human Biology*, 54, 421–453.

Ackerman, R. J. (1987). *Same house, different homes—Why adult children of alcoholics are not all the same.* Pompano Beach, FL: Health Communications.

Adler, R., & Raphael, B. (1983). Children of alcoholics. *Australian and New Zealand Journal of Psychiatry*, 17, 3–8.

Amark, C. (1951). A study in alcoholism: Clinical, social-psychiatric and genetic investigations. *Acta Psychiatrica et Neurologica Scandinavica, Suppl.* 70, 1–283.

American Psychiatric Association (1987). *Diagnostic and statistical manual (3rd ed. revised.* Washington: American Psychiatric Association.

Annis, H. M. (1974). Patterns of intra-familial drug use. *British Journal of Addiction*, 69, 361–369.

Aronson, M., Kyllerman, M., Sabel, K. G., Sandin, B., & Olegard, R. (1985). Children of alcoholic mothers: Developmental, perceptual and behavioral characteristics as compared to matched controls, *Acta Paediatrica Scandinavia*, 74, 27–35.

Baldwin, A. L. (1955). *Behavior and development in childhood.* New York: Dreyden.

Barnes, G. M., & Windle, M. (1987). Family factors in adolescent alcohol and drug abuse. *Drug and Alcohol Abuse in Children and Adolescence Pediatrician*, 14, 13–18.

Bauman, P., & Levine, S. A. (1986). The development of children of drug addicts. *International Journal of the Addictions*, 21(8), 849–863.

Baumrind, D. (1967). Child care practices anteceding three patterns of preschool behavior. *Genetic Psychology Monographs*, 75, 43–88.

Becker, P. H., & Burke, S. (1988). Neonatal drug addiction: An analysis from two moral orientations. *Holistic Nursing Practice*, 2(4), 20–27.

Begleiter, H., Porjesz, B., Bihari, B., & Kissin, B. (1984). Event-related brain potentials in boys at risk for alcoholism. *Science*, 225, 1493–1496.

Bennett, L. A., & Wolin, S. J. (1986). Daughters and sons of alcoholics: Developmental paths in transmission. *Alcoholism: Journal on Alcoholism and Related Addictions*, 22(1), 3–15.

Bennett, L. A., Wolin, S. J., Reiss, D., & Teitelbaum, M. A. (1987). Couples at risk for transmission of alcoholism: Protective influences. *Family Process*, 26, 111–129.

Bernstein, V., Jeremy, R. J., Hans, S. L., & Marcus, J. (1984). A longitudinal study of offspring born to methadone-maintained women. II. Dyadic interaction and infant behavior at 4 months. *American Journal of Drug and Alcohol Abuse*, 10(2), 161–193.

Blechman, E. A. (1982). Conventional wisdom about familial contributions to substance abuse. *American Journal of Drug and Alcohol Abuse*, 9(1), 35–53.

Blum, K., Noble, E. P., Sheridan, P. J., et al. (1990). Allelic association of human dopamine D_2 receptor gene in alcoholism. *JAMA*, 263, 2055–2060.

Bohman, M. (1978). Some genetic aspects of alcoholism and criminality: A population of adoptees. *Archives of General Psychiatry*, 35, 269–276.

Bryant, B. K., & Crockenberg, S. B. (1980). Correlates and dimensions of prosocial behavior: A study of female siblings with their mothers. *Child Development*, 51, 529–544.

Cable, L. C., Noel, N. E., & Swanson, S. C. (1986). Clinical intervention with children of alcohol abusers. In D. C. Lewis & C. N. Williams (Eds.), *Providing care for children of alcoholics* (pp. 65–80). Pompano Beach, FL: Health Communications.

Cadoret, R. J., Cain, C. A., & Grove, W. M. (1980). Development of alcoholism in adoptees raised apart from alcoholic biologic relatives. *Archives of General Psychiatry, 78,* 561–563.

Cadoret, R. J., Troughton, E., & O'Gorman, T. W. (1987). Genetic and environmental factors in alcohol abuse and antisocial personality. *Journal of Studies on Alcohol, 48,* 1–8.

Cadoret, R. J., Troughton, E., O'Gorman, T. W., & Heywood, E. (1986). An adoption study of genetic and environmental factors in drug abuse. *Archives of General Psychiatry, 43,* 1131–1136.

Calabrese, A. R., & Gulledge, A. D. (1985). The neotatal narcotic abstinence syndrome: A brief review. *Canadian Journal of Psychiatry, 30(12),* 623–626.

Carr, J. N. (1975). Drug patterns among drug-addicted mothers: Incidence, variance in use, and effects in children. *Pediatric Annals, 4,* 408–417.

Chouteau, M., Namerow, P. B., & Leppert, P. (1988). The effect of cocaine abuse on birth weight and gestational age. *Obstetrics and Gynecology, 72(3 Pt 1),* 351–354.

Cloninger, C. R., Bohman, M., & Sigvardsson, S. (1981). Inheritance of alcohol abuse: Cross fostering analysis of adopted men. *Archives of General Psychiatry, 38,* 861–868.

Cloninger, C. R., Reich, T., & Wetzel, R. (1979). Alcoholism and affective disorders: Familial associations and genetic models. In D. W. Goodwin & C. K. Erickson (Eds.), *Alcoholism and affective disorders: Clinical, genetic, and biochemical studies* (pp. 57–86). New York: SP Medical & Scientific Books.

Coppolillo, H. P. (1975). Drug impediments to mothering behavior. *Addictive Diseases International Journal, 2(1),* 201–208.

Corder, B. F., McRee, C., & Rohrer, H. (1984). Brief review of literature on daughters of alcoholic fathers. *North Carolina Journal of Mental Health, 10(20),* 37–43.

Cork, M. (1969). *The forgotten children.* Toronto: Addiction Research Foundation.

Cotton, N. (1979). The familial incidence of alcoholism. *Journal of Studies on Alcohol, 40,* 89–116.

Croughan, J. L. (1987). The contribution of family studies to understanding drug abuse. In L. N. Robins (Ed.), *Series in psychosocial epidemiology, Vol. 6, Studying drug abuse* (pp. 93–116). New Brunswick, NJ: Rutgers University Press.

Davis, D. I., Berenson, D., Steinglass, P., & Davis, S. (1974). The adaptive consequences of drinking. *Psychiatry, 37,* 209–215.

Deitrich, R. A., & Spuhler, K. (1984). Genetics of alcoholism and alcohol actions. In R. G. Smart, H. D. Cappell, F. B. Glaser, Y. Israel, H. Kalant, R. E. Popham, W. Schmidt, & E. M. Sellers (Eds.), *Research advances in alcohol and drug problems, Vol 8.* (pp. 47–98). New York: Plenum Press.

Earls, F., Reich, W., Jung, K. G., & Cloninger, C. R. (1988). Psychopathology in children of alcoholic and antisocial parents. *Alcoholism: Clinical and Experimental Research, 12(4),* 481–487.

Elderton, E. M. & Pearson, K. (1910). A first study of the influence of parental alcoholism on the physique and intelligence of the offspring. *Eugenics Laboratory memoir series X* (pp. 1–46). London: Cambridge University Press.

El Guebaly, N., & Offord, D. R. (1977). The offspring of alcoholics, a critical review. *American Journal of Psychiatry, 134,* 357–365.

El Guebaly, N., & Offord, D. R. (1979). On being the offspring of an alcoholic; an update. *Alcoholism: Clinical and Experimental Research, 3,* 148–157.

Eron, L. (1982). Parent-child interaction, television violence, and aggression in children. *American Psychologist, 37,* 197–211.

Ervin, C., Little, R., Streissguth, A., & Beck, D. (1984). Alcoholic fathering and its relation to child's intellectual development: A pilot investigation. *Alcoholism: Clinical and Experimental Research, 8,* 362–365.

Fawzy, F. I., Coombs, R. H., & Gerber, B. (1983). Generational continuity in the use of substances: The impact of parental substance use on adolescent substance use. *Addictive Behaviors, 8,* 109–114.

Fine, E. W., Yudin, L. W., Holmes, J., & Heinemann, S. (1976). Behavioral disorders in children with parental alcoholism. *Annals of the New York Academy of Sciences, 273,* 507–517.

Frederick, C. J., Resnik, H.L.P., & Wittlin, B. J. (1973). Self-destructive aspects of hard core addiction. *Archives of General Psychiatry, 28,* 579–585.

Gabrielli, W. & Mednick, S. (1983). Intellectual performance in children of alcoholics. *Journal of Nervous and Mental Disease, 171,* 444–447.

Gabrielli, W. F., Mednick, S. A., Volavka, J., Pollock, V. E., Schulsinger, F., & Itil, T. M. (1982). Electroencephalograms in children of alcoholic fathers. *Psychophysiology, 19,* 404–407.

George, C. & Main, M. (1979). Social interactions of young abused children: Approach, avoidance, and aggression. *Child Development, 50,* 306–318.

Goodwin, D. W. (1976). *Is alcoholism hereditary?* New York: Oxford University Press.

Goodwin, D. W. (1985). Alcoholism and genetics: The sins of the fathers. *Archives of General Psychiatry, 42,* 171–174.

Goodwin, D. W., Schulsinger, F., Hermansen, L., Guze, S. B., & Winokur, G. (1973). Alcohol problems in adoptees raised apart from alcoholic biological parents. *Archives of General Psychiatry, 28,* 238–243.

Goodwin, D. W., Schulsinger, F., Knop, J., Mednick, S., & Guze, S. B. (1977). Alcoholism and depression in adopted-out daughters of alcoholics. *Archives of General Psychiatry, 34,* 751–755.

Goodwin, D. W., Schulsinger, F., Moller, N., Hermansen, L., Winokur, G., & Guze, S. B. (1977). Drinking problems in adopted and nonadopted sons of alcoholics. *Archives of General Psychiatry, 31,* 164–169.

Gravitz, H. L. & Bowden, J. D. (1985). *Recovery: A guide for adult children of alcoholics.* New York: Simon & Schuster.

Gutzke, D. W. (1984). The cry of the children: The Edwardian medical campaign against maternal drinking. *British Journal of Addiction, 79,* 71–84.

Haberman, P. W. (1966). Childhood symptoms in children of alcoholics and comparison group parents. *Journal of Marriage and the Family, 28*(2), 152–154.

Hayford, S. M., Epps, R. P., & Dahl-Regis, M. (1988). Behavior and development patterns in children born to heroin-addicted and methadone-addicted mothers. *Journal of the National Medical Association, 80(11)*, 1197–1200.

Henderson, C., & Blume, S. (1984). Genetic factors in alcoholism. In M. Russell, C. Henderson, & S. Blume (Eds.), *Children of alcoholics: A review of the literature* (pp. 1–26). New York: Children of Alcoholics Foundation.

Herjanic, B., Herjanic, M., Wetzel, R., & Tomelleri, C. (1978). Substance abuse: Its effects on offspring. *Research Communications in Psychology, Psychiatry and Behavior, 3(1)*, 65–75.

Hinde, R. A. (1980). Family influences. In M. Rutter (Ed.), *Scientific foundations of developmental psychiatry* (pp. 47–66). London: Heinemann Medical.

Hirschi, T. (1969). *Causes of delinquency.* Berkeley and Los Angeles: University of California Press.

Hrubec, Z., & Omenn, G. (1981). Evidence of genetic predisposition to alcoholic cirrhosis and psychosis. *Alcoholism: Clinical and Experimental Research, 5*, 207–215.

Hughes, J. M. (1977). Adolescent children of alcoholic parents and the relationship of Alateen to these children. *Journal of Consulting and Clinical Psychology, 45*, 946–947.

Jacob, T., & Seilhamer, R. A. (1987). Alcoholism and family interaction. In T. Jacob (Ed.), *Family interaction and psychopathology: Theories, methods, and findings.* New York: Plenum.

Jacob, T., Favorini, A., Meisel, S., & Anderson, C. (1978). The alcoholic's spouse, children, and family interactions: Substantive findings and methodological issues. *Journal of Studies on Alcohol, 39*, 1231–1251.

Jeremy, R. J., & Bernstein, V. J. (1984). Dyads at risk: Methadone-maintained women and their four-month-old infants. *Child Development, 55*, 1141–1154.

Johnson, J. L., & Bennett, L. A. (1988). *School aged children of alcoholics: Theory and research.* Center of Alcohol Studies, Rutgers University. New Brunswick, NJ: Alcohol Research Documentation.

Johnson, J. L., & Bennett, L. A. (1989). *Adult children of alcoholics: Theory and research.* Center of Alcohol Studies, Rutgers University. New Brunswick, NJ: Alcohol Research Documentation.

Johnson, J. L., & Rolf, J. E., (1988). Cognitive functioning in children from alcoholic and non-alcoholic families. *British Journal of Addictions, 83*, 849–857.

Jones, K. L., & Smith, D. W. (1973). Recognition of the fetal alcohol syndrome in early infancy. *Lancet, 2*, 999–1001.

Kaij, L. (1960). *Alcoholism in twins: Studies on the etiology and sequels of abuse of alcohol.* Stockholm: Almqvist & Wiksell.

Kandel, D., Kessler, R., & Margulies, R. (1978). Adolescent initiation into stages of drug use: A developmental analysis. In D. Kandel (Ed.), *Longitudinal research on drug use: Empirical findings and methodological issues.* Washington: Hemisphere-Wiley.

Kaplan, H. B., Johnson, R. J., & Bailey, C. A. (1988). Explaining adolescent drug use: An elaboration strategy for structural equations modeling. *Psychiatry, 51*, 142–163.

Kern, J., Hassett, C., Collipp, P., Bridges, C., Solomon, M., & Condren, R. (1981). Children of alcoholics: Locus of control, mental age, and zinc level, *Journal of Psychiatric Treatment and Evaluation, 3,* 169–173.

Keynes, J. M. (1910–1911). Influence of parental alcoholism. *Journal of the Royal Statistical Society, 74,* 339–345.

Klagsburn, M. & Davis, D. I. (1977). Substance abuse and the family. *Family Process, 16(2),* 149–173.

Knop, J., Teasdale, T., Schulsinger, F., & Goodwin, D. (1985). A prospective study of young men at high risk for alcoholism: School behavior and achievement. *Journal of Studies on Alcohol, 46,* 273–278.

Kosten, T. R., Rounsaville, B. J., & Kleber, H. D. (1985). Parental alcoholism in opioid addicts. *Journal of Nervous and Mental Disease, 173(8),* 461–469.

Kumpfer, K. L. (1987). Special populations: Etiology and prevention of vulnerability to chemical dependency in children of substance abusers. In B. S. Brown & A. R. Mills (Eds.), *Youth at high risk for substance abuse.* Rockville, MD: U.S. Dept. of Health and Human Services, DHHS Publication No. (ADM) 87–1537: 1–72.

Lang, P., Stimmel, B., & Brown, F. (1972). Psychological testing as a predictive index of success in methadone maintenance treatment of heroin addiction. In *Proceedings of the Fourth National Conference on Methadone Treatment, January 8–10, 1972* (pp. 433–434). New York: National Association for the Prevention of Addiction to Narcotics.

Littrell, J. (1988). The Swedish studies of the adopted children of alcoholics. *Journal of Studies on Alcohol, 49(6),* 491–499.

MacNicholl, T. A. (1905). A study of the effects of alcohol on school children. *Quarterly Journal of Inebriety, 27,* 113–117.

Maddux, J. F., Desmond, D. P., & Costello, R. (1987). Depression in opioid users varies with substance use status. *American Journal of Drug and Alcohol Abuse, 13(4),* 375–385.

Marcus, J., Hans, S. L., & Jeremy, R. J. (1984). A longitudinal study of offspring born to methadone-maintained women. III. Effects of multiple risk factors on development at 4, 8, and 12 months. *American Journal of Drug and Alcohol Abuse, 10(2),* 195–207.

Marcus, J., Hans, S. L., Patterson, C. B., & Morris, A. J. (1984). A longitudinal study of offspring born to methadone-maintained women. I. Design, methodology, and description of women's resources for functioning. *American Journal of Drug and Alcohol Abuse, 10(2),* 135–160.

Mayer, J., & Black, R. (1977). The relationship between alcoholism and child abuse and neglect. In F. Seixas (Ed.), *Currents in alcoholism, Vol. II* (pp. 429–445). New York: Grune & Stratton.

McCord, J. (1988). Alcoholism: Toward understanding genetic and social factors. *Psychiatry, 51(2),* 131–141.

McDermott, D. (1984). The relationship of parental drug use and parents' attitude concerning adolescent drug use to adolescent drug use. *Adolescence, XIX(73),* 89–97.

Meller, W., Keafer, S., & Widmer, R. (1986). The Oakdale sample: A description of the modern substance abusing population. *Journal of Iowa Medical Society, 76,* 354–362.

Mondanaro, J. (1975). Mothers on methadone—Echoes of failure. In *Proceedings of the National Drug Abuse Convention* (pp. 41–49).

Monnelly, E. P., Hartl, E. M., & Elderkin, R. (1983). Constitutional factors predictive of alcoholism in a follow-up of delinquent boys. *Journal of Studies on Alcohol, 44(3),* 530–537.

Moos, R. H., & Billings, A. G. (1982). Children of alcoholics during the recovery process: Alcoholic and matched control families. *Addictive Behaviors, 7,* 155–164.

Morehouse, E. R., & Scola, C. M. (1986). *Children of alcoholics: Meeting the needs of the young COA in the school setting.* South Laguna, CA: National Association for Children of Alcoholics.

National Institute on Alcohol Abuse and Alcoholism (1979). *Services for children of alcoholics.* Research Monograph No. 4. DHHS Publication No. (ADM) 81–1007.

National Institute on Alcohol Abuse and Alcoholism. (1985). *Alcoholism: An inherited disease.* U.S. Dept. of Health and Human Services, DHHS Publication No. (ADM) 85-1426.

National Institute on Drug Abuse (1987/1988). *Drugged in the womb: What harm to babies?* NIDA Notes, 13–14.

Nichtern, S. (1973). The children of drug abusers. *Journal of the American Academy of Child Psychiatry, 12(1),* 24–31.

Noll, R. B. & Zucker, R. A. (1983). Developmental findings from an alcoholic vulnerability study: The preschool years. Paper presented at the Annual Meeting of the American Psychological Association, Anaheim, CA.

Nylander, I., & Rydelius, P. A. (1982). A comparison between children of alcoholic fathers from excellent versus poor social conditions. *Acta Paediatrica Scandinavia, 71,* 809–813.

Patterson, G. R., & Stouthamer-Loeber, M. (1984). The correlation of family management practices and delinquency. *Child Development, 33,* 1299–1307.

Pearson, K. (1910). Supplement to the memoir entitled: The influence of parental alcoholism on the physique and ability of the offspring. A reply to the Cambridge economists. *Questions of the day and of the fray, no. I.* 1–3. London: Cambridge University Press.

Pearson, K., & Elderton, E. M. (1910). A second study of the influence of parental alcoholism on the physique and intelligence of the offspring. *Eugenics Laboratory memoir series XIII,* 1–35. London: Cambridge University Press.

Peele, S. (1986). The implications and limitations of genetic models of alcoholism and other addictions. *Journal of Studies on Alcohol, 47(1),* 63–73.

Piaget, J. (1963). *The origins of intelligence in children.* New York: Norton.

Pollock, V. E., Teasdale, T. W., Gabrielli, W. F., & Knop, J. (1986). Subjective and objective measures of response to alcohol among young men at risk for alcoholism. *Journal of Studies on Alcohol, 47(4),* 297–304.

Regan, D. O., Ehrlich, S. M., & Finnegan, L. P. (1987). Infants of drug addicts: At risk for child abuse, neglect, and placement in foster care. *Neurotoxicology and Teratology, 9,* 315–319.

Reich, T., Cloninger, C. R., Lewis, C., & Rice, J. (1981). Some recent findings in the study of genotype-environment interaction in alcoholism. NIAAA Research Monograph No. 5.

Reilly, C. J. & Homel, P. J. (1988). Awareness of AIDS in young high risk drug abusers. *Medical Journal of Australia, 49,* 164.

Rice, J., Cloninger, C. R., & Reich, T. (1978). Multifactorial inheritance with cultural transmission and assortative mating: I. Description and basic properties of the unitary models. *American Journal of Human Genetics, 30,* 618–643.

Rimmer, J. (1982). The children of alcoholics: An exploratory study. *Children and Youth Services Review, 4,* 365–373.

Rounsaville, B. J., & Kleber, H. D. (1985). Psychotherapy/counseling for opiate addicts: Strategies for use in different treatment settings. *International Journal of the Addictions, 20(6),* 869–896.

Russell, M., Henderson, C., & Blume, S. (1985). *Children of alcoholics: A review of the literature.* New York: Children of Alcoholics Foundation.

Rutter, M. (1971). Parent-child separation: Psychological effects on the children. *Journal of Child Psychology and Psychiatry, 12,* 233–260.

Rutter, M., & Madge, N. (1976). *Cycles of disadvantage.* London: Heinemann Educational.

Rutter, M., Quinton, D., & Liddle, C. (1983). Parenting in two generations: Looking backwards and looking forward. In N. Madge (Ed.), *Families at risk* (pp. 60–98). London: Heinemann Educational.

Sack, W. H., Seidler, J., & Thomas, S. (1976). The children of imprisoned parents: A psychosocial exploration. *American Journal of Orthopsychiatry, 46(4),* 618–628.

Sardemann, H., Madsen, K. S., & Friis-Hansen, B. (1976). Follow-up of children of drug-addicted mothers. *Archives of Disease in Childhood, 51,* 131–134.

Schuckit, M., & Chiles, J. (1978). Family history as a diagnostic aid in two samples of adolescents. *Journal of Nervous and Mental Disease, 166,* 165–176.

Schuckit, M. A., Goodwin, D. A., & Winokur, G. (1972). A study of alcoholism in half siblings. *American Journal of Psychiatry, 128,* 1132–1136.

Schuckit, M. A., Li, T.-K., Cloninger, C. R., & Deitrich, R. A. (1985). Genetics of alcoholism. *Alcoholism: Clinical and Experimental Research, 9,* 475–492.

Schuckit, M. A., Parker, D. C., & Rossman, L. R. (1983). Ethanol-related prolactin responses and risk for alcoholism. *Biological Psychiatry, 18,* 1153–1159.

Sher, K. J. (1987). What we know and do not know about COAs: A research update. Paper presented at the MacArthur Foundation Meeting on Children of Alcoholics, Princeton, NJ, Dec. 2, 1987.

Simcha-Fagan, O., Gersten, J. C., & Langner, T. S. (1986). Early precursors and concurrent correlates of patterns of illicit drug use in adolescence. *Journal of Drug Issues, 16(1),* 7–28.

Singer, A. (1974). Mothering practices and heroin addiction. *American Journal of Nursing, 74(1),* 77–82.

Skiffington, E. W., & Brown, P. M. (1981). Personal, home, and school factors related to eleventh graders' drug attitudes. *International Journal of the Addictions, 16(5),* 879–892.

Steinglass, P., Bennett, L. A., Wolin, S. J., & Reiss, D. (1987). *The alcoholic family.* New York: Basic Books.

Steinglass, P., Weiner, S., & Mendelson, J. H. (1971). A systems approach to alcoholism: A model and clinical application. *Archives of General Psychiatry, 24,* 401–408.

Steinhausen, H., Gobel, D., & Nestler, V. (1984). Psychopathology in the offspring of alcoholic parents. *Journal of the American Academy of Child Psychiatry, 23,* 465–471.

Stenmark, D. E., Wackwitz, J. H., Pelfrey, M. C., & Dougherty, F. (1974). Substance use among juvenile offenders; relationships to parental substance use and demographic characteristics. *Journal of Addictions, 1,* 43–49.

Sullivan, W. C., & Scholar, S. (1899). A note on the influence of maternal inebriety on the offspring. *Journal of Mental Science, 45,* 489–503.

Sutherland, E. & Cressey, D. (1970). *Criminology.* New York: Lippincott.

Tarter, R. E., Hegedus, A., Goldstein, G., Shelly, C., & Alterman, A. (1984). Adolescent sons of alcoholics: Neuropsychological and personality characteristics. *Alcoholism: Clinical and Experimental Research, 8,* 216–222.

Tarter, R. E., Jacob, T., & Bremer, D. A. (1989). Cognitive status of sons of alcoholic men. *Alcoholism: Clinical and Experimental Research, 13(2),* 232–235.

Ulleland, C. N. (1972). The offspring of alcoholic mothers. *Annals of the New York Academy of Sciences, 197,* 167–169.

U.S. Department of Health and Human Services (1988). *AIDS update,* December.

Warner, R. H., & Rosett, H. L. (1975). The effects of drinking on offspring. *Journal of Studies on Alcohol, 36(11),* 1395–1420.

Werner, E. E. (1986). Resilient offspring of alcoholics: A longitudinal study from birth to age 18. *Journal of Studies on Alcohol, 47,* 34–40.

West, M. O., & Prinz, R. J. (1987). Parental alcoholism and childhood psychopathology. *Psychological Bulletin, 102(2),* 204–218.

Wieland, W. F., & Sola, S. (1970). Depression in opiate addicts measured by objective tests. In *Proceedings of the Third National Conference on Methadone Treatment, November 14–16,* Public Health Service Publication 2172, NIMH, Rockville, MD, pp. 75–78.

Wilson, G. W., Desmond, M. M., & Verniaud, W. M. (1973). Early development of infants of heroin-addicted mothers. *American Journal of Diseases in Childhood, 126,* 457–460.

Wilson, G. S., McCreary, R., Kean, J., & Baxter, C. (1979). The development of preschool children of heroin-addicted mothers: A controlled study. *Pediatrics, 63(1),* 135–141.

Wilson, C., & Orford, J. (1978). Children of alcoholics: Report of a preliminary study and comments on the literature. *Journal of Studies on Alcohol, 39,* 121–142.

Windle, M. (1989). *Children of alcoholics: A comprehensive bibliography.* New York State Division of Alcoholism and Alcohol Abuse, Research Institute on Alcoholism, Buffalo, NY.

Wolin, S. J., Bennett, L. A., & Noonan, D. L. (1979). Family rituals and the recurrence of alcoholism over generations. *American Journal of Psychiatry, 136(4B),* 589–593.

Wolin, S. J., Bennett, L. A., Noonan, D. L., & Teitelbaum, M. A. (1980). Disrupted family rituals: A factor in the intergenerational transmission of alcoholism. *Journal of Studies on Alcohol, 41(3),* 199–214.

Worden, M. (1984). The children of alcoholics movement: Early frontiers. *U.S. Journal, 8(9),* 12–13.

3

Young Children of Substance-Abusing Parents: A Developmental View of Risk and Resiliency

Mary Ellin Logue, Ed. D.
Timothy M. Rivinus, M.D.

Increasingly, public attention and concern are being directed toward children with chemically dependent parents. And it should be. Current estimates show that six and a half million children under the age of 18 live in households with a substance-abusing parent (Russell, Henderson, & Blume, 1985). Public and, in particular, maternal outrage over the effects of male alcoholism on children, women, and family life culminated in the Temperance Movement of the last century, which led to prohibition in the United States (McCarthy & Douglas, 1949; Gusfield, 1955). And yet formal studies of children of chemically dependent parents did not begin until the 1940s. In a retrospective study of adult children of alcoholics (COAs), Row (1944) compared a group of COAs who were raised in foster homes with a control group of children of nonalcoholic parents, who also were raised in foster homes. In this group, there appeared to be no increased rate of alcoholism in the COAs who were raised in foster homes and away from their alcoholic parents. It was postulated that environmental factors played an important part in "protecting" this group from the development of alcoholism or other problems. The confusion that parents' alcoholism caused no damage to a child's physical or mental health was suggested in another early study by Nylander (1960). This study did conclude, however, that when the behavior of the parents was abnormal, whether or not as a result of alcoholism, children were affected.

Recent studies suggest a strong genetic component, particularly for early onset of alcoholism in males (Goodwin, 1985). This finding does not explain, however, why some COAs, well over 50%, do not go on to develop chemical dependency and appear to have normal adjustments of the kind that Roe described in 1944.

The effects of parental substance abuse on children's functioning may not be direct

55

and easily measurable. Research on the effects of substance use on family functioning has aided our understanding of the effects on children. Haberman (1966) documented a greater frequency, when compared with control children, of stuttering, fears, bed wetting, and social isolation after the age of six. The control group was a group with abdominal pains. Behavioral difficulties also were significantly different, with the COAs having more temper tantrums, trouble in school, and fights with peers.

R. Margaret Cork (1969) noted behavioral patterns of children of alcoholic families typified by anger, resentment, low self-esteem, and hopelessness. She showed high degrees of family stress and parental fighting and quarreling, and a significantly higher concern of children of alcoholic families to stop the fighting in their families than in children in the control group.

A study by Chafetz et al. (1971) reviewed case records in a child-guidance clinic and compared COAs with a matched control group. The former showed a higher incidence of school problems, involvement with the law and courts, and disturbed family functioning. However, Kammeier (1971) compared adolescents with alcoholic parents with a matched control group of adolescents and found few differences. Wilson and Offord (1978) point out that although family stress may not be directly related to alcohol use, it is significantly higher in alcoholic families than in non-alcoholic families. Their caution that alcoholism and family fighting may be unrelated variables seems unwarranted, in light of the present understanding of the effects of alcohol and preoccupations with alcohol on family systems function (Steinglass et al., 1987).

A number of studies on communication skills in chemically dependent families (Cork, 1969; Wilson & Offord, 1978; Steinglass et al., 1987; Jacob et al., 1978) have shown that the social relationships of the children are impaired by the presence of ongoing family chemical abuse.

Earlier studies (Goodwin, 1975; Robbins, 1966; Glueck & Glueck, 1950) showing increased problems of conduct disorder, truancy, behavior disorder, attention-deficit disorder with hyperactivity, and oppositional disorder in COAs have been corroborated by very recent studies (Earls et al., 1988; Buydens-Branchey et al., 1989). Past research on the legacy of being a child of an alcoholic parent leads to the conclusion that some COAs may be at higher risk than others. Those with more powerful and more numerous risk factors may be those at higher risk. The assessment of risk and resilience among COAs, however, requires consideration of multiple factors and frames of reference. The conclusions drawn by Wilson and Offord (1978) still hold:

1. The intensity of alcohol-abuse and other substance-abuse involvement in a child's life and in a family's life vary the effect on both child and family.
2. Gender effects, including paternal alcoholism as opposed to maternal alcoholism and its effect on boy versus girl children, are an important variable that must be better understood;

3. The impacts of related problems, such as gambling, infidelity, fights, and mood differences, also are important variables although difficult to measure because they are so often combined with addictive chemical and alcohol use.
4. The role of physical and sexual abuse and other violence often associated with alcohol or other chemical abuse is another important variable.
5. The potential ameliorating fact of extended family, adult friends, siblings, and school performance may provide "protective" factors.
6. The child's individual strengths and defense mechanisms and their employment may buffer the effects of parental addiction.
7. The actual exposure to the alcoholic parent and/or the degree to which the child "idealizes" the alcoholic parent, either present or absent, must be considered.

RISK AND RESILIENCY

What is the relationship between risk and resiliency? At one end of the spectrum, Farber and Egeland (1987) conclude that both abused and neglected children show an extremely poor prognosis, particularly relative to very early abuse or neglect. Certain kinds of psychological abuse (Farber & Egeland, 1987; Garbarino, 1980) may indeed be more pernicious than physical abuse alone. At the other end, based on a core city sample of 456 men originally studied by the Gluecks (1950), Felsman and Vaillant (1987) show that young people who were considered to be at "high risk" in early life may go on, despite periods of limitation and regression, to reflect mastery and competence in adult life. No matter what the stress, some young people were able to develop a sense of mastery and seem to be the ones who are stress survivors. It is most likely that that the combination of genetic and environmental factors at critical periods can serve to weaken or strengthen children's mastery of the developmental tasks necessary for optimal development.

Child Factors: Psychological and Physiological Contributions

The relationship between physiological and psychological factors related to later addiction or psychopathology is not clear. We do know that sons of alcoholic fathers are at fourfold risk compared with the male offspring of nonalcoholics (Goodwin, 1985, Chapters 1 and 2). For this group, certain cognitive deficits have been identified for the sons of alcoholics that may heighten their risk status (Ervin et al., 1984). Children with alcoholic mothers have been shown in controlled studies to be similarly at risk for lower cognitive scores on IQ tests (Aronson, et al., 1985). However, another study of nondisadvantaged families showed that children of recovering alcoholic parents have no differences from non-COAs in performance, verbal, and full-scale IQs, or on reading, spelling, and arithmetic subtests (Johnson and Rolf, 1988).

This study suggests that active recovery by a parent may play a key role in conferring resilience on COAs. Nevertheless, it can be inferred that a generalized protective or resiliency factor, in children of alcoholic parents as well as of nonalcoholic parents, is to have average or above-average intelligence and achievement.

SCHOOL ACHIEVEMENT

Investigations of the relationship between parental alcoholism and children's school performance suggest moderate adverse effects (West & Prinz, 1987). Yet if the alcoholic parents is in recovery and the family has no other major risk factors, the adverse effects of being a COA may disappear (Johnson & Rolf, 1988). The difficulty with school performance as an outcome variable is that the factors contributing to poor school performance are not limited to intellectual ability or aptitude. COAs as a group display higher rates of hyperactivity (Goodwin, 1975), conduct disorder (Nylander, 1960), delinquency (Miller & Jang, 1977; Rimmer, 1982), and truancy (Robbins et al., 1978; Rimmer, 1982), and may be at increased risk for experiencing abuse, neglect, parental discord, divorce, and criminality (Noll & Zucker, 1983; Robbins et al., 1978; Rutter, 1979).

SOCIAL AND EMOTIONAL ADAPTATION

The discussion of biological and environmental markers and variables of substance abuse risk is fully treated in Chapters 1 & 2; only the psychological, cognitive, and behaviroal variables for substance abuse risk will be introduced here.

Little work has been done comparing preschool or younger children of alcoholics with typical peers. Noll and Zucker (1983) have reported on a prospective 20-year investigation of initially intact, community-recruited families with an untreated alcoholic father. A group of four-year-old boys of these families who are considered to be at elevated risk for alcoholism themselves, when compared with control boys, were found to score significantly lower on indices of language, personal/social, fine-motor, and adaptive development. The parents in the alcoholic sample had been more antisocial themselves as children, and continued that pattern into adulthood in their work life, in direct aggressive activity, and in continued trouble with the law. The less adaptive behavior reported for the COAs in testing situations may have been quite adaptive within the contexts of their own families, and may not have been seen by the subject parents as problematic.

Precursors of antisocial behavior have been found in other studies with latency-aged children of alcoholic parents. Fine et al. (1976) found that preadolescent COAs were rated higher than normal controls or children with psychologically disturbed parents on the "unethical behavior" subscale of the parental Devereux Behavior Rating Scale. These children differed from a psychologically disturbed nonalcoholic group on scales for emotional detachment, social aggression, pathological use of senses (indicative behavior seen in schizophrenic children), and inadequate need for independence. Children of alcoholics scored significantly higher than controls on scales measuring proneness to emotional upset and anxious-fearful ideation but not differently from children of emotionally disturbed parents in those areas. Rimmer (1982) reported elevated rates of lying, stealing, playing with matches, fighting, truancy, and discipline problems at school among COAs.

Emotional and social functioning differences have been reported in other studies of COAs. Steinhausen et al. (1982) compared frequencies of various symptoms seen in alcoholic, epileptic, and normal mothers, and concluded that COAs were significantly more impaired than either comparison group in the areas of dependency and difficulty with peers. Anderson and Quast's (1983) sample of six- to 12-year-old COAs scored higher on test norms for anxiety and adjustment scales than did control children. Scores for depression approached significance when the two groups were compared.

Self-concept and locus of control are other areas of socioemotional functioning frequently studied when COAs are compared with control children. Prewett et al. (1981) administered the Norwicki-Strickland Locus of Control Scale to COAs and controls matching for socioeconomic status (SES). COAs were found to be more external in orientation than controls. Kern et al. (1981) found both sons and daughters of alcoholic parents, ages eight to 13, to have higher external locus of control than controls, which is to say that these children considered the power for change as lying outside themselves. In a recent well-controlled study, carefully matching for the confounding effects of SES, significant differences were found in COAs' self-concept scores as compared with controls (Bennett et al., 1988). Johnson and Rolf (1988) found that COAs did not differ from controls in their school achievement but did differ in perceptions of their competence. The discrepancy between self-perception and objective perception is potentially a serious one, and one that may underlie many problems of the adult COAs reported in the clinical literature (e.g., Black, 1979a; Wegscheider, 1981).

GENDER-RELATED DIFFERENCES IN COAS

Living with an alcoholic parents may have different effects on girls and on boys. A gender bias has been evident in many studies of COAs. Sons of alcoholics have been reported to have higher rates of addiction, attention-deficit disorder, and conduct disorders than have daughters of alcoholics, and because of their risk status, are more frequently studied than daughters. Perhaps the negative effects on boys are more overt and immediate than the effects on girls, and so when tested, girls appear to be invulnerable to the stresses of familial alcoholism. Are the daughters in these families invulnerable or do they display their distress differently? Girls from alcoholic families have not shown the overt distress shown by their brothers but clinical findings suggest that the effects of other family disruption may be later for girls than for boys (Wallerstein, 1987; Newcomer & Undry, 1987). Reports of female adolescent and adult depression, eating disorders, and/or marriage to alcoholics suggest that girls may not be as invulnerable as was once thought (Nici, 1979; Silvia et al., 1988). Are the behavioral effects of parental alcoholism indeed hidden for girls, or can patterns indicative of later dysfunction be identified in childhood? Because so much of the existing literature has studied only boys, or has focused on outcome measures that seem to affect boys differentially, the impact of parental alcoholism on girls' development is less well documented.

Gender-related differences in COAs appear in the area of physical health. There seems to be a tendency for female family members in alcoholic families to report health problems at a higher rate than do comparison families. Roberts and Brent (1982) combined children's and adults' use of medical services for both alcoholic and nonalcoholic families and found that females in alcoholic families, when matched with controls, had significantly higher physician-utilization rates and higher numbers of distinct diagnoses. Putnam (1987), however, separated children from adults and divided children by age and gender. She found that preadolescent sons of alcoholics had significantly higher rates of illness, psychosomatic problems, and injury than matched controls. Daughters of alcoholics showed no significant differences when compared with control girls. Further research is needed in this area.

FACTORS RELATING TO LATER SUBSTANCE ABUSE IN CHILDREN

A general profile suggests that those at risk for development of later alcoholism demonstrate higher degrees of social and impulsive behavior, reduced self-confidence, childhood hyperactivity (Rydelius, 1983a, 1983b), and a tendency to consume drugs and alcohol at an early age (Tarter, 1982). These findings have been confirmed and advanced by Kandel and Raveis. (1989), who showed that individuals who are at risk for the development of early substance-use disorder, particularly alcoholism, are more antisocial, more involved with drug-using friends, and more dependent on marijuana. Those who were able to give up substance use despite experimentation were those who committed fewer antisocial acts, had fewer drug-using friends, stopped using marijuana or used it only rarely, and had assumed adult roles, thus giving up or altering the social influences of the drug-using peers from adolescence. A recent study on risk (Buydens-Branchy et al., 1989) showed that those with early onset of alcoholism, particularly before age 20, were more likely to have histories of higher paternal alcoholism, incarceration for violent crimes, and depression and attempted suicide than later-onset alcoholics. For many high-risk individuals, prevention of substance use/abuse may not be possible. However, the results of these new studies suggest that delaying the onset of these behaviors may have important positive consequences for the quality of life of these individuals.

In a developmental, longitudinal study of a nonclinical sample of preschoolers, Block et al. (1988) found different personality profiles for girls and boys who abused drugs in adolescence. Boys who later developed problems with drugs showed behavioral profiles similar to the COA sample in Noll and Zucker's (1983) sample. In nursery school, they were unable to delay gratification, and were very active, were emotionally expressive and labile, were overreactive, and had a low frustration tolerance. As preschoolers, girls who later abused drugs were uneasy with themselves and others, self-protective, unexpressive, detached, devious, hostile, and unlikable, having personality patterns that, according to Block et al. (1988), constrain the development of competence. Whether or not the children who later abused drugs were children of substance-abusing parents is unknown. However, early family environment was related to adolescent drug use in girls but not in boys. Adolescent girls who abused drugs tended to be raised in homes characterized as unstructured and laissez-faire, where there was little pressure to achieve. Additionally, Bianco and Wallace (see Chapter 8) have studied polysubstance-abusing girls referred for residential treatment and have demonstrated a high incidence of family crisis and dysfunction—specifically, parental alcohol abuse, sexual or physical abuse of the female child by parent or caretaker, and parental abandonment and neglect.

Kellam's (1982 & 1988) longitudinal study of children showed gender-specific influences for later substance use. Early psychiatric symptoms were a strong first-grade antecedent of teenage substance use in females but not in males. Shyness in first-grade males, but not females, inhibits delinquency and drug, alcohol, and cigarette use in adolescence. First-grade aggressiveness was a strong predictor for males of delinquency and drug, alcohol, and cigarette use, and aggressiveness coupled with shyness for males was associated with more delinquency and substance use than aggression alone.

EFFECTS OF PARENTAL SUBSTANCE USE ON FAMILY FUNCTIONING AND CHILD DEVELOPMENT

Gender of Substance-Abusing Parent

It appears as though gender is a critical variable in differentiating effects of parental alcohol use on children's functioning. The gender of the alcoholic parent is a variable that often is left unexplored. It continues to be easier to recruit samples of male alcoholics, and thus most research with COAs concerns the effects of living with alcoholic fathers. It is assumed that maternal alcoholism is far more detrimental for young children than is paternal alcoholism when attachment relationships are formed and when safety needs require alert parental supervision. However, this question has not been studied systematically. The growing attention to family systems theory in studying and treating alcoholism, however, would suggest that alcoholism of either parent could/would affect the quality of a child's attachment to the primary care-giving parent, whether that parent is actively drinking or not.

EFFECTS ON ATTACHMENT

A basic tenet of attachment theory is that the quality of mother–infant attachment serves as a prototype for other relationships in the child's life (Bretherton, 1986;

Bowlby, 1982). The degree to which alcohol affects the family system has implications not only for the mother–infant attachment relationship, but also for the child's relationships with peers, teachers, and others. To the extent that alcohol consumption or preoccupation with another's alcohol consumption interferes with a mother's capacity to respond consistently to her baby's needs, the quality of the attachment is jeopardized. O'Connell et al. (1987) studied attachment behavior of infants with over-30, middle-class, alcohol-consuming mothers and showed that a significant proportion of the babies whose mothers drank an average of three drinks per day exhibited a disorganized/disoriented attachment pattern. The long-term effects of maternal drinking on attachment and later development remain unclear, and yet advances in attachment theory suggest that children who display disorganized/disoriented attachment relationships with their parents often show patterns of role reversal and depression, characteristics frequently cited in the clinical literature on COAs. If prospective, longitudinal studies of attachment behavior would, as part of the research protocol, include measures of parental substance use, the relationships among familial substance abuse, attachment, and subsequent development could be further clarified.

Family Roles and Risk and/or Resiliency

The growing body of clinical literature suggesting that the children of chemically dependent parents adopt certain roles (Wegscheider, 1981; Black, 1981) also suggests that those children who become the "heroes" in the family may be those who, in addition to having the roles of responsibility and "heroism" conferred on them, demonstrate a kind of resiliency at an early age despite a stressful situation. Those youngsters who become "lost," victimized, or "scapegoated" in the family system may be those without the internal strengths to turn a stressful situation into one that results in mastery. Such an explanation, however, may be simplistic. Perhaps the family "heroes" have merely adopted more socially acceptable coping mechanisms than their siblings, and the costs of this adaptability may, in the long term, be equally damaging. If this hypothesis is true, it is important to examine some of the socially sanctioned ways in which "heroes" cope, and evaluate the risk of such adaptation to later development (see also Chapter 13).

Time spent in structured activity seems to have important implications for children's functioning. Carpenter et al. (1988) showed, with a normative sample, a positive relationship between the amount of time children spent with adults in predictable, structured activity and their achievement at school. The nature of that activity also has an important influence on functioning. Whiting and Edwards (1988), in their cross-cultural study on the formation of social behavior, suggest that the nature of activities assigned to children helps shape their personality. For instance, they showed that children assigned child-care tasks were more nuturant and prosocial in their behavior than children assigned other tasks. While their findings are used to explain gender differences (i.e., girls are more likely to be assigned child-care tasks than boys and girls tend to be more prosocial than boys), they showed that the nature of the activity exerts a powerful effect in shaping the behavior of children regardless of gender. In this country, girls have been found to spend more time on household chores than do boys (Long & Henderson, 1973). Girls' greater experience with structured daily activities may contribute to their greater compliance with adult rules and their generally higher levels of verbal and reading skills in elementary school (Maccoby & Jacklin, 1974). If the Whiting and Edwards model of human development holds, children, regardless of gender, who participate in household chores will be more similar and perhaps more "protected," than children who do not.

How and in what contexts children assume adult responsibilities are developmentally and culturally determined. The ability to assume adult responsibility is socially condoned, and such children are often considered "responsible" and "independent." The structure implicit in performing adult activity may provide a buffer for the children such that involvement in the activity furnishes the structure necessary to protect academic and social functioning. Several researchers have found that children (particularly girls) who are assigned household responsibilities (e.g., child care) cope well in spite of poverty and discrimination (Werner & Smith, 1982; Clark, 1983; Garmezy, 1983; Rutter, 1979). Is there a point at which assuming adult responsibility in childhood is harmful? Anecdotal clinical evidence about adult COAs suggests that many children in alcoholic families assume adult roles (Wegscheider, 1981). The role reversal observed between mothers and babies classified as having an insecure disorganized/disoriented attachment pattern suggests that precocious adultlike behavioral patterns may indeed be problematic. The distinction between role reversal and the ability to assume adult responsibilities remains unclear. Many daughters of alcoholics, who appear to be highly responsible and independent, could be quite vulnerable. The difference between assuming adult tasks oneself and assisting adults in the same tasks may contribute to different psychological outcomes for all children, but particularly for girls, because of the increased likelihood of girls' participating in household chores. This distinction between involvement in adult activity with and without adult supervision may be a subtle but important one for differentiating "invulnerable" children from those with quiet impairment.

Protective Factors in Families That Contribute to Child Resiliency

PARENTAL RECOVERY FROM SUBSTANCE ABUSE

An obvious buffer for a child from an alcoholic family is the recovery of the alcoholic parent from alcoholism. Little is known about the changes in child functioning relative to parental abstinence. In families whose communication and interaction patterns revolve around the alcoholic, abstinence and its new accompanying behavioral patterns may represent a dramatic change in the roles and behaviors of all family members. A family systems approach assumes that change in one family member necessitates changes in the family system. Recovery, while ultimately in the best interest of each family member, may be traumatic at the early stages. As the habits of one family member change, it can be expected that the habits, and perhaps the roles, of other family members will also change. Recovery, then, may not be a linear process. McCrady et al. (in preparation) found that couples who underwent family therapy showed an initial decrease in marital satisfaction preceding reported increased satisfaction. We do not know whether children in alcoholic families also show patterns of disorganization preceding improvement, but there is evidence suggesting that during periods of trauma (e.g., divorce) children experience approximately a year of disrupted behavior exemplified by increased conflict and lower rates of compliance with parental demands before stabilization (Hetherington et al., 1976, 1979). If changes in children's behavior following parental recovery involve a nonlinear process similar to that of the couples in the McCrady et al. (in preparation) study, it is important to conduct longitudinal studies in order to document the developmental course of recovery.

The effects of parental recovery may be evident in recent comparative studies of COAs and controls. In the sample of COAs from the Bennett et al. (1988) study, more than half had parents who had been abstinent for up to two years. Children of these abstinent alcoholics were grouped with children of active drinkers to form the COA group. The researchers found that COAs scored lower than controls (but still within normal limits) on measures of school achievement. Johnson and Rolf (1988), who studied otherwise low-risk subjects and control families, found no significant differences in cognitive functioning according to testing and school achievement between children of recovering alcoholics (abstinent at least six months) and controls. However, COAs scored lower on measures of self-esteem (Bennett et al., 1988) and perceived competence (Johnson & Rolf, 1988) than did controls. At present, we do not know if, in the developmental course of recovery for school-aged children, improvement in school achievement precedes improvement in psychological functioning.

Moos and Billings (1982) found that when parents abstain from alcohol, their children improve on measures of psychological functioning such that they resemble control children at the end of two years. These and other findings (Johnson & Rolf, 1988) offer hopeful evidence as to the moderating effects of parental recovery on the family system.

FAMILY RITUALS AND PREDICTABLE STRUCTURE.

Stability of family rituals and routines has been associated with the transmission of alcoholism from one generation to another. Steinglass et al. (1987) suggest that when predictable, protective family rituals and routines break down, children are at higher risk for becoming alcoholic themselves than are children from families who maintain their rituals and routines despite an alcoholic parent.

It has been suggested that the children's particular experiences within their families can increase or decrease the likelihood of their developing cognitive, physical, or emotional problems (Bennett et al., 1988). Participation in predictable family rituals, particularly meals, serves to buffer children against the negative consequences of parental alcoholism (Wolin et al., 1980). Wolin and his colleagues found alcoholic families, when compared with nonalcoholic families, to be generally less successful in establishing well-planned, stable, and meaningful family rituals. The lack of such a family environment is reflected in more problems among the children. Bennett, Wolin, and Reiss (1988) found that COAs, when compared with nonalcoholic controls, scored lower on measures of school achievement and self-esteem. Rolf and Johnson (1988) found that the psychological profiles of COAs differed from those of children of nonalcoholic controls in the degree to which they perceived themselves as competent and effective in changing or controlling their environments. More than simply eating together, it may be that the predictable structured activity shared by children and adults is what is important to psychological health and school achievement.

ASSESSMENT OF CHILD RISK

One of the main difficulties in studying or working with young COAs is that the ways in which children are affected by alcoholism are so varied. The age and gender of the child, gender of the alcoholic parent, severity and duration of the alcoholism, extent of family disruption, socioeconomic factors, family size, the child's relationship to the nonalcoholic parent and other supports, and the child's temperament all play a role in influencing the child's vulnerability and resiliency. Attempts to predict adolescent or adult functioning from childhood antecedents have been disappointing and may speak to the impossibility of discerning a simple risk formula for a multifaceted social problem.

In an attempt to "unpackage" the variables of socioeconomic status (SES), Sameroff et al. (1987) assessed four-year-olds on a set of ten environmental variables that are correlated with but not equal to SES. They found major differences in cognitive and socioemotional functioning between children with low multiple-risk scores and children with high scores. The same outcomes were the result of different combinations of risk factors. No single factor was regularly related to poor or good outcomes. The weight of positive versus negative factors, on balance, was the best predictor of outcome. Although parental chemical abuse was not specifically identified as a risk factor in this study, the logic of this analysis suggests that the probability of children becoming alcoholic themselves is also the result of a disrupted balance between stress factors and protective factors. Werner's longitudinal study of high-risk children, many of whom were COAs, appears to bear out this logic by showing the shifting balance between stressful life events that heighten children's vulnerability and the protective factors that enhance their resiliency (Werner, 1988).

HELPING TO BUFFER RISK FOR CHILDREN OF SUBSTANCE-ABUSING PARENTS

Consistent and responsive adults are providing more for many children of substance-abusing parents than they may realize. In a 30-year longitudinal study of high-risk infants, Werner identified several protective factors professionals can utilize in working with such children (Werner & Smith, 1982; Werner, 1988). She found that the "invulnerable" adults in her sample, as babies and young children, received nurturance from substitute care givers within the family, made active use of informal networks outside the family for advice and assistance, had positive classroom experiences that helped develop an achievement orientation, and acquired a sense of meaning and faith about life. Rutter (1979), in studying children at risk for psychopathology, also noted that positive influences at school and coping skills to allow maintenance of self-esteem separated vulnerable from invulnerable children.

Substance-abusing families have been characterized in the clinical literature as having rigid boundaries within which members assume static roles (Steinglass et al., 1987; Wegscheider, 1981; Black, 1979a). Sameroff et al. (1983), in their work on psychopathology and early intervention, found that parental beliefs and attitudes are important mediators between environmental stress and child competence. If the roles children play in alcoholic families become rigid and inflexible, they can be detrimental to the child regardless of whether they are positive or negative roles. Roles are related to family myths, which are beliefs that go unchallenged in spite of reality. Family myths are not readily recognized as distortions, and developmental problems arise when a child must accept a distorted myth in order to remain in the family. Professionals working with children can serve a valuable role by illuminating the myths about children and reframing and challenging them gently but repeatedly.

Children found to be resilient also have other characteristics that are either more difficult or impossible for teachers and clinicians to combat. Resilient children in Werner's (1982) sample grew up in families with four or fewer children with a space of two or more years between siblings. For boys, being first-born was an important protective factor. As infants and toddlers, resilient children were very active, affectionate, regular in functioning, and social in orientation. Family size, birth order, and child spacing may not be variable, but temperamental characteristics may be modified. Kagan (1984) suggests that adults are reluctant to try to change a child's basic style. Accepting the fact that "that's just the way he/she is" may be a disservice to high-risk children, whether they are passive victims or hostile aggressors. High-risk children, among them many COAs, are children whose future health may depend on being able to recruit other caring people into their lives. Those children who do not "appeal" fare less well. Lost, acting-out, or scapegoated children need to be reached out to actively. Social-skills training has proved to be effective in helping children develop the skills necessary to be competent social agents in their worlds (Asher, 1981; Spivak & Shure, 1974).

If growing up with a chemically dependent parent is risk producing, regardless of the roles children assume within the family, a "corrective" environment is necessary. For some children, early exposure to treatment programs such as Alateen may be corrective (Chapter 13). The effect of these programs in conferring a "corrective experience" and a sympathetic environment for children who have the capacity for mastery has not yet been tested.

CONCLUSIONS

In general, the heightened risk status of COAs as a group is becoming more widely recognized by professionals. How the specific characteristics of COAs differ for the characteristics of children from non-substance-abusing dysfunctional families, and how treatment should or should not differ for such children, is an area in which further research is needed. For those endorsing the disease concept of alcoholism, a growing body of material is available to help educators and clinicians in treating COAs (Deutsch, 1982; Landers & Hollingdale, 1988; Black, 1979b; Bingham & Bargar, 1985; Al-Anon, 1983). Research on the effectiveness of such treatments is needed in order to best meet the needs of COAs, who represent a diverse population.

Further developmental research with children of substance-abusing parents is needed in many areas. Much needed research is being conducted in related areas and must be integrated into the substance-abuse field. There is a growing body of literature suggesting that the nature of an infant's attachment to his or her primary parent has long-term consequences for later development. Because parental substance abuse may interfere with the attachment process, those researchers studying attachment would be wise to inquire about substance use as part of their protocol.

Another area in which research is needed is to address the gap between empirical knowledge and clinical practice. Predictable and potentially damaging family roles have been identified by clinicians as characteristic of substance-abusing families. The existence of these roles, upon which much of today's treatment and the work of many of the self-help groups are based, has not been proved empirically. Can the roles of family hero, scapegoat, lost child, and mascot (Wegscheider, 1981) be identified in empirical studies? If they do exist, how stable are the roles? What factors alter the roles?

Treatment-effectiveness studies of the self-help programs for children of substance-abusing parents are needed. Because of the anonymous nature of these programs, well-controlled studies are difficult to conduct. However, efforts must be made to identify the active ingredients of effective treatment.

Identification of the gender differences in ways that parental addiction affects children is also needed. The lack of any differences at one age must not be regarded as a lack of negative effect. Longitudinal studies of girls and boys with substance-abusing families (mothers and fathers) are needed in order to identify critical developmental periods and potential buffers.

Among children who later abuse substances themselves, factors such as parental substance abuse, physical or sexual abuse, depression, temperament, school failure, self-confidence, and aggression have been identified as correlates (see Chapters 7 and 8). The interaction between biological and environmental factors needs to be better understood in order better to assess risk status for children. Attempts to develop a "risk formula" for later substance use or for psychopathology have not proved beneficial. Further research on the impact of cumulative risk appears to be a more valuable line of inquiry.

Children's experiences in their families, schools, and community can exacerbate or mediate the consequences of living in a substance-abusing family. Consistent, concerned adults can play important roles in identifying those children in need of intervention, as well as in acting as a support to families. Bell and Pearl (1982) noted that individuals are likely to move in and out of risk status across developmental phases. As long as the balance between stressful life events and protective factors is manageable for children, they can cope.

In order for adults to intervene effectively in strengthening children's resiliency, knowledge of child development and the ability to make subtle distinctions in behavior is imperative. It is relatively easy to identify the children at risk for conduct disorders, school failure, or physical injury, who are more likely to be the sons than the daughters of substance-abusing parents (see Chapter 7). More difficult but no less important is the ability to make subtle distinctions that may underlie the risk for quiet but damaging outcomes. For example, empathetic care-giving behavior or independent, responsible behavior may be socially acceptable but not necessarily developmentally appropriate for young children if the pattern interferes with necessary autonomy or mastery of age-appropriate social and learning skills. Because these patterns can be so helpful to adults, their harmful effects on "convenient" children may be overlooked. Observational skills allowing one to make difficult distinctions between subtle adaptive behavioral patterns that either promote growth or hinder the behavior within a developmental context can prove helpful in identifying and intervening with "convenient" at-risk children.

There are no simple formulas for predicting substance abuse or related psychopathology in COAs. Nor are there formulas for protecting these children. The situation is far from hopeless, however. Concerned adults offering consistent patterns of interaction, making age-appropriate demands on children, and providing opportunities for children to develop realistic self-perceptions can make a difference.

REFERENCES

Al-Anon Family Group Headquarters, (1983). *Alateen: Hope for children of alcoholics*, New York: Al-Anon.

Anderson, E., & Quast, W. (1983). Young children in alcoholic families: A mental health needs assessment and an intervention/prevention strategy. *Journal of Primary Prevention*, 3, 174–187.

Aronson, M., Kyllerman, M., Sabel, K. G., Sandin, B., & Olegard, R. (1985). Children of alcoholic mothers: Developmental, perceptual and behavioral characteristics as compared to matched controls, *Acta Paediatrica Scandinavia*, 74, 27–35.

Asher, S., & Renshaw, P. (1981). Children without friends: Social knowledge and social skill training. In Asher & Gottman (Eds.); *The development of children's friendships*. Cambridge, England: Cambridge University Press.

Bell, R. & Pearl, D. (1982). Psychological change in risk groups: Implications for early identification. *Prevention in Human Services*, 1, 45–49.

Bennett, L., Wolin, S., & Reiss, D. (1988). Cognitive, behavioral and emotional problems among school-age children of alcoholic parents. *American Journal of Psychiatry*, 145(2), 185–190.

Bingham, A., & Bargar, J. (1985). Children of alcoholic families: A group treatment approach for latency age children. *Journal of Psychology of Nursing*, 23, 13–15.

Black, C. (1979a). Children of alcoholics. *Alcohol Health and Research World*, 4, 23–27.

Black, C. (1979b). *My dad loves me, my dad has a disease*. Denver, CO: MAC Publications.

Block, J., Block, J., & Keyes, S. (1988). Longitudinally foretelling drug usage in adolescence: Early childhood personality and environmental precursors. *Child Development*, 59, 336–355.

Bowlby, J. (1982). Attachment and loss: Retrospect and prospect. *American Journal of Orthopsychiatry*, 52, 664–678.

Bretherton, I. (1986). Attachment theory: Retrospect and prospect. In I. Bretherton & Waters (Eds.), Growing points of attachment theory and research. *Monographs of the Society for Research in Child Development*, Serial no. 209, vol. 50, nos. 1–2.

Buydens-Branchey, L., Branchey, M. H., & Noumair, D. (1989). Age of alcoholism onset and relationship to psychopathology. *Archives of General Psychiatry*, 46, 225–230.

Carpenter, C. J., Houston, A. & Spera, L. (in press). Children's use of time in their everyday activities during middle childhood. In M. Block & A. Pellegrin (Eds.); The ecological context of children's play. New Jersey: Ablex.

Chafetz, M. E., Blane, H. T., & Hill, M. J. (1971). Children of alcoholics: Observations in a child guidance clinic. *Quarterly Journal of Studies in Alcohol*, 32, 687–698.

Clark, R. M. (1983). *Family life and school achievement: Why poor black children succeed or fail*. Chicago: University of Chicago Press.

Cork, R. M. (1969). *The forgotten children: A study of children with alcohol parents*. Toronto: Paper Jacks.

Deutsch, C. (1982). Broken bottles, broken dreams. New York: Teacher's College Press.

Drake, R. E., & Vaillant, G. E. (1988). Predicting alcoholism and personality disorder in a 33-year longitudinal study of children of alcoholics. *British Journal of Addiction*, 83, 799–808.

Earls, F., Reich, W., Jung, K. G., & Cloninger, C. R. (1988). Psychopathology in children of alcoholic and antisocial parents. *Alcoholism Clinical and Experimental Research*, 12, 481–487.

Ervin, C., Little, R., Streissguth, A., & Beck, D. (1984). Alcoholic fathering and its relation to child's intellectual development: A pilot investigation, *Alcoholism: Clinical and Experimental Research*, 8, 362–365.

Farber, E. A., & Egeland, B. (1987). Invulnerability among abused and neglected children. In E. J. Anthony & B. J. Cohlers (Eds.), *The invulnerable child*. New York: Guilford Press.

Felsman, J. K., & Vaillant, G. E. (1987). Resilient children as adults. In E. J. Anthony & B. J. Cohlers (Eds.) *The invulnerable child*. New York: Guilford Press.

Fine, E., Yudin, L., Holmes, J., & Heinemann, S. (1976). Behavioral disorders in children with parental alcoholism. *Annals of the New York Academy of Sciences*, 273, 507–517.

Garbarino, J. & Gilliam, G. (1980). Understanding Abusive Families. Lexington, Mass.: Lexington Books.

Garbarino, J., Guttman, E., & Seeley, J. W. (1986). *The psychologically battered child*. San Francisco: Jossey-Bass.

Garmezy, M. (1983) *Stressors of childhood*. In N. Garmezy & M. Rutter (Eds.), *Stress, coping and development in children* (pp. 43–84). New York: McGraw-Hill.

Glueck, S., & Glueck, E. (1950). *Unraveling juvenile delinquency*. Cambridge, MA: Harvard University Press.

Goodwin, D. (1975). Alcoholism and heredity: A review and hypothesis. *Archives of General Psychiatry*, 36, 57–61.

Goodwin, D. W. (1985). Alcoholism and genetics. *Archives of General Psychiatry*, 42, 171–174.

Gusfield, J. R. (1955). Social structure and moral reform: A study of the Women's Christian Temperance Union. *American Journal of Sociology*, 61, 221–232.

Haberman, P. W. (1966). Childhood symptoms in children of alcoholics and comparison group parents. *Journal of Marriage and Family*, 28, 152–154.

Hetherington, M., Cox, M, & Cox, R. (1982). Effects of divorce on parents and children. In M. Lamb (Ed.), *Nontraditional families*. Hillsdale, NJ: Erlbaum.

Hetherington, M., Cox, M., & Cox, R. (1979). Family interaction and the social, emotional and cognitive development of children following divorce. In V. Vaugn & T. Brazleton (Eds), *The family: Setting priorities*. New York: Science & Medicine.

Jacob, T, Favorini, A., Meisel, S., & Anderson, C. (1978). The spouse, children and family interactions of the alcoholic: Substantive findings and methodological issues. *Journal of Studies in Alcohol*, 39, 1231–1251.

Johnson, L., & Rolf, J. (1988). Cognitive functioning in children from alcoholic and non-alcoholic families. *British Journal of the Addictions*, 83, 849–857.

Kagan, J. (1984). *The nature of the child*. New York: Basic Books.

Kammeier, M. D. (1971). Adolescents from families with and without alcohol problems. *Quarterly Journal of Studies on Alcohol, 32,* 364–372.

Kandel, D. B., & Raveis, V. H. (1989). Cessation of illicit drug use in young adulthood. *Archives of General Psychiatry, 143,* 109–116.

Kellam, S., Anthony, J., Hendricks Brown, C., Dolan, L., Carran, D., Crockett, L., Edelsohn, G., Werthamer-Larsson, L., & Wilson, R. (1988). Prevention research on early risk behaviors in cross-cultural studies. Paper presented at Task Force on Alcohol and Drug Related Disorders, WHO/ADAMHA, Mexico City.

Kern, J., Hassett, C., Collipp, P., Bridges, C., Solomon, M., & Condren, R. (1981). Children of alcoholics: Locus of control, mental age, and zinc level. *Journal of Psychiatric Treatment and Evaluation, 3,* 169–173.

Landers, D., & Hollingdale, L. (1988). Working with children of alcoholics on a college campus: A rationale and strategies for success. In *Alcoholism, chemical dependency and the college student.* New York: Haworn.

Long, B. H., & Henderson, E. H. (1973). Children's use of time: Some personal and social correlates. *Elementary School Journal.* Jan., 193–199.

Maccoby, E., & Jacklin, C. (1974). *The psychology of sex differences.* Stanford, CA: Stanford University Press.

McCarthy, R. G., & Douglas, E. M. (1949). Prohibition and repeal. *Alcohol and social responsibility.* New York: Crowell.

McCrady, B., Stout, R., Noel, N., Abrams, D., & Fisher-Nelson, H. (unpublished). Comparative effectiveness of three types of spouse-involved behavioral alcoholism treatment outcomes at 18 months.

Miller, D., & Jang, M. (1977). Children of alcoholics: A 20-year longitudinal study. *Social Work Research and Abstracts, 13,* 23–29.

Moos, R., & Billings, A. (1982). Children of alcoholics during the recovery process: Alcoholic and matched control families. *Addictive Behaviors, 7,* 155–163

Newcomer S. & Undry R. (1987). Parental marital status effects on adolescent sexual behavior. *Journal of Marriage and the Family, 49* (2), 227–240.

Nici, J. (1979). Wives of alcoholics as "repeaters," *Journal of Studies on Alcohol, 40,* 677–682.

Noll, R., & Zucker, R. (1983). Developmental findings from an alcoholic vulnerability study: The preschool years. Paper presented at the Annual Meeting of the American Psychological Association, Anaheim, CA.

Nylander, A. (1960). Children of alcoholic fathers. *Acta Paediatrica, 49,* suppl. 121(1), 1–34.

O'Connell, M. J., Sigman, M., & Brill, N. (1987). Disorganization of attachment in relation to maternal alcohol consumption. *Journal of Consulting and Clinical Psychology, 55,* 001–006.

Putnam, S. (1987). The effects of parent's alcoholism treatment on children's injury rates: An HMO study. Paper presented at the AMERSA national conference, Washington, D.C.

Prewett, M., Spence, R., & Chaknis, M. (1981). Attribution of causality by children with alcoholic parents. *International Journal of the Addictions, 16,* 367–370.

Rimmer, J. (1982). The children of alcoholics: An exploratory study. *Children and Youth Services Review, 4,* 365–373.

Robbins, L. (1966). *Deviant children grown up.* Baltimore: Williams & Wilkins.

Robbins, L., West, P., Ratcliff, K., & Herjanic, B. (1978). Father's alcoholism and children's outcomes. In F.A. Seixas (Ed.), *Currents in alcoholism* (Vol. 4, pp. 313–327). New York: Grune & Stratton.

Roberts, K., & Brent, E. (1982). Physician utilization and illness patterns in families of alcoholics. *Journal of Studies on Alcohol, 43,* 119–128.

Row, A. (1944). The adult adjustment of children of alcohol parents raised in foster-homes. *Quarterly Journal of Studies on Alcohol, 5,* 378–393.

Russell, M., Henderson, C., & Blume, S. (1985). *Children of alcoholics: A review of the literature* (pp. 1–2.) New York: Children of Alcoholics Foundation.

Rutter, M. (1979). Protective factors in children's responses to stress and disadvantage. In M. W. Kent & J. E. Rolf (Eds.), *Social competence in children.* Hanover, NH: University Press of New England.

Rydelius, P. A. (1983a). Alcohol abusing teenage boys: Testing a hypothesis on the relationship between alcohol abuse and social background factors, criminality and personality in teenage boys. *Acta Psychiatrica Scandinavica, 68,* 368–380.

Rydelius, P. A. (1983b). Alcohol abusing teenage boys: Testing a hypothesis on the relationship between alcohol abuse and personality factors, using a personality inventory. *Acta Psychiatrica Scandinavica, 68,* 381–385.

Sameroff, A., Seifer, R., & Barocas, R. (1983). Impact of parental psychopathology: Diagnosis, severity, or social class effects? *Infant Mental Health Journal, 4,* 236–249.

Sameroff, A., Seifer, R., Barocas, R., Zax, M, & Greenspan, S. (1987). I.Q. scores for 4-year old children: Social-environmental risk factors. *Pediatrics, 79,* 343–358.

Silvia, L., Sorell, G., & Busch-Rossnagel, N. (1988). Biopsychosocial discriminators of alcoholic and nonalcoholic women. *Journal of Substance Abuse, 1,* 55–65.

Spivak, G., & Shure, M. (1974). *Social adjustment of young children: A cognitive approach to solving real-life problems.* San Francisco: Jossey-Bass.

Steinglass, P., Bennett, L., Wolin, S., et al. (1987). *The alcoholic family.* New York: Basic Books.

Steinhausen, H., Nestler, V., & Huth, H. (1982). Psychopathology and mental functions in the offspring of alcoholic and epileptic mothers. *Journal of the American Academy of Child Psychiatry, 21,* 268–273.

Tarter, R. (1982). Psychosocial history, minimal brain dysfunction and differential drinking patterns of male alcoholics. *Journal of Clinical Psychology, 38,* 867–873.

Wallerstein, J. (1987). Children of divorce: Report of a ten-year follow-up of latency-age children. *American Journal of Orthopsychiatry, 57*(2), 199–211.

Wegscheider, S. (1981). *Another chance.* Palo Alto, CA: Science & Behavior Books.

Werner, E. (1988). Individual differences, universal needs: A 30-year study of resilient high risk infants. *Zero to Three: Bulletin of National Center for Clinical Infant Programs,* 8(4), April.

Werner, E., & Smith, R. S. (1982). *Vulnerable but invincible: A longitudinal study of resilient children and youth.* New York: McGraw-Hill.

West, M. O., & Prinz, R. (1987). Parental alcoholism and childhood psychopathology. *Psychological Bulletin, 102,* 204–218.

Whiting, B., & Edwards, C. (1988). *Children of different worlds: The formation of social behavior.* Cambridge, MA: Harvard University Press.

Wilson, C, & Offord, J. (1978). Children of alcoholics. *Journal of Studies on Alcohol, 39,* 121–142.

Wolin, S., Bennett, L., Noonan, D., & Teitelbaum, M. (1980). Disrupted family rituals: A factor in the intergenerational transmission of alcoholism. *Journal of Studies on Alcohol, 41,*(3), 199–214.

4

Children of Chemically Dependent Parents: A Theoretical Crossroads

Stephanie Brown, Ph.D.

In the late 1970s and 1980s, a new social movement and a new legitimate treatment population were born (see also Chapters 13 and 14). The acronyms ACAs and ACOAs (adult children of alcoholics) and COAs (children of alcoholics) are now part of common social language. Originated in the vocabulary of the chemical-dependence-treatment field, they also have become familiar to professionals in the mental health field. Yet recognition and acceptance of the legitimacy of these new treatment populations have been slow in both groups.

Research on young children of alcoholic parents dates back to 1945 (Roe & Burks, 1945), with an established literature base, focused on genetics and psychiatric disturbance, developed during the 1960s and 1970s (Schuckit et al., 1972; Goodwin, 1971; Goodwin et al., 1973; Nylander, 1960; Hawkins, 1950; Bosma, 1972; Fine et al., 1976). Despite this early research, which established that young COAs do have psychiatric problems, the findings did not translate into clinical theory, practice, education, or prevention. In fact, acknowledgment of the realities and legitimacy of this group was largely ignored or denied by professionals (Brown, 1988; Morehouse, 1984; Black, 1981), matching the denial also prevalent among alcoholic parents and families (Hunter, 1963).

Recognition was accomplished by a phenomenal grass-roots social movement originated by a subgroup of professionals in the chemical-dependence field and spread by the popular media (see Chapters 14–16). "Children of alcoholics" was an idea whose time had come, an idea that rapidly developed a base of literature, a national association, a foundation, a rapidly expanding network of self-help groups independent of and affiliated with Al-Anon, and many public-interest groups.

ACOAs and COAs have always existed, but could not be identified and legiti-

74

mized. Asking why is an important first step toward understanding the critically important implications that their recognition and legitimacy bring to the separate fields of chemical dependency and mental health.

Denial and conceptual bias also appear to have characterized the professional treatment fields in a way similar to the distorted beliefs developed in the family to deal with the reality of parental alcoholism and deny it at the same time. The distortion and denial required in the family are significant factors in the pathology that develops as a result of living with an alcoholic parent (Brown, 1988; Black, 1981). A very similar distortion, denial, or narrow theoretical bias has characterized professional theory and practice (see also Chapter 5).

The mental health field viewed alcoholism as a secondary consequence to other problems. The diagnosis of alcoholism was often missed or minimized. The chemical-dependence field focused only on the primacy of the alcoholic or chemically dependent individual, with those close to the addicted person not given separate status. Dynamic theories of psychopathology also focused narrowly on the individual, highlighting the significance of intrapsychic conflict and childhood fantasy as determinants of disturbance and omitting the environment and familial context. Therefore, it was impossible to relate childhood and adult disturbance to parental illness and pathology.

Even if these conceptual biases had been recognized, there still would have been a major problem. Acknowledgment of ACOAs requires a bridging of disparate disciplines *within* mental health—the behavioral, cognitive, dynamic, and system points of view—and *between* the separate, and frequently hostile, fields of chemical dependence and mental health. This bridging requires a collaboration and integration of theory and practice, moving toward a much more complex theory of development and psychopathology. Acknowledgment of ACOAs reveals the lack of any such unifying theory, as well as institutional denial of the realities and consequences of alcoholism.

This chapter explores the phenomenon of professional denial and its relation to established theory and theory development in the chemical-dependence and mental health fields, and then outlines a more comprehensive, complex theory or ordering framework to understand ACOAs grounded in the recent developments of cognitive-constructionist and control-mastery theories.

INADEQUACY OF TRADITIONAL THEORIES

The Primacy of the Diagnosis

Because of a narrow theoretical bias, misleading emphasis, or misattribution, parental alcoholism could not be labeled or treated directly, and thus its consequences understood. Faulty beliefs about the primacy of alcoholism lead to a failure to label and diagnose it as the central issue for the alcoholic and for the adult children of alcoholics. The failure to label it as central maintains faulty thinking patterns of patients and therapists. The childhood reality and trauma of parental alcoholism and the nature of relationships within this traumatic context cannot be acknowledged or appropriately connected to the source. Instead, pathological adjustment or problems in childhood or adulthood must be improperly understood in a way that maintains the denial of parental alcoholism or its reduction to a secondary, consequential status. Arguments about the validity of the disease concept illustrate these problems. The separate chemical-dependence-research and -treatment field, representing a belief in the disease model of etiology and total abstinence as prescribed treatment, was born partly out of this controversy.

Split Between Chemical Dependence and Mental Health

The chemical-dependency field initially had no research base, but a well-established treatment philosophy developed out of personal experiences of treatment personnel and the model of Alcoholics Anonymous (AA). The 1970s saw a proliferation of treatment centers that accepted individuals with a primary diagnosis of alcoholism or chemical dependency in the hospital setting, reflecting the significance of the disease concept, the acceptance of the primacy of the diagnosis, and the legitimacy of a medical frame. Diagnosis and treatment of alcoholism did not spread into the mainstream of medicine or mental health and are still outside the typical bounds of medical education and practice. For many professionals, the acceptance, diagnosis, and treatment of chemical dependency remain baffling and grossly inadequate (see, for example, Chapter 7). In medical and other health settings, the failure to diagnose led to or was a consequence of misattribution. People were treated for the physical and emotional consequences of the primary illness, which was itself not diagnosed.

How, then, could traditionally based professionals possibly recognize the presence or consequences of parental alcoholism while remaining so ignorant about its origins, denying the reality, failing to diagnose it, or treating something else?

Overemphasis on the Individual

Not only have the reality and primacy of parental alcoholism been overlooked by traditional psychotherapy and medicine, but, with several major exceptions (Thurman, 1985; Lidz, 1973; Rutter, 1966), the impact of parental illness on children has been widely ignored. Physical and sexual abuse, chemical dependence and other addictions, and parental disability were not viewed as central factors in a child's development, if they were acknowledged at all (van der Kolk, 1987). For many years, psychiatric and developmental theory focused instead on the controversy between intrapsychic psychodynamic models and behavior or cognitive theories. In each, the isolated individual was the center of interest and little attention was paid to the significance of the environment and interpersonal factors (Laing, 1988; Thurman, 1985), in this case, the reality of parental alcoholism and its effect on children within the family context. Part of this omission has been attributed to an overemphasis on childhood fantasy versus reality (Masson, 1984; Stern, 1985; van der Kolk, 1987) and the Freudian psychoanalytic model of intrapsychic drive and conflict (Laing, 1988; van der Kolk, 1987).

While the concept is still controversial and oversimplified, many theorists and practitioners agree that the realities of a child's experience with alcoholic or ill parents could not be recognized because the trauma was considered to be based on the child's fantasy as related to intrapsychic conflict rather than on interpersonal parent, child, and family reality. Again, the narrow bias or emphasis of a particular theory diverted attention from the primacy of parental illness and behavior and frequently resulted in a denial of the reality. The massive social movement accomplished acknowledgment of the reality, which automatically required a different kind of intervention, theory, and practice. Parental alcoholism—denied, unlabeled, and untreated by traditional mental health and medical practitioners—is now being diagnosed by the adult children of these alcoholics, who are demanding recognition and treatment. Professionals are faced with the consequences of their own denial and inadequate theoretical frameworks (see also Chapter 5).

Denial of Trauma

The range of limited theory development extends further. Since the reality of parental alcoholism was denied, minimized, or diverted, it was impossible for clinicians in the traditional mental health or chemical-dependence fields to recognize that parental alcoholism constitutes a chronically traumatic environment for everyone in the family.

Recognition of the traumatic environment provided the first piece of the puzzle to be labeled and described by the popular media and by that segment of the chemical-dependence field that focused on family issues or codependence. Margaret Cork (1969) poignantly and powerfully led the way. Descriptions of the environment form the background for the first studies on role assumption and defensive adaptation by Black (1981), Wegscheider (1981), and Nardi (1981), and the more recent comparison to the post-traumatic stress syndrome outlined by Cermak (1984, 1986).

While parental alcoholism was now labeled as primary, an understanding of the impact of a chronically traumatic environment on the normal tasks of individual development was still missing (see Chapters 6, 7 and 8). There was little consideration of or emphasis on the function and impact of the family as a whole, or on interpersonal relationships within the family as governing agents in a child's development. Acknowledgment of the significance of these factors also required recognition of reality. What really happened? What was it like? What sort of environment provided the context in which childhood and adult development took place? These questions are implicit in the terminology "children of alcoholics"—the child is to be understood in relation to the parent and to the central significance of parental alcoholism within the family.

The Centrality of Alcoholism as a Systems Issue

One of the major difficulties in theory formulation between the chemical-dependence field and traditional mental health concerns the view of the centrality of chemical dependence for the individual and the family. Those in the alcoholism field believe that alcoholism is the primary diagnosis, with all other disorders, such as depression, anxiety, or marital conflict secondary, and frequently a consequence of the addiction (Vaillant, 1981). These professionals view alcoholism as the central organizing principle (Brown, 1985, 1988; Steinglass, 1980, 1987) in the individual's life, virtually determining the person's view of self, others, and the world. The core of this primary pathology is cognitive and behavioral: the individual denies that he or she is drinking too much while at the same time maintaining the behavior. Such distortion forms the heart of what is called "alcoholic thinking," a system of logic that skews basic premises, altering cause and effect (Brown, 1985).

Professionals in traditional medical and mental health disciplines have tended to follow the same pattern of logical distortion, viewing alcoholism not as *the* primary diagnosis, but as a secondary problem, a consequence of the individual's response to another primary problem or diagnosis (Vaillant, 1981), or as a symptom of a deeper problem. Thus, these therapists often fail to recognize the central organizing function of the addiction for the individual, believing instead that the addiction will vanish or become controlled with the solution of the primary problem. This thinking is more likely if the therapist also challenges the disease concept, which automatically assigns primacy. It involves the same faulty logic that drives the alcoholic and family into deeper and more extensive pathology. The main problem cannot be recognized or openly acknowledged, and yet must be maintained.

It is extremely difficult to accord legitimacy to the problems children and adults experience as a direct result of living with parental chemical dependence if the addiction is not recognized as primary (also see Chapters 5–12). The consequences simply cannot be attributed to the proper source. It is exactly this difficulty that children and adult children have suffered all their lives: their efforts to name or pinpoint the reality of parental alcoholism were squelched, deflected, and explained as something else. There could be no concept of "children of alcoholics" because it too squarely and directly labeled the source.

For many years, professionals operated according to the same logic, failing to appreciate the centrality of parental alcoholism as a governing agent in a child's development. Only when parental alcoholism is acknowledged as primary can the child's experience within the family context be fully understood and related to adaptation, coping, defensive adjustment, and the various tasks of individual develop-ment. The labels COA and ACOA pave the way for this acknowledgment and the necessary break in denial that accompanies it.

Oversimplification

Professionals in the chemical-dependence field had no experience in diagnosing or treating this new population, though many individuals in treatment for their own chemical dependence are also COAs. Early treatment within the chemical-dependence model relied on the value of personal experience, as it had for treatment of the alcoholic. While useful, it was soon clear that both the model and the level of skill required to treat ACOAs were inadequate. These professionals recognized the primacy of alcoholism, but they could not incorporate it into understanding the child or adult child of an alcoholic parent. This can be a troubling shortcoming in the treatment of the chemically dependent individual who is also an adult child (or young child) of a chemically dependent person (alcoholic).

With few exceptions, treatment of the alcoholic ironically has followed and incor-porated the pathology of the family system organized around the denial and the maintenance of someone's chemical addiction. In an alcoholic family, the alcoholic is most often dominant, overtly or indirectly. Those close to this individual become reactive and submissive (what is called codependent) to the dominance of the alco-holic and the organizing function of the alcoholism. They, too, order their lives around maintaining the pathological system (Brown, 1985).

Until recently, the treatment focus was entirely on the chemically dependent person, with family members included *only* to the degree that they might help the dependent person recover and maintain abstinence. Treatment thus replicated the family pathol-ogy: those close to the alcoholic continued to feel dominated by the alcoholism, which was now related to the alcoholic's recovery, rather than active use. But still, these indi-viduals were caught in pathological systems dynamics, emphasizing inequality and the assumption of responsibility for others' behavior.

The alcohol-treatment community failed to recognize or provide treatment for the families of alcoholics as patients with a primary diagnosis of their own. Therefore, they were unable to acknowledge or address the needs of these individuals. The sudden over-whelming recognition of ACOAs posed a threat to the stability and simplicity of the alcoholic-treatment model. How can families and ACOAs be treated in a way that does not replicate the pathological system? The chemical-dependence field has responded to this dilemma by establishing family programs "separate" from the primary treatment of the chemically dependent person, with family members given primary status as codependents. In practice, however, the separateness is weak, if legitimate at all. Treatment for family members in most centers is still included without charge as a part of the "primary patient's" treatment and family members are not registered as separate patients with separate charts or files. So, although the problem was recognized, the system perpetuated it. The chemical-dependence-treatment field must find a way to incorporate a systems perspective into its theory and treatment structure, focusing on the centrality of the addiction as an organizing principle not only for the chemically dependent person, but also for other individuals and the family as a whole. Unless treatment design reflects this shift, the chemical-dependence field will continue to replicate the family pathology.

Expanding Theory and the Structure of Treatment

In establishing the Stanford Alcohol Clinic in 1977 (now the Stanford Alcohol and Drug Treatment Center), we anticipated this problem and built a correction into the system. Treatment was available to anyone with any concern about drinking and other substance use, their own or someone else's. Thus, any person could seek treatment as a primary patient with legitimate treatment needs as a consequence of being chemically dependent, living with someone chemically dependent, growing up with an alcoholic parent, or all three. This model (Brown, 1985) also integrates theory and practice from the chemical-dependence field and traditional psychiatry and psychology, recognizing the need for a merger, and it extends the focus of treatment into recovery. In a structure in which treatment is designed to accord primacy to the diagnosis of alcoholism, and also primacy as well as identified-patient status to those close to the alcoholic, a much larger, more diverse, and more complex treatment population emerges.

Recognition of this new treatment population, ACOAs, has illuminated the need for a more complex theory of human development—one that incorporates both systems and individual developmental perspectives, and that focuses on the significance of interactional patterns and relationship to subsequent development, as well. Such a new theory requires greater complexity and integration, rather than a more simplified "correct" view. It does not mean that any traditional theory should be discarded, but rather that it be incorporated into a new, expanded model. Each theory now becomes important as a smaller piece of a whole. Clinicians and theoreticians must now hold macro and micro points of view at the same time, and build research designs with more complex methodology to consider many more variables. The clinician must assess the family environment and system as a whole, determining what it was really like and the nature of relationships within the system in order to understand the effects of both on the developing child.

The COA movement poses a serious dilemma for all professionals because it reveals the absence of any integrated theory of development—and the essential need for one. In addition, the recognition and acceptance of COAs illuminate the bias and inadequacies of current theory and the controversies between fields that hinder integrated theory development. It is impossible fully to understand the consequences of parental alcoholism for the child's development without incorporating multiple perspectives.

Traditional Values and Beliefs: The Loss of Control

It is difficult to separate value and belief from traditional theory because each influences the other (see also Chapter 5). For example, controversy regarding the disease model of alcoholism is often tinged with remnants of a moral or cultural model in which alcoholism was considered a highly stigmatized disorder resulting from poor control, lack of will, or a weak heritage. Although the disease concept has gained wide acceptance, the strength of the moral model remains. In many quarters, alcoholism is still considered to be within the individual's control and so a matter of will, which makes it difficult to diagnose and treat as a primary illness or to recognize as of primary importance in a COA's development. Beliefs and values related to the origins of alcoholism, the most appropriate treatment, and now the COAs all relate, in turn, to the key issues of self-power and self-control.

SELF-POWER AND SELF-CONTROL

The theory and treatment of addictive disorders pose a great threat for traditional theorists of any single persuasion—behavioral, cognitive, psychodynamic, or systems. The addictions also pose an indirect threat to other professionals and the public alike because they represent a fundamental human condition—the frailty or ultimate failure of human will or control. Acceptance of this shared human condition runs counter to much of current psychological, philosophical, and social theory (Bateson, 1971; Tiebout, 1944, 1949, 1953).

Much of Western culture rests on the belief in the ultimate power of the self, with achievement of that power the organizing principle in life. Thus, individuals strive toward increased power over themselves and others obtained through a purposeful, goal-oriented approach to others and to life situations. Although useful and appropriate to many situations and problems, such a philosophy can also lead to simplistic solutions for difficult problems, which in this case involve an improper emphasis on strategies for regaining control.

The view of alcoholism as a secondary diagnosis or as a consequence of another problem identified as primary, and the belief that alcoholism can be undone with self-control restored, reinforce denial and all of the consequences of denial: inability to accept reality, improper theory development, inadequate or misattributed diagnosis, and improper treatment.

Failure to accept loss of control leads to a predominant interest in regaining it. The chemically dependent person vests energy and attention in maintaining the privilege of using without incurring any of the problems—and fails. The codependent or ACA vests energy and attention in controlling the alcoholic, and also fails.

The beliefs in power and control are also a threat to feelings of personal and professional competence on the part of the therapist. Drug use, and particularly the use of alcohol, is socially sanctioned as a part of normal adult behavior, and is even closely associated with prestige and success as part of a "good life" (Brown, 1982).

Acquiring the right and privilege to drink is important to the ritual of adolescent and postadolescent development in Western culture. Central to these rights is the belief that adults *should* be able to drink, and to control their drinking. Hence, the influence of the moral model and beliefs about control enter into, and frequently collide with, reality. The mechanism of control is the power of the will of self. When there is a failure in one's ability to control, the problem is explained as a lack of personal strength, ego, or will. Treatment efforts are aimed at improving one's moral character or self-control. Alcoholism may be identified as a primary problem, but it is considered one that can be addressed by utilizing efforts to regain control rather than by accepting the loss of control.

These treatment efforts typically remain in the framework in which alcoholism is viewed as a secondary consequence of another, major problem. Therefore, it does not require primary attention because it will be solved when the primary problem is addressed. Or the addiction is labeled as primary, but the loss of control is not viewed as permanent. Within this framework of belief, it is almost impossible for an alcoholic patient or an ACOA to break denial. The reality of one's alcoholism, parental alcoholism, and the loss of control must be named and must be given primacy. The labels "alcoholic" and "ACOA" accomplish both.

THERAPIST BIAS AND BELIEF

In addition to beliefs about power and control and about the etiology and primacy of alcoholism, the therapist's personal experience with drugs and alcohol and with familial alcoholism are critical variables in maintaining a narrow theoretical position and the denial of the reality of a patient's alcoholism or parental alcoholism. The therapist may be struggling with or denying a chemical addiction, a partner's addiction, or a parent's addiction. If so, the therapist maintains the same distorted belief in self-control that characterizes the patient. Neither patient nor therapist can face the reality of the primacy of alcoholism and loss of control. In teaching therapists, it is not uncommon to hear them acknowledge that their own bias, or blinders, as noted by Googins (1984), personal or professional, severely restricted them from diagnosing alcoholism or parental alcoholism, and also influenced their understanding of a patient's dynamics and the subsequent emphasis and course of treatment.

Lackie (1983) outlines in detail the kinds of family experiences that precede and influence a social worker's entry into the profession, accenting the tendency for these therapists to have occupied the role of parentified child, a dynamic common to the alcoholic family in pathological form (Black, 1981). He suggests that the dynamics of the therapist's family of origin play a significant role in the choice of profession, self-view, and interactions with clients, all of which need to be examined and understood by the therapist.

Finally, denial of alcoholism or misattribution serves the needs of the therapist who does not know what to do about a person's drinking, yet feels responsible for the patient's abstinence if the diagnosis is made. In this case, the therapist assumes the typical stance of the codependent: "If I label it, I will be responsible for fixing it." This is particularly true for a therapist or physician whose usual role is to cure disease.

In many instances, maintaining a narrow theoretical framework or improper focus provides an escape for the therapist who cannot or does not want to make a diagnosis of alcoholism or parental alcoholism. Unfortunately, many teaching and training centers reinforce professional and personal denial (Bissell, 1982). Others are looking at these difficulties and building in an evaluation of personal background or characteristics as a part of accepting a therapist into their training programs (Laundergan et al., 1986).

Why Now?

Although traditionalists may have viewed, and continue to view, alcoholism as a secondary diagnosis and to reject loss of control as a reality, due to the ACOA movement and its accomplishments, it is now difficult to continue to miss the centrality of parental alcoholism as a governing agent in childhood development, and the powerlessness and inability of the child or adult child to control or change the behavior of the parent. This is particularly true now that patients are seeking treatment designated for ACOAs, and are armed with knowledge that may surpass that of the professional, thereby challenging the therapist's own denial, beliefs, and preferred schema. Thus, acknowledgment of ACOAs and COAs as legitimate patients highlights the longstanding, though rarely articulated, theoretical conflicts and controversies between chemical-dependence and mental health practitioners. It must be a source of continuing dissonance for therapists to hold one set of beliefs and theory about the alcoholic, including denial of the reality of a patient's alcoholism, and another about COAs, particularly when many of the latter grow up to become alcoholics themselves and when they make up a significant proportion of the mental health and chemical-dependency populations.

Fortunately, there has been a move in traditional psychiatric theory development toward greater complexity and toward the incorporation of multiple variables. There is much greater acceptance of the need for an integrated behavioral, cognitive, dynamic, and systems-oriented theory of development to explain all kinds of adjustment, normal and problematic. Bateson (1971) anticipated this need, linking systems and individual developmental theories.

The recent work of Steinglass et al. (1987) also offers a major contribution to theory expansion and integration. They outline a detailed framework for understanding the centrality of parental alcoholism within a systems context and the implications of the systems view for individual development.

Of greatest significance is the focus on cognitive processes in the development of self. This emphasis opens the way to identifying the prominence of denial and the structure of distorted thinking in alcoholics, in COAs, and in those who treat them. The recent formulations of cognitive-developmental and psychodynamic theorists start from the base of childhood reality and emphasize the profound significance of attachment and the interpersonal context of belief to later emotional health or pathology.

ADVANCES IN THEORY DEVELOPMENT

Cognitive-Developmental Theory and Its Application to ACOAs: The Constructionists

Over the past ten to 15 years, a new body of theory has been developed that links cognitive and developmental theory. In this movement, there is greater interest in the cognitive domain—ordering schemas, personal meanings, and belief systems, and their relationship to human development. This view stresses knowledge organization and development, that is, how an individual develops a sense of self and the world.

Mahoney, 1988 notes that this movement accents constructivism—the belief that humans actively create and construe their personal and social realities. It expands on the rational view that focuses on a single objective reality, moving instead toward acknowledgment of complex systems, reciprocal interdependence, and codevelopment over time. Central to this recognition of complexity is the need for a comprehensive theory of the dynamics of interactional systems, particularly in terms of how they facilitate the personal construction of meaning (Guidano, 1988).

According to Mahoney, the developmentalists and constructionists are challenging traditional concepts of reality, knowing, and rationality that have informed theory and practice. Whereas the rational view emphasizes a "pure truth," the developmental position takes a relativistic and multiplistic approach to reality, with "knowing" not tied to absolute levels of objectivity and certainty. This is not to say that the reality of parental alcoholism is unimportant or indeterminant, but rather that explained and known reality will be based on the family's needs and experiences in relation to it. "Truth" becomes a family or a systems affair (Brown, 1988). The alcoholic family constructs an adaptive view of reality that maintains, explains, and denies the drinking at the same time. In the constructivist view, reality is what works to maintain this contradiction.

In the developmental view, individuals survive because their self-images and world view are viable, not because they are valid. They note that technically inaccurate beliefs may afford adaptive behavior patterns and technically correct beliefs may engender the opposite—maladaptive consequences. As noted, this is of critical significance in understanding the alcoholic family. Denial of the alcoholic reality and the distorted beliefs about the self and family constructed to preserve denial are adaptive for survival in the family (Brown, 1988; Black, 1981; Brown & Beletsis, 1986).

The radical constructionists view reality as an ordering and organizing of a world constituted by our experience. Mental representations are not to be judged by their validity (which is unknowable) or their power to control, but by their capacity to promote or inhibit adaptation and development. Reality is what a person or family says it is. Therefore, in many families, the objective reality of parental alcoholism will not be translated into personal reality for members of the family. What is real cannot be known. Guidano and Liotti (1985) also challenge traditional psychodynamic and behavioral theories, suggesting that they share a mechanistic, one-dimensional attitude toward correlations between abnormal early experience and adult psychopathology. The psychodynamic model explains pathology as libidinal and the behavioral explains it according to conditioned learning schedules. These examples, and any other one-dimensional theory, are bound to result in oversimplification and omission of critical causal or organizing variables. The constructionist view includes interaction and context in understanding the development of self. Social learning theory is a part of this new complex, process-oriented approach. In Bandura's terms (1985), people are neither driven by inner forces nor shaped and controlled by external stimuli. In his model of triadic reciprocality, behavioral, cognitive, and personal factors and environmental influences affect one another bidirectionally.

The constructionist, developmental view emphasizes the importance of belief and knowing processes and the significance of interactional influences in the development of self. The significance of denial—for the alcoholic, the ACOA, and the professional—and distortion and misattribution in the development of self-knowledge are addressed in this complex model. All of these factors are essential first to recognizing the reality of parental alcoholism and then to developing a comprehensive theory to understand its consequences.

From these frameworks, grounded in the earlier work of Piaget, Guidano and Liotti (1983), Mahoney (1977, 1985), Rosen (1985), and Guidano (1987), examine the ways in which children acquire self-knowledge; that is, how they learn who they are and how, through the predominantly cognitive processes of knowledge construction, they acquire deep beliefs and a view of self and others that will be the source of later emotional health or pathology. The notion of stages, as originated by Piaget, information processing, and theories of knowledge construction are central to these formulations. Also fundamental is the link to the attachment theories of Bowlby (1980, 1985). It is this piece that provides the dynamic or developmental link and greatly expands the complexity and explanatory power of the model. It is also this piece that links the systems view. The family or the system provides the structure for belonging and maintaining individual bonds of attachment.

Guidano (1988) emphasizes the significance of attachment. He suggests that attachment theory provides an integrative paradigm of human development that affords an inclusive and organizing vision of all factors that contribute to the structure of self-knowledge. He stresses the need to look at the child as a coherent whole to understand how the unitary development of self-knowledge comes about. Stroufe and Waters (1977) concur, noting that attachment must be seen as an organizing construct whose value lies in its integrative power. Mahoney (1988) emphasizes the relationship of social learning theory to attachment, linking the interdependence of social relationship and personal belief and behavior. He notes that personal meaning systems are generated, maintained, and transformed in the context of emotional attachment.

The child's basic need for an emotional attachment is fundamental to human development and survival. The need for attachment to begin with, and the need for continuing preservation of that primary affectional bond, is a central organizing principle that affects all aspects of a child's physical, emotional, cognitive, and social development. The infant and child are totally dependent on their key figures of attachment and the maintenance of those bonds to negotiate successfully all succeeding tasks of development. The maintenance of a primary affectional bond is the goal of human development (Bowlby, 1980, 1985). Thus, the course of development, including the child's acquisition and construction of self-knowledge and deepest core beliefs, will be determined in large part by the demands required by the parents and the system to maintain the attachment. The process of information gathering and the construction of a view of self (personal identity) is dictated and limited by the parental view of self and the world. Children must develop a personal identity—a view of self, others, and the world—that fits in with or matches the parent's view, no matter how inaccurate or distorted that view may be. Recognition of reality (i.e., parental alcoholism) poses a severe threat to the family's equilibrium. Thus, in disturbed families, there is no room for cognitive, affective, or social development that veers from the narrow view constructed by the family to preserve its status quo and the attachments based on it. Children are forced to exclude information about the outside world and their private world of feelings (Bowlby, 1985) to match the preferred view of their parents.

The seeds for the development of pathology are sewn by the parent's need for denial (Guidano & Liotti, 1983), cognitive exclusion (Bowlby, 1980, 1985) or distortion, and the more active construction of a version of reality or beliefs about the parent and others that denies or explains the pathology while maintaining it and its attachments.

Cognitive-developmental theory stresses active construction—the child is reactive to his or her environment and actively constructs a view of self and the world directed by the parent's preferred view. It is thus a theory of development and pathology based on the centrality of attachment preserved by the acquisition and sharing of basic beliefs about the self and others. In essence, the child's development takes place within the limited context of shared beliefs. In a family dominated by the centrality of parental alcoholism and its denial, that development is shaped by the need for denial and distortion of reality and by the need to preserve false premises. Mental health and chemical-dependence theories suffer from the same mechanism of distortion, which also maintains false premises or a narrow or diverted focus, as illustrated earlier.

The cognitive-developmentalists advocate a systems process-oriented approach to understanding human development (Guidano, 1988), accenting the centrality of the ordering processes of self-knowledge and the challenge of these beliefs as the core of therapy. In exploring the particular knowledge organization of any individual, they ask two questions: (1) What kind of developmental stages brought about this individual knowledge organization? (2) In what way is that knowledge organization determining the shape of moment-to-moment experiences?

The cognitive-developmental-systems view enables the individual to delineate basic assumptions about the self and the world upon which the individual's sense of reality and deepest sense of self rest. Truth or reality is regarded as stemming from the core of an individual's knowledge organization, and, therefore, belongs uniquely to each individual (Guidano, 1988). Psychotherapy does not aim at persuading clients to adapt other standards for truth, which is exactly what happened to them in their families. Children had to accept a standard of truth grounded in denial of parental pathology and of reality. This is also what has happened to many COAs in therapy prior to the birth of the ACOA movement and subsequent beginning realignment of psychotherapy theory and practice. In Guidano's view, the objective of psychotherapy is to help clients better conceptualize their own personal truths, a method that offers the only possibility for making reality real. With the biases existing in the chemical-dependence and mental health fields, the reality of parental alcoholism and its organizing function could not be recognized.

Therapy must be a collaborative venture, enabling the client to identify basic assumptions or core beliefs that underlie his or her way of experiencing reality (see also Chapters 9 and 11). For the children of alcoholic parents, these basic pathogenic assumptions or beliefs are the very ones required to preserve the family's status quo and the maintenance of attachments (Brown, 1988). To the degree that parents must narrow, distort, or deny aspects of reality or their own beliefs will the child be required to match the distortion. It has long been recognized by cognitive theorists and developmentalists that the challenge of faulty belief is essential to behavior change and emotional growth.

Control-Mastery Theory

Recent developments within psychoanalytic theory have led toward a greater emphasis on cognitive theory. Led by Weiss (1986), who developed the theory, and Sampson, who developed the research design, control-mastery theory emphasizes the role that pathogenic belief plays in the development of psychopathology. Weiss also emphasizes the significance of the reality of childhood experiences and the importance of interpersonal learning and attachment. He has shifted emphasis away from drive theory and instinctual conflict. By accenting the power of belief, acquired through interpersonal learning, he has developed a theoretical frame that can incorporate the realities of childhood experience with alcoholic parents as a primary determinant in subsequent development of the self.

Weiss (1986) suggests that psychopathology stems from certain grim, unconscious pathogenic beliefs that the patient acquires by inference from early traumatic experience. The individual suffers unconsciously from these beliefs and the feelings of guilt, shame, and remorse that stem from them. It is in obedience to these beliefs that individuals maintain repression and pathology. Weiss also emphasizes that pathogenic beliefs are acquired through normal inference from subjective experience. In contrast to fantasy, these beliefs are not wishful, but grim and constricting. They are not opposed to reality, but represent reality. The core of therapy involves testing these deep beliefs within the context of a safe therapeutic alliance in order to disconfirm them. Internal and external factors are included in the development of pathogenic beliefs, linking intrapsychic and interpersonal factors. For example, survivor guilt depends on internal motivation and experience with others. Weiss also accents the importance of guilt and attachment, noting that all varieties of guilt arise from the child's fear of disrupting the tie to the parent. For example,

> If a child infers and comes to believe that his attempts to gratify certain critically important impulses or to reach certain vital developmental goals will threaten his all-important tie to his parents, he may decide to repress or inhibit these impulses or goals. Thus he may seriously damage himself in order to maintain his tie to his parents. He may also develop symptoms that are intended to maintain these ties. The child's wish to maintain his ties to his parents is his most powerful motivation. Much of the adult's psychopathology expresses the wish to maintain such ties (Weiss, 1986, p. 67).

In further elaborating the significance of pathogenic belief to childhood development, Weiss states that the pathogenic beliefs developed in childhood are concerned with the major motives of childhood such as the child's dependence on his parents, his libidinal attachment to them, his wish for independence from them and his wish to compete with them. He quotes Freud (1930, p. 124):

> A child must come to fear any motive or behavior that he infers would seriously hurt a parent, provoke severe punishment from a parent or seriously threaten him with loss of parental love.

Telling the truth about parental alcoholism is just such a threat. This intense fear is illuminated by a child in a group for COAs for whom the acknowledgment of the reality of parental alcoholism was a severe threat to the stability of the attachment to the parents. As described by Lovaglia (1988):

> Before Steven joined the group, he and his mother participated in an intake interview with Kids Are Special. The first part of the interview was between him and a Kids Are Special counselor. When asked about his parents' alcohol or drug use, he meekly responded that his parents didn't use alcohol or drugs.
>
> It wasn't until the second part of the interview, when both he and his mom were talking with the counselor, that he heard his mom say for the first time that his dad had a drinking problem and that the family was suffering. Steven's eyes lit up, he looked at the counselor and asked, "Can I speak with you alone again, please?" When alone with the counselor, he said, "I lied to you before when you asked about alcohol and drugs in my family. My dad does do that. I was scared to tell you before."

Weiss (1986), like Guidano and Liotti (1983), Mahoney (1977, 1985), and Bowlby (1980, 1985), notes the difficulty of challenging the faulty beliefs as a child. "The child who filters his experience through the lens of a particular belief, like the scientist who perceives his world in terms of a particular theory, may not be able to make observations that run counter to the belief and may have trouble disconfirming it" (p. 170).

Weiss (1986) suggests that there are two circumstances that cause the development of pathogenic beliefs. In the first, the child attempts to gratify an impulse or reach a goal and discovers that he or she is threatening the tie to the parents. In the second, the child experiences an inherently traumatic event, such as illness or the death of a parent. The child then retrospectively blames himself or herself for the event. Both factors chronically affect COAs. The essence, therefore, of the therapeutic approach is the disconfirmation of pathogenic beliefs. The patient works in accordance with his or her unconscious plan to disconfirm the belief. This process takes place in the context of a collaborative therapeutic alliance, in which both patient and therapist are working in accordance with the unconscious plan.

The Narrative

Daniel Stern (1985), a developmentalist from the psychoanalytic tradition, writes about the therapeutic process of constructing a developmental past, which he calls a "narrative." Stern suggests that the patient and therapist search for the potent life experience or event that provides the key therapeutic metaphor for understanding and changing the patient's life. He calls this experience the "narrative point of origin" of the pathology, regardless of when it occurred in actual developmental time. Once identified, the therapy proceeds forward and backward in time from this point of origin.

This theory is compatible with the cognitive-developmental attention to the significance of an ordering schema. According to Guidano and Liotti (1983, 1988), the personal identity tends to become a historical form of life. The "plan of life" or "life theme," similar to the concept of narrative, indicates the progressive unification that an individual's self-knowledge and actions assume in life. The child of chemically dependent parents accepts pathogenic beliefs in order to adapt to the family's functional equilibrium and to maintain attachment (see Chapters 6 and 9).

The systems point of view is compatible and synergistic with the work of the cognitive constructionists and control-mastery theorists. According to Steinglass et al. (1987), the "essence of the systems approach is an attention to organization, that is, the relationship between parts, to a concentration on patterned rather than linear relationships and to a consideration of events in the context in which they are occurring, rather than in isolation from their environment" (p. 44). It is also similar to viewing parental alcoholism as a central organizing principle around which therapeutic reconstruction takes place. It is precisely the reconstruction of an individual and family-systems narrative that incorporates the realities of parental alcoholism that constitutes the main therapeutic work of recovery (see also Chapter 11).

The cognitive-developmentalists outline the ordering and organizing processes by which a child develops self-knowledge, accenting, as does control-mastery theory, the significance of attachment and the centrality of beliefs. Both theories deal directly with denial. The process of therapy involves making tacit knowledge or unconscious pathogenic beliefs conscious and challenging their validity in the present and the past. Bowlby (1980, 1985) notes further that the curative process of therapy enables the patient to restore memories and gives the individual permission to talk about something he or she has always known. The process of therapy and recovery for the ACOA follows the same path.

THE PROCESS OF RECOVERY

This chapter has outlined the birth of a new social movement and clinical treatment population, the biases and blind spots in traditional theory that previously made recognition of ACOAs difficult, and elements of several recent theoretical formulations combining cognitive and developmental approaches that offer a new framework for understanding the complexities and multiple variables that characterize ACOAs.

This section outlines an integrated developmental theory of recovery accenting what was missing in earlier theories or hidden by professional bias. Included are the significance of the break in denial, the importance of acknowledging the reality of the childhood experience with alcoholic parents, the significance of viewing parental alcoholism as an organizing principle (the primacy of the diagnosis of alcoholism), the acquisition of a new personal identity that incorporates what was denied (labeling oneself the child of an alcoholic[s]), acceptance of loss of control (the inability to fix, alter, or control the drinking of the parent), and reconstruction of the past and new construction of one's identity in the present based on incorporating the realities of parental alcoholism. Much of this process is cognitive in emphasis. However, dynamic issues of attachment and family systems are closely linked in the development of pathology and the process of recovery as Bowlby, Steinglass, and cognitive-developmental and control-mastery theories emphasize.

Whereas the object of attachment for the alcoholic is alcohol, the object for the ACOA is the alcoholic. The ACOA may also be attached to the nonalcoholic parent (if there is one), and to alcohol as the organizing principle in the family's beliefs about itself, the individuals in the family, and the relationship with the outside world. For the child of an alcoholic, the processes of development are bound to and structured by the emphasis on alcohol and the beliefs maintained by the family. The centrality of alcohol as an organizing principle must be incorporated into the new personal identity as an ACOA. This incorporation, which includes the challenge of denial and deep beliefs that were necessary to maintain attachment and the restructuring of one's identity, forms the core of the process of recovery.

Alcohol as the Organizing Principle

In building a theory of a developmental process of recovery in alcoholism, the author focused on alcohol as the central organizing principle, ordering the construction of a view of reality and self that maintains denial of the drinking and explains it at the same time. With the break in denial and acceptance of loss of control, the alcoholic moves out of the drinking phase into a period of transition introduced by abstinence. Central to the theory of recovery is the continuing focus on alcohol as the organizer of a new construction of reality based on the new identity as an alcoholic.

The individual begins a process of new knowledge construction and reconstruction of core identity in the past and present. The process of reconstruction involves acknowledging and incorporating the reality of the past in a manner that is congruent with the new identity as an alcoholic. This reconstruction process is what is known in AA as developing one's "story" or "drunkalogue," or, in Stern's terms, the narrative.

The process of new construction continues through the developmental phases of early and ongoing recovery. It involves incorporating the reality of one's past into one's story in the present. "Who I am" today is continually defined and redefined according to uncovering self-exploration ordered by the new identity as an alcoholic. It is the new schema or ordering provided by the new identity and framework of beliefs that provides the structure for the process of reconstruction and for making sense of the past. These views are consistent with those of the cognitive-developmental and control-mastery theorists, who also accent the significance of challenging or reordering knowledge structures and deep beliefs.

The greater the need for denial (e.g., of alcoholism), the greater is the restriction of cognitive and affective range. The individual cannot see or integrate information from the environment that challenges the "story" constructed to preserve denial or certain core beliefs. The break in denial of alcoholism and change in identity open the process of cognitive and affective expansion because the need for restriction is eliminated. The new story incorporates the realities of the past and present, ordered around the central organizing principle of the new identity as an alcoholic.

The Process of Recovery for ACOAs

The process of recovery for ACOAs follows a similar progression. Denial or distortion of parental alcoholism organizes the range of cognitive and affective experience that can be incorporated. The child develops a sense of self and family congruent with the beliefs required to maintain denial and preserve attachments. If alcoholism is not denied, the child cooperates in the distortion of belief, perception, and affect required to maintain the family's balance, however pathological that may be. Where alcoholism or other problems are longstanding, that balance is the "normality" that children grow up with and incorporate as their own view. When parental alcoholism or other problems are of recent origin, the new balance may be seen as "abnormal."

The child adapts on many levels. Early issues of attachment, including the building of basic trust, symbiotic bonding, and emerging autonomy, are affected by the realities of a chaotic, uncertain, and out-of-control environment *and* the nature of the parent–child relationship. Core issues in identity formation and later separation individuation are also related to the same issues: the environment and the particular nature of the parent–child bond (see also Chapters 3 and 6).

The process of recovery for the ACOA is also developmental, unfolding in levels and stages. The ACOA in the "drinking phase" is bound by continuing denial or distortion of parental alcoholism and the problematic behaviors and beliefs that maintain attachment around its organizing function.

The move from the drinking phase into recovery is characterized by the break in denial. The individual, as a child or adult, "sees" that the parent is or was alcoholic, a recognition that profoundly affects the individual's entire view of self and the world. Many may move no further than recognition. They receive no treatment or exposure to the shared experiences of others. Or they are intentionally or inadvertently diverted from pursuing their new knowledge of parental alcoholism as a central organizing principle, accepting an identity as an ACOA, and beginning a reordering process based on this framework. This diversion may be spurred by threatened family members or a therapist who lacks knowledge or who is caught in personal or professional denial or distortion, as described earlier. Recognition in itself may be extremely important and beneficial, but unless individuals pursue an uncovering reconstruction process, they are likely to maintain core beliefs about the self and patterns of behavior that reinforce pathological adjustment.

The transition phase involves a beginning incorporation of the recognition of parental alcoholism, more clearly and definitively, into one's sense of self. Like the process for the alcoholic, the incorporation is one of "fits and starts," with the ACOA shifting back and forth between acknowledgment of parental alcoholism and denial. The individual may spend years in the process of breaking denial and confirming the reality by incorporating evidence from the past and present. As cognitive (Guidano & Liotti, 1983) and dynamic (Bowlby, 1985) theorists note, this process of reconstruction and new construction involves making tacit knowledge explicit, exploring and challenging deep beliefs, and reorganizing one's beliefs and attitudes toward reality (see also Chapters 6 and 9–11).

The early recovery phase parallels that of the task for the alcoholic as well. The individual begins a process of construction of a new personal identity based on acknowledgment of parental alcoholism and the new identity as a COA (see Chapters 9–12). The person focuses on reconstruction of the past, altering the family story to incorporate the reality of parental alcoholism. He or she also focuses on behavioral change, learning to alter behaviors that supported denial or maintained a problematic or pathological attachment, what is called loosely "codependence." The active codependent position is one of reaction to the dominance or directive of another with little opportunity for initiative. The child "fits" in behaviorally, cognitively, and affectively in a way that maintains attachment to the dominant parental figure(s).

At the core of recovery are the tasks of detachment and disengagement, not only from the behaviors that supported and maintained the codependent position, but from the very attachment itself. Whereas the alcoholic "detaches" from the reliance on alcohol, the ACOA detaches from the destructive reliance on the reactive attachment to the alcoholic and nonalcoholic parents. The ACOA detaches from the beliefs and behaviors that maintained the attachment. The process of recovery is a threatening one from start to finish because it represents a loss of the parental bond (see also Chapters 6, and 9–12).

It is difficult, if not impossible, to sustain the uncovering process and construction of a new identity without a new attachment and a holding environment (Winnicott, 1953) that provide the safety and structure for reconstruction. This alternative attachment may be provided by individual or group therapy or by self-help, 12-step programs. The Al-Anon groups for ACOAs furnish an environment that acknowledges the reality of parental alcoholism and offers a structure and map (through the 12 steps) for the developmental process of recovery (see also Chapter 13). In a setting that validates the new childhood view of reality, ACOAs will strengthen their identities and examine the difficulties in their own adult lives related to the childhood experience of living with alcoholism.

The significance of a new ordering schema that provides a new emphasis and new attribution is clear. The process of recovery involves an expansion of one's cognitive and affective range and equilibrium with greater flexibility grounded in the new schemata of the identity as an ACOA that organizes perceptions and affect, reconstruction and new construction. As denial of parental alcoholism and the beliefs that maintain attachment are challenged, the individual can relinquish more primitive cognitive distortions and defenses and can incorporate and tolerate greater complexity and range of emotion.

Thune (1977) indicates that AA therapy for the alcoholic involves more than a shift in understanding about the essence of the self. It must also lead to the resolution of paradox. Individuals discover that what is paradoxical and problematic is only so when viewed within one body of presuppositions about the self and world. For the ACOA, that body of presuppositions involves the beliefs and defenses constructed to maintain denial and attachment. For the professional, it involves the same beliefs and defenses.

In outlining the importance of the "story," Thune (1977) emphasizes that what is altered are not isolated meanings, patterns, or implications, but a total body of structural integration, definitions, and understanding of experienced reality. Through the process of relabeling and reanalysis, the past and present acquire pattern and coherence that formerly were lacking. This process of total reorganization occurs under the direction of the new identity as an alcoholic or an ACOA. As Kegan (1984) notes, the process of redevelopment involves moving from the security of the old self through uncharted waters toward the construction of a new self.

Cognitive theory is an important cornerstone because it provides a guide to the processes and sequences by which a child or adult comes to know about the self and the world. The therapy involves not only challenging and altering core beliefs, but eliminating feelings based on inaccurate or arbitrary interpretations that are maladaptive (Rosen, 1985). However, the challenge of core beliefs and the elimination of feelings grounded on maladaptive beliefs are not enough. A focus on the development of attachment as outlined by dynamic and developmental theorists—specifically, how those beliefs structure and maintain a core attachment—must be integrated as well. In the process of recovery for the ACOA, the challenge of faulty, distorted, or maladaptive cognitions involves a continuing threat to the core of attachment. As such, cognitive and dynamic theory proceed hand in hand. The individual acquires a new object of attachment—the therapy group, ACOA 12-step programs or ACOA Al-Anon, the principles of Al-Anon, and/or a belief in a higher power—that provides the structure for challenging old beliefs and ordering new ones.

The alcoholic relinquishes the object of attachment—alcohol—entirely and relies heavily on the substitute attachment and dependence on AA. The ACOA or codependent may not relinquish the attachment to, reliance on, or active relationship with the object—the alcoholic—or with alcoholic and codependent parents.

Thus, the process requires the relinquishing of an emotional attachment and of the behaviors and cognitions based on the distortions while not necessarily abandoning the relationship. Finding a working balance between a strong new identity and real involvement with actively alcoholic and codependent parents is often the core struggle of recovery (see also Chapters 9–12). How can one maintain an attachment while altering all the beliefs that maintained it?

IMPLICATIONS

The Label

The ACOA movement, both popular and professional, has profound implications for patients and therapists. Through the popular press and self-help groups, many people are labeling themselves, thereby breaking denial of the reality of parental alcoholism and beginning a process of therapeutic reconstruction independent of treatment. These people may also seek professional help, but of a kind that is labeled and is directed at the central organizing function of parental alcoholism.

The significance of the label is extraordinary. It names childhood reality, establishing its primacy, and so links childhood experiences and the consequences of parental alcoholism to the proper source. This factor alone may provide clarity and new linkages between past and present that could not be recognized or understood when denial or distortion had to be maintained.

For many, the label is even more significant, providing the catalyst for a move from a first-order organizing schema to a second-order framework (Mahoney, 1985; Watzlawick et al., 1974). Under previous theoretical schemas, knowledge about childhood reality could be assimilated into one's view of self and the world only to the degree that it matched or was consistent with prevailing beliefs. As noted throughout, the beliefs of patients and their therapists have been rooted in maintaining denial of parental alcoholism or minimizing its centrality and organizing function. Thus, the individual in the therapeutic reconstruction process could only uncover and assimilate new knowledge that maintained this skewed framework. The break in denial and the acquisition of the label facilitate a second-order move in which the individual steps out of or moves beyond the prevailing knowledge structure, broadening the focus or shifting it entirely.

The label "ACOA" provides a higher-order context (Piaget, 1954, 1970; Mahoney, 1985) or new ordering schema that facilitates a change from first- to second-order thinking and a corresponding therapeutic reconstruction process that acknowledges childhood reality and challenges deep beliefs constructed in the past on a foundation of denial and faulty premises required to maintain attachment. The patient who has labeled himself or herself is poised to make the full move to a second-order frame, but needs a facilitating or "good enough" (Winnicott, 1953,

1960) environment in which to do so. The ACOA-labeled 12-step group and the ACOA-labeled therapy provide legitimacy and reinforcement for maintaining the new identity, and the new version of reality that comes with it (Schwartzmann, 1985). The therapist, skeptical or threatened by the reality or the label, may unwittingly interfere with the reconstruction process, forcing the patient to return to a first-order schema (to the degree that it denies or minimizes parental alcoholism) in which the exploration of self and others reverts to distortion, diversion, or minimization. Or as Mahoney (1985) suggests, the individual will succeed in superficially reordering his or her attitude toward reality without revising the deeper personal identity, which thereby alters the structure of cognitive models of the self and the world. The deeper restructuring process requires an alternative view of the problem. The label and the new identity as the adult child of an alcoholic(s) provide a format and a new ordering frame for structuring and assimilating emerging knowledge and feelings. As a therapist put it: "Things make so much more sense when you label parental alcoholism."

The Unlabeled ACOA in Treatment

Not all patients seeking treatment are already self-identified as ACOAs. For many, that task will be undertaken in collaboration with a therapist who is knowledgeable about alcoholism and about the effects of parental alcoholism on children and adults. It requires a shift in theoretical framework for the therapist who, in the course of beginning therapeutic work, actively must seek information from the patient that will illuminate the reality of parental alcoholism when it is still hidden to the patient. The therapist's sensitivity and clinical judgment remain critical factors in this uncovering process. Knowledge about the reality and organizing function of parental alcoholism is not a proscription for rooting it out and insisting that the patient see it and acknowledge it. Rather, the knowledge provides a new framework for the therapist who, depending on the needs of the individual patient, can gently or aggressively point out the linkages between the past and the present, accenting the significance of parental alcoholism to the individual's development (determined from the history of this *particular* patient). As Weiss (1986) illustrates, the patient provides the leads and the therapist, by responding to the patient's leads, provides support and reinforcement for deepening the process of uncovery. In many cases, when the patient knows that the therapist will not collude in maintaining denial, it becomes safe enough to know the truth.

Many traditional mental health professionals question whether the treatment itself must be labeled ACOA. A good percentage, and frequently a majority, of their patients may be COAs, but as the therapists are not specialists in chemical dependence, they do not want to identify with what appears to be a narrower framework. The question arises as to whether it is possible or desirable to treat ACOAs in an unlabeled traditional setting, as opposed to an ACOA-labeled treatment.

The answer is not yet clear, although it is evident from theory development, research, and clinical experience (Guidano & Liotti, 1983; Mahoney, 1985) that the beliefs and theoretical frame of the therapist are critical factors. Individuals can acknowledge parental alcoholism, label themselves ACOAs, and reconstruct their "stories" from this organizing perspective within a traditional framework if the therapist is not personally threatened or does not undermine the process by accenting an opposing theoretical schema (Burk & Sher, 1990). A person can undertake the same reconstruction process within a chemical-dependence framework if the therapists can take a longer-term, dynamic view in addition to using their chemical-dependence knowledge and skills. The same principles can be true for group, couples, and family therapy; and there is no question but that the ACOA-labeled group is a powerful (Brown & Beletsis, 1986) and popular mode of therapy in the chemical-dependence and mental health fields.

Bridging of Disciplines

This chapter has stressed the importance of crossover and the bridging of disciplines between chemical dependence and mental health and within mental health (see also Chapters 5, 13, and 14). The task of history-taking symbolizes this bridge. Whether the history is a standard structured procedure, undertaken as part of an initial evaluation, or it unfolds during treatment, the therapist will be attentive to taking an "alcohol-focused" history in addition to a broad-based individual and family portrait. The integration of behavioral, cognitive, dynamic, and systems theories, plus the bridging of mental health and chemical-dependence disciplines, is of profound importance. The therapist must hold multiple theoretical frames, gathering an intrapsychic individual history *and* an interpersonal systems portrait at the same time. The latter emphasizes the environment, the context in which development took place, as well as the nature and quality of interpersonal relationships. This framework is spatial rather than linear. It emphasizes pattern rather than internal impulse, wishes, fantasies, or other motivating determinants. It emphasizes interpersonal adaptation, defenses, or characteristic styles of relating, such as roles that were required for survival and for maintaining the family's bonds but are now the very problems causing the individual to seek help.

Because of the complexity and crossover of disciplines required, the role of the therapist cannot be seen as simple or one-dimensional. The term "eclectic" takes on new significance, as therapists must be able to shift back and forth among behavioral, cognitive, dynamic, and systems frames, often in a single session. A therapist dedicated to one school will fail to understand the complexity and unintentionally impede the patient from acquiring a fuller understanding.

Chemical-dependence therapists are skilled in behavioral assessment and intervention, dealing directly with the behaviors that maintain an active addiction to a chemical or person (codependence). They are also skilled in a cognitive mode, helping patients uncover the faulty thinking patterns and beliefs that maintain the addictive behavior. Chemical-dependence therapists may or may not be skilled in systems theory and practice. Typically, they are weakest in developmental and dynamic theory and practice, even eschewing the need for or validity of a dynamic perspective.

The mental health profession is more divided within its ranks, though most therapists maintain a predominant stance, be it behavioral, cognitive, dynamic, or systems. Professionals with a dynamic perspective are more likely to miss the required behavioral and cognitive emphasis. Few mental health therapists understand the absolute need for such a focus at the point of intervention in an active addiction. Those who maintain a behavioral or cognitive focus may provide the proper emphasis at the point of intervention, but fail to understand the dynamic factors related to the addiction, particularly in ongoing recovery. Or they may focus on helping the patient to regain control, rather than to accept abstinence. Few therapists in either field can integrate multiple modalities and perspectives at various times. For many therapists in both fields, the incorporation of the theory and practice of another discipline feels like a betrayal or sacrifice of a professional identity. Over the years, many trainees have reported that they cannot tell their academic supervisors what they are learning in the addictions field because they will lose their credibility. The patient, of course, frequently gets caught in between.

Diagnosis

Part of the theoretical difficulties revealed by the ACOA movement and the problem of bridging disciplines relates to diagnosis. One of the most important unanswered questions is whether being the child of an alcoholic is a diagnosis in itself, or should be (Cermak, 1986), and, if so, what the defining characteristics are (see also Chapters 9 and 12).

The ACOA phenomenon raises tremendous difficulties with the current diagnostic structure and nomenclature because it requires a crossover of disciplines and categories not yet possible within the categories set forth in the *Diagnostic and Statistical Manual of Mental Disorders*. In essence, there is no diagnosis for environmental or systems pathology. Yet ACOA is a family-systems or interpersonal diagnosis because it links generations—parent to child, child to parent, and child to the system as a whole.

The term ACOA is descriptive of the family and of a relationship of child to parent, but it is being invested with the properties of an individual diagnosis. Patients and therapists alike are using the term inappropriately in this way. The label indicates only that a person grew up in a family with an alcoholic parent(s) and alcoholism, or chemical dependence, as a central or dominant organizing factor. To imbue the term with more meaning is to risk oversimplification. To use ACOA as a diagnosis runs the risk of minimizing or significantly muting vast and deep individual differences.

Another danger lies in overgeneralization (see also Chapter 3): Is ACOA a specific term for children of alcoholics or is it generic, referring to children of chemically dependent parents, and perhaps of parents with other kinds of disorders as well? Or is it really referring to certain kinds of systems? In the clinical and popular realms, chemical dependence is now an umbrella term, encompassing all manner of substance abuse. But beyond chemical dependence, the extent of valid generalization remains unclear.

What is clear is that the child-to-parent systems designation of "adult child" is appealing. The ACOA movement and label already have acquired flagship status, providing the model for other categories, such as "children of dysfunctional families." However, the similarities and the differences remain unknown.

As the ACOA movement matures and as knowledge is expanded and integrated into theory and practice, the questions of diagnosis and individual difference surely will become of primary significance.

REFERENCES

American Psychiatric Association. (1987). *Diagnostic and statistical manual of mental health disorders*, (3rd ed., rev.), Washington, D.C.: American Psychiatric Association.

Bandura, A. (1985). Model of causality in social learning theory. In M. Mahoney & A. Freeman, (Eds.), *Cognition and psychotherapy* (pp. 81–101). New York: Plenum Press.

Bateson, G. (1971). The cybernetics of self: A theory of alcoholism. *Psychiatry, 34*(1), 1–18.

Bissell, L. C. (1982). Recovered alcoholic counselors. In E. M. Pattison & E. Kaufman (Eds.), *Encyclopedic handbook of alcoholism*. (pp. 810–821). New York: Gardner Press.

Black, C. (1981). *It will never happen to me*. Denver, CO: M.A.C.

Bosma, W. (1972). Children of alcoholics: A hidden tragedy. *Maryland State Medical Journal, 21*, 34–36.

Bowlby, J. (1980). *Attachment and loss*, Vol. 3. New York: Basic Books.

Bowlby, J. (1985). The role of childhood experience in cognitive disturbance. In M. Mahoney & A. Freeman (Eds.), *Cognition and psychotherapy* (pp. 181–203). New York: Plenum Press.

Brown, S. (1982). Alcohol: Servant or master? *Stanford Magazine, 10*(2), 26–34.

Brown, S. (1985), *Treating the alcoholic: A developmental model of recovery*. New York: Wiley.

Brown, S. (1988). *Treating adult children of alcoholics: A developmental perspective*. New York: Wiley.

Brown, S., & Beletsis, S. (1986). The development of family transference in groups for adult children of alcoholics. *International Journal of Group Psychotherapy, 36*(1), 97–114.

Burk, J. P. & Sher, K. J. (1990). Labeling the child of an alcoholic: Negative stereotyping by mental health professionals and peers. *Journal of Studies on Alcohol*, 51(2): 156–163.

Cermak, T. (1984). Children of alcoholics and the case for a new diagnostic category of co-dependency. *Alcohol, Health and Research World*, 8, 38–42.

Cermak, T. (1986). *Diagnosing and treating co-dependence*. Minneapolis, MN: Johnson Institute Books.

Cork, M. (1969). *The forgotten children*. Toronto: Addiction Research Foundation.

Fine, E. W., Yudin, L. W., Holmes, J., & Heinemann, S. (1976). Behavioral disorders in children with parental alcoholism. *Annals of the New York Academy of Sciences*, 273, 507–517.

Freud, S. (1930/1961). Civilization and its discontents. *Standard edition*, Vol. 21 (pp. 57–243). London: Hogarth Press.

Googins, B. (1984). Avoidance of the alcoholic client. *Social Work*, 29, 161–168.

Goodwin, D. W. (1971). Is alcoholism hereditary? *Archives of General Psychiatry*, 25, 545–549.

Goodwin, D. W., Schulsinger, F., Hermansen, L., Guze, S. B., & Winokur, G. (1973), Alcohol problems in adoptees raised apart from alcoholic biologic parents. *Archives of General Psychiatry*, 28, 238–243.

Guidano, V. F. (1987). *The complexity of the self*. New York: Guilford Press.

Guidano, V. F. (1988). A systems, process-oriented approach to cognitive therapy. In K. Dobson (Ed.), *Handbook of cognitive-behavioral therapies*. New York: The Guilford Press.

Guidano, V. F., & Liotti, G. (1983). *Cognitive processes and emotional disorders*. New York: Guilford Press.

Guidano, V. F., & Liotti, G. (1985). A constructivistic foundation for cognitive therapy. In M. Mahoney & A. Freeman (Eds.), *Cognition and psychotherapy* (pp. 101–143). New York: Plenum Press.

Hawkins, H. N. (1950). Some effects of alcoholism of the parents on children in the home. St. Louis, MO: Salvation Army Midland Division.

Hunter, G. (1963). Alcoholism and the family agency. *Quarterly Journal of Studies on Alcohol*, 24, 61–74.

Kagan, J. (1984). *The nature of the child*. New York: Basic Books.

Kegan, R. (1982). *The evolving self*. Cambridge, Mass.: Harvard University Press.

Lackie, B. (1983). The families of origin of social workers. *Clinical Social Work Journal*, 11 (4), 309–322.

Laing, R. D. (1988). In F. Capra (Ed.), *Uncommon wisdom: Conversations with remarkable people*. New York: Simon & Schuster.

Launergan, J. C., Flynn, D., & Gaboury, J. D. (1986). An alcohol and drug counselor training program: Hazelden Foundation's trainer characteristics and outcomes. *Journal of Drug Education*, 16(2), 167–179.

Lidz, T. (1973). *The origins and treatment of schizophrenic disorders*. New York: Basic Books.

Lovaglia, D. (1988). *Kids are Special Newsletter*, San Jose, CA, p. 1.

Mahoney, M. (1977). Reflections on the cognitive learning trend in psychotherapy. *American Psychologist, 32*(1), 5–13.

Mahoney, M. (1985). Psychotherapy and human change processes. In M. Mahoney & A. Freeman (Eds.), *Cognition and psychotherapy* (pp. 3–49). New York: Plenum Press.

Mahoney, M. (1988). The cognitive sciences and psychotherapy: Patterns in a developing relationship. In K. Dobson (Ed.), *Handbook of cognitive-behavioral therapies* (pp. 357–387). New York: Guilford Press.

Masson, J. (1984). *The assault on the truth: Freud's suppression of the seduction theory.* New York: Farrar, Straus & Giroux.

Morehouse, E. (1984). Perspectives. *Alcohol, Health and Research World, 8,* 35–36.

Nardi, P. (1981). Children of alcoholics: A role-theoretical perspective. *Journal of Social Psychology, 115,* 237–245.

Nylander, I. (1960). Children of alcoholic fathers. *Acta Pediatrica, 49*(1), 9–27.

Piaget, J. (1954). *The construction of reality in the child.* New York: Basic Books.

Piaget, J. (1970). Piaget's theory. In P. Mussen (Ed.), *Carmichael's manual of child psychology* (3rd ed.) (pp. 700–732). New York: Wiley.

Roe, A., & Burks, B. (1945). Adult adjustment of foster children of alcoholic parents and psychotic parentage and the influence of the foster home. In *Memoirs of the Section on Alcoholism Studies,* no. 3. New Haven, CT: Yale University Press.

Rosen, H. (1985). *Piagetian dimensions of clinical relevance.* New York: Columbia University Press.

Rutter, M. (1966). *Children of sick parents.* London: Oxford University Press.

Schuckit, M., Goodwin, D. W., & Winokur, G. (1972). A study of alcoholism in half-siblings. *American Journal of Psychiatry, 128,* 1132–1136.

Schwartzmann, J. (1985). Alcoholics Anonymous and the family: A systems perspective. *American Journal of Drug and Alcohol Abuse, 11* (1 & 2), 69–89.

Steinglass, P. (1980). A life history model of the alcoholic family. *Family Process, 19*(3), 211–226.

Steinglass, P. Bennett, L., Wolin, S., & Reiss, D. (1987). *The alcoholic family.* New York: Basic Books.

Stern, D. (1985). *The interpersonal world of the infant.* New York: Basic Books.

Stroufe, L. A., & Waters, E. (1977). Attachment as an organizational construct. *Child Development, 48,* 1184–1199.

Thune, C. (1977). Alcoholism and the archtypal past: A phenomenological perspective on Alcoholics Anonymous. *Journal of Studies on Alcohol, 38*(1), 75–88.

Thurman, S. K. (1985). Ecological congruence in the study of families of handicapped parents. In S. K. Thurman (Ed.), *Children of handicapped parents: Research and clinical perspectives* (pp. 1–8). Orlando, FL: Academic Press.

Tiebout, H. M. (1944). Therapeutic mechanisms of Alcoholics Anonymous. *American Journal of Psychiatry, 100,* 468–473.

Tiebout, H. M. (1949). The act of surrender in the psychotherapeutic process with special reference to alcoholism. *Quarterly Journal of Studies on Alcoholism, 10,* 48–58.

Tiebout, H. M. (1953). Surrender vs. compliance in therapy with special reference to alcoholism. *Quarterly Journal of Studies on Alcohol, 14*, 58–68.

Vaillant, G. (1981). Dangers of psychotherapy in the treatment of alcoholism. In M. Bean & N. Zinberg (Eds.), *Dynamic approaches to the understanding and treatment of alcoholism* (pp. 55–96). New York: Free Press.

Van der Kolk, B. (1987). *Psychological trauma.* Washington, D.C.: American Psychiatric Press.

Watzlawick, P. Weakland, J., & Fisch, R. (1974). *Change.* Palo Alto, CA: Science & Behavior Books.

Wegscheider, S. (1981). *Another chance: hope and health for the alcoholic family.* Palo Alto, CA: Science & Behavior Books.

Weiss, J. (1986). In J. Weiss & H. Sampson, *The psychoanalytic process: Theory, clinical observation and empirical research.* New York: Guilford Press.

Winnicott, D. W. (1953). Transitional objects and transitional phenomena. *International Journal of Psychoanalysis, 34*, 89–97.

Winnicott, D. W. (1960). The theory of the parent-infant relationship. *International Journal of Psychoanalysis, 41*, 585–595.

5

Psychoanalytic Theory and Children of Chemically Dependent Parents: Ships Passing in the Night?

Timothy M. Rivinus, M.D.

Why was the study of children of chemically dependent parents neglected for so long in psychoanalysis and developmental psychology? Part of the answer to this question may lie in the very nature of *denial* within the addictive system and in a society that has been called "an addict" itself (Schaef, 1987). Three developments have conspired to bring about a better understanding of the chemically dependent system's impact on the developing child. First is the nature of addiction itself. Without a clear understanding of how alcohol (or any addictive chemical) affects the developmental psychology of the individual, little progress could be made clinically or theoretically. Second, without an understanding of how the behavior of one individual within a closed system, over time, affects the psychology, behavior, and spirit of others within that system, there simply could not be an adequate understanding of the effects on the children of substance-abusing parents (COSAPs). This understanding has come about only in the past 50 years, largely inspired and spurred by the self-help and family-psychiatry movements. Third, an essential factor in the liberation of COSAPs has been the powerful force of wave upon wave of minority groups, the traumatized, and the oppressed demanding and slowly being granted more recognition in our society.

We are part of a cultural revolution in which the acknowledgment of being a COSAP is a relatively new phenomenon. It is the purpose of this chapter to discuss developments that preceded this acknowledgment and to suggest how they at first contributed to denial of the special needs and understanding of children of chemically dependent parents.

ANALYSIS AND ADDICTIONOLOGY: PARALLEL BUT SEPARATE DEVELOPMENTS

Contributions of the Temperance Movement

The Temperance Movement—its politics, pamphleteering, literature, and art—contributed much to our understanding of addiction and its effects on addicted individuals and those close to them. It drew from the pioneering writings of Benjamin Rush (1790), who was the first to characterize alcoholism as an addictive disease. At its best, the Temperance Movement highlighted the progressive nature of addiction as a disease leading to the deterioration of the body, mind, and spirit. At its worst, but no less accurately, it proclaimed alcoholism (and, by extension, the addictive process) as a scourge, a plague. The Temperance Movement also highlighted the worst of the effects of an addicted family member on the family. The victimization of wives by alcoholic husbands and of children by alcoholic fathers and the abandonment and neglect of children by alcoholic mothers were first described by the Temperance Movement (Lender & Martin, 1982).

The taking of the temperance "pledge," an admission of a spiritual and moral conversion (Tiebout, 1954) and a pledge to abstinence and to membership in a group dedicated to sobriety and the assistance of others affected by alcohol, became the basis for today's important principles of treatment of the addictions. These are the principles used in Alcoholics Anonymous (AA), Narcotics Anonymous (NA), and Alanon, and in most successful treatment programs for the addictions (Lender & Martin, 1982; Kurtz, 1979).

However, the moral and political rigidity and doctrine of the Temperance Movement weakened its ability to stimulate formal research and social growth in the understanding of addiction. The backlash, by promoters and users of alcohol, was great. The freedom to choose to drink alcohol was felt to be a basic American right. Alcohol had been part of our culture too long to abolish its social and economic power. Furthermore, the nature of chemical dependency was too embroiled in moral controversy to allow it to be considered from a more clinical point of view. However, controversy is necessary for the growth of ideas and knowledge. As a result of temperance efforts and of the effects of the prohibition of alcohol, the addictions today are seen as diseases and as human afflictions worthy of compassion and help.

The Cart Before the Horse: The Impact of Prohibition and "Addictive Personality" Theories

Many psychiatrists still follow the precepts of the early psychoanalysts and consider "depression," "anxiety disorder," or long-standing neurotic or personality problems to be a root cause of addiction (Wurmser, 1978). However, ironically, from the experience of addictionologists, none of these so-called "underlying" disorders, where they coexist with an addiction, can be treated until the patient gives up use of the substances themselves.

In the study of the addictive process, we are often faced with the nature-versus-nurture question. But if there is one thing physicians have learned about the treatment of physical illness, it is that nature must be respected first. Once the disease has been recognized, respected, and brought under control, then its origins in one's relationship to parents, family, and culture can be addressed. This has been the liberating legacy of recognizing alcoholism and other chemical dependency as a disease (Jellinek, 1960). The disease concept externalizes and naturalizes the basic problem in such a way that the addicted can be considered treatable and not, therefore, hopeless.

It is no coincidence that toward the end of Prohibition, the failure of that movement to help individuals deal with the runaway aspects of their addiction (whether the alcohol was legal or illegal) became starkly apparent. In fact, Bill W., the founder of AA, spent his actively alcoholic years as both a businessperson and an "out-of-control" alcoholic during the 1920s, the Prohibition era. It was clear to him that neither medicine nor the law could help him. His was a disease for which no purely medical cure could be found and which no legal sanction could prevent. Treatment had to come not only from within; it also had to take place in the company of others similarly afflicted. Bill W. rediscovered that interacting with other alcoholics attempting to recover was basic to the "cure" (Kurtz, 1979). The first volume of the AA *Big Book* (largely written and inspired by Bill W.) was published in 1939 and contained much of the early data on the new psychological and spiritual findings related to recovery from alcoholism (AA, 1939).

From the accounts of the recovering alcoholics came the movement to recognize alcoholism as a disease, led by E. M. Jellinek (1942, 1960). The disease concept of addiction was adopted by the American Medical Association in 1956, and the World Health Organization soon followed suit. The relative newness of these developments suggested that it would take time to develop the body of self-help experience and the disease concept into psychological theory. The use of ordinary psychological theories and techniques in the attempt to cure the addictions had been largely unsuccessful. Many of the early statements in the psychological literature regarding addictions reflected an ignorance or hopelessness based, perhaps, on the repeated failures of patients to recover and of their therapists to help them.

The first psychoanalytic thinkers emphasized the early and preoedipal injuries and deficits they felt were present in the groups of addicted patients whom they tried to treat (Rado, 1933; Glover, 1956; Knight, 1937). Feinichel (1945) observed that the "superego is soluable in alcohol." This statement reflects the importance of recognizing that the drug itself can dissolve psychological structures and function.

Much confusion about the addictions on the part of psychological and psycho-analytic therapists arose from the fact that these practitioners (as well as their patients) could not separate the psychology of the addiction itself from the premorbid psychology of the individual. These issues could only be clarified by the prerequisite recommended by AA (and by Freud [1974/1912] as a general principle applying to psychoanalysis): *abstinence*. Abstinence from addictive chemicals allows the practitioner and the patient to study the patient's psychology free of toxic effects of the drug. During prolonged abstinence, the psychology of craving and the psychology of the individual can be, in large part, separated.

The quest for an "addictive personality" consumed much of the early literature on the subject. Longitudinal studies began to show that there is relatively little to be gained by discussing an "addictive personality." A profusion of addictive personalities, many opposed to one another, arose from research. In addition, these theories did not explain the large number of individuals with personality profiles similar to those proposed for addicted people who did not become addicted themselves. Longitudinal studies showed that there are few, if any, premorbid personality traits that would predict an addiction when separated from adverse environmental circumstances. Middle- and upper-class groups, otherwise relatively free of adverse social circumstance, when studied longitudinally did not have personality features that would predict later addiction (Vaillant, 1983).

Contributions of Genetic Epidemiology

Further research demonstrated that susceptibility to alcoholism appears to be genetically predisposed (Goodwin, 1988). The effects of nurture were separated in the important genetic studies by focusing on children adopted away from their biological parents. Cross-adopted sons of alcoholic fathers are four to nine times more likely to become alcoholic, if exposed to alcohol, than are sons of nonalcoholics. Cross-adopted daughters of alcoholic mothers are four times more likely to become alcoholics than are those of nonalcoholics. There are 27–30 million children of alcoholic parents (who are genetically susceptible to this disorder) in the United States alone (Russell, Henderson, & Blume, 1985). Therefore, the number of children "at risk" is large.

Additionally, it has been shown that there is significant overlap among propensities for depression, personality disorders, and some forms of addiction to alcohol or other drugs (Meyer, 1986). A large group of children at risk may be prone to depressive spectrum disorder (Winokur et al., 1975). If these hypotheses, based on the reasonable evidence provided, are to be believed, there are considerable numbers of people in our society who either have biological disorders or have problems with their ability safely to use socially available drugs—namely, alcohol and, perhaps, many widely dispensed prescription and illicitly used depressants and other psychoactive chemicals.

The Chemicals Themselves

The rapid growth in the availability, potency, and number of addicting sub-stances other than alcohol has provided abundant evidence of their terrifying power to addict those who use them no matter what their genetic predisposition. Some chemicals are capable of addicting mammals almost immediately following first exposure. Irrespective of genetic succeptibility, the capacity of psychoactive substances such as cocaine and opioids to addict and intoxicate depends on their chemistry, their potency, and the rapidity of their delivery to the nervous system. Among those chemicals that are rapidly addicting are heroin, injected or smoked cocaine and other stimulants, nicotine, and alcohol, for those genetically predisposed.

We can also anticipate that there are other so-called "designer" drugs yet to be designed and new substances yet to be discovered. Some chemicals pro-duce biochemical alterations, over time, that condition the human nervous system to addiction. Alcohol is the best example of this kind of drug, although marijuana, prescription drugs, and the benzodiazepines also belong to this group. The power of psychoactive chemicals to addict resides not only in the users' genetic and physical constitutions, but in everyone, and is directly related to the power of the chemical itself, the amount of drug(s) used, and the duration of the exposure.

Trauma and the Addictions

Many factors predictive of addiction are largely social and environmental. A trau-matic, painful, or disorganized early environment can lead to higher rates of addic-tion. This does not refer so much to early "ego deficits," as suggested by the early analysts, as to traumatic conditions of various kinds, including the stress of growing up in an environment that itself was alcoholic (Fawzy, Coombs, & Gerber, 1983; Wegscheider, 1981; Black, 1981; Brown, 1987). Recent research suggests that early physical and psychological trauma and disruption lead to disorders of attachment and identity (Van der Kolk, 1987). This may be the common pathway shared by those COSAPs who are prone to the addictions, as well as by children from all trau-matizing early environments that lead to morbidity of any kind.

Alcoholism, both in an individual and in the family system, can result in major trauma for children (Bean-Bayog, 1986; Steinglass, Bennett, Wolin, & Reiss, 1987) and is an important public-health issue (Russell et al., 1985). Among certain seg-ments of our population, an entire generation of children is being exposed to the chemical, physical, and psychological trauma caused by parental cocaine and other drug addictions. The casualties among these children are many and will be for some time to come (Chapters 14 and 15).

Psychoanalytic Efforts: Contributions and Historical Oversight

Sigmund Freud was addicted to cigars for most of his adult life and died of cancer of the soft palate, a complication of tobacco addiction. He also was briefly addicted to cocaine at one point, and recommended its use to his friend Fleiss as a treatment for Fleiss' habituation to morphine (Gay, 1988). Nevertheless (and perhaps partly as a result of his experience), Freud struck at the very heart of the psychology of addictions in his theoretical pronouncements. His treatise on the *pleasure principle* versus the reality principle provides an understanding of the early part of the addictive process (Freud, 1974/1911, 1974/1915). Furthermore, his emphasis on the impact of early childhood development and of parental figures (Freud, 1974/1909) is essential to the basis of the science of attachment and child–parent relationships and why they go so terribly wrong in many chemically dependent families.

Yet, in emphasizing instinctual drives and the clash between internal psychodynamic mechanisms in the origin of the psychoses and neuroses, Freud and his successors overlooked the powerful effect of alcohol and other addicting, psychoactive chemicals on a parent's ability to provide an adequately nurturing environment. Because early psychoanalytic treatment of addiction did not focus on abstinence and the powerlessness of the individual to fight the chemical, it was rarely successful. The American psychoanalyst Knight (1937) observed that exposure to alcohol caused personality regression to pregenital levels of functioning, which often became fixed in character structure. He also noted that many people who developed alcoholism had had defects in their early development. What he did not recognize was that many of these defects can be caused by alcohol and can be reversed, in part, by abstinence and a recovery program (Kurtz, 1979). Furthermore, while considering that such defects in early development are present in the addicted person, Knight and other psychoanalytic thinkers did not consider that these defects might have their origin in genetic susceptibility or in an addictive family history. Nevertheless, Knight can be credited with recognizing that the early developmental environment is important in the genesis of the addictions.

In our review of the topic, we have not found any psychoanalytic authors who have commented on the fact that alcoholism runs in families, or any writers in the psychoanalytic tradition who have commented on the situation of the child of an alcoholic parent (Mosher, 1987). The annals of psychoanalysis are littered with reports of unsuccessful treatment of those considered neurotic who were addicted to chemicals of various kinds—a lack of success that perhaps spawned a nihilism about the treatment of the addictions by psychotherapy. In fact, psychoanalytic thinkers, dismayed by their failures, often echoed the prevailing nihilism of society at large regarding the treatment of the addictions (Feinichel, 1945).

Early psychoanalytic treatment held out hope that if sources of psychic pain could be elucidated, then the patient could give up the addictive "self-medication." Many were treated with therapy, with substitute (often addictive) medicines, and without an insistence on abstinence or on an abstinence program. Though well intended, these treatments were largely failures. They put the cart before the horse. These experimental therapeutic failures of the psychoanalysis of the addicted, however, led historically to our understanding that the focus in the treatment of an addict and of the child of an addicted family must be on the stressor (the addiction) that brings the patient into treatment in the first place.

Although addictionologists and AA take the position that the individual is responsible for his or her own abstinence and recovery, the predisposition to become an addict and the progression of the addiction itself are, in fact, disease-related and out of the addict's control. Causes of the disease may be genetic or constitutional, or they may be chemically induced, inspired by early life or ongoing traumata, the result of deprivations, major life stress, or exposures to chemically abusing parental or peer models. The causes may be some combination of these—or they may be unknown. The experience of the self-help groups has paralleled the thinking of classical psychoanalysis in recognizing that an understanding of early life pain and conflict *may* be important in identifying contributing factors to an addictive life-style. However, according to the addictionologist, although the clarification of childhood pain is necessary, it is not sufficient to explain or treat the addictive process.

The Power of Individualism in Psychoanalysis and the "American Mind"

The psychoanalytic movement, as it flourished in the United States, also combined with a strong American value of individualism. Emphasis on the role of the individual in recovery may be, in part, rooted in this tradition; it may have even provided the backdrop for early members of AA to emphasize the need to surrender to a conversion experience (Tiebout, 1954) and to an admission of powerlessness (the first of the "twelve steps" of AA) over the drug of addiction (AA, 1976). It also may have emphasized the necessity for the individual member to surrender to the group.

In the psychotherapeutic situation, however, a focus on the individual may have led to two products of psychotherapy that were not helpful to the addict. The first, rightfully (but righteously) dramatized by Miller (1983), was the overemphasis placed by early psychoanalytic thinkers on the psychic fantasy of the individual, which caused psychoanalysts to miss many examples of early childhood trauma. If analysts and their patients held the individual responsible for having fantasized an early trauma or injury that had in fact happened, this may have resulted in a tragic failure of empathy and a rejection of the patient's real experience.

The second issue is one of "control." Western culture, as well as the psychoanalytic movement, places a high value on an individual's ability to control his or her life and to take responsibility for it. In spite of the importance of this concept to psychoanalytic treatment, it has not been the organizing principle in the understanding of the addictions and in early steps toward recovery of addicted persons. Its antithesis, the admission of loss of control and powerlessness ("the surrender") as a way of regaining some control over the addictive process, has played a key role in the psychological commitment to recovery (Bateson, 1971). The psychology of the self-help movement has been based on the principle that the individual must "give up control," acknowledge his or her "powerlessness" over the drug of addiction (AA, 1976), and admit that he or she is "not God" (Kurtz, 1979). By admitting that control is not the issue, the personal sense of failure of not being able to exercise control by will may be forgiven in oneself. Paradoxically, by acknowledging the loss of control over a psychoactive substance, a control of abstinence is gained. Both therapists and clients must be prepared to admit the ultimate power of the addiction over their lives as they come together in therapy; they will need to accept abstinence as the only path to productive therapy—and ultimately, to a productive life.

A powerful reactionary movement (Fingarette, 1988) strives to show that addicted people can gain enough control over addictive substances to be able to use them "safely." This position is usually taken by those who have had little direct experience with addiction and who wish to express a philosophical, rather than a clinical, position. Control is a very powerful issue, particularly in American psychology. Although the literature on "controlled" drinking or drug use has not been supported by evidence from the follow-up studies of the addicted subjects, there still appears to be a strong but, for the most part, futile effort to show that controlled use of addicting substances by demonstrated addicts may be possible.

Reductionistic Psychoanalytic Thinking and the Addictions

In the course of psychoanalytic treatment, the mind was expected to become responsible for the body. The patient was to take charge of feelings for his or her past. The early psychoanalysts perhaps sensed an omnipotent power in their new method. They felt that psychoanalysis might be capable of changing physical and emotional reactions to childhood events. In the process, psychoanalytical thought engendered ideas that were not helpful in the understanding and healing of addiction and of children of addicted parents. For example, according to the early psychosomatic theories, certain mental states or character configurations could cause physical disease, including addiction to alcohol or other drugs. That the addictions were "oral" fixations and, therefore, highly resistant to cure or that those who became addicted did so because they were latently homosexual were early psychoanalytic hypotheses (Feinichel, 1945). There were also hypotheses that addiction was a perverse outcropping of preoedipal and pregenital sexuality and that the addictions were the only possible "oral" manifestation of these perverse sexual drives. Despite the cramped reductionism of these early hypotheses, the study of the analogy between addiction and sexuality forshadowed studies of their shared pleasure-producing neurochemical mechanisms and their similar capacities to become compulsive, obsessional, addictive, and destructive. Refutation and the reworked incorporation of these early psychoanalytic hypotheses concerning the ramifications and meaning of addictive behavior has led to greater basic scientific and therapeutic understanding of addiction.

The Other 23 Hours: Overemphasis on Process

A further pitfall in the early psychoanalysts' efforts to understand the effect of addiction may have stemmed from an overfocus on the process of the analysis rather than on the process of a patient's life. The primacy of the individual experience of the analysis itself may have tended to block analysis of the other 23 hours of a patient's day. Dealing with parental introjects initially and primarily may have underemphasized the actual effect of the behavior of the parents on the child's development. It is the experience of most therapists who deal with COSAPs that the *trauma* of addicted or codependent parenting must be believed, examined in detail, and put into perspective by both patient and therapist before introjects and repetition–compulsion can be dealt with. The delineation of the child's role in the addictive system is also essential to successful psychotherapy.

Without an understanding of how the addictions work to change character and nervous-system responses, analysts may have focused either too much on the individual and his or her parental introjects or too much on the weaknesses of the parent as a person. The analysand, patient, or client may have come away from therapy feeling too responsible for a parent's behavior—a recapitulation of every child's grandiose wish to be all-powerful, all-responsible for the addictive family process. Conversely, the patient might have held the parent all-responsible, thus blaming the parent, even a sometimes "good" parent, for a disease that was in need of diagnosis and definition.

Addiction Is a Disease

As so often happens in medicine when a disease, such as substance dependence, has no widely accepted etiology, (see also Chapter 4), names are invented that take on a life of their own. For example, if an individual and his or her "personality" structure were held responsible, the label "borderline personality" or "narcissistic personality" (see Chapter 6) might have been applied by the therapist, whereas the diagnosis of post-traumatic stress disorder with borderline or narcissistic traits might have been more appropriate (Herman, Perry, & Van der Kolk, 1989). Terms such as "schizophrenogenic mother" (Fromm-Reichmann, 1952) may have been used by analysts striving to conceptualize the behavior and nature of parents who were actually addicted or codependent.

Failures of Understanding and Empathy

Much of early psychoanalysis was based on the efforts of analysts to apply the brilliant hypotheses proposed by Freud and his successors to the problems that patients brought to them. Analysands' stories were often rigidly pressed into the procrustean bed of Freudian or other psychoanalytic theories (Peterfreund, 1983). One can only imagine the tragedy of the COSAP bringing his or her story of parental trauma into analysis and then having that story reframed in terms of the anxiety supposedly stemming from oedipal or castration issues. Furthermore, if stories of trauma were minimized, denied, or reinterpreted as patient fantasy by the analyst, the patient's version of the truth would have been rejected in a fashion reminiscent of the painful childhood experience. Much of the child's painful experience had already been traumatically denied by the chemically dependent parent. To have pain again be denied by having it recast in theoretical terms that did not adequately apply to the patient's sense of reality might have recapitulated in therapy a primary childhood trauma (Miller, 1983).

Failures of Transference Interpretation

A patient might angrily reject an analyst's theoretical proposal that the patient's story of physical and psychological trauma was fantasy or was a manifestation of issues based on sexual wishes.

If a patient's anger at the analyst's inability to understand was then interpreted by the analyst as a transference issue (e.g., anger that recapitulated "oedipal anger" felt toward the parent or as the "castration fantasies" or "penis envy" of the child with regard to the substance-abusing parent), the situation may have deteriorated further. Analyses or therapies may have failed at this point and analysands may have fled therapy because they experienced the trauma of misunderstanding and misinterpretation. Analysts and therapists may have believed that their patients had avoided crucial issues in therapy or transference when, in fact, the critical issues of trauma and addiction had never been identified.

As a child, Dora had been sexually molested by an alcohol-abusing friend of her father when left alone with him while on family vacations. In analysis, her dreams and her memories of childhood brought this material to the fore. Her analyst then reframed these memories in terms of infantile wishes for both this man's and her father's penis. The analyst framed these events in terms of a child's wish to be united with the men sexually so as to make her a rival to her mother and the man's wife. At this point, Dora sensed that her analyst was accusing her of fantasizing child molestation and her father's and his friend's drunkenness. She also sensed that he was accusing her of somehow having invited sexual assault as a child. At this point, questioning, yet again, her own sense of reality, Dora fled analysis, never to return.

THE BIOPSYCHOSOCIAL ASPECTS OF DENIAL

Practitioners working with addictions agree that the most common defense used by addicted patients or COSAPs is denial. Not only does the afflicted patient deny his or her illness, but spouses, family members, friends, colleagues, doctors, therapists, and society at large deny the seriousness of the problems resulting from the addictions to or dependencies on mind-altering chemicals. Most mind-altering chemicals with addictive properties reinforce denial and the impulses of the pleasure principle.

Biology of Denial

The biological capabilities of alcohol to produce amnesia and memory impairment are well known. Other addicting drugs produce similar memory impairments or alterations in human beings. This blurring of reality is part of the allure of these substances. They alter reality, dull pain, and minimize oppressive thoughts and life situations. Partly because they succeed initially, they are used and used again. This is the cycle of addiction.

Amnesia and altered perceptions by mind-altering chemicals are biologically induced properties. They are linked to the denial process that tells the user, and causes the user to tell himself or herself and the world, in the face of contrary evidence: "No problem!" Denial is the human defense mechanism that rigidly prohibits understanding of present, past, and future reality. Alcohol and other addictive drugs, when used pathologically over time, produce permanent memory impairment on a biological basis (Adams, Victor, & Mancall, 1959; Oscar-Berman, 1987).

Psychology of Denial

Inherent in developmental psychology's denial of the impact of family alcoholism on the developing child was an implicit bias that these were problems of the mind and the will. Psychoanalysis and developmental psychology overemphasized the effect of internal drives and psychological mechanisms on external events—such as trauma or family alcoholism—in the production of denial as a defense.

The early analysts and therapists rarely considered that the parents' pathology may have arisen from an addictive process. Many parents of COSAPs have grown up with addiction. This fact requires that the patient and therapist come to grips with the addiction's intergenerational aspects. Therapists and analysts, limited by the rigid intrapsychic constructs of early psychoanalytic thought, almost certainly failed to help their patients to understand fully the effect of addicted parenting. The advent of behavioral, interpersonal, transactional, and multigenerational family-systems psychologies helped to pave the way for a better understanding of these processes.

Sociology of Denial

The power of denial to produce further denial within a family system, or even within a larger social system, is prodigious. It is those who use alcohol pathologically who often defend it most stoutly. For them, it has properties that are useful. Whether one is addicted to alcohol and is unwilling to admit the destruction it causes or whether one uses alcohol socially only for pleasure, the denial of its deleterious aspects is understandable, if not defensible.

How the addictions affect family systems by producing alterations in interpersonal interaction in the "wet" as well as "dry" state (Steinglass et al., 1987) is better understood. The paradoxical ability of intoxication to produce short-term beneficial alterations in family systems, while, at the same time, generating chronic pathology, has also come to be widely appreciated. Also increasingly appreciated is the extraordinary political, social, and economic aspects of alcoholic denial (Russell et al., 1985; Woodside, 1988; also see Chapter 14).

Politically, throughout the history of the United States, alcohol has been hotly contested. It has bought votes, and has fueled the candidacy and resulted in the victory or defeat of many political figures. It has been an extraordinarily important part of the fabric of American political life (Lender & Martin, 1982).

The economic ramifications of the alcohol (and now the illicit-drug) industry are enormous. Combined, alcohol and illicitly used drugs are *the* major industry in the United States, and are beginning to assume a similar position in other Western countries; in the Middle East and South and Central America, they are a major force in politics and government. It is not difficult to understand that politically, economically, and socially, it is extremely difficult to combat the denial that surrounds alcohol and other drugs.

To oppose this denial is to be a rebel, and even eventually a victim in some U.S. subcultures. Therefore, it is understandable that the therapeutic and psychoanalytic community, without the support of a mass movement, may have been reluctant as a group to take a stand. It is only since the emergence of a political agenda by AA and its supporters, combined with the medical recognition of alcoholism and other substance dependence as "disease," that there has been enough of a rational consensus to enable a stand to be taken against the powerful forces of individual and social denial.

Systems Theory and Denial

Systems theory provides the essential stepping-stone to the understanding that addiction is not just a personal problem—a question of morality or will. This is especially true for the child growing up in a chemically dependent family. As a COSAP, one can swear to oneself that it will "never happen to me," and still end up repeating the same patterns of behavior that one saw while growing up in a dysfunctional family (Black, 1981). What are normal and adaptive interactions in chemically dependent households become maladaptive when the child leaves the family and exports these family survival and coping mechanisms to new relationships in the "outside" world. As the COSAP moves from one set and system into another, he or she begins to feel and appear abnormal. What could be more "normal" to a COSAP than denial as a defense for painful feelings arising from two conflicting realities?

The heuristic power of systems theory to explain the effect of the shift from one system to another has been a major contribution to our understanding of the pathology of the COSAP. If blame for current difficulty is placed on a lack of intrapsychic responsibility without prior clarification of how these difficulties may be based on early family systemic adaptive and survival mechanisms, psychological change in psychoanalytic psychotherapy may be difficult to attain. The self-help movements have shown that much of the "corrective experience" of the COSAP is a symptomatic and systemic understanding of the addictive family acquired through information presented in educational form. Education on this phenomenon is validating for those who have been numbed by amnesia and years of denial, who have been unable to trust, and who are rigidly defensive about their early family life.

The Faustian Bargain—Pharmaceutical Industry and Psychiatric Prescribing

The psychiatric profession has been blessed with increased neurochemical understanding and powerful pharmacological tools. However, psychiatrists and other doctors have had difficulty recognizing and admitting the liabilities of the addictive qualities of some of humankind's oldest neurochemicals (alcohol, the opiates, and the hallucinogens). To balance this view, prescribing doctors have only to review the history of the development of many of the most potently addictive drugs. Heroin, the barbiturates, benzodiazepines, lysergic acid (LSD), the amphetamines, and cocaine were all introduced into the medical and psychiatric pharmacopoeia as "nonaddicting" chemicals. It requires a shift in logic to see that many psychoactive chemicals can relieve human suffering and also themselves be the cause of pathology. The traumas induced by addicting chemicals are states that are not just unwanted side effects (a lesser evil), but come to have a pathological life of their own. Some physicians actually supply addicted patients with the stuff of addiction. Others, unwittingly, supply patients who are at high risk (because an addictive substance blocks or numbs painful memory) and so abet the addictive process.

The Scientific Method as an Inhibitor of Progress

A major source of denial of the problems of the addicted and their children has been the scientific process embraced by medicine and by psychiatry itself. Up to 1950, many of the advances of medicine and psychiatry were based on empirical and individual findings. Since that time, various discoveries that have come from clinical sources have been subjected to intensive scientific scrutiny. The scientific method provides an extremely valuable source of information and validation of theories and of practice (Kuhn, 1970). However, the methods employed (e.g., epidemiological surveys or biochemical or pharmacological hypothesis testing) often tend to repeat the obvious or to make obvious psychosocial causes inscrutable in psychological medicine.

A force that has deterred medical science from coming to grips with addiction as a human process is the hope that a "magic bullet" will soon be discovered that will subvert or tame the addictions—a role that, in the past, had been envisioned for such chemicals as cocaine, LSD, heroin, the benzodiazepines, methadone, lithium, and the tricyclic antidepressants. Although the future may actually see biochemical and pharmacological breakthroughs, the addictions essentially constitute a human process for which human solutions must be socially sought.

Although research into high-risk groups, such as COSAPs, should continue, it would be unconscionable to deny services to those in need because clear diagnostic criteria have not been developed or because the heterogeneity of their symptom presentations defies correct statistical analysis and synthesis. Not to provide help because of the need to subject clinically established facts to repeated scientific scrutiny is to overlook what we already know: there is a cycle of addiction for many of us and we now have an opportunity to interrupt it.

A NEW SYNTHESIS

"Developmental Arrest" as an Organizing Construct for Psychoanalysis and AA

The concept of "developmental arrest" is an important contribution of psychoanalytically oriented thinking to the understanding of the developmental problems of the child of a chemically dependent family (Brown, 1987). The term was originally used in an early classification of childhood disorders prepared by the Group for the Advancement of Psychiatry (1966), and the self-help movement has employed similar terms. From a developmental perspective, events such as trauma or parental addiction can arrest a person's development at the stage below his or her chronological and psychological age. Specific therapies aimed at looking at the causes of that arrest can liberate the client to progress to further growth. Many COSAPs and children of trauma have suffered a developmental arrest as a result of their childhood environment. The impact of parental alcohol or other substance abuse is the focus of specific therapies that help the COSAP to become developmentally unstuck and to grow along "corrective" developmental lines (Brown, 1987; Gonzales, 1988).

Contribution of Behaviorism

Behavioral psychology has helped refocus developmental psychology on external events and cues in the environment. It not only has provided a greater understanding of the formation of the addictions by reinforcement, but also has led to a deeper understanding of how people adapt defensively to the external environment and become developmentally stuck. In the context of the COSAP, certain behavioral cues are rewarded. The silence, the secrecy, the tolerance of intramural family chaos and violence, and the inability to talk about the pain of family chemical dependence are deeply embedded behaviorally in the child's (and adult child's) psychology by continuous family reinforcement. Speaking, feeling, and trusting are punished. Silence, dissociation from feelings, and counterdependence are rewarded. The model of using chemicals to deal with feelings and to quell pain is the norm in chemically dependent families. These are all behaviorally learned events that are continually reinforced during a COSAP's development.

The Contributions of Self Psychology

The failure of therapists to achieve success is a major pitfall in work with traumatized patients. Empathetic failure results from lack of information and collective memory of the effect of trauma on humans. It also results from the absence or denial of direct experience with trauma by therapists. The history of trauma shows that its psychological costs are forgotten by the next generation. Nevertheless, these costs tend to linger, as a result of denial, and become delayed, post-traumatic stress.

Many symptomatic adult COSAPs suffer from a form of post-traumatic stress disorder (Cermak, 1986). Certain external circumstances, therefore, can trigger the appearance of symptoms of the disorder. The COSAP, by puberty or early adolescence, begins to abuse alcohol or other drugs or to find himself or herself in relationships that replicate the abuse known in his or her childhood (see also Chapter 6). Unless the therapist knows this in advance, it is very easy to collude with the denial systems of the patient as a way of empathizing with the patient's outlook.

Recent developments in the field of trauma theory and self psychology have resulted in major contributions to reversing denial and therapists' failure to achieve proper empathy (Van der Kolk, 1987). Alice Miller (1983) and Heinz Kohut (1984,

1985) have played an important part in shedding light on the misunderstandings that parents bring to a child's psychology, and have elucidated the collusive role that therapists may assume in that process. Traumatic and defective parental mirroring, when clarified and corrected, can lead to therapeutic progress for COSAPs and other victims of parental trauma or deprivation. Kohut has shown how the narcissistic parent, in fact, evokes a highly polarized and idealized response in the child to both that parent and others. The narcissistic parent is unable to meet the child's needs, and an "idealized" parent is formed in the mind of the child as compensation for what the parent cannot give. This idealized parent has a good and a bad "introject" in the child's personality; in other words, the child learns either to expect too much or to expect the worst of himself or herself and others (see also Chapter 6). Rarely is the symptomatic COSAP's response well modulated or balanced in his or her expectations.

The Contributions of Interpersonal Theory

Many of the early behavioral and emotional responses of the child of a chemically dependent parent—and, by extension, the later personality development of that child—can be understood in terms of relationship psychology. The early practitioners, Harry Stack Sullivan and Eric Berne, demonstrated that much of what goes on in behavioral manifestations of relations between people has to do with the transaction between them. Furthermore, infancy research and the careful analysis of interactions between a child and his or her parent by Bowlby and a host of others (Stern, 1985) who have followed this line of research have demonstrated that the development of the early responses, and, indeed, the character of the child, is evoked in the early parent–child relationship.

A chemically dependent parent is, by definition, a narcissistic parent— particularly at those times when the parent is preoccupied with getting, using, and recovering from the chemical of addiction. In the cycle of addiction, the addicted parent has little time for a relationship with the child. The other parent may be addicted or absent, and if neither, is likely to be a "codependent" whose parenting is crippled by the constant demands, rebuffs, and traumata of the addicted partner. The child develops idealized "good" and "bad" introjects and models of behavior relative to the codependent parent (see also Chapter 6).

It is rare that a chemically addicted or codependent parent can consistently meet the psychological needs of a child. A child's needs are egocentric, narcissistic, and dependent, requiring parents to delay the satisfaction of their own needs and impulses to meet those of the child. Since addicted and codependent parents are rarely able to fulfill this obligation, the child is left to his or her own devices in coming to terms with unmet needs. The child looks on the chemically dependent parent as an idealized, and the only, caretaker, for better or worse. These internalized parents and parent–child interactions are carried into adult life and require many corrective experiences and clarification to be changed.

The pattern of expected needs and unmet needs provided to us as a template by our parents is, as we become adolescents and adults, transferred to other individuals: spouses, friends, co-workers, and society in general. Much of the turbulence of growing up in an alcoholic or other substance-abusing, chemically dependent family revolves around the fact that basic human needs are not being met, are disregarded, or are minimized. What results is either vigorous protest or withdrawal or some other type of "heroic" adaptation to compensate for the absence of parental care. The child thus assumes various roles within the family structure to counter these deficits interpersonally in the stereotyped homeostasis of the chemically dependent family (Wegscheider, 1981). These roles persist adaptively, or maladaptively, in the child and "adult child's" relations with others outside of the family and often with their own partners and children.

Contributions of Transactional Analysis

The theories of Eric Berne (1964) have provided a significant link between psychoanalysis and the field of addiction. Berne used a simplified model of Freudian (Freud, 1974/1923) structural psychology to outline the ego states of the developing human being. Within us, according to Berne, we contain, as normal structures, a child, a parent, and an adult as internalized figures. Concentration on the parentified "imagos" within us, the child within us, and the mature adult within us and their interactions is part of transactional psychotherapy. Much Freudian theory has been incorporated into theoretical and practical constructs that have helped many COSAPs come to terms with the child and the parent within them, as a way of developing the adult within them (Whitfield, 1984, 1985), and has been an important part of the individual and therapeutic group experience of the COA movement.

Contribution of Family and General Systems Theory

Freud anticipated much of what has been contributed by the movement in his classic paper "Family Romances" (Freud, 1974/1909). In this seminal paper, Freud points out that all children idealize their parents and are likely to act in ways that model those idealized parents or that they hope will reconcile them with their parents. Many of the symptoms of children of chemically dependent families both show a high adaptation within the addictive family system and represent the COSAP's exaggerated psychological needs to idealize or romanticize his or her parents in service in adaptation (Freud, 1974/1909; Kohut, 1984, 1985). Furthermore much action in the addicted family is organized around the denial of addiction. COSAPs may unconsciously "act out" secrets they experienced as children or defensively respond to new situations relative to their own families of origin.

The family-therapy movement has led to an understanding that every person in a family is part of a system, and that there is not necessarily a "sick" or addicted person in this system, but the system itself is dysfunctional (Minuchin, 1974). Addicted parents can be loving and caring at one time, and at another, be abusive and oppressive. All members of an addictive system are affected, but in different forms. This kind of understanding of family "disease" needs clarification before the plight of the individual COSAP can be recognized fully within that system. Helplessness, dependence, addiction, or rebellion can be learned in such systems. Childhood family roles become subsumed within individual personality structures by adolescence and early adulthood. These roles and personality types then may be repeated from generation to generation. The intergenerational aspect of family-generated illness has led to a better understanding of how alcoholism and addiction perpetuate themselves in families and that the afflicted need not be just the addicted (Dulfano, 1982; Elkin, 1984; Fossum & Masson, 1986; Treadway, 1989).

The Contribution of Role Theory

Role theory also has contributed to our understanding of the roles and positions in the addicted family (Satir, 1972; Wegscheider, 1981; Black, 1981; also see Chapter 12). The child "hero" attempts to emulate the idealized, "good" parent and becomes a "little parent" himself or herself. This child often acts as the family ambassador and is rarely able to separate from the family. The hero "pseudoseparates" by dint of accomplishments whose prime purpose is often to put the family in a favorable light and so obscure family pathology.

The "lost" child withdraws and takes on aspects of the classic anaclitic depression or reactive attachment disorder (American Psychiatric Association, 1987, pp. 91–92). He or she sometimes drops out of the system, hoping to find his or her needs met elsewhere. This child attaches quickly to others, usually failing to get needs for nurturance met, particularly if object choices are poor. In situations where a surrogate parent is available, such as a grandparent or a friend's parent, this person may be the child's salvation by providing primary parenting. In other cases, "lost" COSAPs band and bond with peers from similar backgrounds. Members of these peer groups make false promises to one another; they use drugs, seek excitement and quick gratification, and take risks.

The "mascot" child tends to exaggerate his or her childlike qualities, constantly striving to gratify the unmet needs for nurturance within the family. This child often becomes a child "caricature," has difficulty separating, and may be unable to leave the family, attempting to protect by maintaining the child-centered, albeit imbalanced, distribution of nurturance there.

The child who "acts out" is, in many ways, the earliest protester against the imbalance of nurture. This child, sensing the lack of response to his or her own assertiveness, becomes aggressive as a way of attracting attention with the hope of having needs for nurture met. It is basically an acting out of the time-honored principle, "The wheel that does the squeaking is the one that gets the grease."

The chemically dependent or codependent parent who is narcissistically preoccupied is unable to meet either assertive or unassertive cries for nurture. For acting-out children, assertiveness becomes exaggerated and soon is noticed by others. At this stage, it is rarely seen as a cry for help but is more likely to be labeled as pathological or a character problem. These are the children who come to the attention of school, mental-health, and legal authorities. It is this level at which appropriate identification, diagnosis, and intervention may be possible.

When an assertive response in the young child is met with a nurturing response from the environment, the assertiveness generally decreases. When assertiveness that requires a nurturing response goes unmet, it turns into aggressiveness. For children whose parents (dependent or codependent) are generally reacting to the needs of the addicted parent rather than to those of the child, the assertive, then aggressive, acting out can become the norm. This child, too, like the others, may turn to similarly affected peers, to risk taking, and to addictive chemicals as ways of (temporarily) assuaging those unmet needs. What is, in childhood, a cry for nurture and attachment, in adolescence and early adult life becomes characterological—an action-oriented, maladaptive way of life driven by an old, unheeded cry.

The Contribution of the Group-Therapy Movement

The self-help movement required a coalition. The formation of AA as a healing movement, in response to the end of Prohibition and the waning influence of the Temperance Movement, signaled the beginning of a new and positive group coalition. The power of individualism in American life lessened with the depression and World War II, which suggested to many that we are "all in this together." The group-therapy movement resulted from the necessity to treat groups of people— namely, veterans with similar experiences. Since World War II, groups of all types have been meeting to identify and pursue their particular needs. The self-help and group treatments for COSAPs have relied on these historical developments for their strength and direction.

The special issues and developmental arrests experienced by the COSAP require time and a corrective experience in order to produce change. A corrective experience is often best provided in a group-healing environment; and it is no surprise that other COSAPs, who have grown up in an addicted family or currently are going through this process, are the most helpful to other COSAPs. The self-help movement, Alanon, COA groups, and Alateen have provided healing for COSAPs.

Group therapy of the COSAP focuses on breaking down denial, the deliniation of trauma of being a COSAP, and the building of trust. This may result in alienation or a temporary separation from the family of origin, particularly if other members of the family do not also seek treatment. The regressive pull of untreated family members may be too strong to allow the individual to progress, especially if there is ongoing contact with them. For those COSAPs who have left their families but have not separated from their pathological influences, an effective way to change those patterns is for them to reexperience primary relationships within a corrective group. Prior to the group experience, the COSAP may recapitulate the dependent and/or abusive nature of the addicted family in the choice of friends or partners.

Group therapy of COSAPs often has the function both of identifying the individual's place in the family of origin and of redefining that role within the group as a new and corrective "family" system. Because other group members are also COSAPs, they, too, have had similar roles in pathological family systems and so are able to provide good modeling and brief, "good enough" parenting experiences to new group members. In groups, the COSAP learns to recognize patterns and roles in the chemically dependent families of origin of others by identifying with others in the group. The controlled relationships and confidential nature of the group experience allow long-awaited safety and dependency needs to be met without exploitation or overinvolvement (Blume, 1985).

The Contribution of the Liberation of Oppressed Groups

The recognition and self-liberation of COSAPs have overlapped historically with, and been empowered by, the recognition of various suppressed and traumatized minorities. First, the liberation of African-American slaves in the United States overlapped with the efforts of the Temperance Movement. Then, working children were emancipated from their roles as servants of industry and mandated to be educated. The growing power of the labor movement soon began to liberate working people of all backgrounds. The women's movement gained for women the right to vote, and, pushing to liberate them further, has played an important part in focusing on the special injustices that women suffer. Retarded persons, veterans, homosexuals, the traumatically injured, battered children, and sexually abused children are among those who have succeeded in identifying themselves as minority groups with overlooked needs. The resurgence of emancipation and of minority-group representation set the stage for the COSAP movement. African-Americans, Native Americans, Hispanics, Orientals, women, and Vietnam War veterans have demanded another cycle of liberation in the latter part of the 20th century. The emergence of AA, Alanon, Alateen, and Adult-COA groups and the recognition of addiction as a disease have paralleled the recognition of the aspirations of these other groups. Liberation from oppression has represented the essence of American ideals and social evolution. Until oppressed minorities began to speak out and to organize themselves to represent their minority status, the issue of oppressed children could not be addressed. It was not until the 1960s and 1970s that the abuse of children, physically and sexually, could be openly discussed. This further paved the way for the acceptance of the COA movement.

Contributions of Trauma Theory

The history of psychoanalysis has overlapped political history—World War I, the prohibition of legal alcohol in the United States, the Great Depression, World War II, and continuing conflicts throughout the world. Much of the locus of psychoanalytic thinking and thinkers shifted from Europe to the United States as a result of political events. Psychotherapy with Holocaust and war victims played a major part in calling attention to the role of external traumata in changing the psychology of an individual. It was hoped that the results of trauma could be healed by psychoanalysis, but it was soon recognized that much of the trauma could only be acknowledged by those therapists trying to produce or foster change. After a flurry of attention to trauma following World War II, the therapeutic community's interest in the subject waned.

Despite the Holocaust and the exposure of much of Western civilization to the horrors of war, as well as the psychological effects of the nuclear detonations at Hiroshima and Nagasaki and their aftermath, the impact of trauma was still largely unrecognized by therapists and by society in the 1950s. Incest, trauma to children, and the oppression of women and minorities were generally denied. It took the forces of social revolution and the protests of traumatized Vietnam veterans to set the liberation of these oppressed groups in motion so that their social and therapeutic concerns could again be studied and addressed.

Incorporation of Spirituality and Spiritual Concepts Into Therapy

Although Freud (1974/1927) had little positive to say about the contributions of spirituality to psychoanalysis, except in terms of how spiritual concerns arose from the human psyche and how religious movements could often oppress the human spirit, his disciple Carl Jung (1970) made major contributions to the understanding of the spiritual basis of human psychology and to the birth of the 12-step programs (Kurtz, 1979). The AA movement has embraced a spiritual aspect in its second step, which reads, "We came to believe that a power greater than ourselves could restore us to sanity" (AA, 1976, p. 59). The surrender of the egocentric self to a "higher power" is the beginning of a relationship to the outside world, to the group, and to forces outside the self, leavening the obsessional preoccupation with internal feeling states and the egocentricity of the addictive process. That spirituality has a place in psychiatry and in transpersonal approaches to therapy has become increasingly accepted (Whitfield, 1985; Fleischman, 1989). The need for release from obsessionally inwardly directed, egocentric concerns to wider, more cosmic, and universal concerns that embrace relationships with others and life in general has come to be understood by workers in addiction and by psychotherapists as part of the healing process. Much of the inspiration for the acceptance by psychoanalysis of spiritual concerns has come from the field of addictions (Fleischman, 1989).

In turn, much of the early inspiration for the addict's acceptance of a "higher power" came from sources directly derivative from Jung (AA, 1968).

SUMMARY

The psychoanalytic movement has made major contributions to the psychological spirit of our age and to the efforts of people of many nations to construct a correctional experience to counter a traumatic childhood. It should not be forgotten that the first case histories and "stories" of the modern psychotherapy movement were those told to and by Sigmund Freud himself. Of course, AA, Alanon, and other self-help and mutual-aid groups have drawn greatly from this tradition of people "telling stories" in the company of others and obtaining a healing or dressing of psychic wounds through that experience.

Early psychoanalysts and therapists did not know the power of addiction and of addicted family life to disrupt the lives of children. Without a theory of addiction based on chemicals as disease-causing agents, undue emphasis may have been placed on the psychological causes of the addictions, both in those directly afflicted by them and in their children. Today, however, greater understanding of the addictive process and an understanding of the traumatic effects of growing up in substance-abusing families have come together to balance these misperceptions.

REFERENCES

Adams, R. D., Victor, M., & Mancall, E. (1959). Central pontine myelinolysis: A hitherto undescribed disease occurring in alcoholic and malnourished patients. *Archives of Neurology and Psychiatry, 81*, 136–145.

Alcoholics Anonymous (1939). *The AA big book.* New York: Author.

Alcoholics Anonymous (1968, Jan.) The Bill W.–Carl Jung letters. AA *Grapevine,* 17–20.

Alcoholics Anonymous (1976). *The AA big book* (3rd ed.). New York: Alcoholics Anonymous World Services.

American Psychiatric Association (1987). *Diagnostic and statistical manual of mental disorders* (3rd ed., rev.). Washington, DC: Author.

Bateson, G. (1971). The cybernetics of "self": A theory of alcoholism. *Psychiatry, 134*(1), 1–18.

Bean-Bayog, M. (1986). Psychopathology produced by alcoholism. In R. E. Meyer (Ed.), *Psychopathology and addictive disorders* (pp. 334–345). New York: Guilford Press.

Berne, E. (1964). *Games people play.* New York: Grove Press.

Black, C. (1981). *It will never happen to me! Children of alcoholics: As youngsters—adolescents—adults.* Denver, CO: Medical Administration Corp.

Blume, S. B. (1985). Group psychotherapy in the treatment of alcoholism. In S. Zimberg,

J. Wallace, & S. B. Blume (Eds.), *Practical approaches to alcoholism psychotherapy* (2d ed., pp. 73–86). New York: Plenum Press.

Brown, S. (1987). *Treating adult children of alcoholics: A developmental perspective.* New York: Wiley.

Cermak, T. (1986). *Diagnosing and treating co-dependence of alcoholics.* Minneapolis, MN: Johnson Institute Books.

Dulfano, C. (1982). *Families, alcoholism, and recovery, ten stories.* Center City, MN: Hazeldon.

Elkin, M. (1984). *Families under the influence: Changing alcoholic patterns.* New York: Norton.

Fawzy, F. L., Coombs, R. H., & Gerber, B. (1983). Generational continuity in the use of substances: The impact of parental substance use on adolescent substance use. *Addictive Behaviors, 8,* 109–114.

Feinichel, O. (1945). *The psychoanalytic theory of neurosis* (pp. 375–380). New York: Norton.

Fingarette, H. (1988). *Heavy drinking: The myth of alcoholism as a disease.* Berkeley, CA: University of California Press.

Fleischman, P. R. (1989). *The healing zone: Psychotherapy and spiritual issues.* New York: Paragon Press.

Fossum, M. A., & Mason, M. J. (1986). *Facing shame: Families in recovery.* New York: Norton.

Freud, S. (1974/1909). Family romances. In *The standard edition of the complete psychological works of Sigmund Freud* (James Strachey, Trans.; Vol. IX, pp. 235–244). London: Hogarth Press.

Freud, S. (1974/1911). Formulations on two principles of mental functioning. In *The standard edition of the complete psychological works of Sigmund Freud* (James Strachey, Trans.; Vol. XII, pp. 213–226). London: Hogarth Press.

Freud, S. (1974/1912). Types of onset of neurosis. In *The standard edition of the complete psychological works of Sigmund Freud* (James Strachey, Trans.; Vol. XII, pp. 227–238). London: Hogarth Press.

Freud, S. (1974/1915). Instincts and their vicissitudes. In *The standard edition of the complete psychological works of Sigmund Freud* (James Strachey, Trans.; Vol. XIV, pp. 109–140). London: Hogarth Press.

Freud, S. (1974/1923). The ego and the id. In *The standard edition of the complete psychological works of Sigmund Freud* (James Strachey, Trans.; Vol. XIX, pp. 65–144). London: Hogarth Press.

Freud, S. (1974/1927). The future of an illusion. In *The standard edition of the complete psychological works of Sigmund Freud* (James Strachey, Trans.; Vol. XXI, pp. 1–56). London: Hogarth Press.

Fromm-Reichmann, F. (1952). Some aspects of psychoanalytic psychotherapy with schizophrenics. In E. B. Brody & F. C. Redlich (Eds.), *Psychotherapy with schizophrenics* (pp. 143–168). New York: International Universities Press.

Gay, P. (1988). *Freud: A life for our time* (p. 169). New York: Norton.

Glover, E. (1956). The aetiology of alcoholism. In *On the early developmental mind* (pp. 81–90). New York: International Universities Press.

Gonzales, E. V. (1988). Integrated treatment approach with the chemically dependent young adult. In T. Rivinus (Ed.), *Alcoholism/chemical dependency in the college student* (pp. 147–176). New York: Haworth Press.

Goodwin, D. W. (1988). *Is alcoholism hereditary?* New York: Ballantine.

Group for the Advancement of Psychiatry (GAP) (1966). *Psychopathological disorders in childhood: Theoretical considerations and a proposed classification* (pp. 183–194, 225–228). New York: Author.

Herman, J. L., Perry, J. C., & Van der Kolk, B. A. (1989). Childhood trauma in borderline personality disorder. *American Journal of Psychiatry, 146*(4), 490–495.

Jellinek, E. M. (1942). An outline of basic policies for research programs on problems of alcohol. *Journal of Studies on Alcohol, 3,* 103–124.

Jellinek, E. M. (1960). *The disease concept of alcoholism.* New Haven, CT: College & University Press.

Jung, C. G. (1970). The undiscovered self. In *Collected works of C. G. Jung* (R. E. C. Hull, Trans.; 2nd ed.; Vol. 10). Princeton, NJ: Princeton University Press.

Knight, R. P. (1937). The psychodynamics of chronic alcoholism. *Journal of Nervous and Mental Disease, 86,* 538–548.

Kohut, H. (1984). How does analysis cure? In A. Goldberg (Ed.), *How does analysis cure?* Chicago: University of Chicago Press.

Kohut, H. (1985). *Self psychology and the humanities: Reflections on a new psychoanalytic approach.* New York: Norton.

Kuhn, T. (1970). *The structure of scientific revolutions.* Chicago: University of Chicago Press.

Kurtz, E. E. (1979). *Not–God: A history of Alcoholics Anonymous.* Center City, MN: Hazeldon.

Lender, M. E., & Martin, J. K. (1982). *Drinking in America: A history.* New York: Free Press.

Meyer, R. E. (1986). *Psychopathology and addictive disorders.* New York: Guilford Press.

Miller, A. (1983). *For your own good: Hidden cruelty in childrearing and the roots of violence.* New York: Farrar, Strauss, Giraux.

Minuchin, S. (1974). *Families and family therapy.* Cambridge, MA: Harvard University Press.

Mosher, P. W. (Ed.) (1987). *Title, key word, and author index to psychoanalytic journals, 1920–1986.* New York: American Psychoanalytic Association.

Oscar-Berman, M. (1987). Neuropsychological consequences of alcohol abuse: Questions, hypotheses, and models. In O. A. Parsons, N. Butters, & P. E. Nathan (Eds.), *Neuropsychology of alcoholism: Implications for diagnosis and treatment* (pp. 256–272). New York: Guilford Press.

Peterfreund, E. (1983). *The process of psychoanalytic therapy: Models and strategies.* Hillsdale, NJ: Analytic Press.

Rado, S. (1933). The psychoanalysis of pharmacothymia (drug addiction). *Psychoanalytic Quarterly, 2,* 1–23.

Rush, B. (1790). *An inquiry into the effects of spiritous liquors on the human body.* Boston.

Russell, M., Henderson, C., & Blume, S. B. (1985). *Children of alcoholics: A review of the literature*. New York: Children of Alcoholics Foundation.

Satir, V. (1972). *Peoplemaking*. Palo Alto, CA: Science & Behavior Books.

Schaef, A. W. (1987). *When society becomes an addict*. San Francisco: Harper & Row.

Steinglass, P., Bennett, L. A., Wolin, D. S. J., & Reiss, D. (1987). *The alcoholic family*. New York: Basic Books.

Stern, D. N. (1985). *The interpersonal world of the infant: A view from psychoanalysis and developmental psychology*. New York: Basic Books.

Tiebout, H. M. (1954). The ego factors in surrender in alcoholism. *Journal of Studies on Alcohol, 15*, 610–621.

Treadway, D. C. (1989). *Before it's too late: Working with substance abuse in the family*. New York: Norton.

Vaillant, G. E. (1977). *Adaptation to life* (pp. 73–192). Boston: Little, Brown.

Vaillant, G. E. (1983). *The natural history of alcoholism: Causes, patterns and paths to recovery*. Cambridge, MA: Harvard University Press.

Van der Kolk, B. A. (1987). The separation cry and the trauma response: Developmental issues in the psychobiology of attachment separation. In B. A. van der Kolk (Ed.), *Psychological trauma* (pp. 31–62). Washington, DC: American Psychiatric Press.

Wegscheider, S. (1981). *Another chance: A hope and help for children of alcoholics*. Palo Alto, CA: Science & Behavior Books.

Whitfield, C. L. (1984). Co-alcoholism: Recognizing a treatable illness. *Family and Community Health, 7*, 16–27.

Whitfield, C. L. (1985). *Alcoholism and spirituality*. East Rutherford, NJ: Perrin.

Winokur, G., Cadoret, R., Baker, M., et al. (1975). The depression spectrum disease versus pure depressive disease: Some further data. *British Journal of Psychiatry, 127*, 75–77.

Woodside, M. (1988). Research on children of alcoholics: Past and future. *British Journal of Addiction, 83*, 785–792.

Wurmser, L. (1978). *The hidden dimension: Psychodynamics in compulsive drug use*. New York: Aronson.

PART II

DIAGNOSTIC PERSPECTIVES

6

The Relationship Between Codependence and Narcissism

Timmen Cermak, M.D.

Being aware that a client was raised by a chemically dependent parent is extraordinarily useful information for a therapist. But it is never diagnostically sufficient to limit one's description of an individual to the fact that they are a child of an alcoholic/drug addict (COA). A full psychological evaluation is still in order (Cermack, 1990).

At the Genesis Psychotherapy and Training Center, where the author serves as clinical director, we have developed an evaluation procedure that automatically assesses adult COAs on six different axes. This chapter focuses mainly on one of these axes (codependence) and introduces the other five in order to provide an overall perspective.

There are four primary sources of psychopathology that may contribute to the clinical picture of any given COA. First, there is the *biological* propensity to alcoholism and drug addiction that a significant minority inherit from their chemically dependent parent. As a result, the mere fact that a client is an adult COA raises a high enough index of suspicion (in the same way that a history of blackouts might) that a full chemical-use history is in order. In actual practice, this history is generalized to include an exploration of all compulsive behavior or obsessive mental activity. Second, the *stress* that many COAs experience throughout their childhood often leads to characteristics that are the primary and direct result of trauma. Recent work by Terr (1983) and Eth and Pynoos (1985) documents the fact that symptoms of post-traumatic stress (and, indeed, the full-blown disorder itself, PTSD) exist in children and adolescents (see also Chapter 7). Such symptoms include an intrusive state, in which thoughts, images, affects, and behavior well uncontrollably into awareness, and a state of psychic numbing, in which affect is constricted, amnesia

131

exists, and dissociation is prevalent. PTSD also produces hypervigilance, a chronic state of autonomic and psychological arousal, and a foreshortened sense of the future (see also Chapter 7). I call these influences "the wound." Third, there is the characteristic way of *coping* with problems and stresses that is learned in a wide variety of dysfunctional homes, but in none more intensely than those rendered dysfunctional by active chemical dependence. I call these influences "the wound care." Just as any laceration can be worsened by inadequate care, so can the effects of stress be compounded by a self-defeating strategy for dealing with that stress. It is this facet of the COA's experience, currently referred to as codependence, that is the focus of this chapter. Fourth, there is the fact that chemically dependent families do not provide children with the full complement of experiences normally expected in our society. As adults, people are often unaware of random *lacunae in their learning*. As a result, they may complain of not knowing what "normal" is. Rather than automatically interpreting such a complaint from a client as resistance, it is sometimes useful to recognize that the client may, in fact, never have seen a birthday party, a family vacation, or an argument that did not lead to physical violence. I label this "underlearning," and attempt to respond to it with education, rather than introspection, when appropriate.

Readers familiar with Theodore Millon's (1981) work may recognize the parallel between the framework above and his assertion that the etiology of personality disorders lies in a combination of the following factors.

- Temperament (i.e., biology)
- Pathological learning, from:

  —events that create intense anxiety;
  —emotionally neutral models of behavior that reinforce coping strategies that are deleterious when generalized to settings for which they are unsuitable;
  —insufficient experiences requisite to learning adaptive behaviors.

This parallel is intentional, and reflects the author's belief that a family environment disrupted by chemical dependency is fertile ground for the production of personality pathology.

Two additional axes for evaluating COAs include probing for *dual diagnosis* and estimating the *stage of recovery*. "Dual diagnosis" is simply a further reminder that COAs can have clinically relevant issues and pathology that are not directly related to being from an alcoholic home, such as being vegetatively depressed, manic-depressive, borderline, schizophrenic, etc. The "stage of recovery" refers to progress that a client may have made primarily through participation in self-help recovery programs. A thorough understanding of the healing dynamic activated by the self-help modality provides therapists with either an invaluable adjunct to therapy to recommend, or a base on which to begin the therapeutic process if the client has already entered a program of recovery. The remainder of this chapter focuses on the third axis—"the wound care."

Diagnostic clarity has been hindered by confusion regarding the concept of codependence, including its definition, etiology, and relationship to the full spectrum of characteristics seen in adult children of alcoholics/drug addicts. I approach this confusion by defining codependence within the general *Diagnostic and Statistical Manual of Mental Disorders*, revised third edition (American Psychiatric Association, 1987) framework of personality traits/disorders and proposing that it exists in a complementary relationship to narcissism. I further propose that codependence successfully fills a theoretical void suggested by Freud (1914/1963), and that the genetic sources of codependence and narcissism are, on one level, identical. Both have their genesis in defective mirroring during the phases of symbiosis and separation-individuation. An interplay between two factors determines the mixture of codependence and narcissism which develops in any given individual: the *context* within which defective mirroring occurs (i.e., the amount of affect attunement available from parents), and the *specific needs* which are defectively mirrored (i.e., the relative traumatic frustration or overstimulation of two primary interpersonal needs—to be the center and to merge with an idealized parent).

EXPANDING THE MYTH OF NARCISSUS

Just as the prototype of narcissism is found in Greek mythology, so is the prototype for codependence. The following myth, which might best be called the "Myth of Narcissus and Echo," encapsulates more ancient wisdom than often meets the eye.

Echo was the fairest of the wood nymphs, but had been condemned by Hera (the jealous wife of Zeus) never to speak except to repeat what had been said to her. This curse was hardest to bear when she fell in love with Narcissus, a young man of great beauty. It is a misconception that Narcissus' fatal flaw lay in becoming enamored of his own reflection; this was actually the punishment visited on him by Nemesis (the goddess of righteous anger). He was punished because he refused to return love to anyone showing affection for him. He scorned those who adored him, and never responded to their affection. Therefore, Nemesis caused him to fall in love with his own reflection in order to experience the same fate.

After Narcissus' death, Echo's fate was that her flesh became insubstantial, while her bones turned into cold stone. Today, all that can be found of Echo is her voice, in canyons and caves, still repeating what others have said.

The myth of Narcissus and Echo outlines a complementary relationship between two partners, one of whom is mirrored predominately by the other. Narcissus is to Echo as narcissism is to codependence. Their complementary relationship did not escape Freud (1914/1963), who wrote that ". . . one person's narcissism has a great attraction for those who have renounced part of their own narcissism and are seeking after object-love" p. 70. Freud further said, "The disturbances to which the original narcissism of the child is exposed, the reactions with which he seeks to protect himself from them, the paths into which he is thereby forced—these are themes which I shall leave on one side, as an important field for work which still awaits exploration . . ." (p. 72). To date, most of the work that has occurred in this field has focused on individuals in whom narcissistic traits become solidified and excessive. Less work has been done on those who seek object-love by renouncing their narcissism. Alice Miller (1981) and others have broken important ground in this incompletely explored field, particularly in focusing on the intergenerational effects of narcissistically wounded parents.

It is remarkable that the specific effects of growing up with an alcoholic parent have been so pervasively ignored throughout the history of psychoanalytical thought, including Miller's work. Although there can be no simple equation of active alcoholism with clinically significant narcissism, the following passages from the *Big Book* of Alcoholics Anonymous (AA, 1976) point to a direct connection between the two that should not be ignored:

Selfishness—self-centeredness! That, we think, is the root of our troubles.
. . . We invariably find that at some time in the past we have made decisions based on self which later placed us in a position to be hurt. . . . The alcoholic is an extreme example of self-will run riot. (p. 62)

Heinz Kohut (1977) supports AA's assertions (see also Chapter 5). He sees narcissistic issues at the center of psychopathology in all addictions, writing: "It is the structural void in the self that the addict tries to fill. . . . It is the lack of self-esteem of the unmirrored self, the uncertainty about the very existence of the self, the dreadful feeling of fragmentation of the self that the addict tries to counteract by his addictive behavior" (p. 197). Whether narcissism preceded a client's chemical dependence, or developed during the active stages of addiction, it is ultimately of therapeutic importance during sobriety to face it directly. Levin (1987) has outlined how self psychology's understanding of narcissism is particularly useful during the therapeutic process that follows diagnosing the addiction and educating patients well enough that they attain abstinence.

The threads being gathered above begin to weave into a tapestry. Narcissism is a strong element in addiction, and exists in a complementary relationship with something, currently called codependence, in the chemical dependence field. As difficult as the narcissistic stance of an addict is to deal with for other adults, its power is raised exponentially for developing children, for whom the addict is parent and primary role model. Before proceeding with exploring the tapestry further, it is best to study one of the threads in greater detail—the diagnostic criteria for codependence.

ECHOISM: CODEPENDENT PERSONALITY TRAITS AND DISORDER

Within the chemical dependency community, the concept of codependence (or coalcoholism, as it was originally known) has been accepted as an important phenomenon ever since the systems theory of family therapists began to affect the field. In *I'll Quit Tomorrow*, Johnson (1973) described the "ism" of alcoholism as being the same illness as codependence. Overstating the case a bit, he writes: "The only difference between the alcoholic and the spouse, in instances where the latter does not drink, is that one is physically affected by alcohol; otherwise both have all the symptoms" (p. 30).

As long as the "ism" of alcoholism remained only vaguely defined (despite the fact that any good chemical dependency therapist can identify its clinical manifestations), and as long as codependents were largely identified through their relationship to an alcoholic, the concept was bound to remain parochial and of solely empirical value. However, recently it has become clear to some clinicians that codependence exists in family systems with no history of addiction; and work with COAs has demonstrated the extent to which individuals can develop a codependent personality structure early in life and subsequently carry it into a series of dysfunctional relationships throughout adulthood. Therefore, codependence has no essential relationship to the addictions and can be wholly internalized. It does not require that an individual be in active relationships to exist.

Two major roadblocks to including codependence in our formal diagnostic nomenclature are its apparent ubiquity and the continued lack of a clinically useful definition. Described by some critics as "a condition of the 20th century," codependence is often dismissed as social commentary. If nearly everyone appears to be codependent, the argument goes, then how can it be considered a disease?

The answer to the problem of ubiquity lies in DSM-III-R's distinction between personality *traits* and personality *disorders*, a distinction that is directly applicable to codependence. According to DSM-III-R (American Psychiatric Association, 1987), personality traits are "enduring patterns of perceiving, relating to, and thinking about the environment and oneself . . . exhibited in a wide range of important social and personal contexts" (p. 335). Personality traits only become disorders when they are "inflexible and maladaptive and cause either significant functional impairment or significant subjective distress" (p. 335).

The critical point for our purposes is that, while codependent traits may be widespread, the diagnosis of codependent personality disorder can only be made in the face of identifiable dysfunction resulting from excessive rigidity or intensity associated with these traits. Similarly, narcissistic traits are nearly universal, but narcissistic personality disorder only exists in the face of objective dysfunction. There seems to be no reason why the same reasoning cannot be applied to codependence.

DIAGNOSTIC CRITERIA FOR CODEPENDENCY

In an earlier publication (Cermak, 1986), I attempted to address the vagueness in definitions of codependence by advancing a set of specific criteria. As with the criteria for current personality-disorder categories, it is as much the distinct pattern of these criteria as it is the criteria themselves that define the diagnosis. The criteria as set down in my 1986 book (p. 11) are as follows:

A. Continued investment of self-esteem in the ability to influence/control feelings and behavior, both in oneself and in others, in the face of serious adverse consequences.
B. Assumption of responsibility for meeting others' needs, to the exclusion of acknowledging one's own needs.
C. Anxiety and boundary distortions around intimacy and separation.
D. Enmeshment in relationships with personality-disordered, chemically dependent, and impulse-disordered individuals.
E. Exhibits at least three of the following:
   1. Excessive reliance on denial
   2. Constriction of emotions (+/− dramatic outburts)
   3. Depression
   4. Hypervigilance
   5. Compulsions
   6. Anxiety
   7. Substance abuse
   8. Recurrent victim of physical or sexual abuse
   9. Stress-related medical illnesses
   10. Has remained in a primary relationship with an active substance abuser for at least two years without seeking outside support

If codependence were accepted as an Axis II DSM disorder, what would be its relationship to the other personality disorders? To begin with, codependence would fit into cluster B (dramatic, emotional, or erratic) or C (anxious or fearful) of DSM-III-R more than cluster A (odd or eccentric) (American Psychiatric Association, 1987, p. 337). Cluster C includes dependent, avoidant, obsessive-compulsive, and passive-aggressive personality disorders, each of which has some elements in common with codependence. Dependent personalities overlap considerably with codependence, especially in their fear of rejection, preoccupation with fears of abandonment, and willingness to do things that are unpleasant or demeaning in order to get other people to like them. There is one primary distinction between codependent and dependent personalities without which the two might collapse into the same disorder—the secretly active, manipulatory, and willful nature of the codependents' relationship to the world. Dependent personalities are passive, submissive, self-effacing, and docile. Whereas codependents may appear to be this way on the surface, they are nonetheless taking full responsibility for trying to control their world, or feeling deep guilt for being unable to do so. This apparent internal contradiction in codependence between feeling impotent while assuming a grandiose sense of what willpower ought to be able to accomplish is parallel to the internal contradiction within narcissistic personalities between their grandiosity and depression. This distorted relationship to willpower is also identical with the alcoholic/drug addict's prideful need to maintain self-esteem by denying a loss of control. This results in codependents' being more vulnerable to narcissistic wounds than dependent personalities.

Although codependent personalities possess many of the same social discomforts as avoidant personalities, being easily hurt by criticism and fearing embarrassment in front of other people, they generally demonstrate a degree of enmeshment in relationships that is not seen in avoidant personalities. Avoidance of social contact in codependence is usually counterphobic behavior, and not a core dynamic. While codependents can also demonstrate many obsessive-compulsive qualities (especially perfectionism, indecisiveness, and the use of preoccupation with a variety of matters to avoid underlying affect), there is usually no lack of generosity (begrudging as it may be) in giving when no personal gain is likely to result. In a similar way, codependents can be quite passive-aggressive, but their style is likely to be the opposite of protesting, without justification, that others make unreasonable demands on them or avoiding obligations. When passive-aggressive behavior is seen in codependents, it is more the result of years of resentment accumulating without an avenue for direct expression rather than a definition of their core dynamic. These last three personality disorders also do not speak in any way to the central themes within codependents of a distorted relationship to willpower and sacrificing identity for intimacy.

Cluster B contains antisocial, histrionic, borderline, and narcissistic personality disorders. Antisocial personalities are almost the antithesis of codependents. Even such features as a disregard for the truth, which codependents demonstrate vis-à-vis their own inner feelings, stem from an entirely different internal dynamic. The other three overlap with codependence. Histrionic personalities are similar to codependents in their turning to others for protection, their constant requirement for acceptance and approval, and their exquisite sensitivity to the moods and thoughts of those whom they wish to please. However, the lack of tolerance for the frustration of delayed gratification is quite different from the tendency of codependents to be long-suffering martyrs, and may be a reflection of the general shallowness characteristic of histrionics, but not necessarily of codependents.

The distinction between borderline and codependent personality disorders can be extremely difficult to make, especially when the latter is particularly severe. It must be kept in mind that the two syndromes can, and do, coexist. The features that are most commonly shared by the two are chronic feelings of emptiness, efforts to avoid real or imagined abandonment, and a blurring of interpersonal boundaries. For the codependent, this blurring of boundaries takes place most often during periods when the interpersonal distance from others is in flux, or requires negotiation. Like borderlines, codependents do best when stable boundaries are maintained by the external environment. In general, the greater severity of disturbance in borderlines creates a qualitative difference between the two categories. This severity leads to an intensity of affective instability, a depth of polymorphous identity disturbance, and a tendency to cycle between overidealizing and devaluing others that is not usually seen in codependents, who are far too involved in maintaining a façade of normality. There is a confusion between fusion and intimacy in both disorders. But while the borderline is often incapable of maintaining stable interpersonal boundaries, the codependent just as often has this capability, but chooses to dismantle these boundaries in a misguided search for intimacy.

Narcissistic personality disorder is inextricably bound to codependent personality disorder, but the exact nature of their relationship still needs to be addressed. The same core dynamics seem to operate in each, although often in opposite directions, and the same life issues are cathected. These issues include specialness, grandiosity/insignificance, continuous hypersensitivity to the evaluation of others (although the narcissist breaks contact with critics and the codependent tries harder to please critics, both are similarly obsessed), entitlement or lack thereof, fantasies of power, and the existence or lack of empathy in relationships. Narcissists are concerned about a partner's empathy for them, and codependents are concerned about their own empathy for their partners. Because both focus on the same person, the two syndromes interact synergistically.

There is the same element of existential all-or-nothingness in both narcissism and codependence. If the people surrounding the narcissist stop mirroring him or her, so the narcissist can no longer bask in his or her own reflected glory, the relationship ceases. Others are no longer related to as fully human if they become truly autonomous. For the narcissist, it is the other who ceases to exist. For the codependent, who has sought relationship by becoming the mirror that confirms the narcissist's specialness, it is his or her own existence that is jeopardized by cessation of the relationship. The conundrum for codependents is that they do not achieve the pseudo-autonomy of the narcissist, and feel their existence threatened by any movement in the direction of real autonomy.

The essential relationship between codependence and narcissism being postulated here raises many questions. Are the two complementary in the sense of being two ends of an identifiable continuum? Such a relationship implies the existence of a common dynamic process underlying both. Is codependence a variant of narcissism, perhaps the result of a defensive posture in response to narcissistic traits? Is it simply narcissism itself, in need of being called what it is? Or does some other relationship to narcissism exist that is not yet clear as a possibility?

As we clarify these questions and rely on our understanding of child development and self psychology to answer them, the concept of codependence will begin to be seen as an inevitable part of any psychology of personality, with an essential, complementary relationship to narcissism. The following sections continue developing the concept of codependence with an eye toward fitting it into a long unfilled gap in our theoretical framework.

THE INTERFACE BETWEEN NARCISSISM AND CODEPENDENCE

The cause of Narcissus' imperviousness to affection is unclear, but may stem from the oracle at Delphi's response when Narcissus' mother asked how long her son would live. "As long as he shall not know himself," was the answer. Was it in search of eternal life that Narcissus withheld himself from bonding to others? It is, after all, through allowing ourselves to be loved that we come to know much of who we are. And Narcissus apparently felt that true relationship with another was a threat to his life.

Without presuming to do justice to the voluminous literature on narcissism, for the purposes of this chapter, I conceive of narcissism as a disorder of bonding, leading to significant amounts of psychic energy arrested in the symbiotic phase. Movement into the separation-individuation phase is blocked. As opposed to the borderline, who is constantly warding off separation anxiety stemming from attachment followed by abandonment, the narcissist is left to ward off the panic and depression of nonattachment.

Existence and connection to others are inextricably intertwined, and it is in this dynamic that narcissism and codependence find their meeting ground. What differentiates the two is whose existence is threatened when connection with others is broken. Narcissists cannot see others as existing separately from themselves. The codependent cannot see himself or herself as existing separately from others. These are two sides of the same coin. The currency is the same, which is to say that the interpersonal dynamics entered into by each is the same. What is different is that the valence of this currency is in opposite directions, and so the subjective experience each has can be quite different.

Narcissistic individuals have great difficulty in forming human connections, *except* when they see aspects of themselves mirrored in the other. Codependent individuals gain their sense of self through connecting with others they mirror. Together, they form the perfect couple for demonstrating what Melanie Klein (1946) called projective identification.

Bonding with autonomous individuals is outside the realm of conception for the narcissist, since such people provide inadequate mirroring. Existence without mirroring someone else is out of the realm of conception for codependents. The powerful attachment between codependent and narcissist is illustrated nicely in mythology. Other maidens had fallen in love with Narcissus, but he could not have cared less. However, when confronted by Echo's exact mirroring, Narcissus was touched emotionally for the first time. We know this is true because he stormed up to Echo at one point, saying, "I will die before I give you power over me!"

Exhortations such as this are generally good evidence that one member of a couple has penetrated the defensive armor of the other. Echo's response, of course, was, "I give you power over me." Narcissus was disgusted. And what disgusts us more than those parts of ourselves that we have rejected? Recall again what Freud (1914/1963) said, "One person's narcissism has a great attraction for those others who have renounced part of their own narcissism and are seeking after object-love. . . ." This explains, through the mechanism of projective identification, how it is that the codependent often experiences the disowned self-disgust of the narcissist.

The "chemistry" that exists between the narcissist and the codependent can be experienced in a variety of ways, from falling in love, to an immediate sense of familiarity ("It's as though we had known each other for years"), to the excitement and drama of compulsive attraction to each other. The phrase "addiction to relationship," commonly seen in the popular press, captures the subjective quality of being harmfully enmeshed in the complementarity of a narcissistic/codependent dyad.

NARCISSISM, CODEPENDENCE, AND CHILD DEVELOPMENT

Assuming that codependence is a legitimate constellation of personality traits that are capable of crystallizing into a true disorder, it is useful to reflect on its developmental origins. This would be considerably easier if both the nature and genesis of traditional personality disorders were fully delineated. But such is not the case. We immediately enter an area of fluctuating controversy. For the purpose of narrowing the focus of this chapter, I shall restrict myself to the development of primary codependence, which becomes integrated into a child's core identity, versus secondary codependence, which results from regressive use of less mature defenses during adulthood, often in response to a gradually deteriorating relationship with a chemically dependent spouse.

Masterson's work (1981) on the narcissistic and borderline disorders serves as a useful point of entry, because he has placed each into the generally accepted developmental work of Mahler (1975). Even as Masterson (1981) outlines the main clinical characteristics of narcissistic personality disorder, he opens the door for its relationship with codependence. The narcissistic patient is described as being grandiose, being extremely self-involved, lacking interest in and empathy for others, and being endlessly motivated "to find others who will mirror and admire his/her grandiosity" (p. 7). The question facing us involves the diagnostic and etiological delineation of those personalities that are overly involved in mirroring and admiring the narcissist's grandiosity.

Narcissism presents with a variety of clinical pictures. For example, Meissner (Masterson, 1981, p. 8) lists the following:

1. Phallic-narcissistic
2. Nobel-prize narcissistic
3. Manipulative or psychopathic
4. Needy, clinging, and demanding

And Masterson adds:

5. Closet narcissists (who present as timid and shy, but reveal their arrogance in the course of therapy)

If narcissism can indeed present as "needy, clinging, and demanding" behavior, this raises the possibility that Narcissus and Echo are simply two manifestations of the same underlying process.

Within the perspective, advanced by Masterson (1981), Kohut (1977), and Miller (1981), the etiological agent in narcissism is defective mirroring. This defect occurs when a primary caretaker withdraws emotionally as the child begins to develop his or her own unique self. The autonomy of the child is impermissible because it resists resonating with the projections the parent tries to place on the child in order to shape him or her for use as an object essential to maintain the parent's own intrapsychic equilibrium (Masterson, 1981, pp. 22–23). As Miller (1981, p. 85) poignantly writes, probably the greatest of narcissistic wounds is not to have been loved just as one truly is.

The etiological agent for narcissism, as described above, would initially appear to be exactly the same as that for codependence. Children from alcoholic homes who satisfy the criteria for codependence as adults often have vivid memories, with intense affective associations, of the painful moments when an intoxicated parent was unable to focus on their needs, and instead demanded, either overtly or covertly, that the child attend to the parent's needs if there was going to be any substantial connection between the two. Since a narcissism and codependence are distinguishable, other factors must come into play in their genesis. The two additional factors proposed are that different aspects of the child can be defectively mirrored (*specific needs*) and that different kinds of mirroring defects exist (*the context*). In the last case, narcissism and codependence would result from the same general class of etiological agents (i.e., defective mirroring), but the specific way in which mirroring was defective could account for the development of distinct personality structures. Furthermore, if the ways in which mirroring was defective, or the needs that were defectively mirrored were themselves complementary, it would rationalize the complementary relationship that seems to exist between the narcissist, who only connects with people willing to mirror him or her perfectly, and the codependent, who is particularly skilled at taking on other people's characteristics.

The defective mirroring leading to narcissism is postulated to happen during Mahler's symbiotic phase. The most severe defects of mirroring would necessarily come earliest and take the form of an inability, or unwillingness, on the parent's part to enter into the child's psychological state of symbiotic union with the parent. The child's efforts to bond with the parent are met by a parent who does not bond in return. A lesser defect would exist at the other end of the symbiotic phase, when the dual process of separation and individuation begin to take the child out of symbiotic union. It should be seen that the parent who resists a child's developmentally driven urge to leave symbiosis would be dealing from a very different set of internal needs than the parent who resists entering into a bond with the child from the beginning. Obviously, "defective mirroring" can be motivated by very different parental needs and can take very different forms as far as the child's experience is concerned.

In general, the Masterson–Mahler approach to narcissism and its etiology fails to delineate the *range* of defects of mirroring that exist and the need to specify more clearly the different effects each has on developing personality structures. The following framework outlines the various disturbances that can affect the processes of symbiosis and separation/individuation and lead to personality pathology: Mahler (1975) postulated separation and individuation to be two complementary, intertwined, but not identical processes. They can proceed at different paces, and can be partially achieved in innumerable degrees and forms. Separation is *driven* by physical development and "consists of the child's emergence from a symbiotic fusion with the mother" (p. 4). Facets of separation include differentiation, distancing, boundary formation, and disengagement. Individuation, on the other hand, is *pulled* by the developing sense of self, and "consists of those achievements marking the child's assumption of his own individual characteristics" (p. 4). Facets of individuation include the evolution of intrapsychic autonomy, perception, memory, cognition, and reality testing.

The verbs "driven" and "pulled" are vividly suggestive of the two competing frameworks of traditional psychoanalytic theory and self psychology. Traditional psychoanalytic theory focuses on the internal forces that "drive" human development, and outlines how these drives can come into conflict with each other. On the other hand, self psychology focuses on the emerging organizations within individuals that coalesce into deeper and deeper levels of self, which pulls development into new areas (Stern, 1985).

Figure 6-1 visually demonstrates the dual processes of separation and individuation. In healthy development, the child and the parent mature in tandem, and the dual processes of separation and individuation proceed in such harmony that there is little to distinguish the two from each other. It is in the pathological situation that the differential between separation and individuation becomes more important. The figure may help conceptualize the difference between these two processes by showing the opposite of being individuated as being identical and the opposite of being separate as being dependent.

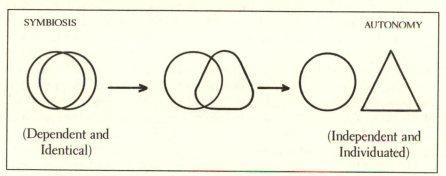

Figure 6-1. *The dual processes of separation and individuation*

Figure 6-2 begins to explore the matrix of potential parental attitudes toward the development of the child from dependence to independence (i.e., separation) and from being identical to being individuated (i.e., individuation). The total lack of separation and individuation is labeled symbiosis. The achievement of independence and individuation is labeled autonomy. The matrix assumes that parents can have a variety of attitudes toward each element of a child's development, creating a complexity that almost outstrips our capacity to conceptualize the phenomena in question.

Parent's Attitude	Child's Development	Parent's Attitude
	SYMBIOSIS ────────────→ AUTONOMY	
Unaware Intolerant Needing Unpredictable Accepting	DEPENDENT ___(Separation)___→ INDEPENDENT	Unaware Intolerant Needing Unpredictable Accepting
Unaware Intolerant Needing Unpredictable Accepting	IDENTICAL ___(Individuation)___→ INDIVIDUATED	Unaware Intolerant Needing Unpredictable Accepting

Figure 6-2. *Potential parental attitudes toward each part of the developmental process.* Reprinted with permission from T. Cermack's *Evaluating and Treating Adult Children of Alcoholics,* 1990, Vol. 1; 1991, mid-March, Vol. 2. © by Johnson Institute.

The matrix in Figure 6-2 outlines a wide variety of disturbances that can take place during the symbiotic and separation–individuation phases of development, and applies each disturbance to every facet of the process. For example, narcissistic parents may be so self-obsessed that they literally are unaware, or highly intolerant, of a child's dependence and need to develop independence. At the same time, they may give the mixed message that they need the child to be a perfect mirror and not individuate if the bond between them is to remain intact (i.e., "Don't depend on me, but be like me"). On the other hand, codependent parents may define themselves so much through how others relate to them that they need the child's dependence, and remain unaware, or become intolerant, of the development of independence. At the same time, they may give the mixed message, out of their own sense of shame, that they are uncomfortable with the child being a reflection (i.e., "Depend on me but don't be like me"). The narcissistic parent would end up encouraging independence, but demanding an absence of individuation if the child is going to maintain a connection with the parent. The codependent parent might encourage individuation (in order to have something to mirror), but discourage independence. Both narcissistic and codependent parents intensify the emotional charge surrounding issues of separation and individuation; and in both cases, the child is not being loved for who he or she is as a unique individual, "just as one truly is," which is the primary narcissistic wound that generates both narcissistic and codependent personalities.

Other parents, because of intermittent intoxication, psychosis, manic-depressive illness, or borderline instability, may unpredictably take all of these different stances. To the extent that a parent's personality structure is a mixture of narcissistic and codependent elements, there will also be a certain amount of unpredictability and arbitrariness in the messages a child receives (i.e., "Don't be like me, but don't be different"). A multitude of other combinations of disturbances could exist, but are not further explored in this chapter. For example, schizoid parents may be unaware of all facets of the developmental process in their child. And depressed parents may alternate between needing their child to be dependent and to be independent, and may also need their child to individuate as much as possible (i.e., "The more you are like me, the more I have failed as a parent"). The underlying point to be made is that "defective mirroring" exists in enough different manifestations that we should expect the consequences to vary widely.

Although the matrix of different attitudes parents can have toward the beginning and end points of the two processes of separation and individuation seems to be an accurate description of observable clinical phenomena, its complexity creates a theoretical quagmire and has limited clinical usefulness. Rather than attempt to sort through the entire complexity at once, it may be useful to narrow our inquiries. The following section describes the two most important factors determining the genesis of narcissism and codependence.

THE DIFFERENTIAL ETIOLOGY FOR NARCISSISM AND CODEPENDENCE

Alice Miller (1981) has written one of the most valuable books for anyone working with children of alcoholics (*The Drama of the Gifted Child*) without ever mentioning alcoholism or codependence. Her descriptions of how narcissisticly wounded parents in turn wound their children, by not seeing them for who they really are, seem to fit equally well for those children who develop narcissism and those who develop codependence. Within the framework of this basic "narcissistic" wound, we can now explore the two influences that determine whether a particular child predominantly develops a narcissistic or a codependent personality structure: the *context* within which the wound occurs, and the *specific needs* within the child that are most traumatically frustrated.

The Context

As the matrix of parental attitudes toward a child's separation–individuation illustrates, there are several different contexts within which the basic narcissistic wound can occur. Fairbairn (Cashdan, 1988, pp. 10–11) introduced the idea of such differing contexts when he wrote that pathogenic interactions with a parent can be either "rejecting" or "exciting" in nature. In other words, an age-appropriate need can be either traumatically rejected or encouraged beyond the point at which it is still age appropriate. In both cases, the parent is responding mainly to his or her own needs, and not to the unique qualities and needs of the child (i.e., the basic "narcissistic" wound).

It is here that Stern's (1985) descriptions of affect attunement prove invaluable. In his words, "The sharing of affective attunement is the most pervasive and clinically germane feature of intersubjective relatedness" (p. 138). A refinement of the concept of mirroring, affect attunement requires that a parent read the child's feeling state from the child's behavior and respond in a way that goes beyond mere imitation, leading to the child's receiving confirmation that his or her feeling state has been accurately perceived. Stern enriches our understanding of the subtleties of communication between parents and children by describing how it is the embedded attunements, especially with vitality affects (the energetic, kinetic aspects of our feeling experience, such as surging, fading, and bursting sensations) and not just with categorical affects (e.g., sadness, anger, joy), that are most responsible for creating the quality, if not even the substance, of human relationships.

It is through affect attunements, or the lack thereof, that parents unconsciously and inevitably communicate their actual feelings about a child's existence and developmental process. A parent who needs the child to be dependent responds to the feeling of dependence in the child and forms a reinforcing human connection around these feelings—a connection that falls into jeopardy when physical growth drives the child toward independence. All the attitudes of unawareness, needing, intolerance, and acceptance are communicated most effectively through those feelings in a child to which a parent is available to attune. No pretense on the parent's part, such as a forced smile to conceal irritability, can override the actual attunements occurring, or the lack thereof (Ekman & Friesen, 1989). Before a child learns to react primarily to what a parent says, rather than to what parent does, the child's organization of self has to advance to the stage where his or her own false self can enter into duplicity with the parent. From this point on, the relationship is between façades rather than between any important emotional realities. The wounds creating codependence and narcissism occur before such a false self exists, and are largely instrumental in nurturing its development.

When the wounds inflicted by a parent take place within an atmosphere of *deficient* affect attunement by the parent (corresponding to Fairbairn's "rejecting" parental interactions), children must provide greater-than-normal input to the relationship to maintain a sense of connectedness. When children cannot accomplish this, a profound sense of disconnection and chronic depression can result. In the most severe cases, autistic traits may develop. The core sense of inadequacy and low self esteem is of such depth that feelings of emptiness and void occupy the center of one's being. When children *are* capable of supplying enough emotional energy to sustain a bond with their parent, a core sense of inadequacy develops nonetheless. The habit of using excessive empathy in order to maintain relationships begins, but the child continually experiences the inability of even their greatest efforts to earn a response in kind. Affect attunements by the parent are scarce, and usually made to their own projections. If the child is to have any sense of connectedness, the only way of achieving this is to identify with these projections. Narcissus' children never feel entitled to be in a mutual relationship.

On the other hand, when a parent's inability to connect with the individual needs of their specific child occurs within an atmosphere of *excessive* affect attunements (corresponding to Fairbairn's "exciting" parental interactions), children must fight off their parents' continual efforts to fuse with them if any independence is to be achieved. A core sense of grandiosity develops, as the child becomes the center of his/her parent's life. The parents' tendency to be perfect mirrors provides children with unlimited opportunity to manipulate them, with little chance to experience mutuality in their relationships. No empathic connection need flow from the child to the parents in order for their bond to remain intact. Echo's children always feel entitled to be a center of their relationship.

These wounds are inflicted very early during child development, and it is prudent to assume that *no* age is too young to be impervious to their effects. Stern (1985, p. 11) places the development of a core sense of self between the ages of two and six months, during which a child first manifests evidence of a coherent sense of his or her own agency, affect, and history. These feelings must be attuned to by parents if they are to flourish. Then, during the seventh to 15th months, when,

Stern argues, children manifest a sense of self with inner experiences that can be shared with others, it is critical that their own internal reality be reflected back to them. When narcissistic wounds take place during these very early stages of child development, the sense of self on a core and an interpersonal level is affected. It is because codependence exists at this level, within the structure and experience of one's self, and not simply at the level of a conflict among drives or a set of dysfunctional beliefs, that it is justifiable to include it among the personality disorders.

Both the narcissist and the codependent have arrests at the symbiotic phase, or disturbances in the formation of their core and interpersonal self, depending on how one conceptualizes child development. But because they are differentiated by feelings of grandiosity versus inadequacy, they build different defensive structures to contend with the initial wounds.

Narcissists develop a pseudoindividuation, based on feelings of grandiosity, and as a protection against the disowned urge to be dependent. ("You must see my uniqueness.") Because the basis for their "individuation" is an unrealistic omnipotence, they have not discovered or developed their true self (which must be based in reality). Despite their pseudoindividuation, they remain unable to achieve true separation. They cannot relate to autonomous individuals because their only sense of human connectedness comes when they are being mirrored by others.

Codependents take the opposite tack. They discover and develop a pseudoseparation through the overassumption of responsibility for others. ("I become valuable by taking care of you.") This is based on a submerged grandiosity, and is not a separation, which is based in reality. Despite this pseudoseparation, they remain unable to individuate, and continually attempt to find their identity in others. Their only sense of human connectedness comes when they are being the perfect mirror. Autonomous individuals remain unable to relate to them. Buried beneath the grandiosity of the narcissist and the inadequacy of the codependent are the stark emotions of rage and panic. The narcissist's grandiosity more easily admits to feelings of rage. The codependent's sense of inadequacy more easily admits the feelings of panic.

The Specific Needs

Whether a child suffering from the basic "narcissistic" wound will develop a narcissistic or codependent personality structure is also determined by the specific needs that are "defectively mirrored." The possibility exists that the parent of a narcissistic individual resisted the child's separation more than the child's individuation, whereas the parent of a codependent individual resisted the child's individuation more than the child's separation. In either case, the symbiotic phase could not be left without losing the bond with parents.

This line of inquiry proves most fruitful if we look at the two needs Heinz Kohut (Cashdan, 1988, p. 21) identifies as healthy, age-appropriate narcissistic needs during the period in which a child emerges from symbiosis into the separation–individuation phase:

1. The need to have one's developing capabilities validated.
2. The need to form an idealized image of one's parent with which to merge.

Kohut (1971) acknowledges that these two needs "are, of course, antithetical. Yet they coexist from the beginning and their individual and largely independent lines of development are open to separate scrutiny." I propose that these two needs be reframed as age-appropriate "interpersonal needs," consisting of the complementary narcissistic need for omnipotence and the echoistic (i.e., codependent) need for dependence and merging. When the narcissistic need fails to mature into adult forms of self-confidence, it remains in its archaic form of the grandiose self, and narcissism results. When the echoistic need fails to mature into adult forms of appreciation and empathy for others, it remains in its archaic form of the idealized parent, and codependence results.

Therefore, the basic "narcissistic" wound is really a dual phenomenon, including both narcissistic and echoistic wounds. Every human suffers some wounding to each of these basic interpersonal needs. It is perhaps symptomatic of Western society's narrow focus on individualism as the ultimate goal that we have been more cognizant of the line of development, in both its healthy and pathological manifestations, stemming from narcissistic needs. This is supported by the work of Takeo Doi (1973), who has explored the Japanese comfort with dependence and the desire to be passively loved (*amae*), which is seen as a basic human need long neglected in the Western world.

The following framework (see Figure 3) results from separating Kohut's two narcissistic needs into complementary narcissistic and echoistic needs:

If the Parent's Personality is . . .	and the Child's Interpersonal Needs are . . .		then the Child's personality becomes . . .
	Narcissistic	*Echoistic*	
Narcissistic (Narcissus as only parent)	Ignored/Rejected "What I am is inadequate or bad"	Stimulated "I am valuable but only as a reflection of you"	Co-dependent
Co-dependent (Echo as only parent)	Stimulated "I am always enough."	Ignored/Rejected "My needs are unimportant or bad"	Narcissistic

Figure 6-3. Interaction between parental personality structure and child's interpersonal needs. Reprinted with permission from T. Cermack's *Evaluating and Treating Adult Children of Alcoholics*, 1990, Vol. 1; 1991, mid-March, Vol. 2. © by Johnson Institute.

1. Narcissistic parents will invalidate or reject their child's narcissistic needs. The child's "See me" encounters the parent's response, "Only as a reflection of myself." But the child's echoistic needs will be stimulated ("excited"), as the child's "You're great" encounters the parent's "I'm great." The result is that echoistic needs do not mature out of their archaic form and narcissistic needs are disowned. The child develops an echoistic (or codependent) personality structure.

2. Codependent parents stimulate narcissistic needs by responding to a child's "I'm great" with confirmation ("Yes, you're great"). On the other hand, echoistic needs are invalidated or rejected. The child's "You're great" encounters the parent's, "Only as a reflection of you." The result is that narcissistic needs do not mature out of their archiaic form and echoistic needs are disowned. The child develops a narcissistic personality structure.

SUMMARY

A formulation of the complementary relationship between narcissism and echoism based on a reframing of Kohut's two basic interpersonal needs serves five functions:

1. It expands the complementarity of codependence and narcissism across generations. In such a framework, the development of personality structure in children proceeds according to systemic principles, in addition to purely intrapsychic dynamics such as identification and incorporation. A narcissistic adult will not only seek out his or her complement in a codependent mate, but will also mold children in the same direction. Conversely, a codependent adult will mold children toward narcissistic personalities.

2. It answers the question regarding whether one is primary and the other is derivative. If the two needs postulated by Kohut are seen as contemporaneous and equal, and as possessing their own independent line of development, then narcissism and echoism are both primary phenomena. They bear a relationship to each other that is present in the basic needs themselves, which Kohut describes as "antithetical." It is only as these needs mature beyond their archaic forms, and the "self" containing these needs grows in sophistication, that their early incompatibility is transcended.

3. The attraction described by Freud that narcissism has for those who have renounced part of their own narcissism is now given a firm psychodynamic foundation, as well as being balanced by the attraction that echoism must have for those who have renounced part of their own echoism. By a process of mutual projective identifications, both narcissistic and echoistic personality structures serve as the hand for the other person's glove. Narcissists own their need to be seen as capable, but disown and project the need to be dependent.

Echoists own the need to be dependent, but disown and project the need to be seen as capable. Each identifies with the other's projections, and each is attracted to the other's acceptance of the shadow side within themselves. The "chemistry" of human emotional attraction is present in full force.

4. The phenomenon of secondary codependence can now be understood as a process in which a person with codependent personality traits comes into relationship with someone with narcissistic tendencies. Through a gradual process of mutual projective identifications, each has his or her particular traits intensified until they cross the line into becoming full-blown personality disorders. In such cases, both the codependence and the narcissism will ebb significantly, back to their original levels of nondysfunctional intensity, merely by withdrawal from the relationship.

5. Finally, there is the clinical reality that narcissism and codependence rarely exist in pure forms. In most clinical cases, these complementary stances exist as an admixture. While one stance predominates in the underlying character structure, the other stance is disowned and projected onto others. As a result, it is not uncommon to see a narcissistic personality crumbling under the weight of a narcissistic injury temporarily reown its projections, becoming thoroughly codependent. For example, as someone's love (which the narcissistic wears as an achievement badge) is withdrawn, there may be a sudden willingness to be whatever the other person wants in order to regain that love. On the other hand, it is also often easy to see in codependents elements of pomposity and grandiose thinking underlying their belief that they can make anyone love them if they are compliant enough.

CONCLUSIONS AND FUTURE DIRECTIONS

The separation of general mental health and chemical dependence into two theoretical frameworks and treatment infrastructures in the United States is a complex phenomenon. From a historical perspective, it is likely that this separation has benefited both. General mental health workers were free from the frustration of trying to treat chemically dependent patients without effective therapeutic modalities. And the chemical dependence field was freed from the confines of psychotherapeutic tradition to create more effective modalities. The effects of this separation have been far reaching, however, and include the creation of political turf and the narrow education of therapists in one field or the other.

Perhaps codependence was first described by therapists in the chemical dependence field in part because the classical study of personality disorder is often neglected in that field. The result was a fresher view, one uncontaminated by how the pie has already been cut by others, but uninformed as to the progress that has been made in understanding other personality disorders. In focusing on the pathology of patients who are, or have been, in intense relationships with active alcoholics and drug addicts, chemical dependence therapists found themselves working with the most concentrated population of codependents available. They responded by reinventing a valuable variant of the wheel.

Cross-fertilization between the fields of chemical dependence and mental health is now necessary if the concept of codependence is going to be developed further and eventually contribute to our overall framework of personality theory (see also Chapters 4 & 5). Such a cross-fertilization will facilitate further inquiry regarding codependence in several important directions.

First, there is the matter of its epidemiology. How prevalent is codependent personality disorder? If it exists more often in women than in men, as many people suspect, what influences create this differential? Do different kinds of family dysfunction create more codependence than others (see Chapters 4 and 5)?

Second, what does the concept of codependence contribute to our general theories of psychology? I look forward to the possibility that our concept of narcissism will be delineated further by being included in a complementary relationship with codependence. The fact that these personality disorders emerge from psychic wounds during the same period of child development should lead us to be more suspicious of schemata that attempt to make one-to-one correlations between specific disorders and specific stages of development. The need for further exploration of the different kinds of wounds that take place during each stage of development, as well as the different contexts within which each of these wounds occurs, is suggested.

Third, the entire area of treatment for codependence should be greatly enhanced by application of psychotherapeutic approaches that have proved valuable for other personality disorders (see also Chapters 4, 5, and 7–12). In particular, therapy based on object relations theory and self psychology has much to contribute. Questions waiting to be explored include: How does treatment of codependence differ from the treatment of narcissism? What approaches are effective when clients alternate between the two complementary disorders? And what kinds of transference and projective identifications are characteristic of codependence?

The next few years hold the promise of an exciting dialogue as we continue to explore the questions surrounding codependence, its definition, and its relationship to narcissism.

REFERENCES

Alcoholics Anonymous (1976). *Big Book* (3rd ed.). New York: Alcoholics Anonymous World Services.

American Psychiatric Association (1987). *Diagnostic and statistical manual of mental disorders* (3rd Ed., rev.), Washington: American Psychiatric Association.

Cashdan, S. (1988). *Object relations therapy.* New York: Norton.

Cermak, T. L. (1986). *Diagnosing and treating co-dependence.* Minneapolis, MN: Johnson Institute Books.

Cermak, T. 1990. *Evaluating and treating adult children of alcoholics.* Minneapolis, MN: Johnson Institute Books.

Doi, T. (1973). *The anatomy of dependence.* Tokyo/New York/San Francisco: Kodansha International.

Ekman, P., & Friesen, W. (1989). *Journal of Personality and Social Psychology, 54*(3), 414–420.

Eth, S., & Pynoos, R. (1985). *Post-traumatic stress disorder in children.* Washington: American Psychiatric Press.

Freud, S. (1914/1963). On narcissism: An introduction. In *General psychological theory.* New York: Collier Books.

Johnson, V. (1973). *I'll quit tomorrow.* New York: Harper & Row.

Kohut, H. (1971). *The analysis of self.* Madison, CT: International Universities Press.

Kohut, H. (1977). *The restoration of self.* New York: International Universities Press.

Levin, J. D. (1987). *Treatment of alcoholism and other addictions: A self-psychology approach.* Northvale, NJ: Jason Aronson.

Mahler, M. (1975). *The psychological birth of the human infant.* New York: Basic Books.

Masterson, J. (1981). *The narcissistic and borderline disorders: An integrated developmental approach.* New York: Brunner/Mazel.

Miller, A. (1981). *The drama of the gifted child.* New York: Basic Books.

Millon, T. (1981). *Disorders of personality: DSM-III, axis II,* (p. 93). New York: Wiley.

Stern, D. (1985). *The interpersonal world of the infant,* New York: Basic Books.

Terr, L. (1983). Chowchilla revisited: The effects of psychic trauma four years after a school bus kidnapping. *American Journal of Psychiatry, 140,* (12), 14–19.

7

Children in Search of a Diagnosis: Chronic Trauma Disorder of Childhood

David Levoy, M.D.

Timothy M. Rivinus, M.D.

Marilyn Matzko, A.C.S.W.

James McGuire, M.D.

Joe is ten years old. He is angry and defiant, and for two years has been oppositional in school. By the age of ten, he had already lost a year or more of academic progress in relation to his peers. Special education with an emotionally disturbed focus could not control him. An assault on a teacher culminated in his referral to a day-hospital program.

In the day hospital, he repeated the same pattern of behavior. He frequently assaulted his peers and the staff and failed to make therapeutic, academic, or social connections with the program or his peers. Efforts to engage his family in therapy met with limited success. The father missed sessions. Joe's mother and two siblings came to sessions and showed evidence of a family overwhelmed. The mother appeared to have little or no control over her three sons. They fought during sessions, crawled under chairs, and defied the skilled structural family therapist's attempts to "empower" the mother to control them. Toys and equipment began to be broken in the family-therapy room, with Joe appearing to be the main culprit. At this point, inpatient hospitalization was recommended.

The father was asked to appear for an inpatient intake interview—his second appearance (the first being the day-hospital interview) in the six months since patient referral. In the interview, Joe acknowledged that his father was often absent and often returned home drunk, and that he had witnessed his father physically abusing his mother on a number of occasions. Joe's two brothers nodded silent assent. When the therapist suggested that for any treatment for Joe to be effective the father might have to accept a diagnosis of alcoholism, the father erupted: "There's nobody gonna tell me how to run my family. What I do with my family is what I want and nobody ain't gonna tell me to stop drinking. They've told me this before. I don't see anything wrong with it. I bring home a check, don't I? And she [pointing to his wife] don't see anything wrong with it. It's your job to fix my son, Doc; I don't want you laying the blame on me."

After hospitalization and in the initial diagnostic play interview, Joe showed distrust and reticence. He blamed his school and the examiner for his "being here." He exhibited violence and fear in his play. When asked what he thought of his dad's outburst, he cried at first, and then suddenly, angrily, denounced and denied, "You little bastard [the examiner was 5 feet 11 inches tall and weighed 170 pounds], there's nothing wrong with my dad. It's me! it's me!" Whereupon Joe attempted to hit the examiner and had to be held by the therapist for some minutes before he could calm himself.

This case presents not only a therapeutic challenge, but also a diagnostic one. How is a clinician to characterize Joe's symptoms so as to qualify him for hospitalization without mischaracterizing his predicament? To focus on the child's symptoms or mood to the exclusion of the environmental trauma would be to focus prematurely on internalized character and affectual states. Such an approach to diagnosis tends to overfocus on individual treatment and management of the child to the exclusion of the family. Yet this is the situation with which clinicians of large numbers of psychiatrically hospitalized children are faced because of the inadequacy of a comprehensive diagnostic category to fit the children's presentation and to justify the comprehensive services they need. Therefore, the purpose of this chapter is to formulate the plight of these children in such a way as to lead to a new diagnostic category that would better suit their phenomenology and treatment needs.

In the search for etiologies of psychiatric disorders, pathology is often thought to be traceable to past trauma. The phenomenologic/descriptive diagnosis of post-traumatic stress disorder (PTSD) (American Psychiatric Association, 1987, pp. 247–251) reflects the body of clinical and research data that supports this hypothesis. However, there is a question as to whether chronic, extreme environmental stress in childhood qualifies as PTSD. Green (1985) has pointed out that chronic, ongoing pathological child-rearing practices have a cumulatively adverse effect on children. When these children become parents, he says, they in turn pathologically abuse their children, creating a multigenerational cycle of parenting pathology "that underlies the physical violence in the child abuse syndrome." Terr and others have identified a subgroup of PTSD in childhood (Type II) that involves exposure to chronic stressful events (Terr, 1985; Kiser et al., 1988).

EFFECTS OF PARENTAL SUBSTANCE ABUSE

Direct effects of parental substance abuse may include impaired parent–child relationships, physical and sexual abuse, and neglect. A literature documents the increase in physical and sexual abuse and the numerous adverse and behavioral effects on the child of that abuse in alcoholic families (Ackerman, 1983; Black, Steven & Wilder-Padilla, 1986; Flanzer, 1988). Furthermore, the model of a parent who ranks an abused substance (the dependent parent) and the crises related to abuse (the codependent parent) before the needs of child rearing gives a profound message to the child about what is important in life.

Indirect effects of substance abuse include socioeconomic sequelae such as job loss, parental medical illness, marital problems, loss of the family's external support, the disruption of family rituals, and the adoption of constricted and stereotyped assigned and/or assumed roles by family members (Steinglass, Bennett, Wolin, & Reiss, 1987, pp. 220–296). The traumatic effect of parental substance abuse may be transmitted indirectly through a dysfunctional family environment. The roles described by Wegscheider and others of "family hero," "lost child," "rebel," and "mascot" are descriptions of developmental arrests in children resulting from the pathological family dynamics of the alcoholic family (Wegscheider, 1979, 1981; Black, 1981).

DEVELOPMENTAL EFFECTS OF ENVIRONMENTAL TRAUMA

The traumaized child may be predisposed to difficulties in developing internal resources for coping with trauma for a variety of reasons. There may be congenital susceptibility in children exposed to alcohol, drugs, or trauma in utero. Children of substance-abusing parents (COSAPs) may have difficulty coping because of cognitive developmental disabilities that have been associated with the fetal alcohol syndrome (Little, Graham, & Samson, 1982; Ervin, Little, Streissguth, & Beck, 1984). A child can experience the psychological and environmental effects or of trauma or of being a COSAP during infancy, toddlerhood, the preschool years, latency, adolescence, or adulthood, or in all of these developmental stages. Depending on when the insult occurred in a child's development and the severity and duration of the traumatization, parental substance abuse may have different consequences for a child diagnostically and in terms of the therapeutic interventions that are made.

Infancy

In infancy, "basic trust" by children in their care givers (Erikson, 1950) presumably helps cushion the effects of experienced trauma. In COSAPs, however, because of unreliable, inconsistent caretaker responsiveness, basic trust often does not develop. Caretakers' responsiveness may be directly related to a caretaker's intoxication or to the caretaker's having to attend to the intoxication of a spouse. Fluctuations in the caretaker's behavior may lead to the child's becoming overwhelmed and defensively constructing an internal model of reality that protects him or her from the instability of the environment. The infant may mobilize and centralize the processes of denial, dissociation, splitting, hyperarousal, overactivity, and aggression as defenses against the direct or recollected effects of trauma. These symptoms become indicators of a child's difficulty in maintaining psychosocial homeostasis. Withdrawal and/or overactivity may become preferred modes of dealing with stress throughout the child's development unless there is intervention.

Toddlerhood

Toddlers, when confronted with traumatic circumstances, utilize their primary care givers for soothing and to help reassure them that it will be safe once again to explore their environment. Parents who help a child exposed to traumatic events by providing a safe harbor (Freud & Burlingham, 1943) are able to differentiate for the child the external nature of the trauma. The child learns that there are external dangers in the world and that he or she can rely on the parents for relative protection. Children who are helped with external trauma are usually able to internalize protective mechanisms that the parent provides, such as learning to say "no" to one's self before pulling an electric cord and being able to feel increasingly safe in one's independent explorations.

In families of COSAPs, the parents may not regularly provide a safe harbor for the child, let alone such protective instruction, especially in the midst of alcohol- or drug-related crises. The toddler has difficulty in learning to separate from the environmental trauma. The reality of trauma related to substance abuse may be denied by the parents, and the responsively aggressive or overactive child may be scapegoated and identified by the parent(s) as the "cause" of chemical-abuse-related crises. The toddler may incorporate aggression, overactivity, and hypervigilance into his or her early "character" structure (Cantwell, 1972; Steward, De Blois, & Singer, 1979).

The child at this age is unable to learn to distinguish the external trauma brought on by parental substance abuse from trauma brought on by the self. The young child may perceive traumatic circumstances as the norm. The child feels there is little that he or she can do to control the circumstances, except within a traumatic and traumatizing framework. The exhortation to children raised in such circumstances to "just say no," without an enduring and protective corrective experience, is giving advice to children who are psychologically deaf to the instructions presented.

Preschoolers

Preschoolers need parental support and guidance to begin to develop an internal locus of control and to make the transition from the family to the community at large. Preschoolers rely on their growing abilities to engage in symbolic play and thought and rehearsal of roles and to create positive, internal "narratives" about themselves to cope with their environment (Stern, 1985). When parental denial of stressful and traumatic events obfuscates reality, the child's cohesive sense of historical reality is impaired, and the child has difficulty putting his or her experiences into perspective. As noted earlier, the child denies, dissociates, and splits off the experience and there is no consistent historical reality. Without the development of internal representations or models for dealing with trauma, the child is susceptible to problematic sequelae of these trauma and is likely to reproduce, by rote, similar behaviors when the affective experiences tied to the trauma are reexperienced.

Young School-Aged Children

In latency, a growing ability to generalize, including the ability to use rules, may help a child deal with trauma. For example, a child may be comforted by the rule that a person who criminally mistreats the child is likely to be punished. A child may also be reassured that, by being more careful, he or she may be protected from further injury or trauma. Parents reassure the child when the inevitable accident occurs. Even if a child cannot master certain traumatic difficulties, he or she learns that industriousness and good works are rewarded and so may gain mastery in other domains. In traumatic or addicted families, rules are often arbitrary and may depend on the degree of parental intoxication (Woodside, 1988). Children are faced with parental models of dyscontrol that lack conformity to societal rules. The children construct internal models that are overly strict or are without boundaries. Children with symptoms of being "parentified" or who are "hyperactive," "acting out," or "borderline" may present to clinicians for the first time at this age.

Puberty and Adolescence

The major developmental issues of adolescence are the consolidation of identity, education and vocation, separation–individuation from caretakers, and the development of healthy behavior and relationship choices. By the time puberty and adolescence arrive, the COSAP may have little internalized sense of self, considerable practice in a pathological role vis-à-vis family and social systems, little sense of trust in the predictability of anything but traumatic or psychologically upsetting circumstances, a well-developed idea that he or she is in fact the cause of those events, and a behavioral style that tends to reinforce this hypothesis. The adolescent COSAP may also have developed a defensive style that deals with trauma by denial, numbing, dissociation, and repetition–compulsion (Black, Steven, & Wilder-Padilla, 1986). It is no surprise that the adolescent is highly susceptible to severe behavioral, psychological, academic, vocational, and life-adjustment identity problems, as well as to substance abuse itself (Russell, Henderson, & Blume, 1985; Steinhauser, Gobel & Nestter, 1984; Earls, Reich, Jung, & Cloninger, 1988).

COSAPS ON A CHILDREN'S INPATIENT PSYCHIATRIC UNIT

On the children's inpatient psychiatric unit at Bradley Hospital, East Providence, R.I., where mainly latency-aged children are treated, we noticed that a high proportion of patients have substance-abusing parents. On a review of 109 admissions to the unit, we found that over 53% were COSAPs as compared with 33% who were physically and/or sexually abused (P/SA). A total of 69% of the admitted children were COSAPs and/or P/SAs (Table 7-1).

Table 7-1
Study Sample

| | N = 109 | | |
	COSAP[1]	NCOSAP[2]	Total
P/SA[3]	18 (17%)	18 (17%)	36 (33%)
NP/SA[4]	40 (37%)	33 (30%)	73 (67%)
Totals	58 (53%)	51 (47%)	109 (100%)

1. COSAP = child of substance-abusing parent
2. NCOSAP = not a child of substance-abusing parent
3. P/SA = victim of physical/sexual abuse
4. NP/SA = nonvictim of physical/sexual abuse

There was considerable overlap in the mixed-symptom picture of these children and in the diagnoses given (Rivinus, Leroy, Matzko, Seifer, in preparation). Both symptoms and diagnoses could be directly related to environmental trauma—the trauma and/or disruption of substance-abusing family life. Furthermore, interventions directed toward alleviating or preventing the effects of trauma and/or parental substance abuse provided symptom relief.

We believe that these findings support the theory that severe home-based problems, such as trauma and/or parental substance abuse, which we have called chronic trauma disorder (CTD), are a major correlate to psychiatric hospitalization for children. If our sample can be generalized to other settings, it would appear that COSAPs are predisposed to severe psychiatric symptoms and that a background of repeated trauma, including being a COSAP, appears to be a common denominator for many children diagnosed as having, and even labeled as having been hospitalized for, severe psychiatric symptomatology.

DIAGNOSTIC DILEMMA

There is no diagnostic option in the American Psychiatric Association's (APA) *Diagnostic and Statistical Manual of Mental Disorders*, revised third edition (DSM-III-R), to classify the disorder of children of trauma. There is also no real diagnostic framework that recognizes the importance of intrafamilial trauma.

A diagnosis that is directly related to the pathology of parenting is DSM-R-III's *reactive attachment disorder* of infancy and early childhood (APA, 1987, pp. 91–93). This diagnosis may be appropriate in some, but certainly not all, cases of physically or psychologically traumatized children. Reactive attachment disorder does not, in fact, capture the mixed-symptom picture of most hospitalized children with a traumatic home environment, nor does it describe older children and adolescents. It does, however, recognize the chronically traumatic environmental circumstances to which these children are subject.

PTSD (APA, 1987, pp. 247–251) also does not adequately describe the developmental vulnerabilities and the mixed, nonspecific-symptom picture of children who are exposed to chronic ongoing intrafamilial trauma. The diagnosis of PTSD was developed, largely, to describe the responses of adults and children to a past traumatic event. Although PTSD does exist in children, with some features that differentiate it from adult PTSD (Terr, 1985, pp. 51–53), it has been our experience that this diagnosis is not well suited to the more global, undifferentiated responses of children to trauma, especially trauma of an ongoing nature. In children subject to chronic trauma, not only the direct effects of the trauma must be taken into account, but also the effect of the chronic traumatic circumstances on a child's development. This includes their effect on the development of the ability to cope, to form relationships, and to avoid the repetition of traumatic behaviors learned in early life. (See also Chapter 6.)

Mood disorder (affective disorder) diagnoses of DSM-III-R (APA, 1987, pp. 213–233) are often warranted for these child patients who are suffering from chronic environmental trauma and stress, particularly when they are first referred for treatment. These youngsters, including COSAPs, may be severely depressed and have vegetative signs of depression (Rolf, Johnson, Israel, Baldwin, & Chandra, 1988). Depression may also be mixed with symptoms of hypomania or dysthymia in their presentation. At the very least, the mood instability they demonstrate before treatment would often qualify them for the diagnosis of dysthmic disorder. However, in our experience, symptoms of major mood disorder often remit when the child is separated from the source of trauma or when sufficient intervention into the environmental disturbance has taken place. Furthermore, the biological or cognitive treatments often effective for mood disorders in adults are usually not effective in children with affective symptomatology related to chronic trauma, whereas protection and assurance of safety often are. Therefore, we suggest that diagnoses of mood disorder may be warranted in environmentally traumatized children but not without the primary qualifier of a diagnosis that emphasizes the contribution of chronic trauma.

The *adjustment-disorder* diagnoses in DSM-III-R are often applicable descriptively to environmentally traumatized children and in the suggestion that the origin of these disorders is in reaction to environmental events (APA, 1987, pp. 329–331). However, the adjustment disorders do not speak to the diagnostic needs of children with signs and symptoms of being chronically traumatized environmentally. Children with CTD commonly have symptoms of higher severity and longer duration than the six months predicated for adjustment-disorder diagnoses. (See also Chapter 6.)

Other diagnoses within the framework of DSM-III-R may have some relevance for traumatized children in psychiatric settings but are not truly accurate or comprehensive in describing these youngsters. These diagnoses include the *personality disorders* and the *disruptive behavior disorders*. The personality-disorder diagnoses are generally premature for children whose symptoms have not yet become a part of their personalities and autonomous, but rather continue to be reactive to environmental traumata. They also imply a nihilism with regard to treatment. The diagnosis of personality disorder (APA, 1987, pp. 335–358) may also force clinicians and social agencies into premature diagnostic closure that blinds them to the environmentally determined nature of symptoms (Frances, Clarkin, & Perry, 1984). Furthermore, DSM-III-R (APA, 1987) recommends that antisocial-personality-disorder diagnoses generally be reserved for people over 18, except where patterns of symptomatology appear to be of long duration and stable. Antisocial personality disorder has repeatedly been demonstrated to have its roots in a traumatic, often alcoholic, early environment (Robins, 1966, 1978; West, 1982; Rutter & Giller, 1984). Recent studies have shown that other personality-disorder diagnoses, such as borderline and narcissistic personality disorders, are often related to a history of childhood trauma and neglect (Herman, Perry, & van der Kolk, 1989; Kohut & Wolfe, 1978; Miller, 1983). Many personality diagnoses might, by this line of argument, be best characterized as a population of "chronically traumatized children grown up."

The *disruptive behavior disorders* of DSM-III-R (APA, 1987, pp. 49–58) (attention-deficit hyperactivity disorder, oppositional disorder, and conduct disorder) occur more commonly in COSAPs (Cantwell, 1972; Steward et al., 1979, Earls et al., 1988) than in other children and may accurately describe a traumatized child's symptoms up to and at the time of psychiatric diagnosis. Enumerated stressors may suggest an etiology for the disruptive behavior in such cases. However, primary diagnoses of disruptive behavior disorder would not be appropriate in cases of trauma. For example, a primary diagnosis of attention-deficit hyperactivity disorder suggests to many clinicians an organic etiology for a child's symptoms, for which stimulants, other psychoactive drug treatment, or behavioral treatments might be prescribed. To embark on psychopharmacological or behavioral treatments to the exclusion of interventions into the family traumata that are the source of a child's symptoms would be a disservice to the child and family.

Oppositional-defiant-disorder and conduct-disorder diagnoses used as primary diagnoses suggest to many clinicians a source of pathology residing within the child. Furthermore, the conduct-disorder diagnosis is interpreted by many clinicians (and third-party payers) to mean that no primary psychiatric etiology is present and that psychosocial treatment is likely to be ineffective. Disruptive-behavior-disorder diagnosis may be warranted in cases where CTD is present but would only be justified as a secondary diagnosis. The importance of CTD as a separate and primary diagnosis of traumatized children and/or children of substance-dependent parents is that it directs clinical attention to the etiology of the child's symptoms (including disruptive behaviors) and to the appropriate environmental and family interventions that are necessary.

The DSM-III-R's V *code diagnoses* (APA, 1987, pp. 359–362) are the only diagnostic categories in which descriptions of pathological family dynamics are possible. Specifically, code V 61.80, "other specified family circumstances," or V 61.20, "parent–child problem," or V 61.10, "marital problem," can be used, and in the absence of a more descriptive diagnosis at present, should be used to describe the circumstances of these children (APA, 1987, pp. 360–361). However, the use of V-code diagnoses is an inadequate solution to the diagnostic dilemma because they do not link the family pathology *with* the child's symptoms, do not describe the specific symptoms of traumatized children, and do not have true "psychiatric status" in many eyes, including those of many third-party payers.

Because traumatic circumstances of physically and sexually abused children and COSAPs occur within the framework of a relationship, a "systems" diagnosis may be the best way to describe such cases. Not only would such a diagnosis more accurately describe the traumatic environment as it is expressed through the families of these children, but it would be more in keeping with the major contributions made by family psychiatry to the nature of the disorders (McLemore & Benjamin, 1979).

One group of clinical researchers has specifically suggested that an Axis VI rating of family functioning be introduced to accommodate family variables (Frances et al., 1984). The addition of a further axis, however, still does not meet the need to provide specific diagnoses with symptomatic children of trauma (sexual, physical, and/or COSAP), nor does it allow clinicians to frame the plight of such children in more appropriate terms than to continue to classify the child as the source of the problem. It would be bitterly ironic not only to "blame the victim," but also to recapitulate the common addicted and traumatizing family myth that the symptomatic child is the main, if not the only, problem. Until a systems diagnostic category is formulated, a diagnostic trauma to already traumatized children will be the result.

A DIAGNOSTIC PROPOSAL

We propose a new diagnostic category, using the form of DSM-III-R, based on our experience with COSAPs, which would be applicable to most psychiatrically hospitalized and severely symptomatic children of chronic family- and home-related trauma. We suggest that the diagnosis be called "chronic trauma disorder of childhood" (CTD-C). This diagnosis should be reserved for children 12 years of age or under.

CTD=C would be divided into four necessary components: (1) a history of impaired or pathological family functioning and roles; (2) an avoidance-type pattern of emotional response by the child; (3) symptoms consistent with chronic hyperarousal in the child; and (4) symptoms that are environmentally sensitive and remit in a safe context.

Family Pathology

Family impairment can include trauma (either witnessed or directly experienced) or chronic, less discrete stressful events and neglect (for example, accidents resulting from lack of parental supervision). Family discipline and rules are often either rigidly authoritarian or overly lax. Physical or psychological trauma is state-dependent or highly variable; for example, little supervision alternating with harsh discipline when the parent is intoxicated, or vice versa. This, in turn, may alternate with caring and seemingly appropriately involved interactions when the parent is not intoxicated (or intoxicated in another circumstance). The household environment is often chaotic and unpredictable, with few, if any, reliable times when the family is able to focus attention on nurturing children or on the family's developmental issues (e.g., the family may rarely eat a meal together) (Steinglass et al., 1987). There may be no reliable times where family issues can be discussed, or even reliable times for the family to be together without disruption. Predictability of caretaking is impaired by frequent caretaker changes.

The parents or other caretakers who are dependent on alcohol are limited in their ability to recognize the impact of adverse family and household circumstances on the child (e.g., "Sure I get drunk, but it doesn't affect my kids; they know to stay away"). If adverse circumstances are acknowledged by the parents, frequently the blame is placed on the child ("You'd drink like I do if you had a demon kid like this"). The family may be defensive about or deny the picture of themselves that they present to others (e.g., the parents may not be able to identify any difficulties in the family other than the child's behavior).

Child "Roles"

The child in the addicted-family system will tend to assume a stereotyped role or roles within the system (Black, 1981; Wegscheider, 1981). The child who over-compensates for the family, tends to take on parental roles, and denies family dysfunction in action and word is called the "family hero." The child who takes on symptoms of hyperarousal, aggression, and poor social and academic functioning is often called the "acting out" child and becomes a scapegoat in the family system. Children who become withdrawn; dissociate from ongoing stress; show symptoms of depression, apathy, helplessness, and hopelessness; and have poor self-esteem within the context of a traumatic or addicted dysfunctional family system are called "lost children" in that system. Some children remain developmentally arrested in a cheerful, joking, clowning infantile way and are called the family "mascots" or "babies" within the system. Separation from the family is often an issue for the hero–mascot in the adolescent and early adult years. All of these roles represent developmental difficulties in attachment and separation–individuation. These issues achieve a pseudoresolution in the assumption of a family role that begins as a defensive response on the part of the child but that then becomes developmentally rigidified (Wegscheider, 1981; Black, 1981).

Interpersonal–Cognitive–Avoidance Pathology in the Child

The parents' inability to recognize the impact of their own actions or inactions on their child may be echoed in the child's confusion over interpersonal cause and effect. This confusion is a cognitive–interpersonal symptom that may be generalized beyond the child's home situation. In play with a peer at school, for example, an 11-year-old boy might claim he struck the peer because a teacher punished him, whereas the reverse may be true. The child may tend to "catastrophize" things, especially around issues of loss (e.g., the loss of a toy may be experienced as a major loss accompanied by a severe behavioral reaction).

The child often varies widely in his or her locus of control. The child may take no responsibility for behavior in some instances and blame others, but in other instances may feel deeply responsible for events over which he or she had no control. Often, the latter is the case concerning the child's life circumstances (e.g., the child believes that frequent home changes occur because "I am bad" when actually it is because of parental and family difficulties).

A wide variability in thinking about self and others is common. Fleeting grandiose self-images ("I am the strongest") may alternate with feelings of intense self-hate. This is also true of the child's view of others—feelings may alternate between overidealization and devaluation of peers or adults, with concomitant clingy or rejecting behavior. The child may have periods of intense desire to please others, especially adults, alternating with severe defiance and oppositional behavior. This may include episodes of antisocial behavior alternating with rigid rule following.

In addition to their interpersonal–cognitive difficulties, these children may have marked avoidant changes in mood, consisting predominantly of emotional constriction or depressed affect. However, constricted affect may be punctuated by dramatic emotional outbursts, as noted by Cermak (1984). When asked about the positive and negative aspects of their home, including what things they wish could be different, such children may be unable to discuss any negative feelings about their home lives. The question may be received with marked restlessness, efforts to change the topic, and defensive denial and dissociation. The child may disavow his or her own feelings. For example, an adolescent may deny being hurt by a close friend's rejection or a child may cry and deny being upset.

Hyperarousal

Symptoms of hyperarousal are closely linked to avoidance of painful memories and environmental realities. Hyperarousal may appear to be in the service of avoidance, and symptoms may appear most prominent when the child is confronted with affectively charged issues. Difficulties in the areas of lack of concentration, attention deficit, overactivity, hyperactivity, sleeplessness, chronic anxiety, and outbursts of rage or anger may occur chronically, but may worsen in temporal association with affectively charged issues (Cantwell, 1972). For example, a child may become agitated when a peer talks of alcohol abuse in the peer's own family. A child may view the world as a frightening place and may reflect this in his or her play. For example, the child's play may show an obsession with horror movies, weapons, or violence.

Restitution to Higher Levels of Functioning

After an initial exacerbation of symptoms in the new environment, children who are removed from the toxic traumatic environment and are in a safe structured and stable environment for three–four weeks often have a remission of symptoms. Overactivity, sleep problems, chronic anxiety, and rage and anger may remit. Symptom remission taking place in a protective environment suggests the release of environmentally induced symptoms and is highly suggestive of CTD in a younger child. The initial worsening of a child's symptoms may occur in the context of the child's apparently unconscious efforts to "set up" the caretaking environment in such a way as to recapture family trauma and thus test the abilities of the treatment setting to respond to the challenge, consistently and nontraumatically.

Associated Features

Associated symptoms include behaviors that occur in attention-deficit hyperactivity disorder, conduct disorder, and oppositional defiant disorder. Symptoms of mood disorder, including dysthymic disorder and major depression and cyclothymia—and, less often, bipolar disorder—may be present, and may warrant an additional diagnosis. Particularly when discrete, severe traumatic episodes have occurred, diagnostic features of PTSD may be present, and this diagnosis may also be warranted in addition to CTD.

The pathological caretaking environment related to this disorder may also produce a symptom picture in the younger child of the reactive attachment disorder of infancy and childhood. Refusal to attend school and other symptoms of separation anxiety disorder and other anxiety disorders may be seen. The context of the symptomatology can be closely related to the environmental circumstances. For example, although complaints leading to school refusal may be somatic ones (e.g., headaches), the child may be trying to stay home to keep an alcoholic parent from drinking and hurting himself or herself. Learning disabilities and speech and language disorders commonly accompany CTD, as do physiological and developmental delays such as enuresis and encopresis (Earls et al., 1988), and deserve classification as separate but related diagnostic categories when they occur.

Course

Over time, usually by middle to late adolescence, CTD may develop into personality traits and disorders with symptomatology that appears to be unrelated to family circumstances: for example, borderline, narcissistic, passive-dependent, masochistic, and antisocial disorders. In some cases, children with CTD develop psychoactive substance-use disorders with or without comorbid Axis I or Axis II disorders or traits. Other cases appear to develop what has been called "codependency disorder" (Cermak, 1984) or "self-defeating personality disorder" (APA, 1987, pp. 371–374). On the other hand, when the pathological environment is successfully treated or the child is removed from the environment and receives treatment, symptomatology may remit and developmental progress may be made.

DIFFERENTIAL DIAGNOSES

If attention-deficit hyperactivity disorder, conduct disorder, oppositional defiant disorder, anxiety disorder, or mood disorder is present, these diagnoses should also be made. In PTSD, there is sometimes a fairly clearly delineated traumatic "event" around which most of the posttraumatic symptomatology is organized. In CTD, the traumatic events and the resultant symptomatology may not be so clearly focused or defined, and the trauma and symptomatology are intimately intertwined in the everyday life and development of a child.

Recent attachment disorder of early childhood may predispose to CTD and some of the conditions of the pathogenic caretaking are equivalent. However, reactive attachment disorder describes either failed, apathetic, or indiscriminately promiscuous social relatedness in the very young child, whereas in CTD, the pattern of relatedness is characteristically tumultuous, oscillating with "all or nothing" responses accompanied by fairly intense affect in children of all ages.

We suggest that V-code diagnoses that assist in the accurate description of the traumatic environmental circumstances and relationships to which the child with CTD is exposed should be used in *all* cases that apply.

DIAGNOSTIC CRITERIA

The following are the criteria for CTD. The CTD diagnosis is reserved for children 12 years of age or under.

I. A history of impaired family function and/or roles as evidenced by three of the following:

1. Frequent caretaker changes.
2. Family neglect or abuse of the child or another family member and/or parental substance-use disorder.
3. Markedly variable caretaker emotional responsiveness or markedly variable discipline/limit setting/rule making by caretakers.
4. Assumption of rigid, stereotypic role for and by the child (e.g., role reversal, "parentified" child, scapegoat, always blamed, negative attributions, sick or fragile child).
5. Impaired or disruptive family rituals (e.g., the family is rarely, if ever, together for a meal or for other activities such as holidays or birthdays).
6. Family denial or defensiveness of one or more parent figures, which may include the inability to recognize any important family difficulties that may have an impact on the child.

II. Interpersonal and cognitive impairment and avoidance pathology as evidenced by three of the following:

1. Confusion over interpersonal cause and effect.
2. Widely alternating locus of control.
3. All-or-nothing thinking of self and others (e.g., grandiose alternating with self-denigrating expression, clingingness alternating with rejection, willingness to please alternating with defiance and oppositional behavior, rigid rule following alternating with antisocial behavior).

4. Constriction of emotions (with or without dramatic outbursts).
5. Anxiety and inability to discuss home issues in an age-appropriate fashion (e.g., the child offers no complaints or expresses no wishes for a better home situation, or a peer talks about the peer's alcoholic parent and the child becomes very agitated).
6. Disowns own feelings (e.g., cries and claims not to be upset, acts out angrily but denies angry feelings).

III. Hyperarousal as evidenced by two of the following:

1. Concentration difficulties.
2. Overactivity difficulties.
3. Sleep difficulties.
4. Chronic anxiety that increases around issues of caretaking and reminders of home life (e.g., if the child is in the hospital, around parental visits).
5. Play or preoccupations that depict the world as a frightening place.
6. Frequent outbursts of rage or anger apparently unrelated to the immediate circumstances.

IV. Evidence of partial or complete remission of symptoms in a safe, nontraumatic environment, usually following the child's having tested the caretaking system for a safe and consistently nontraumatic response to the child's symptomatic outbursts. This criterion is highly suggestive of the CTD diagnosis but is not necessary in the presence of sufficient criteria in items I–III to make a diagnosis of CTD.

DISCUSSION AND CONCLUSIONS

The theoretical origins of the symptomatology for CTD are related to COSAPs and other chronically stressed or traumatized children's developmental exposure to trauma. The all-or-nothing responses that children with CTD demonstrate may be related to the very early reliance on splitting to retain a modicum of trust in an untrustworthy world. Confusion over cause and effect and variable locus of control in the child may be a cognitive developmental failure resulting from the family's confusing and shifting attributions of cause and effect. Taking this one step further, the child's ability to create a linear personal narrative life story may be impaired when family denial purges true history. The child's diagnostic play may consist of a confused jumble of violent episodes, depicting the world as a dangerous place, in place of normal thematic play. The child may see himself or herself in such a disjointed disarray as if he or she had no history—and may feel alternately grandiosely "great" or "terrible."

Family denial of the impact of chronic adverse circumstances on the child may be translated into the child's denial of or dissociation from his or her own affect. Hyperarousal symptoms may be particularly notable around issues of caretaking or in "routine separations," as noted by Green (1985, p. 143) Hyperarousal may be the result of developmental deficits in the ability to self-soothe, combined with ongoing stressful circumstances that might produce hyperarousal in self-defense for any child. This hyperarousal should not be mistaken for attention-deficit hyperactivity disorder from other causes.

Despite the clinical evidence for a proposal of the diagnosis of CTD, it is, nevertheless, proposed tentatively. Much of the evidence for its existence is based on epidemiological data that find a relationship between traumatized children, including COSAPs, and a high risk for developmental pathology (Earls et al., 1988). This body of data does not explain the etiology of the child's symptoms simply by demonstrating an association with a traumatic environment. Such a position does not explain or take into account those children who may have no severe symptoms, nor does it adequately explain those for whom symptoms are minimal or delayed. However, demonstrating that the majority of children hospitalized for psychiatric reasons in our setting are children of an ongoing and chronically traumatic environment suggests that a new diagnosis such as CTD is needed to describe them. Although our proposal demands replication in other settings, it is consonant with a large body of theory and research in child development that has been sidestepped in our current unipolar diagnostic categorizations with regard to child psychopathology.

CTD encompasses a wide range of symptoms. There is no reason to expect that an often-chaotic traumatic environment will produce a well-defined syndrome in children. Chaos may beget chaotic, or at least varied, symptoms. From a developmental perspective, children in general have a less differentiated response to trauma and stress. However, for children of chronic trauma, the process of diagnosis is difficult and sometimes seems to contribute to the chaos of the child's world. Multiple diagnoses that fail to capture the cause-and-effect relationship of the pathogenic environment to symptom presentation may contribute to that chaos. We hope that this proposed diagnostic description will bring improved clarity to the assessment and ultimately, and most important, to the treatment of these young people. If their lives are filled with obfuscations of reality and with denial, clarity may be an essential piece of what we have to offer them.

SUMMARY

The CTD diagnosis that we have outlined attempts to capture the combined sequelae of developmental deficits caused by a pathogenic environment and the reaction of the child to ongoing stressors and trauma. This is only a preliminary attempt to describe the syndrome. It includes features from the DSM-III-R diagnostic categories of PTSD (such as hyperarousal and avoidance of affect), reactive attachment disorder (pathological caretaking environment), and other childhood diagnoses.

CTD goes beyond these syndromes. We believe that it will better serve the majority of children referred to psychiatric settings with severe difficulties because it suggests the environmental origins and treatments necessary for a systemic rather than just an individual problem.

REFERENCES

Ackerman, R. (1983). *Children of alcoholics. A guide for parents, educators and therapists* (2nd ed.) (pp. 68–69). New York: Simon & Schuster.

American Psychiatric Association (1987). *Diagnostic and statistical manual of mental disorders* (3rd ed., revised). Washington, DC: Author.

Black, C. (1981). *It will never happen to me.* Denver, CO: Medical Administration Company.

Black, C., Steven, B., & Wilder-Padilla, S. (1986). The interpersonal and emotional consequences of being an adult child of an alcoholic. *International Journal of the Addictions, 21*(2), 213–231.

Cantwell, D. P. (1972). Psychiatric illness in the families of hyperactive children. *Archives of General Psychiatry, 27*, 414–417.

Cermak, T. (1984). Children of alcoholics and the case for a new diagnostic category of codependency. *Alcohol Health and Research World, 8*(4), 38–42.

Earls, F., Reich, W., Jung, K., & Cloninger, C. R. (1988). Psychopathology in children of alcoholic and antisocial parents. *Alcoholism: Clinical and Experimental Research, 12*(4), 481–487.

Erikson, E. H. (1950). *Childhood and society.* New York: Norton.

Ervin, C., Little, R., Streissguth, A. P., & Beck, D. E. (1984). Alcoholic fathering and its relation to child's intellectual development: A pilot investigation. *Alcoholism: Clinical and Experimental Research, 8*, 362–365.

Flanzer, J. (1988). Alcohol-abusing parents and their battered adolescents. In M. Galenter (Ed.), *Currents in alcoholism: Recent advances in research and treatment* (Vol. VII, pp. 529–538). New York: Grune & Stratton.

Frances, A., Clarkin, J. F., & Perry, S. (1984). DSM-III and family therapy. *American Journal of Psychiatry, 141*, 406–409.

Freud, A., & Burlingham, D. (1943). *War and children.* New York: International Universities Press.

Green, A. H. (1985). Children traumatized by physical abuse. In E. Spencer & R. S. Pynoos (Eds.), *Post-traumatic stress disorder in children.* Washington, DC: American Psychiatric Press.

Herman, J. L., Perry, J. C., & van der Kolk, B. A. (1989). Childhood trauma in borderline personality disorder. *American Journal of Psychiatry, 146*(4), 490–495.

Kiser, L. J., Ackerman, B. J., Brown, E., Edwards, N. B., McColgan, E., Pugh, R., & Pruitt, D. B. (1988). Post-traumatic stress disorder in young children: A reaction to purported sexual abuse. *Journal of American Academy of Child and Adolescent Psychiatry, 27*(5), 645–649.

Kohut, H., & Wolfe, E. (1978). The disorders of the self and their treatment: An outline. *International Journal of Psychoanalysis, 59*, 413–425.

Little, R. E., Graham, J., & Samson, H. H. (1982). Fetal alcohol effects of maternal alcohol and drug abuse on the newborn. In B. Stimmel (Ed.), *Advances in alcohol and substance abuse* (Vol. I, No. 3/4, pp. 103–125). New York: Haworth Press.

McLemore, C. W., & Benjamin, L. S. (1979). Whatever happened to interpersonal diagnoses? A psychosocial alternative to DSM-III-R. *American Psychiatry, 34*, 17–34.

Miller, A. (1983). *For your own good.* New York: Farrar, Straus, Giroux.

Rivinus, T. M., Leroy, D., Matzko, M., Seifer, R. (in preparation). *Chronic trauma disorder of childhood (CTD): Children in search of a diagnosis.* Manuscript available from first author.

Robins, L. (1966). *Deviant children grown up.* Baltimore, MD: Williams & Wilkins.

Robins, L. (1978). Sturdy childhood predictors of adult antisocial behaviour: Replications from longitudinal studies. *Psychological medicine, 8*, 611–622.

Rolf, J., Johnson, J., Israel, E., Baldwin, J., & Chandra, A. (1988). Depressive affect in school-aged children of alcoholics. *British Journal of Addiction, 83*, 841–848.

Russell, M., Henderson, C., & Blume, S. (1985). *Children of alcoholics: A review of the literature* (pp. 37–65). Buffalo, NY: NYS Division of Alcohol Abuse.

Rutter, M., & Giller, H. (1984). *Juvenile delinquency: Trends and perspectives.* New York: Guilford Press.

Steinglass, P., Bennett, L. A., Wolin, S., & Reiss, D. (1987). Alcoholism and family ritual disruption. In *The alcoholic family.* New York: Basic Books.

Steinhauser, H. C., Gobel, D., & Nestter, V. (1984). Psychopathology in the offspring of alcoholic parents. *Journal of American Academy of Child Psychiatry, 23*, 465–471.

Stern, D. N. (1985). *The interpersonal world of the infant.* New York: Basic Books.

Steward, M. A., DeBlois, C. S., & Singer, S. (1979). Alcoholism and hyperactivity revisited: A preliminary report. In M. Galenter (Ed.), *Currents in alcoholism* (Vol. 5, pp. 349–357). New York: Grune & Stratton.

Terr, L. C. (1985). Children traumatized in small groups. In S. Eth & R. S. Pynoos (Eds.), *Post-traumatic stress disorder in children.* Washington, DC: American Psychiatric Press.

Wegscheider, S. (1979). Children of alcoholics caught in family trap. *Focus on Alcohol and Drug Issues, 2*(8).

Wegscheider, S. (1981). *Another chance: Hope and health for the alcoholic family.* Palo Alto, CA: Science & Behavior Books.

West, D. J. (1982). *Delinquency: Its roots, careers and prospects.* London: Heinemann.

Woodside, M. (1988). Research on children of alcoholism: Past and future. *British Journal of Addiction, 83*, 785–792.

PART III

TREATMENT
PERSPECTIVES

8

The Chemically Dependent Female Adolescent: A Treatment Challenge[*]

Dorothy M. Bianco, Ph.D.
Susan D. Wallace

The "good girl" image lingers from school days in other periods when the girls did better in school than boys, when the girls did their homework while the boys dallied. The girls did what they were supposed to do and were expected to do and then graduated to motherhood, selfless and self-contained with time for everyone else's problems, but, as was expected of them, without problems of their own. This is who we have been taught we are; and this is who some of us are; but we come in many varieties. We are people who have problems like everybody else. But because women have often borne their problems with unusual strength or in concealment, much that affects them has gone unnoticed or unheeded.

(Penelope Russianoff, *Women in Crisis*, 1981)

Chemical dependency in female adolescents is a multidimensional problem. These young women must be understood in the context of self, family, and environment. Each case is unique, complex, and challenging to treatment providers. Nevertheless, there is a fairly consistent profile of chemically dependent adolescent females. This chapter describes the complexities of treating such young women in the residential setting of Caritas House, some actual results of this particular treatment program, and the implications of these findings for future programming. Of particular interest are the roles of the family, the treatment program, and society

*The authors wish to express their appreciation and gratitude to the young women and the family members who participated in this study, especially to those who relived many painful experiences during the interviews. Their sadness, their caring, and their appreciation for Caritas House gave us the determination to complete this study; their thoughts and ideas helped to keep us focused; and their words and feelings breathed life and meaning into what otherwise might have been a routine academic exercise.

173

in the origin, maintenance, and alleviation of chemical dependency in female adolescents.

The teenage years are the usual time for children to make their own choices and deal with separation and the general emotional upheavals of maturation. But for some adolescents, especially those who also face traumas caused by family dysfunction, this stage of life may cause a more serious crisis.

A high percentage of adolescent substance abusers come from dysfunctional families in which there is a history of one or more of the following: substance abuse, violence or sexual abuse, overly protective parenting, excessively rigid family rules, mental and emotional illness, and neglect. Adolescents in dysfunctional families develop fragile self-concepts and may use alcohol and other drugs as a way of relieving tremendous pain, not as a way of fitting in with peers. This use of chemicals as a way of coping gradually develops into a self-destructive pattern.

When adults are in crisis, they may make a choice, but adolescents under such circumstances will not. They think, "I have years to go before I stop." Drug- or alcohol-induced incidents typically precipitate the crisis and are usually life threatening, requiring a new degree of intervention. These troubled children have probably been or are currently involved in community-based treatment, which usually has not focused on substance abuse. Instead, they are treated for a myriad of problems ranging from sexual acting out to suicidal ideation. The children, however, continue to abuse alcohol and other drugs until substance-induced crises occur.

The typical adolescent needing residential care is about 15 years old and in a crisis that has prompted an adult to take action. She can no longer hide her problem. She has usually been in the addiction cycle for at least four years. She started by experimenting with alcohol and marijuana and is now using a variety of other drugs on a daily basis. She is of average or above-average intelligence and has had an uneventful school history until recently. Her grades are now dropping, and her attendance at school is erratic. Her peer group has changed and she no longer participates in school activities.

This female adolescent is confused about her feelings and usually has experienced trauma. For many reasons, she sees her parents as emotionally unavailable and unaware of any problem. She thus buries her feelings and attempts to cope in the easiest way she can. This young girl acts like a victim with a shattered ego and low self-esteem and views her world from this perspective. Adults do not seem to validate her or meet her needs, her family appears to her as uncommunicative and uncaring, her community is a threat. Only the negative peer group seems to be a lifeline, a safe haven. It is nonthreatening, validates her behavior, and supports her dangerous choices and drug-induced methods of instant relief.

This adolescent comes into treatment feeling guilty, confused, and wary of most adults. She sees herself as having no choices and no hope, and she is stuck with the dangerous pattern she has established.

Rhea and Pam exemplify the variety and complexity of chemically dependent female adolescents requiring residential treatment.

RHEA

Rhea was 14 years old when admitted to Caritas House for alcohol and other drug abuse. She was repeating eighth grade and had been in counseling at a family-service agency in an outpatient drug-treatment program. She was drinking on a daily basis and was frequently truant. She complained of "not fitting in," felt angry all the time, and just wanted to "get drunk to relieve the pain." When Rhea came into treatment, she began to work on anger over her childhood deprivation. She disclosed that an uncle had sexually abused her.

Rhea's family situation had been chaotic for many years but was stable at the time of admission. Her mother, one of nine children, had been a victim of sexual abuse and was just beginning to deal with that problem as part of her four-year recovery from alcoholism. Her twin was born with cerebral palsy. All except two of the maternal siblings had severe alcohol problems. The mother's three other daughters are also alcoholic. While Rhea was growing up, her mother had been in several relationships, including a six-year marriage. Rhea's biological father lives out of the state and has little or no contact with her. He was one of six children. Both of his parents and two brothers were alcoholic. Her stepfather moved in when she was 11 and married her mother when Rhea was 13.

PAM

Pam was 16 years old when admitted to Caritas House for substance abuse. Her school referred her when she was caught dealing drugs. She had not been in treatment before. At admission, Pam reported drinking and taking other drugs on a daily basis. She spoke of confusion about her behavior and had no insight into her problems.

Her family did not appear to be dysfunctional. Her parents had been married for 18 years and Pam had one sibling, age 12. Her father, who was disabled due to a heart condition, had been married previously and had one son. He worked part time and her mother worked full time. The parents reported that the family was stable and indicated bafflement over their daughter's behavior.

Pam's therapy initially was uneventful. She was nonverbal, superficially cooperative, and appeared relieved to be in treatment. In time she disclosed that her stepbrother had molested her and that at age 12 she had been attacked by several teenagers. She felt angry, fearful, and unprotected. She expressed anger at both parents—especially her mother—and resented her mother's attempts to get closer to her. She reported that both parents knew about the sexual abuse, were initially angry, but then never talked about it again. Midway through treatment, Pam's mother revealed that she had been sexually abused as a child and that her husband was alcoholic.

PROGRAM DESCRIPTION

Caritas House is a residential treatment program for female adolescent substance abusers and their families. It was originally located at the Rhode Island Medical Center and moved into a community facility located in Pawtucket, R.I., in July 1980. The program is funded by state and federal treatment grants and through contributions and fees for services.

Established in 1972, Caritas House was the first program in Rhode Island to break new ground by treating young people in a residential setting. Previously, the only residential drug-treatment programs were designed for hard-core narcotic addicts. The founders of Caritas House wanted to deal with the rapidly growing problem of drug-involved youth who were not yet hard-core addicts. They thus developed a comprehensive program that met the particular needs of female adolescent drug and alcohol abusers. Treatment could be shorter and the long-term consequences of addiction could be avoided, the founders thought, by working with youngsters who had not established long-term abusing patterns.

Family involvement is an essential part of the Caritas House program. The founders believe that family dysfunction is the main cause of substance abuse, but also consider the family to be a major instrument for positive change. Young girls can usually be treated best within the context of family. They are not successfully treated in a vacuum or as separate entities. In fact, Caritas House attributes its high success rate to parental involvement. The experience of the past 17 years clearly indicates that children get well and change self-destructive behavior if parents participate and firmly agree to be part of the solution. Parental involvement, which the children need and want, motivates the youngsters to complete the program successfully and to lead productive, drug-free lives.

The program takes into account the following factors, which illuminate Caritas House's pragmatic approach to treating adolescents for substance abuse:

- The negative peer group exacerbates the situation—remove the child from the peer group.
- The child is in crisis—defuse the crisis first.
- The child has easy access to alcohol and other drugs—remove access and temptation.
- The child is in pain—help her, through group therapy, to understand the pain.

- The child is reacting to family dysfunction—provide family counseling with a goal toward improved family functioning.
- The child is failing in school—provide a closely monitored tutorial situation aimed at success.
- The child is out of control—provide structure and set limits.
- The child has a fragile ego—design an ego-building program.
- The child does not want help—force the issue.
- The child is making poor choices—adults make temporary choices for her.
- The family is part of the problem—include the family in the solution.
- The parent has lost control—help the parent through therapy to restore the parental role.

The basic philosophy of the Caritas House program could be characterized as a *total-person/total-problem* approach. The adolescent's physical, emotional, intellectual, interpersonal, and developmental dynamics, as well as her family, educational, and other life situations, are all related to her problem.

Caritas House provides a therapeutic milieu in which to address a girl's entire life in an integrative approach. Causes as well as symptoms are dealt with, leading to more lasting and meaningful resolutions. The program is a settling experience in the often chaotic life of a troubled adolescent. It gives her a truly safe haven, unlike the negative peer group, where she can reflect as well as explore her potential and be a kid again.

PROGRAM STRUCTURE

The program has four treatment stages that give each girl a flexible framework for measuring her progress (see Table 8-1). Since each girl comes to Caritas House with a unique combination of problems, a strictly time-based program would be inappropriate.

Each girl's progress depends on her behavior, self-control, and efforts to improve her self-image. As she progresses through the defined stages, she gradually earns more freedom to test her newly found skills. She works in the house on one of many crews. She is expected to continue her education, participate in all therapy groups and family counseling, and meet all other program requirements. She constantly evaluates herself and sets weekly goals. Staff, parents, and other residents—her peer group—help her in this process.

Daily group and individual therapy, led by assigned staff, is required of all residents. Additionally, two ongoing programs, with specific contents and schedules,

Table 8-1
Treatment Stages

Characteristics	Stage
Lasts approximately six weeks. Begins with three weeks without "passes" and ends with three weeks of "passes" progressing from four to 12 hours. This stage is for the purpose of becoming accustomed to the program routine. Residents begin to handle small responsibilities (e.g., answering the door, maintaining bulletin board, watering plants); also is assigned to a "crew" (housework, laundry, or kitchen). Group therapy in this stage is more of a didactic experience, with a focus on communication, trust, listening, verbal skills, and identifying needs. Much of the time is spent on observation, with little or no pressure to "work" (therapeutically). Intense therapy is introduced in later stages.	First
Lasts approximately four weeks with passes ranging from 16 to 24 hours. These passes are spent only with family and are closely supervised by parents. The resident becomes the "head" of a crew and earns privileges for positive behavior. She "works" (therapeutically) to earn longer passes, as her group work becomes more directed and intense at this point. When the resident thinks she has successfully handled all the aspects of this stage, she writes a proposal that describes her progress and explains why she is ready for the third stage. The staff reviews the proposal and a decision is made for acceptance or rejection. Family counseling may begin toward the end of this stage.	Second
Lasts approximately six weeks. Resident is "in-house" from Sunday night through Thursday night. The rest of the week is spent at home with her family. Group counseling sessions become more directed at this point to include any issues the resident faces while at home or out in the community. Future life goals are discussed in depth, and family counseling continues with the focus on strengthening family relationships.	Third

Characteristics	*Stage*
Lasts approximately 16 weeks and is made up of three phases: (a) resident goes to her community school and is given more freedom to see friends and to test herself in the community—Thursday night and weekends at Caritas House for four weeks: (b) Thursday night and every other weekend at Caritas House for four weeks; (c) outpatient requirements are Thursday-night group counseling, family counseling, or any other goal-oriented therapy as per an agreed-upon contract.	Fourth

(Condensed from *Caritas House Policies and Procedures Manual*, 1983).

combine education and counseling about alcohol abuse and human sexuality. Everyone regularly attends Alcoholics Anonymous (AA) meetings. Early in treatment, each girl begins family counseling, which continues throughout her stay in the program.

Each girl is required to continue her junior- or senior-high-school education while at Caritas House through an individualized tutoring system. She also has supervised study hours every day. Other educational programs are added to meet other problems as they arise. Recreational and cultural activities are offered daily. Each girl also learns practical skills as she, with close staff supervision, carries out daily household chores, including cleaning, cooking, and maintenance.

All parents are required to participate in family counseling and parent groups, which are designed to help parents learn about feelings and communication skills. Specific topics, such as alcoholism and substance abuse, sexuality, parenting, denial, and letting go of one's children, introduce parents to family and adolescent issues. Parents learn to communicate with each other about common concerns and soon begin to share their experiences naturally.

The characteristics that make Caritas House an especially effective treatment program include:

1. Homogeneity of client population and homogeneity and constancy of its staff. The resident population and all staff are female. Furthermore, although residential drug-treatment programs traditionally have high staff-turnover rates, it is remarkable that Caritas House has a better staff-retention rate than most outpatient programs (Raky, 1982).
2. Family focus. The identified client is neither the sole nor the major focus of treatment. The primary focus of the program is on changing those behaviors of the individual and the family unit that have resulted in an adolescent female's acting out. The program attempts to help all family members exam-

ine and modify patterns of interaction so that the needs of the individual members can be met in more personally and socially productive ways.

3. Homogeneity and continuity of treatment. Although each girl and her family work out an individualized treatment plan designed to meet their unique situations and needs, each resident and family progress through a structured program in specifically defined stages. All residents are subject to the same rules, regulations, and responsibilities, and all receive the same treatment, that is, individual and group therapy, activities and educational programs, family counseling and parent groups. Furthermore, the nine full-time staff members function as a therapy team and cover the program seven days a week, 24 hours a day. All residents and their families interact with all staff, and all staff members are involved in setting goals, planning treatment, noting progress, and planning discharge for all residents. The team approach provides a continuity of treatment regardless of who is on duty.

FOLLOW-UP STUDY

Overview

In 1983, ten years after the program's establishment, a follow-up study was begun.

The purpose of the study was to determine what criteria contributed to the success of this residential substance abuse treatment program for adolescent females.

Study Participants

The participants in this study were drawn from two sources. The first group was from the pool of 116 adolescent female substance abusers (and their families) discharged from Caritas House between July 1, 1975, and June 30, 1980. A second sample of 90 was drawn from clients discharged between July 1, 1980, and December 31, 1988. Data from this second sample are currently being analyzed. Preliminary findings, as they relate to those of the initial study, are noted.

On the basis of criteria specified in the "Procedures" section, 73 of the 116 clients in the first sample were selected for the study. All participants consented to the use of their social, treatment, and follow-up information in this study, and 37 agreed to a personal interview. To protect anonymity, we omitted all identifying information, referring to participants solely by code numbers.

Ten individuals from the initial pool were discarded. Six could not be rated with maximum confidence because of insufficient follow-up information, three had cyclic periods of successful and unsuccessful functioning following discharge, and one had died.

STUDY METHODS

For the purpose of analyzing data and testing hypotheses, individuals from the final pool of 63 participants were assigned to groups by means of an outcome ratings scale (Table 8-2) that measured each participant's level of functioning following discharge. The rating scale took into account criminal activity, opioid use and treatment, nonopioid use and treatment, alcohol use, productive activities, relationship with parents (or parent substitute), and overall success relative to other participants. On the basis of a composite score derived from these ratings, the participants were assigned to one of three outcome groups: (1) those judged on follow-up as having achieved high success based on six specific outcome criteria and a single global rating of success (N = 24); (2) those judged on follow-up as having achieved moderate success on those criteria (N = 20); and (3) those judged as having achieved low success (N = 19).

The following specific procedures were used to assign persons to these categories:

1. From a list we selected the residents who had spent at least three months in the program and met the following additional criteria: when admitted, they were residents of Rhode Island, were between the ages of 12 and 16, and were involved with alcohol and other drugs to the extent that their family, school, or community functioning was disrupted. In addition, all participants were self-admitted or court referred. They had failed with home or community based treatment and had demonstrated the need to be removed from the home for treatment. A letter describing the nature and purpose of the project was sent to all prospective participants, along with a consent-to-participate form to be signed and returned to the program director. Five individuals or families refused to participate and were excluded.

2. The principal investigator (DMB) conducted three orientation sessions for the Caritas House staff members assisting in this study. During these sessions, behavioral descriptions of "success" categories were developed and the staff was instructed in the use of the Outcome Rating Scale prepared for this study.

3. Using the outcome scale and criteria, five Caritas House staff members independently rated each participant. Their ratings were based on follow-up information obtained from case records, the program director's journal, and personal contacts with the residents after discharge. Each staff member also rated the level of confidence of her ratings (high, moderate, low). After completing the independent ratings, the staff was asked to reach consensus on ten clients about whom there had been disagreement and/or who had received moderate or low confidence ratings. In no case was there greater than one point disagreement, and in no case was there more than one staff member

Continued on p. 183

Table 8-2
Outcome Rating Scale

Area[a]	Ratings[b]
1. Criminality	1—arrests for crimes against persons or crimes of profit, or any illegal support from robbery, burglary, or dealing drugs
	2—illegal support or arrests, but only for so-called "victimless crimes" such as gambling or prostitution
	3—no illegal support or arrests
2. Opioid use and treatment	1—daily use in one or more months, either with or without treatment
	2—any use that was less than daily and/or any drug treatment
	3—no use and no drug treatment
3. Nonopioid use and treatment	1— daily use in one or more months, either with or without drug treatment
	2—any use that was less than daily and/or any drug treatment
	3—no use and no drug treatment
4. Alcohol use	1—average of over 8 oz. of 80-proof alcohol per day
	2—average of 4.1 to 8 oz. of 80-proof alcohol per day
	3—average of not more than 4 oz. of 80-proof alcohol per day
5. Productive activities	1—no employment, school, or homemaking reported since discharge
	2—engaged in employment, homemaking, or school fewer than two-thirds of the months since discharge
	3—engaged in employment, homemaking, or school for more than two-thirds of the months since discharge

Area[a]	Ratings[b]
6. Relationship with parents (or parent substitute)	1—stormy relationship with both parents, communication very poor or absent; conflict and hostility prevail; unable to come to agreement on any issues
	2—fairly stable relationship and good communication with one parent only; poor communication, open hostility, and/or conflict with other parent
	3—fairly stable relationship with both parents; communication is open; little or no hostility; conflict and differences are mutually resolved
Overall success relative to other participants	1—less successful than most other participants
	2—no better or worse than most other participants
	3—more successful than most other participants

[a]Outcomes 1–5 based on studies by Hornick, Demaree, Sells, & Newman, 1977; Simpson & Savage, 1979; Simpson, Crandall, Savage, & Pavia-Krueger, 1980.

[b]All ratings were based on participant's functioning at time of follow-up.

in disagreement. Consensus with maximum confidence was achieved on all but six cases.

4. The principal investigator, without knowledge of staff ratings, gathered all data relevant to the independent variables from the case records, staff logs and journals, and other sources.

5. The principal investigator conducted client/family interviews for a subsample ($N = 37$). These interviews were 60 to 90 minutes long and focused on the criteria described in the Outcome Ratings Scale. Prior to the interview, the client and/or family rated the client's postdischarge functioning on each of the seven outcome criteria. The interviewer also solicited the participants' impressions of the strengths and weaknesses of the Caritas House treatment program and clarified vague or missing treatment or social history information. Five additional participants were interviewed by phone.

6. Using the outcome ratings made by the Caritas House staff, a composite outcome score was derived for each participant. For the purpose of analysis, participants were assigned to one of the three outcome groups. A person unfamiliar with the study and its participants performed the final data analysis.

Variables Studied

The principal investigator collected the following data from each participant's admission forms and case records:

A.   Client admission characteristics
   1.   Age at admission
   2.   Education, including GPA, and school status
   3.   Number of arrests/convictions
   4.   Number of prior admissions
   5.   Previous treatment
   6.   Type of admission
   7.   Source of referral
   8.   Drug-use history (age at onset, type, number, and frequency of drugs used)
B.   Antecedent family characteristics
   1.   Sibling position (only, oldest, middle, or youngest), sex of siblings, and family size
   2.   Socioeconomic status (derived from parents' education and occupation using Hollingshead's two-factor index of social position [cf., Miller, 1983, pp. 300–301])
   3.   Parents' work history
   4.   Family crises having emotional, long-lasting effects (for client, siblings, parents, grandparents, and/or other significant relatives) defined as the occurrence of incest and other childhood sexual abuse; physical abuse; prolonged and/or recurrent parental absences; death; alcoholism; drug abuse; treatment for mental illness, including overdoses and suicidal attempts; and major physical illness
C.   Client characteristics at discharge
   1.   Involvement in productive activities, based on information in discharge reports. Each participant was classified either as:
      a.   engaged in productive activities (attending school, employed, or managing a household at least 20 hours per week)
      b.   not engaged in productive activities
   2.   Involvement in drug use, based on information in discharge reports, staff interviews, and client–family interviews. Participants were classified as:
      a.   still involved in drugs
      b.   occasional use of pot or alcohol
      c.   not known to use drugs
   3.   Congruence of psychosocial goals. Client treatment plans, educational assessments, and discharge plans provided the basis for judging this variable. Each participant was rated according to the following classifications:
      a.   goals consistent across all areas and compatible with self-description (high congruence)

b. some inconsistency across goals or potential incompatibility with self-description (moderate congruence)
c. goals unclear and inconsistent from one area to another and incompatible with self-description (low congruence).

D. Family characteristics at discharge
1. The principal investigator gathered information about family participation in parents' groups, family counseling, visiting, telephone calls, volunteer work for Caritas House, and special events, as well as how families related to staff and other parents, from family counseling notes, parent group notes, staff logs, discharge reports, and staff and family interviews (see Table 8-3). Each family was then classified as:
    a. no or low commitment to treatment
    b. minimal commitment to treatment
    c. meets program expectations
    d. goes beyond program expectations
2. Family type was determined using categorical descriptions based on Fisher's (1979) classification of families.[1] Information contained in family counseling notes, social histories, and discharge summary provided the basis for this variable. An independent rater familiar with the classification schema and the family counselors who had been assigned to the cases during residence (or other staff member familiar with the family) independently rated each family as:
    a. constricted
    b. internalized
    c. object-focused (child or community)
    d. self-focused
    e. impulsive
    f. childlike
    g. chaotic
3. Family environment (composition). On the basis of case-record information, the principal investigator classified each family as:
    a. traditional
    b. single parent
    c. reconstituted
    d. substitute
    e. nontraditional
    f. other
For specific criteria, see Table 8-4.

E. Treatment characteristics
1. Participant's treatment stage at time of discharge was obtained from the discharge reports.

Continued on p. 187

Table 8-3
Family Involvement in Treatment

Characteristics	Rating
• Contact only to complain—negative contact. • Rely on social worker to take care of special needs and emergencies. • Do not provide for basic needs. • No transportation; passes must meet family's schedule. • Little or no participation in parent group. • Little or no participation in family counseling. • Constant cancellations.	None or Low
• Parent group 75%; family counseling 50–60%. • Call to complain, cancel, or reschedule. • Kids call them. • No volunteer work.	Minimum
• Twice-a-week group and visit. • Phone at least three times a week; special visit once. • Call or contact during passes. • Cook once a week. • Question decisions of staff; support other parents. • Often ask for extra time. • Overall, demanding group in terms of staff time.	Meets program expectations
• All of the above plus: donate time, call every day. • Available for special events. • Interested in other CH kids in addition to their own.	Goes beyond program expectations

Table 8-4
Family Enviroment
(Household Composition)

Characteristics	Rating
Intact or extended—parents and child(ren); two or three generations	Traditional
One parent and child(ren)	Single parent
One biological parent and spouse (stepparent) and child(ren) (siblings and stepsiblings)	Reconstituted
Foster home, group home, children's center, adopted children	Substitute
Parent and nonrelated adult (not legal spouse or parent) and child(ren)	Nontraditional
Independent living; sister and brother-in-law; back and forth between separated, divorced or remarried parents; grandparents	Other

2. Whether a resident completed her educational or skill-development programs was obtained from the discharge report.
3. The principal investigator determined the level of informal postdischarge contact with the Caritas House staff using information found in the case record (including follow-up correspondence) and the program director's log, and from interviews with the Caritas House staff. From this information, she rated each participant's level of contact as:
   a.   high (at least twice a week)
   b.   moderate (once every two to three months)
   c.   low (no contact until they encountered trouble), or none.

OUTCOME MEASURES

Composite Scores

Postdischarge outcomes (i.e., ratings pertaining to behavior after discharge) were represented by a composite score calculated as a sum of several independent outcome criteria, which included criminality (arrests and illegal support); opioid (heroin, illegal methadone, or other opiates) use and/or treatment; nonopioid (cocaine, amphetamines, barbiturates or sedatives, hallucinogens, and other nonopiate drugs except marijuana) use and/or treatment; alcohol use (expressed in average daily consumption); family relationships (with parents or parent substitutes); and a global rating of overall success after discharge relative to other participants.[2]

OUTCOME GROUPS

The composite outcome scores were first inspected to determine the range and then trichotomized to yield three fairly equal outcome groups. Participants were assigned to the three outcome groups using the following criteria:

Composite score of 16 or lower = low success group
Composite score of 17 to 19 = moderate success group
Composite score of 20 to 21 = high success group

Data-Analysis Procedures

Information gathered in interviews is summarized separately. All other data were analyzed using the SAS and SPSS statistical packages (Hull & Nie, 1981; Sall & Standish, 1982).

Participants in the study, classified into three outcome groups, were compared on antecedent family characteristics, admission characteristics, length of time in treatment, and length of time since discharge. Whenever substantial differences between outcome groups were observed in means, percentages, or frequencies, chi-square analysis or analysis of variance (ANOVA) was carried out to determine the significance of these differences.

Chi-square analysis was carried out for each of the following variables:

Family involvement in treatment
Family type
Family composition
Client involvement in productive activities at discharge
Client involvement with drug use at discharge
Congruence of client's psychosocial goals
Treatment stage
Educational or skill development program complete
Postdischarge contact

Cramer's phi coefficients were obtained to measure degree of association.
The sections that follow describe the findings concerning characteristics of the

total sample and include statistical analyses and comparisons of the three outcome groups.

RESULTS

Client Admission Characteristics

AGE AT ADMISSION

The findings for client admission characteristics are summarized in Table 8-5. The average for the first sample was 15.62 years (S.D. = 1.29) with a range of 12–19 years. Slightly more than half (54%) of the sample were 15 years or younger; there was one 12-year-old participant and only one 19-year-old. While the average age at admission has remained about the same in the second sample, the range has narrowed to 13–17.

EDUCATION

Most of the participants in this study were in grades 8 through 10 (73%), and only one had completed high school. The mean school grade upon admission for the sample was 9.80 (S.D. = 1.17) with a range of 8–13. A substantial majority (84%) of the sample were still attending school at the time of admission, an interesting finding given the extent of their drug involvement and the near absence of school referrals (see Table 8-5). In the second sample, those attending school increased to about 94%.

ARRESTS

The findings regarding the difference in number of arrests prior to entering treatment across outcome groups are presented in Table 8-5. Eleven of the participants in the sample had records of arrest: nine had one recorded arrest, and two had three recorded arrests.

The only significant differences among outcome groups with respect to admission characteristics was in the number of recorded arrests prior to admission. However, statistical analysis of the data indicated that the group variances were not homogeneous, and heterogeneity was only partially corrected by a square-root transformation of the raw data. This finding, therefore, should be interpreted with caution.

PREVIOUS TREATMENT

Fifty-four percent of the sample had received previous treatment from at least one other source and 24% from two to four other sources. This latter figure is consistent with the percentage of referrals from outpatient clinics (see Table 8-5). Again, the data for the second sample show some notable differences: 87% had received

Table 8-5
Sumary of Client Admission Characteristics

| Variable | Outcome group | | | Total | F^a χ^2 df |
	High Success	Moderate Success	Low Success		
Education					
Grade x̄	9.88	9.72	9.79	9.80	
					0.09 2
Range	8–13	8–12	8–12	8–12	

	f (%)	f (%)	f (%)	f (%)	
In school	21 (91%)	17 (85%)	15 (88%)	53 (88%)	0.41 2
Dropped out	2 (9%)	3 (15%)	2 (12%)	7 (12%)	
N= 23		20	17	60	

Previous Treatment					
x̄	.88	1.05	0.89	0.94	
					0.14 2
Range	0–4	0–4	0–4	0–4	

Age at Admission					
x̄	15.71	15.45	15.68	15.62	
					0.24 2
Range	12–19	14–18	14–18	12–19	

Referral Source					
Family/friend	10 (42%)	9 (45%)	6 (32%)	25 (40%)	
Outpatient clinic	10 (42%)	1 (5%)	5 (26%)	16 (25%)	
					11.91 6
Child welfare/ court/corrections	3 (13%)	5 (25%)	6 (32%)	13 (21%)	
Other	3 (13%)	5 (25%)	6 (32%)	9 (14%)	

Arrests					
x̄	0.04	.50	0.21	0.24	
					14.35* 2
Range	0–1	0–3	0–1	0–3	

*$p < 0.05$

previous treatment from at least one source and 54% from two to four other treatment sources.

TYPE OF ADMISSION (LEGAL STATUS)

Most of the participants had been admitted to treatment on a voluntary basis (83%); only 11 (17%) had been court stipulated.

REFERRAL SOURCE

Most participants in the sample were referred to the treatment program by their own families or family friends (40%). Two other common sources were outpatient substance-abuse and mental-health clinics (25%), and court, correction, or child-welfare offices (21%). Only two participants had been referred to treatment by school personnel. Preliminary analysis of the data from the second sample indicates a number of recent changes in referral source. Approximately 50% of the second sample were referred to Caritas House from 21-day residential programs. Referrals of this type were nearly nonexistent in the initial study. Referrals from school guidance counselors also have increased since the first study but are still relatively low given that nearly every girl in this second sample was attending school just prior to admission.

DRUG-USE HISTORY

The data for drug use were analyzed separately for number of drugs, frequency of use, and type of drugs used.

1. Age at onset: The participants in this sample began to use drugs at a very early age (see Table 8-6). Onset of drug use ranged from ten to 15 years with a mean of 12.48 years (S.D. = 1.09). Half the sample began using drugs at age 12 or younger. Given that the average age at admission was 15.62 (S.D. = 1.29), most participants had been using drugs for about three years before entering treatment or for a quarter of their lifetime. The situation has become even more bleak. In the second sample, onset of drug use ranged from age seven to 15, with an average onset at about age 11. The youngest child in this sample was using alcohol, marijuana, and cocaine at the age of seven.
2. Type, number, and frequency of drugs used: The findings for specific type of drug used, the number of participants using each drug, and the frequency of use of the various drugs (reported in Table 8-7) provide a clearer picture of the drug use pattern of this sample. The most commonly used drugs were depressants (97%) and drugs with mixed effects (95%). They used relatively fewer stimulants other than nicotine (56% and 24%, respectively, for amphetamines and cocaine). For the second sample, the use of depressants, illegal stimulants, and drugs with mixed effects were reported with about equal frequency in the 95% range.

Continued on p. 195

Table 8-6
Drug Use History[a]
(Prior to Admission)

Variable	Outcome Group			Total	Comments
	High Success	Moderate Success	Low Success		
Age at onset					
x̄	12.55	12.33	12.56	12.48	50% (29) 12 yrs. or younger
Range	10–15	11–14	10–15	10–15	
Number of drugs used ever					
x̄	4.25	4.40	4.26	4.30	44% (27) using four or more different
Range	1–6	2–6	2–11	1–11	drugs
Weekly					
x̄	2.36	2.78	3.40	2.78	51% (28) using three or more different
Range	0–6	1–6	0–7	0–7	drugs
Daily					
x̄	1.43	1.44	1.73	1.52	43% (23) using two or more different drugs 83% (45) one
Range	0–5	0–3	0–5	0–5	or more

[a]Excluding nicotine.

Table 8-7
Drug Use History-Type by Frequency of Use

Drug Type	Nᵃ	At Least Daily f	%	Several Times/Wk. f	%	Less Than Once/Week f	%	Users f	%	Non-Users f	%
Depressants/ analgesics (all Ss, all types)	63	21	(33%)	30	(48%)	10	(16%)	61	(97%)	2	(3%)
Alcohol— all Ss	63	14	(22%)	21	(33%)	20	(32%)	55	(87%)	8	(13%)
High success	24	3	(13%)	8	(33%)	9	(38%)	20	(83%)	4	(17%)
Mod. success	20	5	(25%)	6	(30%)	7	(35%)	18	(90%)	2	(10%)
Low success	19	6	(31%)	7	(37%)	4	(21%)	17	(89%)	2	(11%)
Other general depressants—all Ss	63	10	(16%)	11	(17%)	21	(33%)	42	(67%)	21	(33%)
High success	24	6	(25%)	3	(13%)	8	(33%)	17	(71%)	7	(29%)
Mod. success	20	1	(5%)	5	(25%)	7	(35%)	13	(65%)	7	(35%)
Low success	19	3	(16%)	3	(16%)	6	(32%)	12	(63%)	7	(37%)
Narcotics—all Ss	63	0		0		4	(6%)	4	(6%)	59	(94%)
High success	24	0		0		2	(8%)	2	(8%)	22	(92%)
Mod. success	20	0		0		0		0		20	(100%)
Low success	19	0		0		2	(11%)	2	(11%)	17	(89%)
Stimulants (all Ss, all types)	63	48	(78%)	2	(3%)	8	(13%)	58	(92%)	5	(8%)
Nicotine— all Ss	63	44	(70%)	0		1	(2%)	45	(71%)	18	(29%)
High success	24	15	(63%)	0		0		15	(63%)	9	(37%)
Mod. success	20	14	(70%)	0		1	(5%)	15	(75%)	5	(25%)
Low success	19	15	(79%)	0		0		15	(79%)	4	(11%)
Amphetamines— all Ss	63	5	(8%)	10	(10%)	20	(32%)	35	(56%)	28	(44%)

Continued on p. 194

Drug Type	N^a	At Least Daily		Several Times/Wk.		Less Than Once/Week		Users		Non-Users	
		f	%	f	%	f	%	f	%	f	%
High success	24	3	(13%)	2	(8%)	7	(29%)	12	(50%)	12	(50%)
Mod. success	20	2	(10%)	4	(20%)	7	(35%)	13	(65%)	7	(35%)
Low success	19	0		4	(21%)	6	(32%)	10	(53%)	9	(47%)
Cocaine— all Ss	63	3	(5%)	3	(5%)	9	(14%)	15	(24%)	48	(76%)
High success	24	2	(8%)	0		4	(17%)	6	(25%)	18	(75%)
Mod. success	20	0		1	(5%)	4	(20%)	5	(25%)	15	(75%)
Low success	19	1	(5%)	2	(11%)	1	(5%)	4	(21%)	15	(79%)
Hallucinogens (all Ss, all types) (LSD, mescaline)	63	5	(8%)	6	(10%)	14	(22%)	25	(40%)	38	(60%)
High success	24	2	(8%)	0		9	(38%)	11	(46%)	13	(54%)
Mod. success	20	1	(5%)	2	(10%)	1	(5%)	4	(20%)	16	(80%)
Low success	19	2	(11%)	4	(21%)	4	(21%)	10	(53%)	9	(47%)
Drugs with^b mixed effects (all Ss types)	63	39	(62%)	9	(14%)	12	(19%)	60	(95%)	3	(5%)
Tetrahydro- cannabinoids (THC) all Ss	63	39	(62%)	9	(14%)	12	(19%)	60	(95%)	3	(5%)
High success	24	13	(54%)	5	(21%)	5	(21%)	23	(96%)	1	(4%)
Mod. success	20	13	(65%)	3	(15%)	3	(15%)	19	(95%)	1	(5%)
Low success	19	13	(68%)	1	(5%)	4	(21%)	18	(95%)	1	(5%)
Phencyclidine (PCP), all Ss	63	7	(11%)	1	(2%)	5	(8%)	13	(21%)	50	(79%)
High success	24	1	(4%)	0		1	(4%)	2	(8%)	22	(92%)
Mod. success	20	5	(25%)	1	(5%)	1	(5%)	7	(35%)	13	(65%)
Low success	19	1	(5%)	0		3	(16%)	4	(21%)	15	(79%)

[a]The same person appears in each of the general categories (e.g., depressants, stimulants, etc.) and in each of the specific drug categories (e.g., alcohol, nicotine, etc.) as either user or nonuser.

[b]Drugs in this category (mixed effects) have both stimulant and sedative properties and may produce hallucinations when taken in high enough doses. Tetrahydrocannabinol (THC) is the principal psycho-active chemical found in marijuana; phencyclidine (PCP) is a commonly used animal tranquilizer. Both THC and PCP may be taken orally or inhaled after smoking (Bassuk & Schoonover, 1978; O'Brien & Cohen, 1984; Spiegel & Aebi, 1984).

Nicotine and marijuana were used on a daily basis by 70% and 62%, respectively, for the first sample. Daily use of alcohol was somewhat less common (22%) but use of alcohol at least several times a week was reported by 56% of the sample. These rates of nicotine and alcohol use dramatically exceed estimates of the rate of use of these drugs by Rhode Island teenagers in general.[3] The regular use of other stimulants (principally amphetamines), depressants other than alcohol, and hallucinogens (LSD and mescaline) was relatively less common. However, these drugs were being used at least occasionally by 56%, 67%, and 40%, respectively, of the total sample. Furthermore, six participants were regular users of cocaine, and a startling 24% of the sample had used cocaine at least occasionally.

These rates continue dramatically to exceed current estimates of the rates of use of these drugs by Rhode Island adolescents in general.[4] The most notable change in the second sample was a profound increase in the use of cocaine and the increased use of alcohol on both a daily and weekly basis. Almost without exception, alcohol (94%) and marijuana (95%) were the first drugs of use, followed by cocaine (58%) and amphetamines (25%). Furthermore, daily use of alcohol was reported by 31% of the sample and use three to four times a week by an additional 31%. Daily use of cocaine was reported by 19% of the second sample and use three to four times weekly by an additional 17%.

The young women in both of these samples were not just casual users of drugs. Excluding the use of nicotine, the data reveal that 83% of the first sample were daily users of one or more drugs and more than a third of the sample (43%) were daily users of two or more different drugs. On the average, the participants in this study had used approximately five different kinds of drugs ($\bar{x} = 4.30$; S.D. $= 1.56$), with one young woman having used as many as 11, and 27 participants (43%) having used four or more different kinds of drugs. This pattern remained the same in the second sample.

Antecedent Family Characteristics

Sibling Position and Family Size

There were no significant differences among the outcome groups in sibling position, sex of older and younger siblings, or number of siblings. The mean number of siblings for the entire sample was 3.73 (S.D. $= 2.18$), with a range of one to 12. This reflects fairly large family sizes ($x = 6.73$, S.D. $= 2.22$, range 4–15), with a mean family size double the Rhode Island average (3.26 according to the 1980 U.S. Census). The majority of the participants were middle (51%) or oldest (32%) children.

The mean number of siblings for the second sample was 2.83, with a range of one to eight, suggesting somewhat smaller family size than the original sample but still relatively large when compared with state and national averages. There is also a noticeable difference in sibling position, with the second sample having 50% first-born children and an additional 32% first-born female children.

SOCIOECONOMIC STATUS

Participant families distributed fairly evenly across socioeconomic scale (SES) II–V, with only three coming from upper-class families. Although the low-success group was slightly overrepresented among the lower SES levels, this was not statistically significant ($x^2 = 5.36$; df $= 6$; $p > 0.05$). There is a slight upward trend in the new sample, which may be partly due to the overall improvement in the Rhode Island economy and to changes in parental work history, as noted below.

PARENTS' WORK HISTORY

Seventy-seven percent of the fathers and 38% of the mothers were employed on a regular, full-time basis. According to recent U.S. Census data, these rates are slightly higher than the Rhode Island average for paternal (75%) but considerably lower than the Rhode Island average for maternal employment (50%). The high-success group tended to have a greater proportion of working mothers than either the moderate or the low-success groups (46% compared with 25% and 37% respectively), but this difference was not statistically significant ($\chi^2 = 4.92$; df $= 4$; $p > 0.05$).

The data from the second sample reflect a significant change in parental work history, most notably for mothers. Although there is an overall increase for both parents, 79% of the mothers in the second sample were working outside the home.

FAMILY CRISES

The data regarding critical events experienced by the families in the first study were analyzed separately for number of events experienced by each family and type of event. A complete list of the type of family crises reported and the frequency of occurrence in this sample can be found in Table 8-8.

1. Number of family crises. The number of critical events per family in this study ranged from one to 11. All but three families reported multiple crises, with 72% of the families experiencing four or more different crises over a span of three generations (grandparents, parents, and client or siblings). The mean for the total sample was 5.00 (S.D. $= 2.34$). The number of family crises was somewhat higher for the low-success group ($x = 6.00$) than for the moderate and high groups ($x = 4.60$ and 4.54 respectively), but ANOVA indicated that these differences were not statistically significant ($F = 2.42$, df $= 2$, $p > 0.05$). Analysis of covariance further indicated there was no need to adjust for family size, as the regression coefficient was essentially zero.

Table 8-8
Outcome Group Comparisons of Five Most Frequent Family Crises

| | Outcome Group | | | | | | |
Variable	High Success	Moderate Success	Low Success	Total	χ^2	df	ϕ'
	f	%f	%f	%f	%			
N =	24	20	19	63			
Parental divorce	12 (50%)	8 (40%)	12 (63%)	32 (51%)	2.17	2	
Mother remarried	9 (75%)	3 (38%)	3 (25%)	15 (24%)	6.40[b]	2	0.44
Parental alcohol or drug abuse							
Mother	3 (13%)	4 (20%)	6 (32%)	13 (21%)	2.36	2	
Father	10 (42%)	7 (35%)	7 (37%)	24 (38%)	.23	2	
Parental abscence							
Mother	3 (13%)	3 (15%)	5 (26%)	11 (17%)	1.52	2	
Father	3 (13%)	9 (45%)	13 (68%)	25 (40%)	14.19[d]	2	0.47
Client, abuse of							
Any sexual/ [a] physical	11 (46%)	11 (55%)	12 (63%)	34 (54%)	1.44	2	
By Family [a] Member or Friend	5 (21%)	9 (45%)	12 (63%)	26 (41%)	8.01[c]	2	0.37
Abuse of client's mother	8 (33%)	7 (35%)	6 (32%)	21 (33%)	3.11	2	

[a]Occurrences of incest across the three outcome groups were three, four, and three respectively.
[b]Sig at 0.05
[c]Sig at 0.02
[d]Sig at 0.001

2. Type of family crises. The most frequently mentioned crises were sexual and/or physical abuse of the client (53%); parental divorce (51%); parental alcohol or drug abuse (49%); parental absence (46%); and physical and/or sexual abuse of mother (33%).[5]

Although the figures for divorce approximate the national and Rhode Island divorce rates, the frequency of occurrence for the remaining four crises are alarmingly high and substantially greater than those estimated for Rhode Island children in general during the same time frame as our study:

- Sexual abuse, two per 1,000
- Alcoholism and alcohol abuse, estimates of ten to 20 per 1,000 for adult males; less than half these rates for women
- female householder, no husband present, with own children; under 18 years, 17%
- physical abuse, four per 1,000

(Source: 1980 U.S. Census [HHS Executive Summary, 1982] Rhode Island, MHRH, DSA, Alcohol Treatment Needs Assessment, 1982)

The data from the second sample indicate a rise in both parental divorce (62%) and remarriage (46%). There was also a substantial increase in reported parental alcoholism (75%). The reported occurrence of sexual and physical abuse of client or mother remains about the same but is being disclosed and addressed much earlier in treatment. Parental absence was rare in the second sample and may be partly a reflection of the program's strong insistence on parental involvement following the initial study.

Table 8-8 presents the frequency with which each of these crises was reported for the first sample's participants by outcome groups and chi-square analyses of the differences in occurrence across the three groups.

1. Sexual and/or physical abuse of client: Thirty-four of the young women (53%) in the first sample had been sexually or physically abused at some time during their childhood or early adolescence. Although all groups experienced sexual and/or physical abuse to about the same extent (46%, 55%, and 63%), there is a significant association between poor outcome and abuse by family or family friend (21%, 45%, and 63% for the high-, moderate-, and low-success groups, respectively [$\chi^2 = 8.01$, df = 2, $p < 0.02$]).

2. Parental divorce and remarriage: Although the parental divorce rate was highest for the low-success group (63%) and lowest for the moderate-success group (40%), the differences across the three groups were not statistically significant. However, comparison of the outcome groups according to number of divorced mothers who remarried did generate a statistically significant difference among the groups. In the high-success group, 75% of the divorced mothers were remarried compared with 38% and 25%, respectively, for the moderate- and low-outcome groups ($x^2 = 6.40$, df = 2, $p = 0.05$).

3. Parental alcohol or drug abuse: There were no statistically significant differences in parental substance abuse across the three outcome groups. The percentages for paternal substance abuse was quite similar across all groups, with the lowest occurrence being reported in the moderate-

outcome group (35%) and the highest percentage reported in the high-outcome group (42%). With regard to maternal substance abuse, the group differences were somewhat more substantial: alcohol or drug abuse by mother was nearly twice as great for the low-success group as for the high-success group (32% versus 13% respectively) but these differences were not statistically significant.

4. Parental absence: Both paternal and maternal absences were highest for the low-success group (father absent, 68%; mother absent, 25%) and lowest for the high-success group (father absent, 13%; mother absent, 13%). However, the group differences were statistically significant only for paternal absence $(x^2 = 14.19, df = 2, p < 0.001)$. The contingency coefficient $(0')$ of 0.47 suggests a fairly strong association between father absence/presence and treatment outcome.

5. Sexual and/or physical abuse of mother: The reported occurrence of abuse was also high for the mothers of the study participants. The reported family crisis data revealed ten mothers who had been sexually abused as children and 16 who had been physically abused as adults by either husbands or boyfriends. Taken in combination, 21 of the participants (33%) in this study had mothers who had been sexually or physically abused by men, either as children or as adults. There were no significant differences across outcome groups.

SUMMARY OF FAMILY-CRISIS DATA

Table 8-9 combines the most frequently occurring family crises according to the three family members associated with the crisis, that is, father, mother, or client. The table also reports the number of cases accounted for by each of these combinations and for each in combination with the others. Parental divorce is excluded from this analysis because the rates are consistent with state and national figures. Parental remarriage was also excluded from this table because it accounted for only two additional cases.

A substantial majority of the participants in this study (58%) came from families in which fathers were alcoholic and/or absent. Furthermore, a majority of the participants (53%) had been sexually or physically abused as children, and a third of the participants had mothers who had been abused. When considered in combination, 75% of the participants had absent and/or alcoholic fathers and had been sexually and/or physically abused as children; 70% had experienced physical and/or sexual abuse, and/or had mothers who had been abused; and, finally, father absence and/or alcoholism, and/or abuse of mother, and/or abuse of client was reported for 84% of the participants. The occurrence of one or more of six specific critical events was reported in all but nine of the families in this study.

Table 8-9
Combined Effect of Most Prominent Family Crises

Crisis	Total		High Success		Moderate Success		Low Success	
	f	%	f	%	f	%	f	%
	(N = 63)		(N = 24)		(N = 20)		(N = 19)	
1. Absent or alcoholic father	37	(58%)	11	(46%)	12	(60%)	14	(74%)
2. Sexual/physical abuse of client	34	(53%)	11	(46%)	11	(55%)	12	(63%)
3. Sexual/physical abuse of mother	21[a]	(33%)	8	(34%)	7	(35%)	6	(32%)
1 and/or 2	48	(75%)	16	(67%)	16	(80%)	16	(84%)
2 and/or 3	45	(70%)	16	(67%)	16	(80%)	13	(68%)
1 and/or 2 and/or 3	54	(84%)	20	(83%)	17	(85%)	17	(89%)

[a]Includes S cases of childhood sexual abuse.

Client Characteristics at Discharge

LENGTH OF TIME IN TREATMENT AND MONTHS SINCE DISCHARGE

The average number of months in treatment for the total sample was 14.68 (S.D. = 7.17), with a range of three to 28 months. The average number of months from discharge to follow-up was 45.62 (S.D. = 18.19), with a range of 18 to 83 months. As anticipated, there were no significant differences among the outcome groups on either of these variables.

Following the initial study, the inpatient phase of the program was shortened and a more formal, structured outpatient phase was added. The average length of inpatient stay in the second sample was about six months with a range of three to seven months. Time spent in outpatient status ranged from four to six months. Thus, overall contact period remained about the same.

INVOLVEMENT IN PRODUCTIVE ACTIVITIES

As predicted, the data revealed a very strong relationship between involvement in productive activities (school, job, homemaking) at the time of discharge and level of success at follow-up ($\chi^2 = 20.27$, df = 2, $p = .001$). Ninety-one percent of the participants rated high in success of outcome were involved in some form of productive activities at discharge. The percentage was also fairly high for the moderate-success group (74%), but considerably lower (26%) for the low-success group.

INVOLVEMENT IN DRUG USE

The data indicate that 89% of the first sample had little or no drug involvement (other than nicotine) at the time of discharge. With the exception of nicotine, a substantial 48% were totally drug-free. Only 9% of the sample were known to be involved with drug use on a regular basis at the time of discharge. It is worth noting that this variable had the most missing data: we could not obtain reliable information on drug use at discharge for 12% of the sample (four in each of the moderate- and low-success groups). As predicted, chi-square analysis of the distribution of participants across outcome groups indicated a significant relationship between known drug use at discharge and level of success at follow-up ($\chi^2 = 11.03$, df = 2, $p < 0.01$). Inspection of the contingency tables suggests that this relationship is principally due to the disproportionate number of regular drug users in the low-success group (83%).

GOAL CONGRUENCE

As predicted, a strong relationship exists between congruence of psychosocial goals and outcome. A substantial majority of participants in the high-success group had highly congruent goals at time of discharge (65%), whereas a majority of the low-success group were low in goal congruence (56%). For the moderate-success group, goal congruence fell primarily in the moderate category (63%). A chi-square test indicated that these differences across groups were highly significant ($\chi^2 = 26.76$, df = 4, $p < 0.0001$).

Family Characteristics at Discharge

FAMILY INVOLVEMENT IN TREATMENT

The number of families classified into each of the four levels of involvement in treatment were as follows:

Low involvement—four (19%)
Minimum involvement—11 (18%)
Meets expectations—30 (48%)
Goes beyond expectations—ten (16%)

For the purpose of analysis, the first and second levels were classified as "does not meet expectations" ($n = 23$) and the third and fourth levels as "meets expectations" ($n = 40$). As predicted, the analysis revealed a significant relationship between outcome and family involvement in treatment ($\chi^2 = 11.90$, df = 2, $p<$ 0.005). The high-success group had the greatest proportion of families involved at or beyond program expectations (88%), the low-success group had the fewest (37%), and the moderate group fell in between (60%).

Family Type

No constricted family types and relatively few self-focused types (6%) were in the sample. The remaining four types were fairly evenly distributed across the total sample. The most common types were the child/community-focused (24%) and the impulsive (22%) family types. Looking across the three outcome groups, the child/community-focused type was the most common among the high-success families (38%), whereas the impulsive type was most common for the moderate group (30%). Families of the low-success group were fairly evenly distributed across all represented types.

In order to test the prediction that child/community-focused and impulsive family types would be associated with successful treatment outcome, these types were combined ($n = 29$) and compared across outcome groups with all other types combined ($n = 34$). The low-success group had the fewest child/community-focused and impulsive-type families as predicted, but the differences among the outcome groups on this variable were not statistically significant ($\chi^2 = 4.56$, df = 2, $p> 0.05$).

Family Environment

This variable pertains to the composition of the household they entered upon discharge from the treatment program. The greatest proportion of the high- and moderate-success groups had been discharged to traditional families (containing biological parents and siblings), whereas the greatest proportion of the low-success group had been discharged to single-parent families. Furthermore, high-success participants were also more likely than the other two outcome groups to have entered reconstituted families (remarried parent, stepparent, and siblings). A chi-square test of the association between family composition at discharge and level of success at follow-up was significant ($\chi^2 = 16.66$, df = 6, $p = 0.01$) as predicted.

Treatment Characteristics

Treatment Stage

A substantial proportion (70%) of the total sample had progressed into at least the third stage of treatment by the time of discharge. The majority of the sample (62%) were either in, or had completed, the fourth stage of treatment at the time of discharge. This stage permits the most freedom and privileges but also involves the most responsibility and active involvement in the community. Nearly all the participants in the high-success group had progressed into the fourth stage (83%).

The percentage was somewhat lower for the moderate-success group (60%) and the lowest of all for the low-success group (37%). For the purpose of analysis, completion of the third or fourth stage was classified as late stage ($n = 39$), whereas completion of less than stage 3 was classified as early stage ($n = 24$). A chi-square test of the differences in these distributions across the three outcome groups was significant ($\chi^2 = 9.77$, df $= 2$, $p < 0.01$). As predicted, discharge during early stages was associated with low success (63%), whereas discharge during late stages was associated with high success (83%).

EDUCATION OR SKILL-DEVELOPMENT PROGRAM

A substantial majority of the total sample (75%) had completed the educational or skill-development aspect of their treatment programs. However, chi-square analysis revealed significant differences in the distribution of these individuals across outcome groups. As predicted, 100% of the high-success group had completed their educational or skill-development program, compared with 65% and 53% for the moderate- and low-success groups respectively ($\chi^2 = 13.99$, df $= 2$, $p < 0.001$).

POSTDISCHARGE CONTACT

This variable was also strongly associated with high success as predicted: heavy or moderate contact with the program staff following discharge was associated with high success (67%) and moderate success (60%). A striking 90% of those in the low-success group had little (16%) or no contact (74%) with the program or staff following discharge ($\chi^2 = 24.97$, df $= 6$, $p < 0.001$).

SUMMARY OF FINDINGS

Several predictions were made prior to data collection and analysis regarding the relationship of specific family, client and treatment variables to favorable outcome following treatment. A summary of the findings relevant to those variables is presented in Table 8-10, along with the Phi coefficients for the degree of association among variables.

Regarding client characteristics, we predicted that:

1. Involvement in school, employment, or homemaking at time of discharge would be associated with high outcome. This was confirmed. A contingency coefficient of 0.58 suggested relatively strong association among these variables.
2. Little or no drug use at time of formal discharge would be related to high outcome scores. Skewed distribution and missing data made it difficult to test this prediction. Only 9% of the sample were known to be involved in regular use of drugs at the time of discharge. However, high- and moderate-success

Table 8-10
Summary of Findings Relevant to Predictions

Variable	Prediction	Findings			
		χ^2	df	p	ϕ'
Involvement in productive activities at discharge	Confirmed	20.27	2	0.001	0.58
Drug use at discharge	Confirmed	11.03	2	<0.01	0.45
Goal congruence at discharge	Confirmed	26.76	4	0.001	0.47
Family in treatment	Confirmed	11.90	2	<0.01	0.44
Family type		NS			
Family composition at discharge	Confirmed	16.66	6	0.01	0.36
Treatment stage progress at discharge	Confirmed	9.77	2	<0.01	0.39
Education and skills development at discharge	Confirmed	13.99	2	<0.001	0.47
Postdischarge contact	Confirmed	24.97	6	<0.001	0.45

participants tended to have either little or no drug involvement at discharge, whereas regular drug use was associated with low success.

3. High congruence of psychosocial goals at time of discharge would be associated with high outcome scores. This prediction was confirmed and further specified: high goal congruence was associated with high success, moderate goal congruence with moderate success, and low goal congruence with low success. The contingency coefficient (0' = 0.47) suggested a fairly strong association of the two variables.

Regarding family characteristics, we predicted that:

1. High family involvement in treatment would be associated with high outcome scores at time of follow-up. This was confirmed for the sample.
2. Child/community-focused and impulsive family types would be associated with high outcome scores. This was not confirmed. Although the low-success group had fewer child/community-focused and impulsive-type families than the moderate or high-success groups, these differences were not statistically significant.
3. Returning to a traditional family environment at time of discharge would be related to high outcome scores. This prediction was confirmed with further

clarification. Analysis revealed that high-success was associated with return to a traditional or traditionally structured (reconstituted) family at discharge, whereas low-success participants most commonly returned to single-parent families.

Regarding treatment characteristics, we predicted that:

1. Discharge at later treatment stages would be associated with high outcome scores. This prediction was confirmed.
2. Completion of the educational or skill-development aspect of the treatment program would be associated with high outcome scores. This prediction was heartily confirmed. A contingency coefficient of 0.47 suggests a relatively strong association of these variables.
3. High levels of postdischarge contact with the treatment program and/or staff would be associated with high outcome scores. This prediction was confirmed. The contingency coefficient for the association of these variables was also fairly strong ($0' = 0.45$).

As shown in Table 8-10 eight of the nine predictions were confirmed at or beyond the 0.01 level of confidence. The strength of the association of the independent variables to outcome scores, as measured by the contingency coefficient, ranged from a high of 0.58 for involvement in productive activities to a low of 0.36 for family involvement. The frequency distributions for family environment and drug use at discharge were somewhat distorted across outcome groups, and there were eight cases of missing data for the drug-use variable. Therefore, family involvement in treatment, client involvement in productive activities, goal congruence, completion of education or skill program, and postdischarge contact are probably the strongest and most reliable predictor variables for this sample.

Interview Data

We interviewed 59% of the participants and/or one or more members of their families. The remaining 19 participants (31%) were not available at the time of scheduling or had moved out of the state. The three outcome groups were fairly evenly represented (high success, 75%; moderate success, 55%; low success, 53%), and there were no significant differences in the refusals from each group.

PROGRAM WEAKNESSES

The most common weaknesses of the program, mentioned about equally by parents and clients, were: concern about the length of the treatment schedule, the need for a longer transition period, and the need for more formal, structured follow-up. Without exception, each client interviewed mentioned feelings of postdischarge isolation and loneliness and the difficulties associated with fitting back into the community after treatment. Also mentioned were feelings of not belonging either in the community or in the program. The clients commented on the lack of support systems outside of Caritas House and about the relative absence of peers who shared or appreciated the values, attitudes, and interpersonal skills they had developed in the program. They also commented on both a need not to lose connection with the outside world and the importance of a structured aftercare program that gave them a reason to stay in contact with the program after discharge. A number of clients acknowledged that they often felt the need for help after they had left the program, but that "it was hard to ask because I felt badly about not doing okay." Others mentioned thinking that "you can only go back or call if you screw up." This suggests that involvement in some form of productive activity within the community at the time of discharge may provide some structure and direction to clients and facilitate the transition into the community. It also further substantiates the importance of postdischarge contact to maintaining improvement over time.

Clients and parents also felt the program was weak with respect to dealing with issues pertaining to sexuality and alcoholism. Both clients and parents (mainly mothers) referred to a need for greater focus on sexuality issues and male–female relationships. Parents in particular wished for more emphasis on alcoholism intervention. These themes are consistent with the findings of extensive childhood abuse, principally by trusted males, in the early lives of these young women, and with the extensive use of alcohol by such a young population. The interviews further suggest that excessive use of alcohol may be linked with anxiety and confusion about sex and sexuality and that these issues may be more important and difficult treatment areas than drug abuse per se.

PROGRAM STRENGTHS

With but one exception, everyone interviewed cited some aspect of family involvement (e.g., parents' group, family counseling, family support) when commenting on program strengths. The one exception was a father who was a counselor in the field, who acknowledged having, perhaps, a biased view. Interviewees frequently mentioned the program's focus on self-understanding and the development of interpersonal, parenting, and family communications skills. The program strength most frequently mentioned by fathers (father's involvement) was also mentioned under weaknesses by two divorced fathers—"failure to involve father initially." (It is worth noting that one of these fathers initially refused to be involved.) Several remarried mothers mentioned how beneficial the stepfather's involvement had been.

In general, the following clusters capture the essence of the interview comments regarding program strengths:

Of the program:
    routine

rules
discipline
tasks
responsibility
structure
safe

Of the staff:
supportive
understanding
fair
patient
sincere
straightforward
dedicated
compassionate
believe in the program

Of the other clients and families:
understanding
supportive
caring
sharing
loving
comforting
close
accepting

CLIENT GAINS

Judging from the case-history material, the most common characteristic among the young women of this study was disruption of their early psychosocial development. At ages as young as 11 and 12 years, these girls were sexually active, drinking regularly, and high on drugs as often as they could get them. Many had run away from home a number of times, for days, weeks, and sometimes months. During those runs, they would live on the streets with one or more older men. Some had run out of the state, some just down the street. Many were sexually and physically abused on those runs; others were abused at home. Many of them had not run away at all but had remained at home, caring for sick or troubled parents or taking on the role of an absent parent. Some of them would just sneak off during the day or at night without their overburdened parents ever being aware that there was a problem. It seems not so much that these young girls had grown up too quickly, but more important, that they missed out on a critical part of the process of growing up. Shortly after admission, when these young women were asked to respond to the question, "Who am I?" the most common answers by far were, "I don't know," or just a name.

Comments about the program strengths and client gains suggest that Caritas House provides a safe, structured, protected environment in which these young girls could take time out from a confusing, hectic, troubled life situation. It forced them to take a good look at themselves in a trusted, caring, supportive, and accepting environment, and it gave them the opportunity to complete or repair a developmental process that somehow got interrupted or distorted. Answers to the question, "What did you gain most from Caritas House?" bear this out:

". . . took me out of a bad situation and gave me time to think."
"The problems didn't change, but I learned how to cope with them better."
"No one can do it for you, you've got to do it for yourself."
"It's got to come from yourself."
"It put me in perspective."
". . . strengthened my self-image."
"Self-confidence."
"They let you be the kid that you didn't get to be 'cause you grew up too quickly."
"They're your family."

When discussing what they had gained from the program, five of the 16 clients interviewed whose families had not been involved with the Caritas House program mentioned that Caritas House had been their substitute family.

FAMILY GAINS

Clients, parents, and siblings alike repeatedly referred to the family involvement and support as being critical to success. Family involvement not only benefited the client, but also the family and other individual family members. A few examples:

". . . helped my parents to be more together."
". . . got family to open up and talk to one another."
"It especially helped us in dealing with the other, younger children."

The interview comments about family gains were quite numerous and varied, but the common themes were:

1. Parenting skills that helped them in raising their other children as well as the client: "I was able to use what I learned here in dealing with my son." "It especially helped us in dealing with our younger children." "Communication is better with the others."
2. Perspective and support that helped them to stay involved: "Seeing and hearing

other parents and not feeling like such a failure or so responsible."
". . . helped us to better understand the situation and to put things in proper perspective." ". . . let me not be guilty for my daughter." ". . . strength to get through."

OUTCOME GROUP DIFFERENCES

The interviews were scheduled, carried out, and analyzed without knowledge of the participants' outcome scores or outcome group assignments. In writing up the interview material and organizing the data, we discovered distinct differences among the interviews. Some interviews were richer in clinical content than others. Also, striking differences in some parents' attitudes or tone of comments suggested differences in the quality of their involvement with their daughters' treatment programs. These differences turned out to coincide with outcome group assignments.

For example, interviews with clients or parents of clients from the low-success group tended to be longer and richer in clinical content than the others. Reluctance to terminate the interview, and comments such as, "This [the interview] was very good for me," suggested that there may be a lot of unfinished business for these young women and their families. There were also some striking differences in the attitude and tone of comments made by some parents that suggested differences across outcome groups in the qualitative aspect of parental involvement. High-success parents tended to express gratitude for the program that focused on the whole family or the client—"Caritas House saved her life"—and were enthusiastic—"It's a great program, and I would do it again if I had to, or if I had problems with the other kids." Remarks from parents of moderate-success participants, in contrast, tended to be qualified and/or for those who had been heavily involved in the program, to have a tone, if not a direct expression, of resentment for that involvement:

"[the program] helped her, but it didn't change her that much."
"In crude English, it stunk . . . having to be at Caritas House all the time . . . too much involvement. If I had it to do over, I wouldn't."

Finally, and most distinctly, the comments from parents of low-success participants tended to focus on themselves:

"I needed a lot of help for myself. It was a great experience for me."
"All I ever wanted was to have a better relationship with my daughter than my mother had with me."
"Toward the end, I was beginning to resent having to be there so often."

SUMMARY OF INTERVIEW DATA

In general, the interview data provide subjective confirmation of how the main findings relate successful treatment outcome to:

- Involvement of client in productive activities at time of discharge
- Postdischarge contact with Caritas House
- Family involvement in treatment

The interviews also indicated that the program helped participants to develop increased self-awareness and self-confidence, which are important to long-term success. Parental comments during the interviews also suggested that the involvement of the parents of low-success clients may have been directed toward meeting their own personal needs, while the involvement of parents of the high-success clients appeared to be motivated by concern for the client or the family as a unit.

Finally, the interviews strongly indicate that families and family members other than the identified client can and do benefit from their involvement in the treatment program and that some of these benefits have been gained even by families of the low-success participants.

NATURE AND EXTENT OF THE PROBLEM: CAN WE BLAME THE CHILDREN?

What does this study tell us about substance abuse among adolescent females? Most striking is the early onset of substance abuse and the polydrug use of the young girls in this study. For nearly a quarter of their lives, they regularly used several different drugs. A majority of the sample were daily or nearly daily users of the more easily obtained drugs (nicotine, marijuana, and alcohol) but used the more expensive, scarce, and dangerous drugs whenever they could. The early psychosocial development of nearly all these young women was so disrupted that they attempted to live adult life-styles when they barely possessed the necessary skills to function adequately as children. Their reckless-drug-use patterns also underscored the desperate nature of their behavior and their apparent lack of regard for personal safety. At ages as young as 11 and 12, these young girls were sexually active, drinking regularly, and "mellowed out" on drugs as often as they could get them. Many had run away from home for days, weeks, or even months. Yet, surprisingly, few had received previous treatment and nearly all were still attending school.

Given the general characteristics of this sample, any theoretical or programmatic considerations must take into account the complex and varied nature of the problem for this population. Singling out one or another substance as the focus of education, prevention, or treatment efforts does not help. Likewise, youth prevention efforts, though important, are not sufficient to help these young women. Active intervention and treatment services for young females are needed and a reexamination of the role and responsibility of the schools in these efforts is imperative. It is difficult to comprehend how a child could be involved with drugs to the extent that this population is for so long a time without the parents' awareness or intervention, and it is equally incomprehensible that school personnel could be unaware of a 13-year-old's daily ingestion of alcohol and other drugs. Yet only two of the young women in this sample were referred to treatment by their schools.

The problem, then, seems serious, but how widespread is it? Each year, approximately 150 Rhode Island female children between the ages of ten and 19 years are referred to Caritas House, one small program (16–20 beds) in one very small state. It is the only residential program in Rhode Island specifically designed for the treatment of adolescent substance abusers and one of the few such programs in the country. Each year only about 40 of those referred are admitted for treatment. What happens to the approximately 100 youngsters per year who are not admitted? Health-care providers need to address this issue in future research. The more difficult problem is determining how many others in need are never even referred. Comments of professionals in other child care agencies suggest that the numbers are great, but these children are the boisterous, acting-out troublemakers. How many more are hiding in the classrooms?

We must reach a common understanding about the extent and seriousness of the drug problem among young women. Parents, schools, social-service agencies, health-care providers, and those in the judicial system need to recognize that girls are as likely as boys to experiment with, to use, and to abuse alcohol and other drugs. Furthermore, those who are concerned with the drug problems of young people must understand the underlying problems that lead to and complicate drug use by young women. Prevention, intervention, and treatment activities based on male or female stereotypes are inadequate. In spite of the sugar and spice, everything is not nice. All the evidence points to an ever-increasing problem among women in general and among young girls in particular. We must try to discover why, and begin to accept and deal with what girls are really made of.

THE ROLE OF THE FAMILY: CAN WE BLAME THE PARENTS?

Except for those who take a strictly genetic or sociological view of addiction, people in the field generally assume that there is a clearly identifiable, addictive family prototype and that the family plays an important role in the origin and maintenance of drug abuse problems. In general, this study supports the latter but not the former contention. In addition, the findings support an equally important, but long-overlooked, assumption that the family also plays an important role in the treatment and alleviation of drug-abuse problems, at least for a young female population.

The families of Caritas House, like the young women themselves, come in many varieties. Some are families with confused children and child-focused, concerned, and caring parents who somehow lost their way. Some are families with abused and abandoned children of abused and abandoned mothers whose own needs are too strong. Others are families with throwaway children of throwaway parents whom the system considers lost causes. Still others are families with parentlike children and childlike parents who recognize their mistakes but do not know how to change. Some are large, overwhelmed families with not enough attention, support, understanding, patience, or tolerance to go around. They are like my family or your family and the family next door. They are not families with bad children or families with bad parents—they are just families with troubled, confused, and sad children of troubled, confused, and frightened parents who do not understand what went wrong.

No clear type of drug-abusing family emerged from this study, nor did a relationship of family type to favorableness of treatment outcome. We could not identify family types that vary predictably in their responsiveness to treatment. Only one family type was not well represented for the sample, in general and across all outcome groups. However, two characteristics of this sample stand out, namely, family size and family crises.

Although socioeconomic status was of no direct importance as a distinguishing characteristic, family size does appear to be an important consideration in the study of substance abuse among adolescent females and may have interacted with other variables, such as the mother's work history and the daughter's sibling position, to exercise a subtle effect on family relationships and the children's perception of gender roles. The number of members in the families in this study was found to be considerably greater than the average for the state in general (6.73 compared with 3.26). In addition, most of the participants were either middle or oldest children, and, as a group, their mothers' employment rate was relatively low (38% compared with a 50% state average). Even though the impact of family size on financial resources is obvious, the emotional consequences are more subtle: the more children, the greater are the expenses, but the more difficult it is also for the mother to maintain employment outside of the home. With the mother unable to supplement the family income comes the further likelihood that the father will work overtime or have a second job. Thus, the distribution of parental resources in the home becomes strained and the mother's role more constrained. Older children, especially girls, are likely to receive less support and attention and/or to be called on to assist with parenting responsibilities. Furthermore, the mother/female role in such families may not be perceived in a very desirable light.

> I guess a lot of the reasons my mother and I never got along was because she knew me well and all the games; and my father who was at work all day would come home and not know what's going on. So if I asked my father to go some place, he would say "yes," and my mother would tell me "no" a lot more than him; and if my father did say "no," I could usually get him to say "yes." (Caritas House resident)

Children in such families understandably experience considerable emotional stress, role confusion, and fusing of generational boundaries. At times they may feel anxious, inadequate, deprived, and overburdened. It seems quite plausible that such youngsters would be highly attracted to strangers for false nurturance and to chemicals for emotional relief and temporary escape.

The data regarding family crises clearly indicate that drug-abusing adolescent females come from multiproblem families. Although the data do not exist to provide a comparison with the general population, the findings are impressive. All but three families reported multiple crises, and 72% experienced four or more different crises. More than 17 different kinds of family crises were mentioned, but the striking were an absent or alcoholic father and sexual or physical abuse of the client. An alarming 53% of the young teenagers in this sample had been sexually and/or physically abused, most of them by a family member or trusted family friend. Father absence or alcoholism was reported for 50% of the first sample (and 75% of the second sample) and one or the other of these events was reported for over 75% of the participants in the initial study.

This strongly suggests that adolescent substance abuse by girls is a symptom of other dysfunctions in the family and that the running-away behavior of these teenagers may be the classic cries for help or a safety valve for the family. Furthermore, as Davis and Klagsburn (1977) and Steinglass (1987) suggest, individual drug use may be an adaptive behavior within the family. Thus, drug use can be a way for the child to protect herself and the family from increased awareness of painful effects.

> I talk more with my father now, and it feels good to be close to him again. There may be a little more work to do, but I'm not afraid of him now. It's hard to start a conversation between us, and I do feel a little uncomfortable when we talk because I'm not used to it yet. . . . I'm starting to open up a lot more in family counseling. . . . Right now we're talking about the issue of sex, which is a big issue in my family. I feel a little uncomfortable, but I am still sharing my experiences and feelings. My parents seem glad to see me opening up more, and I feel better now that I am. We're really getting some place, and it feels good. . . . I feel family counseling has helped me a lot to understand my parents and for them to understand me and get closer. . . . Sometimes I wonder how hard it must be to sit through my family sessions and counsel. (Caritas House resident, father/daughter incest; both parents involved in treatment)

Although the literature hints at a link between early childhood abuse and alcoholism and addiction in women, the rates of physical and/or sexual abuse found in this study were startling. The finding suggests that the excessive use of alcohol and other drugs may be linked to anxiety and confusion about sex and sexuality secondary to trauma. Regular substance use or abuse may represent one means that physically and sexually abused women and children use to ease the shame, rage, and confusion brought about by their traumatic experiences. Furthermore, other researchers (DeAngelis & Goldstein, 1978) suggest that some drugs (e.g., PCP) may provide respite from the emotional pain and anger suffered by youngsters who have been so abused. The hostile, belligerent, and verbally abusive behavior often exhibited by young female drug abusers is most commonly attributed to the effects either of chemical intoxication or withdrawal. It is perhaps also the case that the chemical controls the rage at some stage of the intoxication and that, as the drug effects diminish, the suppressed anger surfaces in its overt form.

In addition, de Young (1982) suggests that there is a relatively high rate of physical self-abuse (wrist-cutting, overdosing, and other high-risk behavior) among incest victims. The extensive polydrug use and disregard for personal safety demonstrated by the young participants in this study most surely can be described as self-abusive behavior. The findings from this study clearly indicate that program planners and treatment providers need to be aware of these and other possible underlying circumstances, to look for causes other than drug effects, and to intervene beyond the drug problem. The family histories in this study indicate the importance of treating the whole unit rather than singling out the troubled adolescent. Furthermore, the results of treatment also support the value of a family-focused treatment approach and suggest that a supportive two-parent family structure with both parents (or parent substitutes) taking an active interest in working on the problems and the solutions maximizes treatment effectiveness.

As predicted, family involvement in the treatment program was significantly related to successful treatment outcome. For this population, treating more than just the identified client is important from a number of perspectives. At the very least, family involvement indicates to the young client that someone cares, that she is not alone, and that maybe things can get better. Such involvement may also communicate that the family is concerned for the client's well-being, is willing to make sacrifices and concessions in her behalf, and most important, that other family members are willing to take some responsibility for the problem.

Family involvement also helps the parents see that they, too, are not alone and that someone cares about them as well as their child. Involvement provides support and reassurance and helps parents regain their self-respect.

Finally, some parents discover for the first time during the treatment process how necessary and important their involvement is:

> The first time [in family counseling] we worked on what she [mother] wanted from me. Next we talked about her childhood past and about my mother's and father's divorce. The last family counseling was about all the hatred for my mother. . . . When I go home on passes we talk about different things, we communicate very well. She makes me feel really proud to have a mother like her. I don't have that hatred for her anymore. She shows that she cares, and it's not with material things either. She makes me happy. I like

being with her. (Caritas House resident; parents divorced; father in contact but living out-of-state)

THE ROLE OF THE TREATMENT PROGRAM:
WHAT MAKES A DIFFERENCE?

I am putting my fourth-stage proposal [for increased privileges at Caritas] in because I feel I am ready for it. I want to go out there and prove to myself that I can make it. . . . I want to go through more tests and pass them all by saying "no" and coming out stronger each time. But I really don't know what I'm going to do or what it's going to be like out there. I know I'm going to feel lonely once in a while and for now I think I can handle it. (Caritas House resident)

In general, the follow-up data support the general effectiveness of the treatment program for the participants in this study. Overall, we considered only eight of the 63 participants to be in trouble either emotionally, legally, or socially. At the time of follow-up, 54 participants were living what would be considered a middle/lower-middle-class life-style, typical of most young adult females in Rhode Island. Some were attending school, others were working or raising families of their own, and like many of today's young women, a few were involved in all of these activities.

Whether the Caritas House program is more effective than other treatment approaches or modalities, or no treatment at all, is a question for future research. This study was concerned with differences in outcome level. Those differences were found to be related to certain aspects of the treatment program. Program effectiveness, in other words, was enhanced by some treatment variables. Participants who had completed later stages of treatment, who had completed their educational or skill-development programs, and who had planned daily activities at the time of discharge were likely to have better outcomes than those who did not. Thus, it would seem that the opportunity to exercise a certain degree of freedom and self-responsibility successfully is an important aspect of successful adolescent residential treatment. Furthermore, involvement in productive activity within the community at the time of discharge may provide some structure and direction for the adolescent and also facilitate the transition back into the community. It also allows the youngster to test out new behaviors and a new identity with support and backup from the treatment staff.

The importance of careful posttreatment planning is also emphasized by these findings. Often, treatment programs provide adequate psychotherapeutic work during treatment but make little effort or have few resources to plan or provide for the future. Postdischarge contact with Caritas House was associated with positive outcome, which further substantiates the importance of aftercare and follow-up for maintaining improvement over time—especially for those adolescents who have less stable, more fragile family environments.

The extent to which a treatment program can compensate for family involvement is an important question for future investigation. In this study, five participants whose families were not involved in the treatment program came to view Caritas House as a substitute family. These five young women had been placed by the Department of Children and Their Families with foster families at the time of discharge from the treatment program and showed moderate to highly favorable outcome—a cause for substantial optimism. It underlines the importance of comprehensive treatment programming and interagency collaboration in providing effective treatment for this population.

From a systems perspective, involving the total family unit in the change process is essential for a young population still very dependent on a supportive family environment. When a child is brought to treatment by parents or other authorities, the expectation, stated or not, is for change. The parent usually wants and expects the child to change, and that is not always necessary, or sufficient, or even possible. The same is true of the child's expectations for the parent to change. Engaging the whole family in the treatment process not only communicates to the parents that they are in charge of and responsible for the child, but also helps them to understand the process and to be committed to changes that may be different from what they initially expected.

Finally, from a clinical perspective, the family crisis data strongly suggest that the client's drug abuse may just be the tip of the family-problem iceberg. Often, having a child in treatment provides parents with much-needed treatment for their own personal problems that they might not otherwise seek. Viewing their own issues in the context of a total family situation or with the support of others with similar problems may help parents feel less shame and guilt and lead them to a better understanding of their own behavior and that of their children. If professionals view the adolescent drug abuser as the one who is trying to help her family, the family can then use her as the means of entering treatment and change (see also Chapter 9).

Family structure or composition is related to positive treatment outcome. As predicted, clients who had been discharged to two-parent families showed the most favorable outcome on follow-up, whereas those returning to single-parent families showed the least favorable. This finding may confirm the positive aspects of the nuclear family and, thus, reaffirm the important role of a father figure in adolescent female development. A more pragmatic conclusion is that two adults are better able to support (financially and emotionally) or set limits on a child during a difficult and stressful phase of development and to support and console each other. Parents of any teenager at one time or another question their ability to maintain sanity during their children's adolescence. It is not hard to understand that a single parent in a multiproblem family would find it difficult to focus on the needs of a troubled adolescent struggling to gain a new identity.

Lastly, from a family systems perspective, it is difficult for a young client, parent, or family to work through an important treatment issue, such as divorce or separation of the parents, when a key family member is not also engaged in the process.

> I needed something a little more, so I made up this big fantasy of Daddy and I, except it was too fake to ever come true.
>
> I started inviting him up [to Caritas House] and the time we had together grew less and less. I made all the plans and all the calls; the only thing I didn't do was pay for lunch! After a short time of seeing him, I got sick of our relationship because he never really did anything, so I said goodbye to him, on the outside, anyway, only because I felt it was one of those right things to do. I have said goodbye now, though, on the inside, and it's real. (Caritas House resident; parents divorced; father living in same community but not involved)

Availability and involvement, then, would seem to be preeminent treatment considerations. The problem of getting family members—especially fathers—involved in treatment has long been recognized as an obstacle in the family-focused approach to treatment. Program planners and treatment providers need to be more creative and to devote more energy to outreach efforts, especially when the parents are separated.

Families of drug abusers, like any troubled family, can be difficult to work with. At times, a family member's resistance to involvement in treatment may be met with an underlying sense of relief. Nevertheless, when an honest effort is made to engage key family members, the results can be positive and rewarding.

Clearly, these clients and their families may have more important and more difficult issues to treat than drug abuse per se. More rigorous research in this area is necessary. Many questions remain unanswered. For example, if adolescent drug abuse reflects some dysfunction in the family, do other factors predispose a child to choose drug abuse instead of displaying other symptoms? Parental alcoholism was not reported in all cases, so this behavior is not simply transmitted from one generation to the other.

The relationship of family size to family crises also needs further investigation. In this study, the number of family crises was not correlated with family size. But differences in family crises across outcome groups suggest that the specific nature of the family crisis may be a more important consideration than simply the number of crises per se. For example, parental drug abuse or alcoholism and physical or sexual abuse of the client were equally high across all outcome groups. However, parental absence and abuse of the client by a family member or trusted family friend were highest for the low-outcome participants. Thus, it would seem that some critical events may have more severe psychosocial implications and greater long-term effects than others. The relative impact on family and child of physical abuse or sexual exploitation of a child by a family member or friend is intuitively obvious and supported by experts (National Center on Child Abuse and Neglect, 1979). The absence of the father or mother may leave a child more vulnerable to such abuse, whereas the presence of even an alcohol-impaired parent may serve as some minimal deterrent. Furthermore, although it may be necessary initially to separate an abusive parent from the family, having such parents available affords the opportunity to bring them into treatment, and possibly for change.

Future research also needs to consider the specific nature of family involvement in treatment and its relationship to outcome. The interview data hint that involvement alone may be necessary but not sufficient. Parental motivation for involvement (e.g., to meet self-needs versus the needs of the family or client) may be an equally important consideration in the long-term effectiveness of treatment.

The issue of adolescent female drug use and abuse is a varied and complex research and treatment problem. But one thing seems quite clear: if we really want to help the children, we must first try our best to save the families.

AND WHAT ABOUT SOCIETY?

Dear Abby: When a kid goes wrong, would you say it was due to his environment or heredity? D.J., Camden, N.J.

Dear D.J.: It's a toss-up. But one thing is certain. His parents will get blamed for both. (API, January 12, 1979)

In a so-called child-centered society, especially when dealing with emotional and value-laden issues such as child abuse and neglect, we tend to blame the parents and to rescue the child rather than engage and support the family in an attempt to understand the feelings, needs, and patterns that lie beneath everyday family events. We accept myths about ideal families and make assumptions about typical problem families. Holding parents responsible for their offspring is rooted in tradition, and arguments attributing child and adolescent problems to unsatisfactory family conditions have strong logical, intuitive, and moral appeal. Attitudes such as, "If the family were what it used to be and did what it used to do, there would be less drug abuse today," reverberate from the White House and are commonplace even among professionals. Historical evidence, however, lends little support to the notion that American families were once happy, cohesive, or consistent in disciplinary practices.

Furthermore, many problems within a family are clearly caused by pressures originating outside the home. More than 40 years ago, in a time less stressful than today, Reuben Hill (1949 cited in Sussman, 1968) wrote:

The modern family lives in a great state of tension precisely because it is the great burden carrier of the social order. In a society of rapid social change, problems outnumber solutions, and the resulting uncertainties are absorbed by the members of society, who are for the most part also members of families. Because the family is the bottleneck through which all troubles pass, no other association so reflects the strains and stresses of life. With few exceptions persons in work-a-day America return to rehearse their daily frustrations with the family, and hope to get the necessary understanding and resilience to return the morrow to the fray. (p. 441)

Hill later developed a schema presenting the interplay of forces that produce a family crisis, but his basic premise was that a family crisis is likely to have its roots in forces outside the family. Arlene Skolnick (1978) stressed this same point:

The strains of parenthood are not the inevitable battle of wills and the temperamental incompatibilities of adults and children. In part, they are the responsibility of social arrangements that make parents solely responsible for children and fail to provide even minimal assistance for parents as they go about their daily rounds of work and chores. (p. 295)

Even though the role external conditions play in creating family problems has been recognized for years, the family itself remains the predominant target of reform efforts. As Skolnick points out, despite repeated recommendations from numerous White House Conferences, no one has undertaken even the most basic reforms:

For example, the United States is the only industrialized country without a family health-care program that includes prenatal, maternal, and child-care services. This lack may partially explain why our infant mortality is higher than that of many other countries. Other social indicators suggesting that all is not well with American families are: the large number of families and children living in poverty, the unavailability of child-care options, and the high prevalence of child abuse. (p. 383)

Skolnick goes on to propose that "rather than trying to reform the family itself, the best strategy for improving family life would be to reduce the stresses and strains that flow from the larger society to the family" (p. 383).

Professionals in this field of substance abuse must recognize and accept that the family is not, and never has been, an emotional haven. Nostalgia for a nonexistent family tradition has been fabricated and perpetuated by the media and has prejudiced our understanding of families in contemporary society and biased our research and treatment efforts. Furthermore, exaggerating the importance of the family in a child's development can distract attention from other etiological and contributing factors, mask other potential solutions, block treatment efforts, and in general produce a sense of futility about prevention and treatment efforts for adolescents and children. Instead of taking steps to alleviate stressful conditions in society or to modulate their effects, most family-focused programs reflect an underlying assumption that the ability of parents to cope is, and should be, limitless, so long as they are constantly supplied with an ever-increasing, more sophisticated armament of parenting skills.

Other factors in effective treatment planning for adolescent females are as important as family involvement: for instance, helping the client develop a positive identity and self-esteem by providing vocational and career planning, education, and counseling in the areas of alcoholism, sexuality, and the role of women.

Finally, treatment providers can compensate, at least in part, for the lack of family support or involvement by recruiting foster families or family substitutes and involving them in the treatment program. Basing substance-abuse treatment on stereotyped views of the ideal American or typical drug-abuser family and assuming that the family system is the cause (and cure) of adolescent drug-abusing problems will not suffice. We must also focus on aspects of the larger system that contribute to the prevalence of stressful home conditions and to female identity confusion, role ambivalence, and low self-esteem. We must change social systems and policies that interfere with effective treatment and prevention efforts.

WHAT THE PROGRAM LEARNED FROM THE STUDY

The study basically corroborated what we knew to be true—that basic ingredients for meeting the needs of troubled adolescents are family involvement, nurturing, removal from pressure, and structure.

The study identified some weaknesses in the program, such as the length of stay in residence, a too-short transition period, and insufficient structured follow-up and aftercare. Study participants suggested that more attention be given to the issues of human sexuality and the girls' sexual relationships and that more teaching, therapy, and follow-up were needed concerning alcoholism.

Most of the recent changes in the program were an outgrowth of this timely, informative, and useful study. We have already modified the program to address these weaknesses specifically. For example, an outpatient component now provides more structured follow-up, aftercare, and stronger linkages to supportive community programs and other outpatient services; the program has been shortened to a four- to six-month treatment schedule; and new components have been added to address the issues of alcohol use and abuse and of sexuality and sexual relationships.

We learned that our therapeutic direction, target population, and goals were viable approaches and that major changes were not warranted. The study did, however, lead us to consider some philosophical changes. We realized that we could not solve every problem in the allotted time and thus adjusted our self-image to being the first solid step toward real family recovery after long-term family patterns of dysfunction. Parents now continue in groups for sexuality and adult-children issues. Many of the women become involved in consciousness-raising efforts and continue their quests for optimal family functioning and true family solidarity.

We now rely more heavily on the resources in the community and encourage ongoing treatment in programs such as Alcoholics Anonymous (AA). Our recent emphasis on treating alcoholism has greatly affected outcome. Support from AA lessens the relapse rate considerably and provides a meaningful, community-based support system. Before the study, we focused on drugs as being the more dangerous of the two substances, but now realize that alcohol is more insidious, more addictive, and every bit as dangerous to troubled adolescents. We are uncovering the problem more frequently and estimate that 95% of all admissions have families that in some way have been affected by alcohol abuse. AA is now almost always used as part of the contracting and backup system upon discharge.

The study helped us to devise strategies to ease transition problems regarding sexuality. We learned that poor male–female relationships are an outgrowth of poor self-concept, father loss, divorce, family alcoholism, and sexual abuse. These issues are addressed from the beginning of—and throughout—treatment. We have learned that the more we train staff members to work on and uncover threatening issues, the more the girls are willing to work on these issues. We suspect that alcoholism and sexual abuse were underreported in the earlier years of the program because we did not focus on them.

A FINAL NOTE ABOUT PREVENTION

Researchers in the field of substance abuse have recently discovered what the child-welfare system in this country has known for many years, namely, that the rates of incest and child abuse in our society are appalling and are spread across all social classes. The response has been a familiar one—rescue the child and convict the parent. Knowledge about the sexual abuse of children is evolving in a way similar to that of physically abused and raped women. First comes the startling discovery that the problem is more prevalent than had been imagined. Then comes a second disturbing discovery of how society and its care givers further victimize the victims following disclosure. We must examine how our social institutions perpetuate, if not instigate, the problem.

The view of women our society presents to most female adolescents is at best ambiguous and confusing and at worst degrading and demeaning. Young women must cope with images of themselves as less emotionally stable, less capable in certain important functional areas, less responsible, and less able to take care of themselves than are men. Young women are taught not to be too assertive and to concede positions of authority to men. At the same time, many little girls learn how to be provocative, coy, and manipulative. Books, television, toys, family, and friends, wittingly or not, have encouraged them to use feminine wiles to their advantage. Sexiness may be covertly reinforced before they are old enough to understand its meaning or implications, and they may become confused as to its purpose and function. The situation is no better for little boys, most of whom are raised with unfounded views of gender differences, unrealistic expectations of their own traits and abilities, and inappropriate attitudes about sexuality and women in general. The notion that, under certain circumstances, men are entitled to sexual pleasure, or that women and female children ask for it, is still subtly reinforced in our society. In some cases, this attitude is even blatantly and publicly owned by people in responsible social positions.

It is futile to talk about the primary prevention of drug abuse among women without addressing the problem of child abuse in general and the role of females in our society in particular. As long as society views women as subservient sexual objects, and as long as the rights of women are so blatantly disregarded, female children will remain at high risk for all kinds of abuse. If we really want to help the children, we must first save the family. If we truly want to save the family, we must change the prevailing attitudes and practices in our society that allow one gender to exploit the other and that lead one gender inadvertently to become hopelessly trapped in the victim role.

I feel like a seed of some big flower, and I tried so hard to grow; I kept growing until I ran out of water and sunshine, then I would just sag there. Those petals would never open and show people how good I was. (Caritas House resident)

SUMMARY

The results of the follow-up study reported in this chapter indicate general overall favorable outcome following participation in a structured residential treatment program for troubled girls. The study also identified specific family, client and treatment variables that maximize treatment effectiveness. Examination of pretreatment individual client and family characteristics points to major weaknesses in our social system that may foster and sustain the underlying conditions that lead to substance abuse in this population. The findings of this study have significant implications for future research, treatment, and prevention efforts. In particular, attention must be given to the role of the family, the treatment program, and society in the genesis, maintenance, and alleviation of substance-abuse problems for female children.

ENDNOTES

1. In an attempt to integrate all existing family classification schemata, Fisher (1970) developed a system of six clusters of family types. The clusters were created after a thorough review of the literature, "by comparing the various subtypes of each family schema with each other, and grouping together those subtypes that, by my understanding of the original author's description, displayed a reasonable degree of similarity" (p. 4). A table listing each family cluster, the original author, and the specific family subtype involved can be found in Appendix A. The prognosis for families in therapy is postulated to be best for the child- and community-focused subtypes of the object-focused family and the impulsive family.

2. A composite score was derived for each participant by summing the scores on the seven specific components. Since each component could be rated 1, 2, or 3, the maximum score possible was 21, indicating most success in the judgment of the raters; the minimum score, representing least success, was 7. This procedure for assessing treatment outcomes was adapted from the work of Simpson and associates of the Texas Christian University Institute of Behavioral Research. These investigators have carried out follow-up evaluation of drug-treatment programs at more than 50 locations across the United States and Puerto Rico (Chambers et al., 1975; Hornick, et al., 1977; Savage & Simpson, 1979, 1980, 1981, 1982; Simpson, et al., 1978, 1980).

3. According to the Rhode Island Department of Health (1983), in 1978 in Rhode Island, it was estimated that over 3,000 juveniles, age 17 and under, could have drinking problems. This represents about 2% of the population for this age category. A report by the Rhode Island Department of Mental health, Retardation, and Hospitals (1980) reports rates of one to four per 1,000 for diagnosed alcoholism or alcohol abuse for the 15-to-19 age category. There are no sex-specific estimates.

4. A needs-assessment study conducted by the Brown University Center for Alcoholism (1985) reports that 26% of Rhode Island youth have used alcohol and a "best guess" for number of youth with "drinking problems" as 10%. A study by the Harvard School of Public Health (1987) reports the following rates of "ever use" of drugs other than alcohol: marijuana, 25%; cocaine, 5.5%; "painkillers," 5.3%; amphetamines, 3.5%; hallucinogens, 2.7%; tranquilizers, 1.5%; barbiturates, 1.5%. Weekly or daily use of these drugs was reported by less than 1% of the sample. There was very little difference between male and female rates.

5. There was only one reported incidence of abuse to a father during his childhood.

REFERENCES

Bassuk, E L., & Schoonover, S. C. (1978). *The practitioner's guide to psychoactive drugs.* New York: Plenum Medical Book Co.

Brown University Center for Alcoholism Studies. (1985). *Substance abuse treatment in Rhode Island: Population needs and program development.* Providence: State of Rhode Island.

Island: Population needs and program development. Providence: State of Rhode Island.

Chambers, C. D., Inciardi, J. A., & Siegal, H. A. (1975). *Chemical coping: A report on legal drug use in the U.S.* New York: Spectrum.

Delucci, K. L. (1983) The use and misuse of chi-square: Lewis and Burke revisited. *Psychological Bulletin, 94,* 166–176.

DeYoung, M. (1982). Self-injurious behaviors in incest victims: A research note. *Child Welfare,* 61(8), 577–584.

Fisher, L. (1979). On the classification of families. In *Family psychiatry* (pp. 27–52). New York: International Universities Press.

Harvard School of Public Health. (1987). *A drug abuse treatment and prevention plan for Rhode Island.* Providence: State of Rhode Island.

Hill, R. (1949). *Families under stress.* Cited in Sussman, M. B. (1968). *Sourcebook in marriage and family* (pp. 440–451). Boston: Houghton Mifflin.

Hornick, C. W., Demaree, R. G., Sells, S. B., & Newman, J. F. (1977). *Measurement of post-DARP outcomes: The definition of a composite and of differential outcome groups* (Report 77–17). Fort Worth, TX: Institute of Behavioral Research, Texas Christian University.

Hull, C. H., & Nie, N. H. (1981). *SPSS Update 7–9.* New York: McGraw-Hill.

Klagsbrun, M., & Davis, D. I. (1977). Substance abuse and family interaction. *Family Process,* 16(2), 149–164.

Miller, D. C. (983). *Handbook of research design in the social sciences.* New York: Longman.

Miller, J. S., Sensenig, J., Stocker, R. B., & Campbell, R. (1973). Values patterns of drug addicts as a function of race and sex. *International Journal of Addictions,* 8, 589–598.

National Center on Child Abuse and Neglect. (1979). *A curriculum on child abuse and neglect* (DHEW Publication No. OHDS 79-30221). Washington, DC: U.S. Government Printing Office.

National Center on Child Abuse and Neglect. (1982). *Executive summary: National study of the incidence and severity of child abuse and neglect.* Washington, DC: U.S. Department of Health and Human Services.

Newman, J. F., Demaree, R. G., Hornick, C. W., & Sells, S. B. (1977). *Client characteristics and other variables associated with differential post-DARP outcome groups* (IBR Report 77–16). Fort Worth, TX: Texas Christian University.

O'Brien, R., & Cohen, S. (1984). *The encyclopedia of drug abuse.* New York: Facts On File, Inc.

Raky, H. (1982). *Division of substance abuse program evaluation and monitoring report.* Cranston, RI: Department of Mental Health, Retardation, and Hospitals.

Rhode Island Department of Health. (1983). *Health interview survey: 1978.* Interviews of Rhode Island residents. Providence: State of Rhode Island.

Rhode Island Department of Mental Health. (1980). *Substance abuse state plan.* Cranston, RI: Department of Mental Health, Retardation and Hospitals.

Russianoff, P. (1981). *Women in crisis.* New York: Human Sciences Press.

Sall, J. P., & Standish, W. M. (1982) *SAS user's guide: Basic* (1982 ed.). Gary, NC: SAS Institute.

Christian University.

Savage, L. J., & Simpson, D. D. (1980). Posttreatment outcomes of sex and ethnic groups treated in methadone maintenance during 1969–1972. *Journal of Psychedelic Drugs, 12*(1), 55–64.

Savage, L. J., & Simpson, D. D. (1981–1982). Client types in different drug abuse treatments: Comparisons of follow-up outcomes. *American Journal of Alcohol and Drug Abuse, 8*, 401–418.

Simpson, D. D., Crandall, R., Savage, L. J., & Pavia-Krueger, E. (1980). *Leisure patterns of opioid addicts: A six-year follow-up of clients* (DHEW Publication No. ADM 81-1040). Rockville, MD: National Institute on Drug Abuse.

Simpson, D. D., & Savage, L. J. (1979). *Re-entry and outcomes among opioid addicts during a four-year follow-up drug abuse treatment* (IBR Report 79-19). Fort Worth, TX: Texas Christian University.

Simpson, D. D., Savage, L. J., Lloyd, M. R., & Sells, S. B. (1978). *Evaluation of drug abuse treatments based on first year follow-up* (DHEW Publication No. ADM 78-701). Rockville, MD: National Institute on Drug Abuse.

Skolnick, A. (1978). *The intimate environment.* Boston: Little, Brown.

Spiegel, R. & Aebi, Haus-J. (1984). *Psychopharmacology.* New York: Wiley.

Steinglass, P. (1987). *The alcoholic family.* New York: Basic Books.

9

Breaking the Cycle: Treating Adult Children Of Alcoholics

David C. Treadway, Ph.D.

Ann spends her life in relationships with men she hopes to save. She keeps trying to be good enough to make them better. They don't get better, but she keeps trying. She dreams of being in a relationship with a strong and competent man and yet being with such a man always makes her anxious and she doesn't know why. Ann wants to be married and have children. She makes lists of self-improvement projects she's going to start next week. She can never find clothes that fit. Soon she'll turn 40.

Bob brought his daughter a $50 pair of Reeboks. He knew he couldn't afford them and his wife would be mad but he couldn't resist. Bob remembered being a child with two alcoholic parents. The money they might have spent on clothes for the kids went to the liquor store instead. He used to put cardboard in his sneakers to block the holes in the soles. He wanted to make sure that his daughter was going to have the best of everything.

Bob's daughter didn't like the sneakers very much because they were too hard to tie. She lost one of them a few days later.

John is an excellent therapist. He always knows how to handle a crisis and he never loses his cool. Everyone admires John but no one feels very close to him. At home, he takes care of his family in the same way. John's family also admires him but doesn't know how to be close to him either. His six-year-old once asked her mother, "Why does Daddy always get in such a bad mood on his birthday when we give him presents? He never likes anything."

* * *

What these people have in common is an alcoholic parent and the particular kinds of scars left by growing up in an alcoholic family. Nobody escapes childhood unscathed, but for children growing up in the alcoholic family system, the wounds are often scarring and contribute significantly to their problems in adult relationships.

Black (1982), Wegscheider-Cruz (1981), Woititz (1981), Ackerman (1983), and many others have done a superb job of describing the typical patterns that develop in alcoholic homes and the resulting difficulties children from these homes encounter in their adult lives. In writing for a general audience, these authors have promulgated the concept of an adult-children-of-alcoholics (ACOA) syndrome that is valuable for people from alcoholic families and the therapists who treat them. The ACOA concept allows people better to understand their defenses and provides a new perspective on their life experiences that many people find liberating.

It is important to note, however, that most of the descriptions of ACOAs are general and could be considered applicable to adults who have grown up in many different kinds of traumatic family environments. Families in which there is a chronically ill or insane parent, an abusive or incestuous parent, a difficult divorce, the death of a parent, or a marital dysfunction that involves the children will all tend to give rise to patterns similar to those described in the ACOA literature. Abuse of alcohol is not the central variable; rather it is the experience of growing up in a family where there is a significant dysfunction in the adult system that seems to be the catalyst for creating these patterns.

The label *adult child of an alcoholic* is not a diagnostic category and although generalizations about ACOAs are easy to make, in actuality there are significant differences in how children cope with growing up in an alcoholic environment, what their defense systems will be, and the relative degrees of success and emotional health they will achieve. Although the tendency to over-generalize about ACOAs is one that has to be guarded against, there are some specific issues that almost all adult children will have in common regardless of differences in family roles and personality variations.

TRUST

ACOAs grew up in a capricious and inconsistent environment in which it was hard to predict the behavior of others. What will be the long-term effect on Ann of spending her childhood watching her dad to see when he was going to be okay, hating her mom for picking on him, and wishing she could tell him that she loved him anyway? What is the impact on Bob of watching his parents take money out of his sister's piggy bank to buy alcohol when there was not enough food to eat? How does the ten-year-old John integrate the experience of stepping between his parents who are having a fist fight, only to be told the following morning that nothing had happened, that all parents have disagreements, and that he had better not tell anyone about it?

Children of alcoholic parents (COAs) survive by learning how not to trust one, and often both, of their parents to protect them and provide nuturance for them because the parents behave in such an unpredictable fashion. At an early age, children tend to assume that their parents are completely normal whatever they do. It takes a long time for them to learn that their parents are capable of lying to them, manipulating them, and in many instances abusing them without any clear reason. The child never knows how the alcoholic is going to act. Sometimes the parent is abusive and scary, sometimes peripheral, and sometimes the most wonderful parent in the world. Such children develop a wary watchfulness that helps them figure out when it's safe to engage the parent and when it is better to try to avoid him or her.

> One client remembers the relief she experienced when she learned to listen to how her father unlocked the front door when he came home in the evening. On a good night, the key went into the lock, no problem. On a bad night, the key scratched at the lock, then there was angry muttering, often leading to the door being pounded on. At these times she knew to spend the evening in her room away from the family as much as possible. She told the story with a funny kind of proud smile and I had a sudden sense of the little girl from a long time ago being so pleased with herself that she had figured out a way of predicting what was going to happen and how to protect herself.

If the alcoholic parent is confusing, the other parent is frequently more so. Usually, the other parent is the prime source of comfort and nurturance and yet while not adequately dealing with the alcoholic will often take out his or her own frustration on the kids, and will also tend to turn to the kids for emotional support. Children will excuse the parents' failures to cope with the situation by simply assuming that they are as powerless as the children themselves and are doing the best they can. Thus kids learn not to trust or depend on the non-alcoholic parent because you never know when this parent will turn from being a comforting friend ("Don't worry, sweetie, your mommy didn't mean to ruin the party—she's just a little tired, that's all") to being a harsh punitive parent ("I can't believe you're so stupid. You deserved to get hit. How many times have I told you not to talk back to your mother when she is in one of her moods?").

In addition to the inconsistent picture created by the parents' unpredictable behavior, the child has to deal with the discrepancy in how the family members behave with one another and how they present themselves to the outside world. The alcoholic family often will have a public image that is extremely different from the private reality. One client remembers how difficult it was to accept the public image of his mother as one of the finest, most upstanding and generous members of the community while he knew that the minute she was behind closed doors she turned into a vicious, abusive drunk. This charade can lead a child to be unsure about how to relate to the outside world because the injunction in the family about betraying family secrets is usually so strong. The child learns to keep his or her mouth shut. When one client's child broke the family rule, and in response to a class unit on alcoholism acknowledged that his parents were alcoholic, he was completely ostracized him by the family from that day on. Reaching out to the outside world cost him his place in his family.

Regardless of whether the alcoholism is a public or private affair, the unpredictable patterns of behavior that typify the alcoholic system leave the children confused about what is going on, whom to believe, and what to do. The result is that kids learn not to trust anyone, including themselves. Imagine the anxiety created for these children when as adults someone says to them, "I really care about you. You can trust me."

LOW SELF-ESTEEM

Young children naturally think of themselves as the center of the universe and assume that the actions of people around them are on some level their responsibility. Whether the parent beats the child, neglects the child, or simply ignores the child, the child does not assume there is something wrong with the parent but that there is something wrong with himself or herself. Children believe that they deserve what they get. In addition, blaming themselves is a way for children to make sense of a parent's behavior. It is much easier to blame oneself than to risk acknowledging how inadequate, inappropriate, and out of control is the behavior of one's parents.

For many children growing up in alcoholic homes there are also the shame and humiliation of how their family acts in the outside world. Seeing your drunken dad arguing with the umpire and holding up your little league game, or having him come stumbling into your room in his underwear to give you a slobbering goodnight kiss in front of your best friend, or being forced to call the police because your mom is hysterical and threatening to kill herself are humiliating episodes that children take onto themselves. Somehow it becomes their fault. If the parent is embarrassed or ashamed, the child is often given the job of forgiving the parent. Or if the parent does not see that he or she did anything wrong, then the child is left alone with a sense of shame.

Children develop coping mechanisms that enable them to adjust to their low self-esteem and feelings of shame. As adults, however, no matter how successful they become, they still harbor the child within who secretly knows that anything that goes wrong is really their fault.

EXPRESSION OF AFFECT

Therapist: (to woman about her fight with her alcoholic dad when she was seven) "How do you remember feeling when your dad was holding you against the wall by the neck and screaming at you?"

Client: "I would imagine that someone might be upset if that happened to them."

Learning how not to feel one's experience is one of the most successful survival techniques for children growing up in this kind of environment—children who are treated in a harsh and often scary situation over which they have no control and cannot leave develop the ability to become unaware, unfeeling, and unreactive. This is a safer response than speaking out or fighting back.

Since the "see, hear, and speak no evil" approach is the way in which many children protect themselves, it is not surprising that as adults they often are completely blocked affectively. This numbness and lack of connection to one's feelings frequently lead to an amnesia about one's childhood experiences or a subtle revision in which the bad experiences are rationalized and the childhood is rewritten as successful and happy. Clearly, this state of being out of touch with one's feelings can create significant problems for adult children because they frequently do not know some of the motivating feelings that cause much of their behavior and so often have very little understanding of the responses they receive from others. These adults are often unconsciously expressing angry and fearful feelings that elicit from others the very rejecting behavior they fear the most.

Many adult children are able to repress their memories and become emotionally cut off or numb, others are unsuccessful at blocking the feelings of pain, despair, and rage naturally. For some ACOAs, this means an extreme sensitivity to being hurt by others and they are highly reactive. The slightest negative response is considered a personal rejection. Other adult children are likely to turn to compulsive behaviors that are aimed toward reducing or blocking feelings. Alcohol and drug abuse, as well as many other externally focused efforts, are attempts to gain a sense of surcease from the difficult and overwhelming affect. One client stated it very simply when he said, "You know, when I smoke dope the knot in my stomach goes away. I'll never forget the first time it happened. I never felt so good in my whole life."

Whether the compulsive behavior is self-destructive as in drug abuse, promiscuity, or gambling, or productive of success as in workaholism, working out, or perfectionism, the net result is the same. The individual is spending life on the run. The rush does not last. The promotion feels hollow. The knot always comes back.

DEPENDENCY

Therapist: "Was there a point when you sort of gave up on your parents?"

Client: "I don't know about my mother but I remember giving up on my dad. I was about nine and he and Mom were separated. I was spending the weekend with him and I remember him telling me he was just going to step out to get a soda. I knew he was going drinking. I was afraid to be alone in his apartment. I started to cry. I asked him not to go and he promised he would be right back. He told me to make him proud and be his "big, brave little girl." He came in about three in the morning with some woman whom he had found. I was asleep on the couch. He was drunk and laughing. He said he wanted me to meet Helen, who was going to be my new mom, at least for the night. They both thought that was funny. I didn't say anything. I just went to bed. But I knew I didn't have a dad anymore."

After a leg is amputated, the remaining stump has to be cauterized in order for the patient not to bleed to death. It used to be done by simply searing the flesh with a hot instrument. Most adult children have had a similar experience with a parent, and often both parents, in which they, in essence, give up on the notion that they can depend on the parent to be there to take care of them. The ACOA learns not to care anymore and is no longer vulnerable. The nerve endings have been cauterized. The parent is gone.

Most ACOAs are completely unaware of this process of hiding their dependency needs and giving up on reasonable expectations from their parents. Children simply learn to depend on themselves, like the client whose dad brought her a new mother in the middle of the night. She basically avoids any kind of relationship with a man. Is it any wonder that as a single woman she owns two cars? After all, one might break down.

The process of denying one's own needs for nuturance, caretaking, and safety by, in essence, sticking out one's chin and saying, "I don't need that silly old stuff anyway," covers a profound yearning for what has been lost. It is frequently these unconscious needs and denied expectations that lead to tremendous conflict for ACOAs in their adult relationships. To the rest of the world they often manage to communicate the exquisitely mixed message, "I'm fine. I don't need anybody. Why aren't you taking care of me?"

Although most ACOAs adopt the counterdependent position, many will do the opposite and be overtly vulnerable and dependent. They wear their hearts on their sleeves and yet the results are often the same. The adults that they annoint as surrogate parents can never meet their old childhood needs and thus they are always in a position of being hurt and disappointed. Regardless of whether the old wound is sealed over by an ugly scar or it continues to be raw and open, the wound remains.

These legacies from childhood—lack of trust, low self-esteem, blocked affect, and unresolved dependency—clearly have a profound effect on ACOAs' ability to relate to others. Most adult children will have some problems in their roles as intimate partners, as parents, and as professionals.

AS PARTNERS

A strong fear of vulnerability and a desire for intimacy and nurturance are usually the prime motivating forces for ACOAs in their relationships to others. Almost by definition, the needs for safety and for intimacy are mutually exclusive. Successful intimacy is usually based on the partners' being able to be trusting, affectively available, and interdependent. For the ACOAs this is a highly unsafe position that almost always evokes the childhood sense of danger, dread, and entrapment.

ACOAs run the full gamut of possibilities in trying to resolve the dilemma of how to find intimacy without sacrificing safety. Many adult children simply avoid becoming too close to others and will prefer to stay alone rather then risk being hurt in a close relationship. Others will find a way to engage in a kind of self-protective partial intimacy in which they are able to be close without being too endangered. For example, the woman who always engages in relationships with underfunctioning men never has to address her own anxiety about being in the dependent role. Another example is the ACOA who maintains multiple intimate relationships so that he or she is protected from having too much of the emotional self at risk with any one person. Clearly, all couples have to find some idyosyncratic way of achieving a balance around intimacy issues. For couples coming from relatively normal backgrounds, closeness is associated with a sense of safety. For ACOAs who have often been betrayed by those closest to them, closeness is equated with danger. The need for safety is usually the prime motivating force for much of an ACOA's behavior, including behavior that seems transparently destructive to the relationship and destined to create the disaster that the person is trying to avoid.

The problem of needing to be safe is compounded by the twin issues, mentioned earlier, of the adult child having low self-esteem and the tendency to be blocked affectively. As a result, ACOAs, unaware of how they express anxiety and neediness, are sure that, if there are problems in the relationship, it must be their fault. Part of the reason that they are so capable of remaining in abusive relationships is that, on some level, they feel that they deserve whatever they get.

Finally, whether consciously or unconsciously, ACOAs tend to be seeking some kind of resolution of their past pain in their present relationship (see also Chapters 5 and 6). This is normal for all people but for ACOAs it is often more traumatic because of the heightened pain and sense of deprivation they bring into adult relationships.

This process of seeking in adult relationships a form of emotional reparations for the failings of one's own parents is often the primary cause of difficulty for ACOAs and their spouses. No matter how much the spouse loves the ACOA it does not really compensate for the past, which results in feelings of inadequacy and frustration because nothing the spouse does ever seems to be enough. For the adult child, the failure of the loving spouse to heal the past can lead to feelings of further isolation and deprivation, which, in turn, bring back the ACOA's original childhood feelings.

AS PARENTS

All parents want to spare their children from having to go through the difficulties that they themselves experienced as children. Children of alcoholics are both more intense and more insecure as parents. The intensity comes from wanting desperately to give one's own children what was missing from one's childhood. The insecurity is often created by the experience of having negative role models and not having a sense of what is normal and how to do it right. The hardest part of parenting for ACOAs is recognizing that no matter how hard they try, they will end up replicating some of the worst of the old parental behavior.

In trying to sum up some of the characteristics of ACOAs in their role as parents, it is very difficult to cover the uniqueness of each person's relationship to his or her own alcoholic family and how that relates to the bringing up of children. The following series of statements reflect some of the often unconscious feelings many ACOAs have in their role as parents.

1. "It's okay for you to be yourself just as long as you're perfect and you're always happy." Having grown up being helpless and unhappy in an often capricious and even hostile environment, ACOAs tend to have a very strong need to be protective and in control of their own children. This, combined with the desire to give one's children everything that was missing in one's own childhood, leads to very high expectations for the children to look right, feel right, and be right at all times. One client put it quite bluntly when she said. "There's only one thing I really want for my kids. I never want them to have any of the feelings that I had when I was a kid."

2. "Wasn't that a wonderful Christmas? Aren't I a good parent?" Because of their insecurity and need for validation, there is a strong tendency for ACOAs to look to their children for affirmation of their parenting. One parent in treatment kept expecting his child to understand what a great parent she was whenever she punished him.

3. "What do you have to complain about? You never went through what I went through." Tucked away inside the typical overesponsible, overprotective ACOA parent who wants his or her children to have perfect childhoods is the part that is capable of being resentful, and even a little jealous, of the children because they take for granted the stable, nurturing, and protective parenting the ACOA works so hard to give them. This problem is compounded by the ACOA's having grown up not ever really having had his or her complaints, hurts, and angers recognized and so feeling uncomfortable with such openness on the part of the ACOA's own children. The net result is that having created a family in which kids feel safe enough and open enough to complain, to have tantrums, to do what normal kids do, ACOAs tend to resent their sense of entitlement.

4. "I can't believe that you were sent in from recess. You're going to grow up to be an alcoholic!" It is painfully unsurprising that many ACOAs have children who get into trouble with drugs and alcohol. Adult children tend to be hypervigilant about substance abuse, which naturally tends to lead curious children to the forbidden fruit. It does not take long for a child to discover a parent's hot button. Thus, the normal adolescent struggling for autonomy in the ACOA family often becomes entangled in conflict and tension around substance abuse.

5. "You're the only family I have." For many ACOAs, letting their kids become independent and leave home is the hardest task. This is the point at which ACOAs often become aware that they have depended on their children as a substitute for the sense of belonging and closeness that they did not have in their own family. They thus are feeling not only the natural loss of their own children, but also the deeper, older losses from the past. A very high percentage of ACOA clients come in for treatment at the time that their children are getting ready to leave home.

   This feeling of loss combines with most ACOAs' sense of the world as not being a very safe place. Often it leads to giving the kids the underlying message, "Stay here, we're all in this together."

AS PROFESSIONALS

The difficulties adult children get into in the workplace are found at both ends of the spectrum. ACOAs at work either will tend to be too isolated or they will become too emotionally reactive (see also Chapter 12).

Many ACOAs are distant and emotionally restricted and, therefore, have difficulty in developing good working relationships, particularly ones that involve participation in a team effort. They are much more comfortable either with being in charge of projects or with having somebody else clearly in charge. The collegial work situation that does not have a clear-cut hierarchy tends to recreate the confusing and unpredictable circumstances of the past and so can be very anxiety producing for ACOAs. They have difficulty in defining themselves without external guidelines or structures.

On the other hand, ACOAs may invest too much emotional meaning into their relationship to work. It is at the workplace that ACOAs often try to derive a sense of security, power, and competency that they are afraid to struggle for on a more personal level. Work becomes the substitute family and ACOAs will often attempt to have success in the workplace make up for the painful past, much as they do in their relationships. One client summed it up: "My boss treats me like a cog in a machine. He doesn't ever tell me I did a good job. And he never acknowledges that I'm the first to come in and the last to leave. He's just as bad as my father who never noticed anything I did around the house."

It is no coincidence that many adult children gravitate toward the helping professions. Growing up in an alcoholic family is a form of on-the-job training for future clinicians. The survival skills one learns (e.g., to manage crises, to take care of others, and to work hard with little recognition) can be very useful. For the child who struggled to keep the family functioning with little success, becoming a therapist is attractive, as an opportunity to be an acknowledged and powerful leader of families. In addition, being a therapist is a potent way to experience an intense level of intimacy and closeness while staying in control. It is easier to be intimate on a time schedule and by the professional's rules; it is safer to give love than to receive it.

Most people in this field are in recovery. Clearly, they are not in the business for money or fame. They are in it because of their own life experiences, roles they played in their families, and their implicit need to "12-step" as part of their healing. They need to keep asking themselves how they handle their own reactions, values, and feelings in relationship to their clients. How much is their empathy and ability to connect to the pain of others part of the problem rather than part of the solution? How do they know when feelings about their own struggles are impeding the therapy? Caring, commitment, and responsibility are all necessary ingredients of good therapy. How do they know when their caring becomes overinvolvement and their willingness to take responsibility becomes codependence?

Many therapists attempt to suppress the feeling responses that are uncomfortable for them, thus pushing the feelings into the unconscious. They still are played out in the therapy. When a therapist is bothered by a client, it shows, whether he or she inwardly acknowledges the feeling or not. The person of the therapist is never outside the system.

Many of us in the substance-abuse field are former parental children in our family of origin. Instead of retiring, we have continued to play out our old family scripts by becoming professional "heroes." Being a therapist may meet significant emotional needs in our lives. For many of us, closeness in the therapy room is easier than intimacy with our spouses, our parents and siblings, or our children. Our role is more clearly defined. We are more in control. It is safer. Like the therapist John, mentioned earlier, it is sometimes easier to dispense gentle and loving nurturance in the therapy room then to receive it from one's own family.

FIVE-STAGE TREATMENT MODEL FOR ACOAS[1]

Stage 1. Identification

Most ACOAs are unaware of the relationship between their early life experience and whatever their presenting problem treatment might be. It is normal for adult children to come into treatment presenting a host of symptoms that are seemingly unrelated in their minds to their childhood experiences. Therefore, the first step in the treatment of ACOAs is to identify the connection between the presenting problem and the unresolved issues from their childhood. It is not useful to push the identification of ACOAs prematurely because many adult children are in an active stage of denial about the impact of their childhood experience and will find it threatening that the therapist emphasizes their childhood as an explanation for their current life difficulties. If a woman is bringing her husband in for treatment for marital issues and the therapist quickly focuses on her issues as an ACOA, she's very likely to feel attacked by the therapist in a way that completely undermines her relationship to the therapy.

I interview all clients with an awareness of the potential impact of substance abuse. I will ask questions about patterns of alcohol use in the family of origin as a matter of course. When I begin to get evidence that there is a connection between alcohol abuse and a person's family-of-origin experience, I will keep it to myself initially, especially if the connection is not being made by the client. What I am looking for is the opportunity to link the presenting problem to the old issues and so I will ask such questions as: "How is your marriage, better or worse than your parent's marriage? Do you worry as much about your husband's drinking as you used to about your dad's or do you worry less about it? Which of your siblings has had the most success at being able to make a good relationship and which of your siblings has had the most difficulty? How does your drinking compare to your dad's? What was it that you wanted to make sure that your children experience differently than you did when you were growing up?" These questions allow the therapist to develop a series of hypotheses about the relationship between symptoms and family pattern and structure without necessarily making explicit the therapist's presumptions about those connections. These questions will often provide ample evidence of the connection between the family-of-origin issues and the presenting problem.

[1]Most of the material presented in this treatment model is taken directly from the author's book *Before It's Too Late; Working With Substance Abuse in the Family.* New York: Norton, 1989.

Another line of questioning one can use when trying to develop these issues is the more traditional one of asking clients simply to refer back to when they previously had the particular feeling they now have about the presenting problem and in relationship to whom. For example: "With which of your parents did you tend to have the same feeling of frustration as you currently feel toward Bob about this kind of thing?" The value of this identification of the adult child's problem is not at all obvious to most clients. Therefore, the therapist proceeds in small steps while overtly placing the primary focus of the therapy on resolving the presenting problem. This is the appropriate and respectful response that clients request when coming into therapy in the first place. The therapist should not assume that the case will involve the working out of adult child issues. In many instances, the clients' defenses are working well for them and a slight adjustment around solving the presenting problem will be enough to help the couple regain a sense of stability and continuity. When the presenting problem proves to be intractable is often the ideal time for making explicit the linkage between family-of-origin issues and the presenting problems.

Stage 2. Reframing and Restraint from Change

When the presenting problem is not being resolved by treatment strategies, the therapist can reframe the meaning of the problem in terms of how it serves a protective and useful function in the life of the couple or system. For example, if the presenting problem is a lack of intimacy in a relationship, a consequent reframing might be to suggest that a large degree of responsiveness in terms of intimacy and emotional availability on the part of the spouse would actually precipitate anxiety, discomfort, and old pain on the part of the adult child who has requested such closeness because it would, almost by definition, bring up all the loss issues that have been dammed up in the adult child. For example:

A client said he wanted his wife to be more emotionally responsive to him, but when she did, his response was to become distrusting and uncomfortable almost to the point of accusing her of insincere motives and of trying to manipulate him. Investigation of the family-of-origin issues led to a much clearer understanding of his behavior. His mother's alcoholism had clearly involved her in a variety of very manipulative behaviors in relationship to him; she kept him close to her by showering attention and affection on him while, at the same time, engaging him in colluding with her in maintaining her drinking by bringing her alcohol and hiding bottles. Thus the wife's attempts to be responsive to the man were met with anxiety and distrust, causing her to withdraw again to her more distant position. It was safer for him to complain than to get what he was asking for.

The reframing that one uses in treating these cases has to make sense to clients. Since people are torn between the need to change and fears of the destabilization that change creates, a logical reframing that essentially appreciates why and how people need to be doing what they are doing serves as a foundation for later risk taking in the therapy. It is also useful to use the reframe as a rationale for suggesting that the couple or the individual restrain from pushing aggressively for change. Frequently, the way clients try to change actively makes the situation worse rather than better in the way that drivers become stuck more deeply in snow by spinning their wheels. Simply to suggest an interruption of people's problem-solving behavior when it has become repetitive and rigid can have a powerful therapeutic effect of its own.

Restraining from change does not necessarily work by itself, but it frequently allows the therapist time to work on the other issues that have been masked by the particular problem that has been presented. It also may reduce the couple's frustration and anxiety about working on the presenting problem unsuccessfully. I use positive reframing and restraint from change as a holding action that allows me to work on family-of-origin issues.

Stage 3. Supportive Exploration of Affect

If clients allow themselves to open up to the painful feelings from their childhoods, they may experience intense reactions. Very competent and successful people will suddenly seem to be coming apart at the seams as they get in touch with the hurt and vulnerable child of many years ago. When ACOAs give up some of their primary defenses, such as denial, projection, and addictive behavior, they may experience either anxiety attacks or bouts of depression.

EDUCATION

Before opening up the repressed affect that most ACOAs have about their past, I spend considerable time educating clients about the natural history of growing up in an alcoholic family, the roles people develop, and the healthy ways in which children survive. It is very important that ACOAs appreciate the defenses and survival skills they developed as children. It is also important for spouses to appreciate their partners' defenses.

I help each spouse distinguish between being responsive and being responsible. Most spouses of ACOAs feel overwhelmed and inadequate in response to their partners' needs. Ultimately they become discouraged and withdraw. I want the spouses to learn how to be empathic without feeling that they have to make up for the past. Spouses need to learn how to be supportive; their partners need to accept the limitations of their support. Love does not conquer all.

USE OF LITERATURE, GROUPS, AND RETREATS

At this juncture, I help the couple look outside the marriage for additional support. The ACOA literature and the many available ACOA groups and workshops are useful in helping both spouses feel a sense of support, belonging, and normality about their shameful past and the scars they carry into the present. Group support is often essential in helping clients tolerate the flooding into consciousness of years of blocked affect. Just as Al-Anon and Alcoholics Anonymous are essential in the successful treatment of active alcoholism, ACOA groups have proved to be valuable in helping adult children come to terms with their past.

Naturally, most ACOAs are reluctant to engage in any kind of group experience. I encourage such clients to consider a professionally led group first, because there they may feel safer than in the ACOA/Al-Anon groups. The leader will be skilled enough to help clients overcome their initial anxiety.

In the past few years, I have run several retreats for adult children of alcoholics. These have been profoundly moving experiences, as people who have felt isolated in the world and filled with a sense of shame have finally experienced understanding and acceptance. One man said to the group at the end of the weekend, "I feel like I've been welcomed home."

Stage 4. Coming to Terms with the Past

As emotional needs are opened up and the ACOA is supported in exploring the past, expectations of the marriage become less intense. The focus shifts to the family of origin. There is, nevertheless, a payoff in the marriage: This reduction of expectation on the part of the other member of the relationship often means that the spouse feels less pressure and is more responsive and forthcoming. Thus, in most cases, the spouse who expects less gets more.

ACOAs come into treatment with a set of fixed responses to their past. They are usually angry, sad, or numb. Many ACOAs have arrived at a kind of pseudoresolution. They often say that they "understand" that their parents "did the best they could" and that "it was nobody's fault in the end." This healthy defense covers all the appropriate childhood feelings of anger and sadness, which are locked inside of the adult and played out unconsciously in his or her relationships. The task of therapy is to help the adult child to understand the range of feelings that underly such set responses to the past and to see how those feelings inform and direct present behavior.

Helping clients acknowledge and even reexperience some of the charged affect from the past is usually the first step toward opening up the question of what they want to do about making peace with their family of origin. Until the emotion is brought to the surface, most ACOAs simply play out a rigid role vis-à-vis the family, a role learned in childhood. Regardless of how unfulfilling their relationship to the family is, they dismiss both the hope and the need for change. Until clients have become comfortable with their pain and anxiety, they will be too anxious to attempt changing their roles and behavior in the family of origin.

Not all clients need to work through their relationships with their families of origin. Sometimes simply acknowledging the legacy of the past and its impact on the present is enough to allow spouses to become closer and more intimate. I usually pursue active family-of-origin coaching when clients clearly see the link between their present problems and their past relationships, when they are motivated to change their position in the family of origin, and when the spouse is supportive.

I do not believe it is useful to ask clients to do family-of-origin work just on faith. I want them to see that working on the past will help them change patterns of behavior that are hurtful to themselves and their partners in the present. Armor may have been appropriate protective outerwear in medieval England, but not in 20th-century America, and particularly not with an intimate partner. ACOAs survived childhood by donning defensive armor, but those defenses have become suffocatingly cumbersome, as well as obsolete, in adult life. Going back to the family of origin makes sense if the client sees it as an opportunity to take off the old armor and leave it behind.

I have three goals in mind when I encourage clients to address their family-of-origin issues. I want clients:

1. To deepen their understanding of what happened growing up in their family, so that they can better understand themselves and the impact of their childhood on the present.
2. To feel more empowered by taking charge of conducting their relationships with their parents and siblings, rather than remaining trapped in a helpless, reactive, one-down position.
3. To accept the grief of recognizing that no one can make up for the past. Clients should not go into the family-of-origin work with the secret expectation that all their unmet needs of the past will be fulfilled and all their broken relationships healed.

The first step often involves helping clients disengage from the struggle to get from their parents or their siblings the validation, acceptance, and love they have always yearned for. Most ACOAs are in highly reactive relationships with their families. They painfully repeat the part of old destructive patterns with little awareness of their behavior's impact. In order to break the pattern, they must recognize how their way of struggling is perpetuating the tug-of-war. I encourage them to take a one-down position, to give up trying either to change someone else or to win an old fight. Naturally, many of my clients argue with me about this, saying, "It's not fair that I should do all the work. It isn't right that my parent is being let off the hook." I respond, "It's true that it isn't fair, but if you're going to wait for it to be fair, you're going to wait forever. The only way you can break this pattern with your folks is to be willing to do more than your share of the work."

The following is an example of how I help a client "let go of the rope."

Ellen's alcoholic father had been suicidally depressed off and on since she was a child. After her mother died, her father would call Ellen several times a week so that Ellen could cheer him up. Ellen, who is a social worker, would become engaged in lengthy phone conversations in which she would encourage her father to feel better about himself. By the end of these phone calls, the father seemed to feel better, but Ellen would be in a silent rage. Inevitably she would lose her temper with her husband or her children immediately after the call. She felt completely at the mercy of her father's depression.

I advised her to make a list of 20 empathic phrases she might have picked up in social-work training, such as, "I am very sorry that you feel so bad," or "Tell me more," or "It must feel like nobody understands what you're going through." Then I encourage her to stop allowing her father's calls to intrude on her life in a random fashion. She should take the initiative and call her father at a set time each week. If her father called at other times, she could gently but firmly refuse to take the call. She was to prepare for her weekly call by planning a distraction for the kids, making herself a nice snack and a hot cup of tea, and sitting on the sofa with her husband and the list. She was to encourage her father to talk about his depression and see if she could insert into the conversation all 20 of her empathic statements. Once she finished the phone call, she was to talk a little with her husband about how difficult it had always been to feel responsible for her father and how much she wished her father would show some interest in her. Her husband was encouraged to let her have her feelings, no matter how despairing they were.

Ellen was quite resistant to this idea because it seemed to her that I was trying to get her even more involved with her father. She tried it out, however, and found, much to her surprise, that the calls to her father were shorter and that frequently she couldn't get her father to focus on being either depressed or suicidal. In one conversation, he actually asked why Ellen kept worrying about his being depressed and said there must be something else they could talk about. As Ellen checked off her empathic phrases, she and her husband shared a silent conspiratorial chuckle. No longer was Ellen's father able to drive a wedge between them; in fact, they were actually drawn together. She particularly liked his willingness to listen to her sadness about her father. He liked feeling that it was okay to just listen rather than having to say or do something to make her feel better.

Learning how not to react to old family patterns empowers clients and makes them feel more in control of themselves and their relationships with members of their families of origin. They feel more confident that they can engage their family without being swallowed up in it. It is equally important for my clients to educate me about how their families work. When clients tell me that they cannot do a given task, I accept their caution and assume that I have asked them to take too big a step. There is always a smaller step to be taken.

> I once spent several months working with a client, helping him plan and initiate a luncheon with his dad. He decided that the safest topic for discussion was the pennant hopes of the Boston Red Sox. We role-played the initial phone call and the son anticipated all the arguments his father would use in order to reject the lunch invitation. This preparation took a long time because the son had never initiated contact with his dad before; he could not even remember having a conversation alone with his father. Encouraging this client to attempt a "meaningful" conversation with his dad would have overwhelmed him. My client intuitively knew that before he could have a serious conversation with his dad, he needed to be able to have a successful superficial one.

I generally divide the family-of-origin work into four categories, working with (1) the sibling, (2) the alcoholic parent, (3) the codependent parent, and, finally, (4) the inner child. Although it is usually easiest to start with the siblings, I trust my clients' wisdom in making the choices. The clients' own instincts about what they and their family members can handle are usually the therapist's best guide.

WORKING WITH SIBLINGS

ACOAs tend to have two different types of sibling relationships. Some siblings are very close and talk frequently around their feelings about the family and its impact on them. These clients have little difficulty engaging their siblings in the therapeutic process. Most sibling relationships, however, are distant, competitive, and superficial. The siblings' feelings about their shared past are never discussed and they play out their old roles from childhood (e.g., hero, scapegoat) in highly ritualized patterns (Wegscheider, 1981; Black, 1982). In these situations, the siblings do not see each other very often and rarely engage in anything more serious than small talk, except to fight with each other. Naturally, this kind of sibling relationship is protective, since the distance enables the siblings to avoid opening up the old pain around their experiences as children. Depending on which role they played, clients will feel either rejected by their siblings or resentful because they feel responsible for them.

Given the nature of these sibling relationships, it is not surprising that clients react to the idea of engaging their siblings with considerable fear of rejection and doubts about the potential value of reengaging with them. Clients will make such comments as, "I've tried everything," or, "He's hopeless. All he cares about is making money." I accept that their fears are realistic and their resentments appropriate; however, I continue to encourage them to engage their siblings. There are three main reasons.

First, engaging their siblings on their own initiative empowers my clients and moves them out of the hurt, reactive, victim position. Second, learning about their siblings' perspective on what happened in the family helps my clients in turn to develop a broader perspective on their childhood and a more systemic understanding of the effect of alcoholism on the family. Siblings' versions of reality are often strikingly different; however, as with binocular vision, the different perspectives together increase depth perception. Finally, learning about the impact on their siblings of having grown up in an alcoholic family is normalizing. Frequently, my clients, who are addressing old wounds, are actually more at peace with themselves than their seemingly well-put-together brothers and sisters who do not believe in "crying over spilled milk," "digging up the past," or "self-absorbed psychological ruminations."

I discourage clients from thinking that their needs for validation will be met by their siblings. What usually blocks communication between siblings about family-of-origin issues is tension around whose version of reality is more accurate. Clients have to be prepared not to push their own version or to challenge a sibling's story. They have to be willing to do more than their share of work, to meet on the other's terms, and to expect only minimal reciprocity of interest. I tell my clients that, even after they have worked hard to engage a sibling, they may decide that the relationship is too uncomfortable to sustain. Ultimately, they may return to the old level of distance. There is no mental-health rule that states that siblings have to like each other or be close. These depressing caveats help my clients approach the sibling work with their eyes wide open.

Clients frequently tell me that their siblings are unable to talk to them about their feelings and memories about the past; in fact, they do not even acknowledge having feelings. However, once clients establish a working contact with a sibling, they are able to open up the past. I coach clients to use factual and circular questions rather than questions about feelings. A brother who has no memories of the parents' fights may remember his favorite toy, his best friend, or what they did when Dad lost his temper. A sister who says that there was nothing at all wrong in the family will still be able to answer such questions as: "Who was closest to Dad?" "Which of us kids got dragged into the middle of Mom and Dad's fights the most?" "Of all of us, who do you think turned out most like Mom and who do you think is most like Dad?" Every sibling's story of what happened in the past is different; the true story is the composite portrait made up of everyone's different experiences.

One client spent 30 years resenting her older sister because the sister was exempt from their father's beatings. After listening to her sister's shame and guilt about always being the favorite and watching the others being beaten, she was finally able to see that although their experiences were different, they both bore the scars of growing up in an alcoholic family.

When the siblings are very close and have formed a kind of family within a family, it is easy to bring them together to talk about their experiences. It is particularly useful to have siblings who are open about their history talk about how it has affected their current life. For example, if a woman has difficulty forming trusting relationships with men, then it is useful to find out how her sister has handled relationships. Together they might explore a range of options and deepen their understanding about the aftereffects of having had a father who was dangerous.

As an outcome of the sibling work, clients often better understand what happened in their family, better accept their siblings' ways of coping with the old wounds, and, in many instances, feel closer to their siblings. Sometimes the relationships change and are healed. Sometimes they are simply accepted for what they are.

WORKING WITH THE ALCOHOLIC PARENT

There is a harsh scene in the movie *I Never Sang For My Father,* in which the son is trying to make peace with his father, who has been difficult, self-centered, and unapproachable all of his adult life. Now the father is dying. In the scene, we see the son talking to the father about his longing for them to be closer, while the father sits on the sofa looking straight ahead. As the son asks for a response, the picture widens and we see the father lean forward and turn up the sound on the TV set.

Most people die as they have lived. Clients have to come to terms with the likelihood that their alcoholic parents will never fully understand or acknowledge the effect of their behavior on their children.

When I encourage clients to make contact with the alcoholic parent, I have three primary goals for them: (1) to develop an enhanced degree of power and autonomy in relationship to that parent; (2) to grieve the loss of the alcoholic parent and accept that, regardless of whether the alcoholic ever gets sober, nothing will ever completely make up for what happened in the past; and (3) fully to appreciate the disease process and to use that perspective in coming to terms with the destructive behavior of the alcoholic parent.

The necessary steps in coming to terms with an alcoholic parent obviously will vary depending on whether the parent is still alive and, if so, is still drinking or is in recovery. If the alcoholic is still drinking, then the first step involves helping the client to take more control over his or her interactions with the drinking parent. Many ACOAs are still enabling their parent's drinking behavior and have never directly confronted the drinker. I encourage my clients to explore the possibility of doing an intervention with their siblings; if that is not possible, they might consider doing their own confrontation. This might mean that the ACOA openly confronts the alcoholic about the drinking for the very first time. One woman told her alcoholic father that he could no longer drive the car with her children in it because of her concerns about his drinking. Another ACOA told his alcoholic parents that they could not drink when they came to his house. Sometimes the first step is as simple as empowering the ACOA to put an end to phone conversations with a parent who is drunk.

Ironically, the situation is often not much easier for the ACOA if the alcoholic parent is no longer drinking. In this case, ACOAs may be reluctant to bring up the past drinking and its effects because they are afraid to upset the parent and precipitate a relapse. They may be immobilized by the feeling that they are supposed to be happy about a parent's sobriety while part of them bitterly protests that it is all "too little and too late." Additionally, it is often the case that sober parents cannot handle dealing with the past and will avoid addressing any of their children's hurt.

Obviously, the difficulty in dealing with a dead parent is that there is no direct way to come to a resolution. Death, however, does not end the relationship. The clinical challenge is to enable the client to work through that relationship and accept the ultimate lack of resolution.

If the parent is dead, or is still drinking and my client has given up trying to change him or her, I encourage the client to confront grief and anger directly by writing the parent an "I surrender" letter. The purpose of this letter is to allow the client openly to grieve the loss of hope that the relationship with the alcoholic parent will ever change. Since this letter is so difficult to write, many clients make several false starts. It is extremely important for the therapist not to rush the process, but to trust that working on this letter in and of itself will be therapeutic. The value of the work transcends the product. Many clients find that writing merely "Dear Dad" or "Dear Mom" brings enormous pain. The letter is simply a way that the client can put closure on the relationship and for once in the client's life take charge. Death does not end a relationship. Hate does not cancel the yearning for love. Writing the letter does not heal the wound, but simply acknowledges it. The scar remains.

The next step involves helping the client understand the parent and the evolution of the alcoholism. ACOAs tend to have an image of an abusive, obnoxious drunk locked in their heads and not to have any sense of what their parent was like as a person. The best way to help clients fully appreciate the ravaging effects of the disease of alcoholism is for them to find out what their parent was like before he or she became an alcoholic.

I encourage my clients to interview the alcoholic parent (when available), his or her spouse, siblings, and even parents about what the alcoholic parent was like as a child and as a young adult before becoming alcoholic. Our goal is to create a picture of the parent as a whole person with strengths and weaknesses.

Interviewing the alcoholic parent and those who knew the parent before the alcoholism is an effective way for my client to engage that parent on new terms. Usually, the client has alternated between the hostile, reactive position and the trapped, enabling position; now he or she can initiate interaction with the parent as a curious historian. Since all people, including alcoholics, like to talk about themselves, this form of engaging the alcoholic parent is usually successful, although persistence is required.

When the alcoholic parent is dead, interviewing friends and relatives is the primary avenue toward understanding the alcoholic as a person. I encourage the client to bring in pictures of the alcoholic as a way of making him or her more real and accessible. Then I ask the client to engage in a dialogue with the picture of the alcoholic parent.

> One man, looking at a photo of his father standing with his arm around the son at graduation, said: "Dad, I love you and I feel terrible that so little of my life I got to spend with you as you might have been. I know that you couldn't help your problems with alcohol, but speaking as your son I would have wished that there were more moments when you and I were together like this. It just seems so unfair that when you finally stopped drinking you got sick, and then you were in the hospital and then you were dead. It just seems so unfair."

One can feel this son's struggle to express his longing and love for his dad, as well as his frustration and anger.

When alcoholic parents are invited to their adult children's therapy, extensive preparation is essential. The adult child needs to have all of his or her fantasies about resolution worked through in advance of the joint interview, so that no great expectations are harbored.

I conduct a low-key parent-adult child interview, making it clear that the parent's role is to be a consultant to me. Generally I ask all the questions while my client listens. This enables me to join the parent and make him or her feel comfortable. Then later, if my client does want to confront the parent in a session, the parent will feel safe enough with me to try it. I am careful to avoid unleashing years of my client's pent-up resentment, since that could lead to an irreparable rupture.

Clients are likely to be caught between the impulse to forgive and the deeply buried rage from childhood that blocks forgiveness. I differentiate between understanding the alcoholic and forgiving him or her for past destructive behavior. Wounds heal but scars last.

WORKING WITH THE CODEPENDENT PARENT

Clients usually have a variety of conflicted feelings about the codependent parent. On the one hand, the codependent is frequently seen as the parent who was emotionally available and provided what nurturance and support did exist in the family.

On the other hand, the codependent was unable to protect the children from the alcoholic or to confront the alcoholism. ACOAs are usually quick to understand and forgive the codependent because they have had a much better relationship with this parent. They also look at the codependent's inability to deal with the alcoholism or violence from their own perspective of helplessness; therefore, they assume that the codependent is as much a legitimate victim as they were. While this is true, it ignores the difference between an adult who *does* not deal with destructive alcoholism and children who *cannot* deal with it. Part of coming to terms with the codependent is allowing oneself to feel the legitimate anger locked in the unasked question, "Why didn't you do something?"

While many ACOAs have difficulty being angry with the codependent parent, others blame and resent this parent even more than the alcoholic. It is not unusual for ACOAs who have thoroughly dismissed all feelings about the alcoholic to express anger at the codependent for his or her role in the family story. This is particularly true when the codependent was an active enabler who made excuses for the drinker's behavior and was in complete denial.

In one family, the 80-year-old mother still refers to the father as someone who "was a little grouchy, like the man in *Father Knows Best*," when in reality the father was violently abusive when drunk. The children, now in their 50s, are in a rage with their mother and her inability to acknowledge the reality of their lives.

The first step in coming to terms with the codependent parent is to address the stored-up resentment. Sometimes this means helping clients to acknowledge their anger, and sometimes it means helping them let go of it. I usually ask clients to make a "resentment list," which basically addresses their anger at the parent for not having done anything about the alcoholism without the excuses that are normally employed by ACOAs to defuse their own anger.

The rest of the work involves the same interviewing process described above for dealing with the alcoholic parent. It is important for the ACOA to understand the codependent in terms of his or her history and particular context, to create a picture of the codependent as a child and young adult before becoming trapped in the alcoholic marriage. Understanding the particular context in which the alcoholic marriage emerged also defuses any sense the client may have of being destined to follow in the parents' footsteps. The client learns to write a new family script.

A mother and daughter in treatment were painstakingly addressing their mutual hurt and resentment about the roles they played in dealing with the alcoholic father/husband. During one session, they were beginning to see how they had been trapped in the situation and ultimately pitted against each other in a rivalry over this man. The mother finally said to the daughter, "I know that I hurt you. I think I was really crazy at the time. When you got the other kids to confront him, I just thought you were trying to wreck my marriage. I really resented you, especially when you kept seeing him after he left the house and started up with his girlfriend. That was the worst."

The daughter responded, "He was the only father I'm ever going to have. What would you expect? It was the first time in my life that he was ever sober and I'm not supposed to see him because it's going to hurt your feelings?"

The dialogue went on. The angry feelings and buried resentments poured out. Finally the daughter burst into tears and said, "I just wanted to have a father and mother without having to choose sides. Was that such a crime?" The mother moved over to the sofa and put her arms around her daughter. She didn't need to say anything at all.

WORKING WITH THE INNER CHILD

The last part of the family-of-origin work involves addressing the complicated and mixed feelings clients have about themselves as children growing up in dysfunctional or alcoholic families (see also Chapter 5). It always surprises me how much blame ACOAs reserve for the kid they used to be.

All the preceding work in relationship to siblings and alcoholic and codependent parents is designed to help ACOAs and their spouses develop some degree of empathy for themselves, as well as some appreciation for their lack of options and their survival skills. Clients need to accept that, even though the defenses they developed as children have turned out to be self-defeating in adult life, they were useful at the time. Naturally, an emotionally deprived six-year-old might nurture herself with too much food, an abused boy might become a bully, or a scared eight-year-old might become painstakingly shy. After all, they were just kids.

Sometimes I ask clients to conjure up a mental picture of themselves as children under the age of 12 and imagine what they felt like, what their fears were, how hard they tried, how alone they felt. Then I ask them to consider just for a moment what they would like to give to that child if they could go back in time. These are some of their answers:

"I would tell her that it wasn't going to last forever."
"I would be his friend and we could play together."
"That it's okay she doesn't know how to make it better."
"A place she could go where she would be safe."
"Just a hug. That would be good enough."
"I would promise him that I will always love him."

There are a variety of ways to help clients nurture themselves more effectively. I encourage clients to develop some healthy indulgences, practice affirmations, accept their personality flaws, and learn how to grieve for their lost childhood. For example, I have one client who never expressed any of her feelings as a child and who survived by hiding behind a wall of silence. She is currently keeping a daily journal in which she takes herself back into childhood feelings and then writes them down. She brings the journal into the sessions and reads it. Slowly she is learning to let the little girl she used to be say the things that never got said. Adult children bring themselves up the best that they can. Essentially I teach my clients how to be their own parent more effectively and lovingly.

As ACOAs separate their sense of an emerging adult self from the child they once were, they begin to feel more capable of taking risks. The key is recognizing that it is not up to one's partner to be a caretaker and make life safe—that is something one does for one's self. Clients can be helped more effectively and lovingly to parent themselves. As ACOAs separate their sense of an emerging adult self from the child they once were, they are able to engage more fully and with greater vulnerability in their adult relationships.

Stage 5. Acceptance

The last stage of treatment is frequently the most difficult for the ACOA, his or her spouse, and the therapist. It involves giving up the hope that one's adult life can make up for the years of deprivation and abuse. It means risking letting go of a well-learned role that provided some security for the child but has become a burden to the adult. It means having to discover a simple painful truth: deep wounds leave scars.

In this stage of treatment, it is useful for the client and the therapist openly to discuss the natural disappointment that comes at the end of treatment when the limitations of therapy become clearer. Therapy does not provide a cure. It simply provides tools for accepting the past, coping with the present, and, it is hoped, choosing a future. Yet the scars remain. There is no magic wand.

ENDINGS

It did not surprise me that Lynn needed to run the last session. She had always been in charge of her therapy. It was the only way for her to take the enormous risks she had in facing her painful past and her lonely and constricted life. She had worked with me off and on for a couple of years. She had confronted her buried memories of being an abused child, she had reconnected with her siblings, she had blossomed professionally, and she was taking more risks interpersonally. But she was still lonely and still having to confront the possibility that as a single woman in her 40s, she may never have children or find a partner.

She did most of the talking in the last session. She explained to me how she needed to take a break from therapy because she wanted to learn how to handle things alone. She was very positive about all the changes she had made and how much better her life was. She looked sad. It made me sad. We both knew it was time for her to end. We had been talking about it for several sessions but we were both reluctant. We acknowledged the successful parts of the therapy, reminisced over some of the problems we had worked through between us, and shared in the disappointment that therapy didn't solve all of her problems.

Near the end she said, "I used to think, you had all the answers and that if I just worked hard enough and long enough, I'd live happily ever after. But it's just as well that you're not perfect anyway. If you're not, then I don't have to be."

REFERENCES

Ackerman, R. (1979). *Children of alcoholics.* Holmes Beach, FL: Learning Publications.

Ackerman, R. (1986). *Growing in the shadow.* Pompano Beach, FL: Health Communications.

Ackerman, R. (1987). *Same house, different child.* Pompano Beach, FL: Health Communications.

Black, C. (1982). *It will never happen to me.* Denver, CO: Medical Administration Corp.

Fossum, M., & Mason, M.C. (1986). *Facing shame, treating families in recovery.* New York: Norton.

Middleton-Moz, J., & Dwinell, L. (1986). *After the tears.* Pompano Beach, FL: Health Communications.

Schaef, A.W. (1986). *Codependence: Misunderstood-mistreated* San Francisco: Harper & Row.

Sexias, J., & Youcha, G. (1985) *Children of alcoholism: Survivors manual.* New York: Harper & Row.

Treadway, D. (1986). It will never happen to my kids. *Focus on the Family.*

Treadway, D. (1988). The ties that bind. *Family Therapy Networker,* July.

Treadway, D. (1989) *Before it's too late; Working with substance abuse in the family.* New York: Norton.

Wegscheider, S. (1981). *Another chance; Hope and health for the alcoholic family.* Palo Alto, CA: Science & Behavior Books.

Whitefield, C. (1983). *Healing the child within.* Pompano Beach, FL: Health Communications.

Woititz, J. G. (1983). *Adult children of alcoholics.* Pompano Beach, FL: Health Communications.

Woititz, J. G. (1985). *Struggle for intimacy.* Pompano Beach, FL: Health Communications.

10

Short-Term Psychoeducational Group for Adult Children of Alcoholics: Catalyst for Change

Michele Clark, L.C.S.W.
Noel Jette, L.I.C.S.W.

Many adult children of alcoholics (ACOAs) have difficulty using psychotherapy for themselves. The therapy session tends to be filled with the business of others—the feelings, demands, and goals of he, she, them, or it. The focus on self—what one feels about one's own experience, one's own desires and conflicts, one's obligation to self—is brief, and sometimes virtually absent.

This lack of self-focus comes about because, in an alcoholic home, the child's development of a sense of self and a personal agenda is chronically undermined by the family norm: don't be selfish (Subby & Friel, 1984). Encouraged instead, to the detriment of self, is the focus on others. For example, when a child is being verbally or physically abused by an alcoholic parent, the coalcoholic parent may also insist that the child stop making trouble, because the alcoholic parent has had a hard day or is tired or sick. The child is pushed to attend to another's pain and deny his or her own.

If this is a frequent occurrence, as in many alcoholic homes, the child becomes habitually other-focused, waiting for demands or more subtle cues about what to do, want, or think next. This child, and later adult, may be capable of deep empathy for others, but be harshly censorious of herself or himself. Lerner (1986) describes this condition of codependency in the ACOA as "a dependency on people and things outside the self to the point of self-neglect and diminished self-identity."

The individual therapist of the ACOA may be drawn in this direction and that, trying to find the patient's own self in the revelation of one troubled content area after another, to no avail. As long as the therapist, like the client, is focused on content external to the client, the latter inadvertently will talk rings around the therapist. Both will come to puzzle over why the therapy seems to be "stuck." The key is helping the patient first of all to see that the problem and remedy are located largely in the underdeveloped self, that *this* is the lasting bequest of growing up with family alcoholism. However, initially, to ask the ACOA to focus on the self is to ask the ACOA to do a shameful, anxiety-filled act. For many individual therapy clients, this impasse must be broken before successful therapy can progress.

Lerner (1986) and Gravitz and Boden (1986) have noted that it is often a cognitive intervention that releases the ACOA from feelings of isolation and shame and allows self-focus to take place. Lerner further notes that codependence is a "learned" behavior and can be "unlearned." This learning includes understanding the nature of addiction and its impact on family life. Although ACOAs have grown up with alcoholism, and in some ways are experts on this disease, in other ways they may arrive at adulthood with harmful misconceptions about alcohol addiction. For example, they still may be thinking it is a question of will power, which their alcoholic lacks. Or they may have grown up with so many alcoholics that they may not know that the drinking in their family was abnormal. Although they have suffered from their parents' alcoholism and codependence, ACOAs often do not realize what impact the family process has had on their current life problems.

As clinicians, we have noted that some of our individual ACOA patients are responsive to a cognitive approach in treatment. Active learning seems to intervene in their other-focus, forming a wedge through which psychotherapy can begin in earnest. These patients became interested in facts about the disease of alcoholism and the dynamics of family alcoholism that we offer and are willing to read conceptual material. Reading gives them a cognitive framework in which to name their own experience more clearly, and it also introduces them to the feeling of relief from isolation and shame. At the same time, this reading process provides a shared cognitive framework for the patient-therapist therapeutic collaboration. Janet Woititz' (1983) *Adult Children of Alcoholics*, Claudia Black's (1982) *It Will Never Happen To Me*, and Subby and Friel's (1984) article "Co-dependency" are exceptionally useful in successfully challenging the compulsive other-focus of some patients. More than one of our clients has said, after reading Subby and Friel, "I felt like he was sitting in my living room. How did he know?"

Many in the group psychotherapy field (Appolone & Gibson, 1981; Grenvold, 1979; Herman & Baptiste, 1981; Rahe, 1973; Yalom 1985) have noted that education alleviates anxiety and helps people become more able and likely to engage in self-care. Indeed, some ACOAs go directly from forming a cognitive framework through reading to a better use of individual psychotherapy and/or engagement with Al-Anon.

Al-Anon is an important resource because it emphasizes talking about life's difficulties with appropriate feeling and a focus on the self within a supportive group atmosphere. By attending an Al-Anon meeting, an ACOA breaks the "don't talk, don't feel" (Black, 1982) rules that operate in an alcoholic home. Al-Anon offers hope and relief from shame. However, for many ACOAs, going directly to Al-Anon is too big a step. They feel guilty and disloyal when they think of going, or they think Al-Anon will encourage them to go back and save the alcoholic, which they do not want to do, or they have met people who use Al-Anon in a robotic way. For clients who will not attend Al-Anon, another portal into recovery is required.

Gravitz and Bowden (1986) and Lerner (1986) have pointed out that sometimes an experiential or cognitive intervention is the only one that can begin the road to self-focus and growth. This intervention "often occurs as the result of their reading a newspaper story, attending a public lecture, or attending a class specifically for adult children of alcoholics." We decided that a small, short-term group would be a good gateway experience for these harder-to-reach ACOAs. Through a structured educational format, they could receive information about alcohol addiction and codependence. In this context, group members could identify with others from similar backgrounds and find initial relief from isolation. Others have noted that groups are useful in the treatment of children still living with their alcoholic parent (Hawley & Brown, 1981; Deutsch, 1982), of adolescents (Morehouse, 1986), and of young adults (Barnard & Spoentgen, 1986; Downing & Walker, 1987). We posited that such a group would lead to what Gravitz and Bowden (1986) describe as the "emergent awareness" stage, a necessary precursor to further growth and integration. In the emergent awareness stage, the client "espouses the label 'adult children of alcoholics,' and . . . individuals feel permission to accept themselves, to learn a new way, to ask for what they want and to receive what they want . . ." Further, we expected that this process would make people likely to use therapy more effectively and/or engage with Al-Anon or another recovery resource.

THE ACOA EDUCATION GROUP

Over a four-year period (1983–1987), 11 groups were offered. Each group had two coleaders and an average of seven participants. Their schedule varied from four to eight weekly meetings. The groups now undergo five weekly, two-hour sessions. Since, as clinicians, we work primarily with adult women, the groups became all-women's groups. However, this does not mean a similar approach would not be effective with all-male or mixed-gender groups (Barnard, 1986; Downing, 1987). Members have ranged in age from 24 to 58.

Recruitment

Approximately half of the original group members were self-referred from an advertisement in a local newspaper or from seeing the group advertised on a therapist's bulletin board. The remaining participants were referred directly to the group by their individual therapists.

A group leader met with each interested person for a one-hour individual evaluation and orientation. Most interviewees (90%) became group participants. Individuals were excluded (1) who were in an acute life crisis, (2) who were disorganized or psychotic, (3) who were looking for an interactional therapy group, (4) whose own alcohol or substance abuse posed an immediate serious problem, or (5) who were grandchildren of alcoholics or were from other codependent family situations but were not ACOAs.

The goals of the individual meeting were (1) to establish a limited alliance between the group leader and the prospective participant, (2) to orient the person in detail to the content of each of the five group sessions, (3) to evaluate current use of alcohol and other mood-altering drugs, (4) to prepare the individual for anxious reactions to portions of the group's content, (5) to assess whether this was the right group for this person at this time, and (6) to prepare the prospective member for the homework assignment at the midpoint of the group session, which is to attend an Al-Anon meeting. The individual left this meeting with an initial set of readings on the nature of alcoholism and addiction, (Mann, 1987; Prember, 1982; Robe, 1987).

Group Structure and Program

The format of each session is fairly structured, with some time included for personal sharing. Each meeting has a content agenda, which is listed on an instructional board. Group leaders stress competence and hope whenever possible, pointing out ways that coping with parental alcoholism also builds personal strengths along with the psychological problems. During each session group leaders offer sample problems—concrete situations that might arise involving group members and their family alcoholics. We also discuss the recurrent theme of one's own safe and abusive drinking, a topic very much on members' minds.

The first session begins with welcomes, introductions, and a discussion of group rules. Following this, the content focus is on alcoholism, the illness of the alcoholic. In order to begin with members on a competency basis, they are asked to make a list of facts they already know about alcoholism, and, later, a list of things they would like to learn in this group. The leaders answer the specific questions on the second list, questions such as, "What can I do about my father's drinking?" or "How do I know if I'm drinking abusively?" They also offer hopeful information in answer to the more general questions, such as, "Can I get better from this?" The film A Slight Drinking Problem (Southerby, 1979) is shown. Members easily identify with this film, which also evokes a lot of feeling. The discussion that follows is on recognizing the signs of denial and early detachment. Participants leave with a second set of readings on codependence and family roles (Subby & Friel, 1984; Collett, 1988).

The second session begins with a discussion of roles children play in the family: hero, scapegoat, low profile (lost), and mascot (Deutsch, 1982; Black, 1982). These roles are reviewed in detail, again stressing strengths as well as problems. Group participation usually increases during this section. Then the film *Soft is the Heart of a Child* (Hazelden, 1978) is shown. Again, group members easily identify with this film about three children in an alcoholic family, and usually at least one group member is tearful as the film ends. This film is particularly effective with those who are in substantial denial about their family situations. Group members are given more readings on the characteristics of children of alcoholics and are encouraged to reread the codependency article.

The third session focuses on the concept of codependence and its origin in dysfunctional family process. Group leaders discuss the nature of codependence and the family rules as described by Subby and Friel (1984). The homework assignment, attending an Al-Anon meeting, is explained. Members are given meeting booklets from Al-Anon and any participants who have already attended a meeting are asked to tell about their experiences. The leaders stress that not everyone likes Al-Anon and that it does not help everyone; all reactions and doubts are permissible. A group leader does a guided fantasy with participants about their ideal Al-Anon meeting. Members have an alternative homework assignment if they choose not to go to Al-Anon—to observe their feelings about having homework and about the organization that they (by now) have heard so much about.

The fourth session spotlights self-care, homework reports, and a review of recovery-resource options. The importance of self-renewal and fun and pleasure is stressed. Staying within a competency framework, group members are asked to talk about ways in which they already take good care of themselves. The list they generate is long and creative. This is followed by reports from Al-Anon meetings or from the self-observation exercise. Usually about half the group goes to a meeting and half does not. Then a leader does a relaxation exercise as a here-and-now experience in self-care. Finally, a list of other local and national resources is shared and discussed. This list includes Hazelden Press, the Johnson Institute, and Health Communications, as well as local agencies that offer a variety of services for ACOAs and addicted persons.

In the fifth session, participants have an opportunity to bring in concrete problems they are having with the alcoholic(s) in their lives. Group members and leaders brainstorm about alternatives in behavior or in attitude. Next, using a worksheet, the group discusses how to plan for more satisfying holidays and family gatherings. The emphasis here is on self-focus, being realistic, having more than one plan, not being the target of the probable blowout, and garnering small, real moments of closeness with some family members. We then invite feedback from participants about the overall group experience, as well as thoughts about further recovery work.

FOLLOW-UP SURVEY

Our original group participants received an open-ended follow-up questionnaire six months to a year after their group ended. The general aim of the survey was to gather the assessments of group members as to the impact of the group experience on their subsequent recovery processes. Of 73 possible respondents, 51 (70%) answered the anonymous, mailed questionnaire.

The remaining 22 members did not respond despite twice receiving copies of the questionnaire. We have no way of knowing the extent to which the fact that they did not respond was random or reflected different attitudes toward the group experience. Nonetheless, the questionnaire does provide a clear picture of the views of a majority of group participants. It also appears to have provided a useful opportunity for reflection on the group experience to many members, judging by the detail of the replies.

Specific Questions

Question 1: *Do you feel you have changed because of participating in the group? If so, in what ways?*

Almost everyone (48 respondents) reported insight and awareness changes since participating in the group, with only six of these uncertain as to whether to attribute such changes to the group. "I am more aware of the dynamics that went on in my family as I was growing up and the profound influence that had on me. I know what my problems are and though that's hard, it's better." Nineteen respondents reported behavioral changes. For example, "I found Al-Anon through this group and it has changed my life." Another asserted, "I no longer get involved with men who have substance-abuse problems."

Table 10-1
Question 1: Reports of Changes Since Group

Total responses	51	(100%)
Insight and awareness changes	48	(94%)
Behavioral changes	19	(37%
"Uncertain"	6	(12%)

Note: Sum is greater than number of respondents (51) due to multiple responses. "Uncertain" category refers to those unsure of whether group was causal agent of reported changes. All percentages based on $n = 51$.

Question 2: *Have your feelings about your alcoholic parent (or parents) changed?*

Forty-four respondents reported attitudinal shifts and/or changes in feelings. Thirty-two cited more detachment, less denial, or more understanding about the effects of family alcoholism. Twenty-six respondents reported feeling closer, or having more empathy; eight felt more distant or disappointed.

Table 10-2
Question 2: Reports of changes in Relation to Aalcoholic Parent

Total responses	51	(100%)
No, not much, not sure	5	(10%)
Yes (40) and uncertain (six)	46	(90%)
Attitudinal and/or emotional changes	44	(86%
More detachment, less denial, more understanding of effects of family alcoholism	32	(63%)
Feeling closer, having more empathy	26	(50%)
Feeling more distant, disappointed	8	(16%)

Note: See Table 10-1 note.

Question 3: *Have your feelings about your coalcoholic parent changed?*

Of the 46 respondents to whom this question was applicable, 39 reported cognitive, emotional, or behavioral changes. One respondent put it this way: "I'm much more tolerant of my mother—I think because I've been working on my own coalcoholic issues—and I feel clearer about how to interact with her [in a manner] that takes care of me more than before."

Question 4: *Has there been a change in your feelings of being alone or isolated?*

Forty-six respondents cited some shifts. Thirty-five reported feeling less alone; seven said they felt less shamed—"weird," "crazy," "damaged." One respondent said, "I'm getting over the feeling of being damaged. I'm starting to feel proud of the work I've done to change and take care of myself. I feel part of a community [that] knows when to ask for help . . . I don't feel 'all alone in the world.'" Thirteen respondents reported being more in touch with feeling lonely. Nineteen respondents cited other emotional and behavioral changes. For example, one respondent said, "I feel that I communicated my feelings better than I have in the past." Another said, "I am more open with people. I used to be shy but I am not as shy anymore."

Question 5: *Has there been a change in your behavior(s) around taking care of other people?*

Forty-four said they had experienced changes in their caretaking behavior. Among these, 37 noted positive interpersonal growth and twenty-nine found they had a greater capacity to focus on themselves. As one respondent put it: "I'm much more aware of the [caretaking] tendency and I'm getting more 'selfish.' Not bending over backwards to accommodate others . . ."

Question 6: *Do you tell yourself your own history in a different way now?*

Forty-six reported that their views of the past had shifted. Of these, 40 had developed more compassionate attitudes toward their pasts. One person said, "I think now my history seems a little less humiliating to me. I used to bury my family problems but now I seem to be able to discuss my past with a little more clarity—as well as kindness toward myself and family members." Twenty-five respondents said they had more available feeling about the past, that they had broken through emotional numbness. "I am beginning to remember more unpleasant memories and connect them to how I sometimes feel now. I occasionally feel deprived or even emotionally abused when I remember my past."

Table 10-3
Question 6: Reports of Understanding Own Histories in New Ways

Total responses	50	(98%)
No	3	(6%)
Yes, some shifts (42) and uncertain (6)	48	(94%)
more compassionate attitude to past	40	(78%)
more available affect, less numb	25	(49%)

Note: See Table 10-1 note.

Question 7: *Have there been any changes in how you relate to your parents, sisters, brothers?*

Forty-two reported behavioral, attitudinal, or emotional shifts, including five who had "very little contact." Forty tried out new approaches with family members, 24 noted awareness changes, and seven cited changes in their feelings toward family members. One person said, "My relationships are more direct—less triangulation." Another respondent said, "I'm working hard on not immediately falling into old patterns of smoothing the waters but [instead] figuring out what I want and need— and sometimes doing what I want and need rather than appeasing everyone else."

Question 8: *This question asked for specific recovery steps people had taken since the group.*

All 50 who answered this query reported some movement. Thirty-four began or continued to attend Al-Anon meetings, 16 on a regular basis. Seventeen respondents began or continued individual or group therapy. Thirty-eight of those responding availed themselves of other recovery resources, such as books, films, workshops, or conferences.

Table 10-4
Question 8: Reports of Postgroup Recovery Steps

Total responses, including uncertain (6)	50	(98%)
No response	1	(2%)
Began or continued Al-Anon meetings	34	(67%)
on regular basis	16	(31%)
Began or continued psychotherapy	17	(33%)
Used other recovery resource	38	(75%)
(books, films, workshops, conferences)		

Note: See Table 10-1 note.

Question 9: *In this question, respondents were queried about what they had found most helpful in the group experience.*

Fifty responses were received. Among these, thirty-one mentioned factors that enhanced universality, such as sharing similar feelings and experiences and group discussion and support. Thirty-three respondents credited the cognitive inputs as important—the educational presentations, film, articles; 16 responses cited structural elements, such as group size, confidentiality, or the leaders, as significantly helpful. One group member commented, "In a way, going to the group was as big a step as anything I learned in group."

Table 10-5
Question 9: Most Helpful Aspects of Group

Total responses, including uncertain (6)	50	(98%)
No response	1	(2%)
Factors enhancing universality	31	(61%)
Cognitive input	33	(65%)
(presentations, films, articles)		
Structural elements	16	(31%)
(size, confidentiality, leaders)		

Note: See Table 10-1 note.

DISCUSSION

We observed in the course of leading these groups that people were indeed able to gain relevant and helpful information. This was evident in the process of the sessions as participants energetically used the terminology and concepts offered to analyze their families of origin and current life issues. The degree of participation in thoughtful, sometimes very painful, group discussions was striking. The level of commitment to this experience was high; there were few dropouts (under 10%), and there was very good overall attendance (less than 10% did not attend all five sessions).

Participants spoke of sharing their readings and subsequently having productive discussions about family alcoholism with family members and friends. Several members sent a sibling, friend or co-worker to a later group. At least two members did postgroup interventions with their alcoholic parent. Several members spoke of educating their therapists about alcohol addiction and codependence. Indeed, after finishing the group, many participants surged ahead in their individual therapies, a process we observed directly with our own patients and indirectly through other (referring) clinicians' reports.

This progress was characterized for some by the clients' growing abilities to sit still and bear their own affect. When the other-focused "whirring" subsides, often sadness, fear, and loss are present. True grief resolution requires a true, developed self, and, indeed, such work tended to occur late in the therapy process and faster if the person was engaged with Al-Anon.

Members who, upon completion of the group, were still in substantial denial about the way parental alcoholism had affected them, soon after began to accept and integrate the information. This usually occurred at the next visit with parents. One participant, on her next visit home, was shocked and frightened by the way her father drove a car when he had been drinking. Yet her father's habitual drunk driving had not changed; it was her perception of its meaning that had changed. After this visit home, the material we had covered in the education group became part of her understanding of her family. Several group members whose drinking could be called early-stage alcoholism or prealcoholic drinking began, after this group, to observe their own drinking patterns with their therapist in a candid and searching manner.

Our observations of participants' apparent growth in understanding the impact of family alcoholism are borne out by responses to the survey. Eighty-two percent reported the development of insight and awareness in this area. Also significant were the shifts in members' ways of relating to their families of origin; 78% reported trying new approaches and responses. Important to "getting on with it" in therapy and in life is the capacity to focus on the self.

Many respondents cited evidence of positive interpersonal growth, usually involving less caretaking and a greater ability to focus on their own needs. The groups had substantial success in helping members feel less isolated and ashamed. Sixty-nine percent reported feeling less alone. And 78% developed a more self-accepting historical view as a result of being in the group. Sixty-eight percent had some attendance at Al-Anon, with 32% attending regularly. Seventy-six percent availed themselves of further educational resource.

The developmental schema we work with might be described this way: The symptomatic ACOA is given hope and relief from shame through the information and small, structured format of the education group. At the same time, this process stimulates the person's pain. However, it also helps to galvanize the self to cope with pain in a new way; that is, without the former level of denial. The person, probably with outside help, learns how to comfort the self, and also observes her or his increased ability to bear strong feelings without behaving compulsively. Thus, the self is enhanced: it is, and knows it is, stronger. As this process continues, older and deeper losses may surface and be named, grieved, and integrated. The person then can move on, less encumbered by the past, with improved self-esteem and a clearer self-identity. This work sets the stage for further measured risks, challenges, and commitments, which will further develop the self.

SUMMARY

In summary, an educational group model can be a valuable therapeutic tool for ACOAs. The value of relevant education in a supportive atmosphere was borne out by the growth reported by participants. It is important to keep in mind that this kind of group does not constitute a recovery process in itself. Recovery, we have observed, is neither brief nor linear; it is an ongoing dialectical, self-development process.

Thus, the education group model should in no way be opposed to Al-Anon, psychotherapy, or other long-term recovery resources. But it can be a gateway to a deeper, more productive engagement with recovery. This may be especially true for the ACOA who wants to move ahead but is too enmired in codependence to take the next healing step.

REFERENCES

Appolone, C., & Gibson, P. (1981). Group work with young adult epilepsy patients. *Social Work in Health Care, 6*, 23–32.

Barnard, C., & Spoentgen, P. (1986). Children of alcoholics: Characteristics and treatment. *Alcoholism Treatment Quarterly, 3 (4)*, 47–65.

Black, C. (1982). *It will never happen to me*, (pp. 13–27) Denver, CO: Medical Administration Corp.

Collett, L. (July/Aug. 1988) Step by step. *Mother Jones*, 43–48.

Deutsch, C. (1982). *Broken bottles, broken dreams*, (pp. 54–74, 163–177, 178–190). New York: Teachers College Press.

Downing, N., & Walker, M. (1987). A psychoeducational group for adult children of alcoholics. *Journal of Counseling and Development, 65*, 44–442.

Gravitz, H., & Bowden, J. (1986). Therapeutic issues of adult children of alcoholics, (pp. 187–208). In R. Ackerman (Ed.), *Growing in the shadow.* Pompeno Beach, FL: Health Communications.

Grenvold, D. K., & Welch, G. J. (1979). Structured short term group treatment of postdivorce adjustment. *International Journal of Group Psychotherapy, 29,* 347–356.

Hawley, N. P., & Brown, E. L. (1981). The use of group treatment with children of alcoholics. *Social Casework: The Journal of Contemporary Social Work,* 40–46.

Hazelden Productions (1978). *Soft is the heart of a child* (film). Center City, MN.

Herman, E., & Baptiste, S. (1981). Pain control: Mastery through group experience, *Pain, 10:,* 79–86.

Lerner, R. (1986). Codependency: The swirl of energy surrounded by confusion (pp. 113–121). In R. Ackerman (Ed.), *Growing in the shadow.* Pompano Beach, FL: Health Communications.

Mann, G. (1987). *The dynamics of addiction.* Minneapolis, MN: Johnson Institute.

Morehouse, E. (1986). Working with adolescent children of alcoholics. In R. Ackerman (Ed.), *Growing in the shadow* (pp. 125–142). Pompano Beach, FL: Health Communications.

Premer, R. (1982). *Medical consequences of alcoholism.* Minneapolis, MN: Johnson Institute.

Rahe, R., et al. (1973). Group therapy in the outpatient management of post-myocardial infarction patients. *Psychiatry in Medicine, 4,* 77–78.

Robe, L. (1987). *Blackouts and alcoholism.* Minneapolis, MN: Johnson Institute.

Southerby Productions (1979). *A silent drinking problem* (film). Long Beach, CA.

Subby, R., & Friel, J. (1984). Co-dependency—paradoxical dependency. In *Codependency: An emerging issue* (pp. 31–44). Pompano Beach, Fl: Health Communications.

Woititz, J. (1983). *Adult children of alcoholics.* Pompano Beach, FL: Health Communications.

Yalom, I. (1985). *The theory and practice of group psychotherapy* (pp. 9–12). New York: Basic Books.

11

Treatment of Children of Substance-Abusing Parents: Selected Developmental, Diagnostic, and Treatment Issues

Timothy M. Rivinus, M.D.

These are the biases of a psychiatrist who has learned most of what he knows about the addictions outside of formal medical and psychiatric training. I have been exposed to the consequences of addiction during many phases of my clinical and personal life. Yet, during most of my life and training, addiction and its effects on people; on their bodies, minds, development, and spirit; and on their families, children, and friends were never spoken about. Drinking and taking drugs were something that was "done," or not done, but never thoughtfully discussed.

The addictions *are* hard to talk about and write about. Nevertheless, as a psychiatrist, I feel the need to articulate what I have learned—particularly to my colleagues in psychiatry. I am troubled by how much difficulty many psychiatrists have in comprehending the impact of family addiction on the young. I have come to understand that this is a symptom of professional and personal denial. These observations on work with children of substance-abusing parents (COSAPs) are dedicated to challenging professional denial and resistance: my own and that of my colleagues.

DEVELOPMENTAL ISSUES

The Drug-Taking-Parent Model

The basic lesson that the COSAP learns in childhood is that the psychoactive chemicals provide ways to deal with stress and deny reality. This is why children who have seen a parent abuse alcohol or drugs so often resort to the same substances as a way of dealing with emotional states or painful events. They may say to themselves, "I will never drink and become like Dad." Yet many find themselves almost "destined" to deal with reality and emotional events in the same way once they can acquire alcohol or other drugs. Alcohol is often made prematurely available to COSAPs by the abetting alcoholic parent, and such collusive and self-justifying actions by the addicted parent are often the beginning of the addiction for the child. The COSAP may drink or use drugs as a way of "joining" the alcoholic parent in the only way he or she knows how. The repetition of this early learning is so strong that the marriages, especially first marriages, of COSAPs are to alcoholics or drug-abusing individuals.

The Codependent Model

The COSAP looks to the "sober" parent or codependent for stability and sanity while growing up (Whitfield, 1984). This parent provides the only stable model for a child's behavior during childhood. Because of constant denial of the problem, what the child learns from the codependent parent is the "caretaking stance," in which the child assumes responsibilities of and for the alcoholic parent and the family. With this caretaking role, the child also inherits a pervading sense of fatigue, emptiness, lack of personal fulfillment, depression, and hopelessness, often thinly disguised.

The codependent parent may appear martyred, often saintly, but she or he is also "unreal" and essentially unavailable as a parent or partner. His or her efforts are often superhuman, and the codependent parent may turn to the children for nurturing and partnership. This can make a child's separation from this parent a problematic process. The codependent parent may blame a rebellious child for the alcoholic's behavior. So, despite the sometimes outstanding nurturing and caretaking qualities of codependent parents, a child may have angry and ambivalent feelings toward this parent while, at the same time, having an "overcathected" attachment to, idolatry of, and protectiveness toward this same parent, who is the only lifeline in the storm of addictive family life.

The system of allegiance to family and to the family's addictive secret remains so pervasive that the "presenting complaints" of COSAPs in adulthood are usually obscure. Depression of unknown cause and psychosomatic complaints are common. COSAPs, as adults, often seek organic therapies for their complaints. Psychiatric symptoms can appear in the context of troubled relationships, with the COSAP finding himself or herself in the same dependent position that he or she knew as a child, sometimes with an abusive (perhaps chemical-abusing) partner.

The manifestations of identification of a codependent parent appear as an arrest of psychological growth in the COSAP. Adult COSAPs find themselves in marriages that do not grow in love or understanding, arrested in individual psychosexual growth in ways that are justified by a strong feeling that such growth is impossible, that "nobody can really change," and that they deserve no better.

Repetition–Compulsion

The dissociative status of those who have grown up in chemically dependent families is similar to the situation of many traumatized patients with a kind of post-traumatic stress disorder (PTSD) (American Psychiatric Association, 1987, pp. 247-251; see also Cermak, 1986, and Chapter 6, this volume). Such individuals are numbed, chronically disappointed, and in continual pain as a result of dashed expectations for normal developmental handling by their parents. They have often wished to stop feeling and may seek relief of pain in unsatisfactory relationships, self-destructive behaviors, and a kind of "repeat after me" phenomenon in which COSAPs adopt the drugs of addiction of their parents to relieve the pain of child-hood experiences (Black, 1981). In many cases, their decision to come into therapy is precipitated by the realization that they are "unconsciously" repeating patterns that they saw and learned and experienced during childhood. This is a classic example of the repetition-compulsion that was so carefully written and thought about by early psychoanalytic psychotherapists.

Self-Treatment of Chronic Stress Disorder

Among the problems that a COSAP has to face are general anxiety and the constant fear of possible calamity (Kolb, 1987; Van der Kolk, 1987; see also Chapter 7). Many patients describe a sense of impending violence or self-injury as the result of the alcoholic's behavior. D. H. Lawrence (1976/1913) describes this in a moving, largely autobiographical passage describing the young Paul Morel and his sister overhearing the pleadings of their mother and the violence of their alcoholic father above the howling of the wind.

> The winter of their first year in the new house their father was very bad. The children played in the street, on the brim of the wide, dark valley, until eight o'clock. Then they went to bed. Their mother sat sewing below. Having such a great space in front of the house gave the children a feeling of night, of vastness, and of terror. This terror came in from the shrieking of the tree and the anguish of the home discord. Often Paul would wake up, after he had been asleep a long time, aware of thuds downstairs. Instantly he was wide awake. Then he heard the booming shouts of his father, come home nearly drunk, then the sharp replies of his mother, then the bang, bang of his father's fist on the table, and the nasty snarling shout as the man's voice got higher. And then the whole was drowned in a piercing medley of shrieks and cries from the great wind-swept ash-tree. The children lay silent in suspense, waiting for a lull in the wind to hear what their father was doing. He might hit their mother again. There was a feeling of horror, a kind of bristling in the darkness, and a sense of blood. They lay with their hearts in the grip of an

intense anguish. The wind came through the tree fiercer and fiercer. All the cords of the great harp hummed, whistled, and shrieked. And then came the horror of the sudden silence, silence everywhere, outside and downstairs. What was it? Was it a silence of blood? What had he done?

The children lay and breathed the darkness. And then, at last, they heard their father throw down his boots and tramp upstairs in his stockinged feet. Still they listened. Then at last, if the wind allowed, they heard the water of the tap drumming into the kettle, which their mother was filling for morning, and they could go to sleep in peace.

So they were happy in the morning—happy, very happy playing, dancing at night round the lonely lamppost in the midst of the darkness. But they had one tight place of anxiety in their hearts, one darkness in their eyes, which showed all their lives.

Paul hated his father. As a boy he had a fervent private religion.

"Make him stop drinking," he prayed every night. "Lord, let my father die," he prayed very often. "Let him not be killed at pit," he prayed when, after tea, the father did not come home from work.

There is a pervasive sense of impending doom and violence for many COSAPs. Ron is a 1980's version of Lawrence's Paul.

Ron described sleeping underneath his bed throughout his childhood for he feared that his father would come home and pull him out of bed and beat him severely for allegedly wetting his bed (something he had done until age six). This went on years after he had become dry at night. Yet the fear of wetting, a general anxiety at nighttime, and a sleep disorder remained with him as symptoms into adult life—the symptoms he attempted to treat with alcohol and ingestion of illegal drugs.

Trust versus Mistrust

COSAPs who are exposed to parental substance abuse for a year or more in childhood lack basic trust, both in others and in the meaning of verbal communication (Ackerman, 1983). The promises of the alcoholic cannot be trusted. The child's hopes and wishes, awakened by occasionally "good enough" parenting by the substance-abusing parent, are ultimately disappointed and unfulfilled. As life goes on, a flicker of childhood hope remains. As Freud (1974/1908) pointed out, children always would like to hope the best of a parent.

Lucy was a ten-year-old girl who told her therapist that her mother would always come into her bedroom intoxicated, wake her up, hug her, and cry, sobbing uncontrollably, sometimes up to an hour before letting her daughter go, and leave the room and her daughter in a highly agitated state, unable to sleep for many hours. When her therapist asked her if she had been able to tell anybody, the child stated, "I told my daddy, but he said it didn't really happen . . . Another time he said, 'Why don't you just go to another room, and stop upsetting your mother so?'"

The therapist, at that point and for the first time, recalled a similar experience growing up in her own alcoholic family. She realized that until she, too, had gotten therapy, she had long pursued a policy of going into her room, closing the door, and crying alone with her own anxiety. With this knowledge, she felt that she could best validate her patient's experience by putting it in the context of the addicted family. To do so, the therapist acknowledged she, too, had experienced similar denial of communicated reality.

Lucy and her therapist met ten years after completing therapy and agreed that they both felt that this moment was a turning point of trust in the therapy.

The important therapeutic point to note is Lucy's doubt of reality, illustrated by her quotation of her father. Doubt, whether words can "heal anything or mean anything," is pervasive in COSAPs. Words and actions cannot really communicate or help one extricate oneself from inevitable pain of human relationships. This is a view of life that needs to be explored and made explicit in the context of therapy with COSAPs. Often, brief self-revelation by therapists who are COSAPs can assist in this process.

Countertransference problems arise when the therapist recognizes issues from his or her own past with an alcoholic parent and finds himself or herself withdrawing from the patient because of these issues. Similarly, if the therapist has had no such experience, he or she may miss an opportunity to explore the patient's experience of having had a communication of reality blocked by someone. When communication is blocked in childhood, the communicative energy takes behavioral (hyperactivity "acting out"), affective (depression or mania), or cognitive (dissociation, identification with the aggressor) forms (see Chapter 7). Therapy may allow the patient to realize that those symptoms were a cry for help at the time within the context of the addicted family. The corrective experience offered by these therapeutic opportunities is immeasurable.

Codependency and Counterdependency

The COSAP often learns to trust and attach to *no one*. Yet, as children and adults, COSAPs often have extraordinarily strong, unmet dependency needs, which—when remaining unmet—can result in "counterdependent" approaches to life. Initially, while living with chemically dependent parents as a child, hopes for love and nurture may be kept alive by parental promises. But these promises usually are not kept by addicted parents living in a constantly shifting and all-consuming framework of intoxication, withdrawal, and brief periods of "dryness," thus throwing the child onto himself or herself for "self-care."

Newly sober and recovering parents often are no better parents, and sometimes are worse, than addicted ones. Parents may disappear into residential programs or an endless series self-help meetings and adopt the "selfish" rhetoric of the self-help movements. There is little time for "other-oriented" provision of a "holding environment" for children. Parents may be irritable and self-absorbed. The child has a chronic fear that the patient will "fall off the wagon" and revert to active drinking or drug use.

COSAPs learn from addicted parents that instinctual and narcissistic needs are ultimately primary—that the Id, not the Ego, or even the occasionally overexerted Superego, holds sway. COSAPs may adopt this position for themselves in adult life, and expect it of others in relationships. The COSAP may make too few demands on others as a result of counterdependence or make overwhelming demands on relationships or form "codependent" relationships with addicted partners related to the overwhelming dependency needs driven by early childhood learning and survival experience.

Learned Helplessness

Chemically dependent families observe a "pact of denial" that implies: "Don't trust, talk, or feel. There's nothing you can do about it anyway" (Black, 1981). The child victim of this family process comes to understand a principle well honored by law-enforcement personnel, as well as clinicians, that "you can't talk to a drunk." This principle becomes a generalized agreement in chemically dependent families. It then becomes generalized with respect to all meaning or communicative action for COSAPs. In other words, "You not only cannot talk to a drunk, but you cannot 'talk' or 'feel' at all."

A young man, himself an alcoholic and a drug abuser, describes sleeping under his bed so as to avoid his father's wrath. His mother would then chide him for doing so, saying, "There's nothing you can do about him anyway." This young man adopted this view about all aspects of his life prior to coming to therapy.

These repeated messages, within the family context, seem to be an excellent example of how 'learned helplessness' becomes internalized within a human-family structure, and then within the character structure itself (Flannery, 1987). Although the COSAP intends "never to drink, never to become like the dependent parent," he or she finds that this is a promise that "signifies nothing" owing to the meaninglessness of words, resolutions, and promises within his or her internalized, dependent family framework; nor is it difficult to understand the patient's deep, basic mistrust, superficial statements and commitments notwithstanding, of the promise of "talking therapy(ies)" as an endeavor that will produce change or healing.

Isolation

The child's development within the addictive family structure is an extraordinarily isolated process, although it may have the veneer of respectability. In many alcoholic families, the alcoholic parent is known as a "provider" who works and brings money home but is absent from all aspects of family life, including the emotional development of the child. The codependent parent is so busy simply meeting the complex needs of the addicted parent and the basic physical needs of the family that he or she, too, is only aware in passing of important developmental milestones in the children's lives.

The family's biggest and most demanding "child" is, of course, the addicted parent himself or herself. Sibling relationships among COSAPs take on close similarity to the relationship between the parents. Often there is the child who "keeps things together" by joining the codependent parent in a caretaking role—"the parentified child." Other siblings may "act out" or "drop out," adopting aspects of the chemical-abusing parent's role (Black, 1981; Wegscheider, 1981). This should be interpreted by care givers as a cry for help. Too often, it is viewed by the child's world as a symptom of badness or character pathology.

Particularly serious is the lack of trust that children of chemically dependent parents develop. At one moment, a parent may seem loving, attached, and caring. At other moments, the addicted parent or the codependent parent may be totally withdrawn and preoccupied with the addiction, blaming, punitive, and thoroughly distorting of the child's sense of reality. Therefore, intimate relationships are extremely difficult for many children of chemically dependent parents because there is no trust. The young child or adult child often feels that closeness to any figure, including a therapist, would mean betrayal of the type that occurs within the addicted parental system. This leaves a sense of chronic isolation, problems with intimacy, and a resulting feeling of defeat and depression.

The Developmental Arrest

Many aspects of normal childhood development are neglected in the addicted family and many COSAPs find themselves in a developmentally arrested stage (Group for the Advancement of Psychiatry, 1966). The encouragement of normal development through trial, error, reparenting experiences, and the corrective experiences of therapy is the basis for reversing these developmental arrests. For example, socialization, which has been impaired because the child has not dared to share the family's secret, can begin by the relationship of therapy.

> One young man described never wanting to invite people to his home because of the embarrassment of the alcoholic's behavior or family behavior in protecting that individual, not realizing himself that he, too, was protecting that "secret" by shutting himself off from the outside world in relation to his home. By sharing his secret, he began to conclude that a safe relationship might now be possible.

The painful realization during childhood that other children's parents were different and that, therefore, one was somehow different is often a confession that begins therapy. A feeling of "other worldliness" in relationships that proceeds well into adult life requires special consideration in the treatment context, both in the examination of the patient's ongoing relationships and within the transference relationship.

The Self-Holding Environment of the COSAP

While intoxicated, a parent is often unaware of his or her affectionate or hostile actions, or only vaguely aware of them. While withdrawing or between states of intoxication, the parent is constantly and vigilantly seeking to preserve his or her own sense of self-esteem—and planning the next drink or drug. In such an environment, a child comes to realize that his or her needs come second to the overwhelming, narcissistic needs of the parent for the drug. The child is basically deprived of any sort of "holding environment" (Winnecott, 1960) and is taught to provide himself or herself with one of his or her own. This child-generated care system often needs to extend to become the holding environment for the addicted parent (cum child) and for other family members. This is the origin of the well-described role reversals noted in alcoholic and chemically dependent families where "parentification" and the model child, or "little parent," is produced. Yet at all stages of development, "the impostor syndrome" is likely to be present. The COSAP usually feels that more responsibility is required than he or she can possibly "as a child" bring to the situation.

The Self: An Empty Bottle Waiting to Be Filled

The COSAP who constantly identifies as a self-object has little time to develop a sense of self as a person.

> A young girl says, "I spent my whole childhood just looking out for my mother. It was her next move that I was constantly thinking of. School was the only safe place for me. I never really had a feeling for who I was, what

I wanted to be, or what anybody expected of me except to watch out for her next move and try not to get in her way. That's what everybody else (especially my father and my two brothers) seemed to be thinking and saying about *her*. That was the way to survive."

In the absence of accurate and consistent parental "mirroring" (Kohut, 1984), a disfigured sense of self develops. The magical, "preoperational" thinking of the young child translates into the constant question, "Am I the cause of all this?" A painfully parentified but guilt-ridden sense of self-understanding can result in which the mirrored child-parent is alternately seen as defective, intoxicated, grandiosely parentified, and empty of reflected self.

Codependent Defenses

Various childhood defense mechanisms develop within the context of the addictive family: highly compulsive cathexis to work, to caretaking, and to denial of personal self-care are examples of defenses of children who are "survivors." In adult life, workaholic patterns and repeated patterns of pathological familial caretaking are often the symptomatic result. Such traits as explosiveness, dissociative states, memory lapses (similar to "blackouts"), passiveness, and dependence are other defense mechanisms that are learned and adapted within the addictive family system but are maladaptive when the individual emerges from the closed addictive system at the time of adolescence and young adulthood. The young person with these defenses often finds himself or herself without the experience to develop a sustaining relationship, except with those who come from similar backgrounds or are addicted or abusive themselves.

The Depressed-Angry Position

The child of a chemically dependent parent symptomatically takes the depressive position. Helplessness, hopelessness, and worthlessness underlie this position. In the transference situation, the helplessness and hopelessness translate into profound doubts that there is hope or help in therapy. Therapy may go on for months and years, and gains may be apparent but the patient, at bottom, may still doubt whether change is possible or whether anything has changed in life. This reflects the relationship that the child has had to the chemically dependent parent and to the family.

The important finding first made by Freud (1974/1917), and elaborated by others, is that anger is a basic emotion related to depression. Where object relationships are concerned, anger at the dependent and codependent parents (open or suppressed) is often at the root. One of the therapeutic challenges in working with such children is that the anger at the alcoholic parent, the coalcoholic parent, and the entire alcoholic family situation is so great and pervasive that the patient often has great difficulty taking any responsibility for his or her present actions (see also Chapter 6). The ease, in the face of such overwhelming anger, with which the patient feels shame over and blames the addicted family situation and the alcoholic parent not only for what has occurred in the past, but for the patient's present life situation, is an important psychological mechanism of the COSAP (Fossum & Mason, 1986).

The "disease model" of chemical abuse and alcoholism can provide a helpful first step in allowing the patient to "project" and externalize his or her feelings of self-worthlessness onto alcohol or other chemicals as "disease-causing agents" (Wallace, 1985a, 1985b). The therapist needs to be aware that, although the disease model may have limitations in helping the patient take responsibility for change, it is often a crucial neutral and educational catalyst with which both the patient and therapist can reframe painful and affect-laden historical events of the patient's life to promote future change.

Shame-Blame Systems

The tendency to feel shame and blame and to transmit those emotions is unusually strong in children of alcoholic families (Fossum & Mason, 1986). When combined with a feeling of helplessness and hopelessness in terms of life situations in general, brought from the experiences of the alcoholic to therapy, shame combines with the strong tendency to "blame" and "attribute" a whole range of present problems to external causes. Such patients often find themselves, for long periods of time, feeling that they can initiate no real change and that they are not really responsible for what they bring to an interaction. They not only seek out partners and situations that often cause them to feel helpless and ineffectual, but they exercise little judgment and self-analysis in these situations and relationships.

In therapy it is usually corrective to examine these feelings in light of the feelings engendered by past experience in the alcoholic family, and to analyze them as they are brought into the therapeutic situation and transference. It is our experience that this requires a great deal of time and persistence on the part of both patient and therapist in confronting the notion of COSAPs that change is not possible and that they, as individuals, have no responsibility for what they do. A core belief, which growing up with addiction fosters, is the notion that people are not responsible for their actions. The helplessness and projected (and justified) rage that COSAPs feel are a caricature of the behavior that is so common during the active phases of addiction by the addicted parent(s).

Control Issues

Issues of control are constant throughout therapy. At first, the question of whether the patient has any "control" over anything is central. At later stages of analysis of the patient's life, it is clear that the patient is responsible for "controlling" many things as a way of guarding against feelings of "loss of control."

One patient's obsession with time, lateness, the fear of being late himself, and anger toward others for "being irresponsibly late," even if latenesses were only by a few minutes or were unavoidable, accounted for a psychologically consuming proportion of his life. His fear of reliving the behavioral irresponsibility, and temporal disregard of his alcoholic family life had to be carefully dissected before this obsession could be relieved. Chest pain, for which no direct cardiologic origins could be identified, and a careful examination of type A personality traits made this possible from a psychosomatic standpoint. Still later in treatment, resistance to change, interpretation, or suggestion in the therapy became a control issue. The patient's fear that any move would "make things fly apart" was paramount. Yet, the patient's unrecognized impulsive moves and dogmatic stances which, in fact, did make things fly apart, had to be examined. The relationships for which the patient was actually responsible had to be reexamined and decathected from projective identification with members of the patient's family of origin.

Another patient was constantly upset at his wife's occasional and unavoidable delays in arriving home because of commuter traffic. He, for a long time, refused to take responsibility for his infantile behavioral outbursts resulting from the sense of neediness and deprivation caused by these delays. In the course of putting into context the repeated feelings of abandonment that he had as a result of his own mother's drinking, he acted out in the therapeutic relationship by canceling numerous appointments with the therapist, both before and after the therapist's vacation. He also consulted a lawyer, claiming that he "wished to sue" the therapist because of charges made by the therapist for missed appointments. The lawyer advised him to pay these bills. The anger resulting from this interaction took a year to work through in twice-weekly therapy. A favorable result was accomplished when the patient's anger, too, was placed in the context of early abandonment resulting from alcoholic family life.

Stress Points in Developmental Context

Stress points in the life cycle of the patient require careful examination and placement in developmental context. The time at which the alcoholic parent's drinking became a problem is often a stress point for the child.

A young woman recalled her mother's beginning to drink alcoholically after two successive miscarriages. The patient had tremendous fears of decompensation if she herself should become pregnant.

A young man whose mother drank alcoholically after his parents' divorce had severe attacks of anxiety and unrealistic fear that he, too, was "becoming an alcoholic" if he accepted even one drink at the time of his own engagement.

A young man, who learned from his mother that his father had begun to drink alcoholically while in military service, resisted the draft on ideological grounds. Then, when threatened legally by the Board of Draft Registration, he developed psychosomatic respiratory symptoms for the first time in his life.

Favored-Child Status and Responsible-Child Status

The role of the favored child is a particularly difficult one for the COSAP. He or she pays a large price for collusion. Often, denial is lifelong and is recognized only in the course of long-term psychotherapy following referral for seemingly unrelated events, such as losses, divorce, or career collapse. These favored-child survivors often have a kind of survivor guilt syndrome underlying an elaborate defense system.

The COSAP may take on a burden of responsibility and blame for the rapid mood swings and chaotic behavior of the alcoholic parent and the family. Yet, this "neurotic" pattern of self-blame and guilt is often not enough, defensively, to allow the "adult child" to separate from his or her family of origin or to maintain a smooth pattern of functioning in either childhood or adult life. Many of the chapters in this volume and other writings or artistic productions related to children of alcoholics demonstrate the predicament poignantly (Rivinus & Ford, 1990). A recent example that shows that the COSAP's situation is addiction related and not culture bound is the Russian film Little Vera (1988). The protagonist of the film, Vera, is an 19-year-old woman struggling unsuccessfully but touchingly to separate herself from the mythic grip of an alcoholic family. The struggle nearly costs her her life by overdose. What is clear, however, is that the suicidal gesture that she makes is a symptom not only of her own solitary psychological turmoil, but also of the systemic personal and interpersonal violence of the entire alcoholic family.

The child of chemically dependent parents has often been placed in an "overresponsible" position of recognizing reality but not having it validated. In one sense, the responsible child may become the diagnostician of the "sick" and dependent family system before outside clinicians or agencies can help. Such children often try to change their parents or to control their sense of outside reality. If defeated in their efforts to do so, they eventually become chronically depressed and try to numb their feelings by using substances or by attitudes of repression, projection, or dissociation.

DIAGNOSIS AND DUAL DIAGNOSES

Addiction as a Mental Disorder

The chemical dependencies share with no other psychiatric diagnosis, except for the antisocial and borderline personality disorders, the consistent-inconsistent capacity for drug-induced and drug-seeking self-delusion and the delusion of others, particularly children and spouses. Schizophrenia is noted for the primitive defense mechanisms of denial, distortion, and projection, which are readily discernible to others and often are among the symptoms that classify a person as "crazy." The addicted person, however, not only uses these same primitive defenses in an attempt to protect himself or herself, but may revert to other defense patterns and behavior in such a way that makes him or her appear "normal." Denial, distortion, and projection in this case may be perceived by others as lying or self-deception or manipulation but not as the actions of a "crazy person."

Within our cultural and social network, schizophrenia is described as a disease, whereas the addictions often are not. This is part of the problem for children of chemically dependent parents. Perceptions, if help is available, of a crazy schizophrenic parent may be validated by the social network (Rutter, 1966). This validation may seldom be true for the child of the addicted parent without the evidence amassed by the children-of-alcoholics movement, literature, and research.

The "craziness" of the addicted parent is often readily discernible to the children but not to people outside the family. The denial, distortion, and projection of chemically dependent persons (and codependents) and visited on their spouses or children are often accepted as normal in the family and social network of the alcoholic. This can go on throughout one's childhood without one's being allowed to understand that anything is wrong or distorted about the chemically dependent way of life. Alcoholism and the other addictions share with the personality disorders a self-justifying but shifting, unstable, "borderline" quality that the child is compelled to adapt to or reject at risk of parental rejection in turn.

A COSAP is blamed by his or her alcoholic mother and coalcoholic father for being "the cause of his or her mother's difficulties," while the mother is sober or "drying out"; but the same mother claims, "You're the only daughter I ever really wanted . . . You are so much better than I am; why can't I live up to what a wonderful daughter you are?" (tears) during an intoxicated blackout.

COSAPs as Symptom Bearers and Diagnosis Masqueraders

A wide range of diagnostic presentations, which include anxiety disorder, PTSD, depressive disorder, eating disorders, substance abuse and dependence, oppositional disorder, conduct disorder, and other personality aberrations, are often the presenting symptoms of the underlying disorder resulting from exposure to life in a chemically dependent family. Use of 12-step programs, the self-help movement, and individual and, where possible, family counseling based on specific interventions designed for the recovering individual and family are the basis for successful intervention (Stanton & Todd, 1982; Dulfano, 1982; Brown, 1987; Treadway, 1989).

Sam is an eight-year-old boy who was admitted to the hospital for having threatened his sister with scissors and then, when confronted by his mother, turned the scissors' points on his own stomach, scratched his stomach, and stated that he wished his sister and he would die. His two-year-old sister and he had been fighting, both verbally and physically, for the year and a half since his father had left the home after years of physical and verbal abuse of his wife and alcoholism and cocaine dependence. Shortly after the separation, he admitted himself to an inpatient treatment program and had been sober and clean of drugs for over a year prior to Sam's admission to the hospital.

Sam had many symptoms of depression, including thoughts of suicide, which resulted in a referral for outpatient counseling for depression. He had also been truant, threatened others, and had cheated at school. He had lied and stolen, both at school and at home. His admission diagnoses were major depression and conduct disorder. Treatment included antidepressant medication, further definition of learning disabilities, and a resultant psychoeducational prescription of a learning-disabilities classroom and early discharge.

Sam was readmitted three months later; in quick succession, he had tried to poison his sister with rat poison and had filled a bathtub and attempted to lie face down in it, saying, when pulled out by his mother, "I don't want to live anymore." On the second hospitalization, the issues of his parents' separation and impending divorce and his experience, as a child of an alcoholic parent in recovery, were directly addressed. His mother was referred to Alanon, and he began to attend Alateen meetings at the hospital. He was referred to a day hospital where ongoing work with both of his parents that dealt with aspects of their traumatic relationship and the father's alcoholism were addressed in mother-daughter-son sessions and father-daughter-son sessions. Significant improvement occurred over a year, and both symptoms of depression and conduct disorder had abated to the degree that Sam was able to return home and to his local school system, while the family, now divorced, continued to participate in outpatient therapy (father participating with the children one week, mother participating the next week) with Alanon, Alcoholics Anonymous (AA), and Alateen support.

Without further investigation and alternative modes of treatment to address COSAP issues, Sam might have been inappropriately treated as having a childhood-onset depression. A more tragic situation might have evolved if he had been labeled as conduct disordered, which is, too frequently, considered an untreatable disorder (see Chapter 9).

COSAPs and "Anxiety Disorder"

Peg is a 35-year-old woman, single but in a stable relationship that offered the promise of marriage, who had just received an important job promotion. It was at that point that she began to experience symptoms of anxiety, mostly at night, often waking her from sleep. More rarely, she had these symptoms at work in her new office. She experienced sweating, heart palpitations, a feeling of panic, and an overwhelming sensation of doom and of being a failure, thinking that death might be the only relief of her symptoms and the situation that she was in. These feelings would last 15–30 minutes, but would go unnoticed by others. She first sought help for them by seeing a psychiatrist.

The psychiatrist made a diagnosis of panic attacks and prescribed Xanax (a potentially addictive sedative of the benzodiazepine group). Peg, who had grown up with alcoholism and occasional prescription-drug abuse by her father, was reluctant to take medication, but Xanax relieved her symptoms, particularly if she took it morning and night. Soon she found that she could not stop using Xanax, experiencing a recurrence of worse symptoms if she tried to do so. At this point, she consulted a friend, who referred her to a psychologist, who in turn suggested that she stop medicine, begin counseling, and join a group for adult children of alcoholic parents (ACOAs).

Using behavioral and relaxation techniques, she was, with great difficulty, able to be weaned from Xanax, which she had only been taking for two weeks. She felt that she had been addicted and, despite relief, had already, after two weeks, found herself "tempted to take more."

Individual counseling and work in a group for ACOAs helped her recall the abusive relationship that her parents were in and the fear she had of her own relationship becoming an abusive one (although there was little evidence of that being the case). In counseling and in the ACOA groups, she became in touch with arguments between her parents in which her mother was put down physically and verbally by her father. Her mother would, in turn, accuse her father of being a failure at work. These internalized fears in Peg, once acknowledged, led to an understanding that appeared to give her relief from her anxiety attacks, which largely disappeared.

This woman found help because she herself rejected the hypothesis that this was a disorder to be treated by medicine alone. The case is also an example of potential malpractice. A psychiatrist foreclosed prematurely on the psychological origins of Peg's disorder and prescribed an addictive medicine as a palliative measure. The necessary treatment was a combination of psychoanalytically oriented, uncovering technique and the specific referral to the ACOA support system.

The COSAP with Depression

Bob, a 20-year-old college student, turned to the college health center because of increasing symptoms of depression. He felt unmotivated to work, took no joy in activities, found himself turning to alcohol for relief of these symptoms, was having ruminations about suicide, and had concluded that there was very little hope for him except to go to the health service. An internist who saw him, with brief consultation from a psychiatrist, suggested a prescription of a trycyclic antidepressant. As a result of this management, Bob felt more hopeless and rejected and, upon the intervention of a college roommate, went to a therapist in the community.

Diagnostic reevaluation showed that Bob was in the throes of a family crisis in which his alcoholic mother was often calling Bob to complain about a long-standing dysfunctional marriage. Bob felt a need to return home to mend the situation in ways that he had learned as a "go-between" for his parents in the past. But this clashed with his college aspirations and his knowledge that he needed to "grow up and get away from my family, to put them behind me, even though I love them."

Psychodynamically oriented psychotherapy, coupled with group work in a group organized by the college counseling center for ACOAs, allowed Bob to share his predicament with others and to gain mastery over his depressive symptoms without the use of medication.

The depression of the COSAP is rarely biological alone. Antidepressant medication should always be coupled with psychotherapy that focuses on the patient's individual experience as a COSAP, and that, in time, may obviate the need for antidepressant medication.

The COSAP with PTSD

Brent was a 44-year-old Vietnam veteran who had completed a program of inpatient and outpatient treatment to deal with recurrent symptoms of delayed PTSD. He had continued in a support group, and had married, returned to gainful employment, and was generally doing well. On an inpatient program for PTSD, he was reminded of a painful childhood in an alcoholic family with a father who abused him physically and repeatedly while under the influence of alcohol. He did not explore this history to any great extent at that time. While in stable recovery from PTSD dating from Vietnam, he began to find himself, in the company of his own children, increasingly irritable and intolerant of their noise, activity level, and basic needs. He felt consumed by them and became increasingly homicidally rageful toward them. Part of this he could understand as related to the trauma and assault of children that he had witnessed and participated in in Vietnam, but this did not relieve his symptoms, and he found himself turning more and more to heavy use of marijuana to still his feelings of anxiety and his wish to abuse his children physically.

With his therapist, Brent began to explore his own early experience as a child. Gradually uncovered were the specific incidents of an abusive childhood and his father's alcoholic behavior. Clarification of this early experience led Brent to conclude that he did not wish to abuse marijuana in the way that he felt his father had abused alcohol. This allowed him to accept his own growing reliance on and addiction to marijuana. He also was able, with understanding of what the symptoms of PTSD were, to relate some of his own symptoms in the company of his children to the disorder dating from his own childhood. He made a commitment to an abstinence program, stopped using marijuana, and asked his wife to join him in couples' therapy to deal with parenting issues.

The Chemically Dependent Family as a Borderline Family System

The shifting nature of the chemically dependent parent and family system has been described as oscillating between the "wet" and "dry" family system (Steinglass, Bennett, Wolin, & Reiss, 1987). The "wet" stage is the addicted family member's and family's set of behaviors, feelings, and ways of interacting when the chemical is being used. The "dry" phase includes those behaviors, feelings, and interactions that take place when the family member is not currently under the influence of chemicals.

There is no more vivid example of how the direct effects of a chemical can be projected onto the social field during the wet phase than the situation created by the "blackout." In this situation, addicted people can commit physical acts of behavior and express emotions without any conscious awareness that these have transpired. They are "normal" for that phase of family life. There is no memory of the events. The child observes a parent acting in one manner for long periods, either in the haze of intoxication, in a "brownout," or in a complete blackout, and then sees that same person as an entirely different person during withdrawal or between episodes of intoxication, the dry periods.

Often, dry periods in the family with an actively addicted family member are punctuated by a heightened sense of nervousness and irritability—behavior that is often related to anticipation of the next drink and a pervading sense of shame and guilt over the remembered, or partially remembered, events, or the unremembered events that might have taken place during intoxication. A "pseudoperson" emerges as a parent of the child. Variably, during wet or dry phases, parental expressions of love and affection (both genuine and as an expiation of guilt) are directed toward the child but, for the addicted parent, are quickly overridden by the narcissistic necessities dictated by the need for more chemical(s) of addiction.

Personality Disorders and the COSAP

It is not the purpose of this section to suggest that personality problems among COSAPs are psychiatric disorders separate from the struggles and result of being a COSAP. On the contrary, too much emphasis has been placed on the "genetic" coexistence of personality disorders among the addicted and their offspring (e.g., Meyer, 1986) instead of on the intergenerational impact of addictive trauma *in* producing personality problems and emotional problems of living in certain families and their members (Bean-Bayog, 1986).

Many of the problems of personality in COSAPs respond to therapy in group and/or individual format if the adult or late-adolescent COSAP is motivated to find and accept help. If a child or an adolescent is still in the family, the family must be motivated to accept help. Often, child, adolescent, or adult COSAPs show the personality symptoms of family roles adopted adaptively and defensively within the addicted family system (Wegscheider, 1981; Black, 1981). The acting-out child, as a child, is often labeled as oppositional or as having a conduct disorder. With further elaboration during adolescence and early adult life, without intervention, and admixed with substance-use disorder by the COSAP himself or herself, the acting-out adult child is called antisocial, impulsive, borderline, or narcissistic, or is said to have a passive-aggressive personality disorder. In turn, lost adult children are labeled inadequate, passive-dependent, schizoid, masochistic self-defeating, or codependent in their personality styles. None of these labels describes the origin of or a treatment for these "disorders" or traits.

The basic question concerning personality disorders, problems, or traits lies in their formulation. Children whose problems arise from traumatic or abusive family circumstance should not be labeled as having a personality disorder. Yet, as the child victim of unmitigated problems of an addictive family environment grows up, he or she is bound to have had long experience in internalizing learned, adaptive behavior into a personality style. The question is: *Who, having grown up in an abusive, addictive family situation, would not have a distinctive pathological personality style or traits?* The danger of the personality-disorder label is that it gives no clue to etiology, and it expresses, for many, a nihilism regarding treatment. However, treatment, if it is wanted by the patient and/or the family, can effect personality change as long as the traumatic etiology is faced honestly. The company of other COSAPs, group and self-help formats, and therapists experienced with the addictions have proved, so far, the most effective agents of change for this group of patients.

TREATMENT ISSUES

Dual Diagnosis = Dual Treatment

These examples, among the many seen by this author and his colleagues who have had the good fortune to be exposed to classical and family psychotherapeutic techniques and to the recent discoveries of the addictionologists and the self-help movements regarding life with chemically dependent parents, show how an important liaison between these two fields provides the essentials of effective therapy. Alone, neither of these two orientations and disciplines stands to serve patients whose problems, at first, appear to be psychiatric and to require traditional psychoanalytically oriented, uncovering techniques, and yet also require the special understanding afforded by a growing science and therapeutics of and for children of chemically dependent parents, whether as "child children" or "adult children."

COSAPS in Treatment for Substance Abuse/Dependency

Being a COSAP coming for treatment for addiction can be a barrier to sobriety and recovery but it also can be a boon in treatment. Childhood or "adult child" issues can be prominent in early or late stages of the achievement of abstinence from drugs or alcohol. Principles of this work have been outlined by others (Kress, 1989; Kern, 1987), some of which will be emphasized here.

1. Sobriety and complete abstinence from alcohol and other psychoactive substance usually need to be established before childhood work with COSAP issues can begin. Symptoms of PTSD related to COSAP experience and/or other childhood trauma are often too painful and emotionally charged to be dealt with in the sensitive early stages of treatment of an addiction. If abstinence cannot be achieved, COSAP issues may be a crucial block to early recovery or to the establishment of relapse-free recovery in later stages of treatment.

2. Coming to terms with his or her own addiction can often help a COSAP to achieve some understanding of the addiction of a parent or parents. In some cases, forgiveness, understanding, or acceptance of an unalterable painful past or present reality can be accomplished by working through the 12 steps of AA or Narcotics

Anonymous, and individuals recovering from addiction may need to attend Alanon or ACOA or other group meetings at this stage of treatment.

3. Family treatment or the "bringing in" of family members in person or by the use of prescriptive confrontations or written communications to a parent, a sibling, or a child is necessary in some stages of the treatment of COSAPs with substance use disorder of (see also Chapter 10). The roles played by the COSAP within the family system and coming to terms or grips with other addicted family members also require examination (Wegscheider, 1981; Kress, 1989).

4. Young adults and adolescents who are abusing or are addicted to chemicals often require family treatment for successful outcome. Separation, parental addiction, and child or parent physical- or sexual-abuse issues are often prominent in work with addicted adolescents and require identification and, where possible, intervention for the young addict to proceed (Chapter 8).

Pitfalls of Therapist Empathy

The capacity of the addicted parent to compartmentalize alcoholic behavior is infinite. The "good parent" exists for the outside world. The intoxicated, angry, seductive, abusive, irritable, variable parent lives at home. How often has the child of an alcoholic been told, "Your father was always a good worker, and a good friend. We never *knew* he had a problem." Or, "Your mother says your behavior is such a worry to her. Don't you know how much you upset her?" The COSAP often expends great personal effort to maintain these outside appearances of family stability. The lack of validation of the adult child's recall of reality is isolating and devastating, and from a therapist it can be tragic.

Isolation, Transference, and Countertransference

COSAPs often feel acute embarrassment and a sense of isolation from others as a result of the secrecy and denial that characterize growing up in a family with a chemically dependent member. Rules in the chemically dependent family are, "Don't talk, don't feel, and don't trust" (Black, 1981). Because of their isolation, many COSAPs despair of or don't want to enter psychotherapy.

Addicted families have chronic difficulties with the expression and articulation of feelings. There are periods of open anger followed by periods of silence permeated with angry feelings. Anger is often expressed *during* times of stress and *during* intoxicated (wet) states or states of withdrawal from the addictive drug. Sadness and joy also occur erratically and explosively during wet periods. Unarticulated but emotionally charged silences characterize the dry periods in addicted families (Steinglass et al., 1987).

The overwhelming defense mechanism of COSAPs is denial. Denial (Vaillant, 1977; Freud, A., 1968) is a primitive defense mechanism that often arrests development and distorts a sense of true reality. Where the destructive aspects of addiction are denied by the parents and the family system, a child's sense of reality can be distorted and he or she left alone with his or her feelings and perceptions. Without an early investigation of how the addicted family functioned, a therapy experience can fail. If addiction in the family is not diagnosed, denial is replicated in therapy and a bondage to addictive secrecy and denial symptoms is maintained. This may well have been the case in the treatment of many children of alcoholic and other chemically dependent parents before the secret "came out" after being liberated by the self-help movement (see Chapters 4, 5, 13 and 14).

No Language but a Cry

Denial and chemical-induced amnesia make reevaluation and apology by a parent, for mistakes or errors committed, impossible. Shared memory is a requirement for safely developing relationships. Self-medication by a parent obliterates a shared memory, and denial becomes the pervading operational feature in the families of the chemically dependent. Because denial replaces affect, the universal emotions—sadness, anger, guilt, and anxiety—have no meaning that corresponds to a reality-based situation or its emotional response. Deaths, losses, and moments of love and joy in an alcoholic family often are either "numbed" or obliterated from reality by the heavy use of drugs and by the family's denial. Children who are witnesses to such events (which they often are) find themselves confronted with inappropriate affectual outbursts (e.g., a family brawl at a wedding, expressions of sadness triggered by minor events, or denial of affect taking place where affect is appropriate). Affect may be denied even while it is being, or after it has been, expressed. Because there is no predictable way to sort out the relationships between reality and behavioral expression, the overwhelming defensive response of the COSAP is denial. Apparent affect in COSAPs is likely to be mixed with denial at deeper levels. Therapy allows, for the first time, a language to be fitted to behaviors and emotions which were old modes of (childhood) expression in a family where a child's words had no meaning.

Self-Help Groups and Spirituality

A crucial sense of reality and validation is given the COSAP by the self-help movements. The spiritual commitment supplied by the embracing of "the higher power" of groups such as Alanon is also of great assistance in the rehabilitation and therapy of the COSAP (Clinebell, 1981). Because the joining of a group and the acceptance of a higher power so often represent the first sense of being real to the COSAP, the concept of a conversion experience (Tiebout, 1954) or a rebirth experience needs to be respected by therapists.

The Myth of the ACOA "Group Junkie"

Colleagues often inquire whether there is such a thing as "too much" ACOA group participation, "too much" Alanon, or "too much" in a client's seeing himself or herself as "addicted" to food, relationships, a chemical, work, perfection, spending, and so on. What really is being asked is, "Can a client become an addict to the idea of addiction?" The opinion of this author is yes—and no. Both the yes and no of the answer can be a good thing if thoughtfully managed; the only pitfalls of 12-step "junkiedom" occur when the client and/or therapist sees them as such in a pejorative or inflexible way.

To see oneself as a "COA" or a "codependent" has three basic and salutary functions: (1) it may allow the patient to identify a source of trauma in his or her life that has had a personal and developmental impact; (2) it may allow the patient to identify approaches, including self-help and group treatments, and a sense of fellowship with others comparably afflicted to help to deal with the trauma; (3) by giving the trauma a name, a framework of understanding, it may allow the patient to see the source of the problem as external to the self—unencumbered by guilt and shame—and as a problem for which help may be sought and accepted.

Most therapists working with COSAPs regard a patient's identification with the self-help movement as a boon and an opportunity. Membership in the self-help group usually enhances individual or group therapy, and in some cases (particularly when the patient is addicted to a psychoactive substance or continues to be traumatized), it may be a prerequisite for effective therapy. The client's experience with self-identification, self-referral, and experience in a 12-step program is essential information for the therapy process. Twelve-step groups provide support and a sense of community that individual therapy cannot, and should not, provide.

It is important for the therapist to be alert when a patient joins a destructive cult or a cult of personality or forms a destructive relationship. Generally, members of 12-step groups are encouraged *not* to form close or romantic relationships with other group members or to accept sponsors who do not have the requisite years of stability and sobriety. In most cases, a working relationship with a mature sponsor in a 12-step program can greatly enhance therapy, the patient's quality of life, and decision making.

Therapists working with clients who are in the self-help movement should acquaint themselves with the meetings and literature of the movement. Occasional orienting or reorienting attendance at self-help meetings by therapists working with COSAPs is heartily recommended (Vaillant, 1983). Some clients may use therapy to develop some independence from the self-help identity or group over time. Others may need to rely on 12-step groups for years or a lifetime to support their sense of personal identity and to deal with everyday problems. It is important for therapists to take a nonjudgmental stance toward these alternatives, guarding only against the self-destructive nature of a patient's choices and affiliations and the possibility of addictive relapse in the therapeutic work.

SUMMARY

A new view of therapy, which recognizes the importance of the experience of the addictive family situation as equal to the many other vicissitudes and traumata of a young person's life and experience brought to therapy, promises to change the course of many individual cases of psychotherapy. These developments represent a dramatic new contribution to the understanding of many patients, perhaps one in four (Russell, Henderson, & Blume, 1985), who come to psychotherapy.

The 1970s and 1980s have brought a growing understanding of the plight of children of chemically dependent parents, largely based on the accounts of those who have been children of alcoholic families. The recognition that children and women speak with "another voice" has really sprung from the child-treatment and women's movements (Gilligan, 1982). Specifically, with regard to COSAPs, there is another voice that is clearly emerging: one of trauma, of distortion of reality, and of pain. Once that "other voice," with the pain it describes and the defenses it uses, is accurately heard, therapeutic healing of the COSAP can begin.

REFERENCES

Ackerman, R. J. (1983). *The children of alcoholics: A guide for parents, educators and therapists* (2nd ed.). New York: Simon & Schuster.

American Psychiatric Association. (1987). *Diagnostic and statistical manual of mental disorders* (3rd ed., rev.). Washington, DC: Author.

Bean-Bayog, M. (1986). Psychopathology produced by alcoholism. In R. E. Meyer (Ed.), *Psychopathology and addictive disorders* (pp. 334–345). New York: Guilford Press.

Black, C. (1981). *It will never happen to me! Children of alcoholics: As youngsters—adolescents—adults.* Denver, CO: Medical Administration Corp.

Brown, S. (1987). *Treating adult children of alcoholics: A developmental perspective.* New York: Wiley.

Cermak, T. (1986). *Diagnosing and treating co-dependence of alcoholics.* Minneapolis, MN: Johnson Institute Books.

Clinebell, H. (1981). The role of religion in the prevention and treatment of addictions—the growth counseling perspective. In *Man, drugs, and society—current perspectives: Proceedings of the First Pan-Pacific Conference on Drugs and Alcohol* (pp. 206–213). Canberra, Australia: Australian Foundation on Alcoholism and Drug Dependence.

Dulfano, C. (1982). *Families, alcoholism, and recovery, ten stories.* Center City, MN: Hazeldon.

Flannery, R. B. (1987). From victim to survivor: A stress management approach in the treatment of learned helplessness. In B. A. van der Kolk (Ed.), *Psychological trauma* (pp. 117–132). Washington, DC: American Psychiatric Press.

Fossum, M. A., & Mason, M. J. (1986). *Facing shame: Families in recovery.* New York: Norton.

Freud, A. (1968). *The ego and the mechanisms of defense, the writings of Anna Freud* (Vol. 2, pp. 31–34). New York: International Universities Press.

Freud, S. (1974/1908). Family romances. In *The standard edition of the complete psychological works of Sigmund Freud* (James Strachey, Trans.; Vol. IX, pp. 235–244). London: Hogarth Press.

Freud, S. (1974/1917). Mourning and melancholia. In *The standard edition of the complete psychological works of Sigmund Freud* (James Strachey, Trans.; Vol. XIV, pp. 237–258). London: Hogarth Press.

Gilligan, C. (1982). *In a different voice: Psychological theory and women's development.* Cambridge, MA: Harvard University Press.

Gonzales, E. V. (1988). Integrated treatment approach with the chemically dependent young adult. In T. Rivinus (Ed.), *Alcoholism/chemical dependency in the college student* (pp. 147– 176). New York: Haworth Press.

Group for the Advancement of Psychiatry (1966). *Psychopathological disorders of childhood: Theoretical considerations and a proposed classification.* New York: Author.

Kern, J. C. (1987), Management of children of alcholics. In S. Zimberg, J. Wallace, & S. B. Blume (Eds.), *Practical approaches to alcoholism psychotherapy,* (pp. 315–346). New York: Plenum.

Kohut, H. (1984). How does analysis cure? In A. Goldberg (Ed.), *How does analysis cure?* Chicago: University of Chicago Press.

Kolb, L. C. (1987). A neuropsychological hypothesis explaining post-traumatic stress disorders. *American Journal of Psychiatry,* 144, 989–995.

Kress, Y. (1989). Special issues of adult children of alcoholics. In G.W. Lawson & A. W. Lawson (Eds.),*Alcoholism and substance abuse in special populations,* (pp. 139–164). Rockville, MD: Aspen.

Lawrence, D. H. (1976/1913). *Sons and lovers* (pp. 59–60). New York: Penguin.

Meyer, R. E. (1986). *Psychopathology and addictive disorders.* New York: Guilford Press.

Rivinus, T. M., & Ford, B. (1990) Children of alcoholics in literature: Portraits of the struggle. *Dionysos* (University of Wisconsin, Superior), 1 (3).

Russell, M., Henderson, C., & Blume, S. B. (1985). *Children of alcoholics: A review of the literature.* New York: Children of Alcoholics Foundation.

Rutter, M. (1966). *Children of sick parents: An environmental and psychiatric study* (Institute of Psychiatry, Maudsley Monographs No. 16). London: Oxford University Press.

Stanton, M. D., & Todd, T. C. (Eds.). (1982). *The family therapy of drug abuse and addiction.* New York: Guilford Press.

Steinglass, P., Bennett, L. A., Wolin, D. S. J., & Reiss, D. (1987). *The alcoholic family.* New York: Basic Books.

Tiebout, H. M. (1954). The ego factors in surrender in alcoholism. *Journal of Studies on Alcohol,* 15, 610–621.

Treadway, D. C. (1989). *Before it's too late: Working with substance abuse in the family.* New York: Norton.

Vaillant, G. E. (1977). *Adaptation to life* (pp. 73–192). Boston: Little, Brown.

Vaillant, G. E. (1983). *The natural history of alcoholism* (p. 303). Cambridge, MA: Harvard University Press.

Van der Kolk, B. A. (1987). The psychological consequences of overwhelming life experiences. In B.A. Van der Kolk (Ed.), *Psychological trauma.* Washington, DC: American Psychiatric Press.

Wallace, J. (1985a). Working with the preferred defense structure of the recovering alcoholic. In S. Zinberg, J. Wallace, & S. B. Blume (Eds.), *Practical approaches to alcoholism psychotherapy* (2nd ed., pp. 23–35). New York: Plenum Press.

Wallace, J. (1985b). Critical issues in alcoholism psychotherapy. In S. Zinberg, J. Wallace, & S.B. Blume (Eds.), *Practical approaches to alcoholism psychotherapy* (2nd ed., pp. 37–52). New York: Plenum Press.

Wegscheider, S. (1981). *Another chance: A hope and help for children of alcoholics.* Palo Alto, CA: Science & Behavior Books.

Whitfield, C. L. (1984). Co-alcoholism: Recognizing a treatable illness. *Family and Community Health, 7,* 16–27.

Whitfield, C. L. (1985). *Alcoholism and spirituality.* East Rutherford, NJ: Perrin.

Winnecott, D. W. (1960). The theory of the parent-infant relationship. *International Journal of Psycho-Analysis, 41,* 585–595.

Wurmser, L. (1978). *The hidden dimension: Psychodynamics in compulsive drug use.* New York: Aronson.

12

An ACOA Substance-Abuse Counselor: Family-of-Origin Influences on Personal Growth and Therapeutic Effectiveness

Helga M. Matzko, M.A., C.A.G.S.

INTRODUCTION

This chapter consists of two parts. Part I presents a study which examines the influence of an ACOA substance abuse counselor's self-perceived role in the family of origin on the choice of preferred counseling practice. How these roles are carried into the adult professional life of the ACOA therapist and how they may be enhanced by the practice of structured therapies was identified. Part II presents special approaches and techniques for supervision and training for ACOA and non-ACOA counselors based on these findings, a review of the literature and on the author's personal experience.

Ackerman (1978, 1986a), Black (1986), Gade and Goodman (1975), Gravitz and Bowden (1984), Lerner (1986), and others report that there are approximately 28–32 million children of alcoholics living in the United States. Of these, it is estimated that 20–25% become alcoholics and/or other substance abusers (Ackerman, 1978); and there is an increasing awareness in the mental health field of the special treatment needs and issues that are specific to that population and many programs have been developed in the human-services field to accommodate the needs of adult children of alcoholics (ACOAs).

Who specifically are these ACOAs? For the purpose of this research, it is defined as anyone who grew up with an alcoholic parent. While much literature does not differentiate degrees of effect on the growing child, Ackerman (1986a) and Steinglass (1987) do so by examining factors such as which parent is affected by the disease of alcoholism, what stage of alcoholism the adult is in at a given developmental stage of the child, family adjustments and styles of coping mechanisms, and the degree to which the significant others are affected by the family disease (codependency). For the purpose of this research, only the roles of ACOAs will be considered.

Ackerman (1986), Black (1986), Wegscheider-Cruse (1976), and Woititz (1986) have defined and discussed how children adapt to rigid roles in order to survive the alcoholic family systems. In the research, Wegsheider-Cruse's (1976) definition of survival roles was used, which she characterizes as follows:

The *chief enabler* is often the spouse who is most depended on by the alcoholic. This person attempts to provide responsibility by becoming increasingly involved by taking over the afflicted person's responsibilities and functions. This is accomplished through manipulation with an attendant decrease of sense of self.

The *family hero* is the role most typically adapted by the oldest child or the only child in the alcoholic family. This person provides structure for the family and for the self. He or she is the organizer of the family and an expert at manipulation of the environment to achieve goals. While one may develop many leadership qualities in the process, this person achieves by disowning feelings. Feelings of confusion and hurt are often hidden behind visible success.

The *scapegoat* is an acting-out child who is often in trouble. The feelings of loneliness or rejection lead this child to seek recognition in an outside group where he or she can prove worthy. This child provides distraction of focus for the family and is usually the first member to receive treatment.

The *lost child* is a social loner who adapts to an atmosphere of inconsistency in the family by removing himself or herself from it. This child offers relief to the family by being out of the way and never in trouble, and in return stays relatively out of harm. Over time, feelings of anger, isolation, rejection, and distrust of others develop.

The *mascot* learns how to survive by being cute and funny; this child covers hurtful situations with humor and laughter and saves the family from embarrassment and ridicule.

Those who adopt these roles live in a world of relative self-delusion, locked into one or more of these roles to aid the system and to survive in it. Often one role can be replaced by another as one of the children moves on in development or appears in different situations or contexts. The roles that helped these individuals survive their alcoholic home environments do not change simply because they leave the family; rather, they become more or less fixed patterns that are carried into adulthood. At the point in the life of an individual when old ways of coping are no longer working in adult life situations, the effects of having been raised in an alcoholic family begin to show. ACOAs can experience meaninglessness, depression, substance abuse, difficulty establishing intimate relationships, inability to make career choices, and difficulty maintaining productive and satisfying positions in the workforce (Foster, 1976; Nardi, 1981; Cermack, 1986). Often, at this time, the strengths learned while living in an alcoholic family surface more strongly and are put into service and it is not surprising therefore to find that many of the ACOAs enter the human-services professions.

Many ACOAs are working as service providers and are in leadership roles in the substance-abuse-treatment field (Kern, 1986). A paper examining the families of origin of social workers by Lackie (1983) supports the belief that induction into a caretaking role in the family of origin through significant life experiences shapes career choices and colors professional development. He reports a prevalence of identification with roles in the families of origin promoting self-sufficiency among social workers, such as the parentified child, the overresponsible member, the mediator, the good child, the burden carrier, and the infantalized child. Pilat and Jones (1984) report finding, in a study of people taking a course to improve teaching skills, that many therapists who express interest in alcoholism counseling had their first exposure to alcoholism by their parents. These authors identify 35% of all students as ACOAs.

Lackie (1983) and Treadway (1989) believe that good children eventually seek overt validation and approval outside the family, which their covert roles within the family disallowed. The child willing to accept the responsibility for authority abdicated by one or both parents becomes the family rescuer in the process, out of a mixture of premature altruism in addition to the primary concern for survival. COAs are considered predisposed to choose the helping professions as an extension of their childhood nurturing roles. The profession becomes an overt declaration of mastery for these once parentified children (see also Chapter 10). A similar view is held by Miller (1981), who explores the idea that a child growing up in a dysfunctional family loses touch with personal emotional needs and adapts at an early age in order to accommodate the parents' unmet emotional needs instead. Miller believes that the sensitivity and deep interest in human condition required of any therapist have at their roots a home environment that was basically insecure and unstable, requiring the child to take on a pseudo-adult caretaking role prematurely. Counselors are often first introduced to the role of "junior therapist" in the family of origin (Lackie, 1983; Miller, 1981; Pilat & Jones, 1984; Treadway, 1989).

The kind of history the therapist brings into the therapeutic encounter is bound to affect the relationship with the client. The counselor's major tool is his or her personality (Corey, 1976), regardless of theoretical orientation. If the parentified or lost child, the hero, the placater, or the enabler enters the counseling profession, and if the adapted or survival roles continue to require significant efforts of repression or denial of feelings, then it may be that the therapist seeks a cure through work, that is, to gain insight into his or her own emotional and personal difficulties (Gravitz & Bowden, 1984; Pilat & Jones, 1984; Spensley & Blacker, 1976). Many ACOA substance-abuse counselors bring with them the dysfunctional family patterns experienced in the family of origin (Kern, 1986). They recreate dysfunctional families in the workplace by casting themselves and others into the childhood roles with which they are most familiar. Kern found that these conditions are particularly prevalent in alcoholism-treatment centers. He attributes this phenomenon to the large number of untreated individuals who enter the profession, and cites manipulation, blaming, enabling, isolating, secret keeping, lack of cooperation, inability to confront, and lack of introspection as primary issues for these counselors. While supervision is vital for any therapist (Guerin & Fogarty, 1972; Haley, 1976; Minuchin, 1981; Mintz, 1987; Rogers, 1965; Stanton & Todd, 1982; Whitaker, 1982), one can conclude that supervision is imperative in helping these counselors in order to attain high professional standards and to provide the best possible treatment for the substance-abusing population. It is important to realize, however, that all the authors mentioned in this research state explicitly that individuals coming from any dysfunctional families can possess attributes similar to those of the ACOA and can have similar difficulties in the work environment. ACOAs—or, more specifically, ACOA substance-abuse counselors—bring with them into the profession a great variety of strengths, as well as potential difficulties, making the practice of therapy particularly challenging.

STUDY

Purpose

The purpose of this study was to assess whether a relationship exists between the self-perceived dominant role of the ACOA substance-abuse counselor in the family of origin and a preferred counseling theory when treating substance abusers and related issues (ACOA, COA, codependency).

Methods

A questionnaire, designed by the author, was mailed to 76 Rhode Island certified substance-abuse counselors in which they were asked to identify their (1) sex, (2) existence of alcoholism/substance abuse in the family of origin (three generational), (3) self-perceived dominant role as child in the substance-abusing family of origin, (4) preferred theoretical counseling approach, and (5) therapeutic history, if any.

HYPOTHESES TESTED

1. More counselors will identify themselves as ACOAs than as non-ACOAs.
2. More counselors who identify themselves as family heroes will respond to the survey.
3. More counselors who identify themselves as family heroes and lost children will prefer structured therapies than will prefer less structured therapies.
4. More counselors who identify themselves as non-ACOA will have a preference for less structured therapies rather than for more structured therapies.

Methods Used in Data Analysis

The statistical treatment of the study was a nonexperimental type of research (survey). Percentages of different categories or responses were listed for nominal data. Chi-square was implemented to measure the data. The level of significance was 0.05.

FINDINGS

1. Fifty-three people actually participated in the research.
2. Thirty-eight women and 15 men responded.
3. All four hypotheses were statistically confirmed.
4. Analysis of data showed that 66% of respondents identified alcoholism or drug addiction in their family of origin.
5. Thirty-four percent of respondents perceived themselves in the roles of family heroes, 23% as lost children, 17% as family scapegoats, 3% as family mascots, and none as family enablers. Twenty-three percent of respondents did not identify with a role.
6. Of the self-identified ACOA counselors (66%), 31% reported being or having been substance abusers.
7. Lost children and family heroes reported a preference for more structured therapies, whereas non-ACOAs almost exclusively preferred less structured therapies.

Details on statistical analysis and highlights of findings can be obtained from the study (Matzko, 1988).

IMPLICATIONS OF FINDINGS

The results of this study have implications for the field of counseling, particularly as they relate to the role and function of the ACOA substance-abuse counselor. This research supports previous findings that there are more ACOA substance-abuse counselors than non-ACOA substance-abuse counselors providing treatment for substance abusers and related problems (ACOA, COA, codependency). Educators and agency administrators have a significant responsibility for recognizing the strengths and liabilities of ACOA substance-abuse counselors and for preparing them educationally and emotionally and providing ongoing supervision for these clinicians. Agencies would then be able appropriately to match a counselor's professional level of competency and personal development with specific substance-abuse-treatment stages; that is, early treatment with emphasis on structure and cognition or advanced treatment with greater emphasis on awareness and emotional expression. Emphasis on the development of personal growth through seminars, workshops, and more theory-specific trainings is important and should be built into training and career development. Educators should refer students or trainees to therapists if and when it becomes evident that personal emotional deficiencies prohibit effective and therapeutic functioning. An active elimination process screening for readiness of counseling students/trainees is necessary in every substance-abuse-counseling program. Only by setting more stringent requirements will poorly functioning individuals be excluded from entering the counseling profession.

Family heroes' and lost children's preference for more structured therapies could be attributed to the respective needs to manipulate the environment successfully and to use structure as an avenue for presenting oneself authoritatively, safely, and with the greatest probability of successful treatment. This would assure the greatest personal needs gratification in a relatively brief period with less risk of having to engage in a potentially threatening intimate relationship with the client. What must be guarded against by the ACOA substance-abuse clinician is the use of any theory to rigidify familiar ways of being or to cover up personal inadequacies. If the ACOA therapist is unaware of this process in the intra- or interpsychic domain, educators, supervisors, and administrators must join the counselor in constructive ways to help him or her become cognizant of unhealthy behaviors, thinking, relating, or feeling.

To know a counselor's role in the family of origin in combination with his or her preferred way of working with clients can be most helpful in placing counselors appropriately. Partial personal recovery and level of professional development need not necessarily interfere with working effectively if "goodness of fit" in the therapeutic relationship is considered. For example, someone with a more structured and cognitive orientation who is beginning a counseling career could do well with clients in a detoxification facility, inpatient treatment facility, or halfway house when the treatment population benefits most from structure, as in reality and behavior therapy. Thereafter, during a client's more advanced stages of recovery, when the need to relate and focus on affect becomes more relevant, clinicians who are more advanced in their personal development and more able professionally would be a better match for the client.

In summary, the implications of this research illustrate the need to look more closely at the emotional readiness of substance-abuse trainees and counselors. Awareness must be raised, personal and professional growth encouraged, and the worth and integrity of the individual and the profession upheld. Well-trained, self-aware counselors could effect a lower turnover rate of personnel in substance-abuse-treatment centers and agencies; there could be more job satisfaction, higher productivity, and, most important, more positive treatment outcomes for a needy and deserving population.

TRAINING AND SUPERVISION

Overview

Ackerman (1978), Black (1979), Wegscheider (1976), and Woititz (1986) were the pioneers in the movement to bring recognition to the special plight of millions of alcoholics or substance abusers and their families. Supported by personal experiences of growing up in alcoholic families, they identified issues, labeled symptomology, developed theories, and implemented therapies. They supported their findings by some research and, accepted by the target population, have made the treatment of substance abuse (COAs, ACOAs, codependency, and the like) a viable and respected specialty in the mental health field. These pioneers have gained acceptance and support for their work from the target population and mental health professionals, and all this has been accomplished in the relatively short span of ten to 15 years. Not only has a message of hope through treatment been heard by millions of professionals and nonprofessionals, ACOAs and non-ACOAs, but the treatment of this population has grown into a multimillion-dollar business. The myriad of treatment programs available, and the emphasis in EAP programs, the professional journals, at national conferences, on speaking tours, and in television presentations attest to the fact that this movement has grown into a major industry.

These efforts translate into new jobs and, more important, the possibility of self-discovery and self-healing for countless individuals and their families. They purchase self-help books, tapes, and films, and attend lectures, workshops, and seminars. Self-help groups (Alcoholics Anonymous, Narcotics Anonymous, Al-Anon, Alateen, ACOA, and codependency, family, and group psychotherapies) complement and supplement these efforts. These people embark on a painful journey of recovery that is described by many as their first glimpse of hope for stability and is considered a lifelong process.

ACOA substance-abuse counselors are part of this recovering population. Even if denial is still used as a defense and they are not involved in a formal program of recovery, their choice of the counseling profession is an expression of self-healing. ACOA counselors exemplify belief in humankind, a resilience of the human spirit to survive in spite of childhood experiences. These dedicated professionals enthusiastically pursue the cause of recovery, for themselves and others, with perseverance, understanding, and compassion. Their intimate experiential knowledge of substance-abuse issues and dysfunctional family dynamics makes them ideally suited for treating this population.

An ACOA counselor may have inherent weaknesses as well. These will be the topic of discussion of this chapter. Suggestions for training and supervision to accommodate these areas will be outlined to help the ACOA counselor gain optimal personal and professional growth, and examples from the author's experience as trainer and supervisor will be cited in support.

ACOAs at Work

Staff turnover in treatment facilities and agencies is epidemic, in some cases certification for drug or alcohol counseling cannot be delivered to the counselor who has earned it because he or she has already moved on. There are several reasons why; one is the existence of an often unhealthy and turbulent emotional climate among staff and administrators. ACOAs are often blinded by their personal history of living in dysfunctional families and, therefore, do not recognize their individual contribution to the dysfunctional whole of an agency or treatment facility. Family-of-origin roles are recreated and neither administration nor staff is able to deal with resulting disruptive, negative interactions objectively and professionally; feeling stuck as experienced in the family of origin and loyalty to the system prevents staff members from breaking out of individual pathological interactions.

Dysfunctional families are constantly created or recreated as new and old staff find an available niche. Stress leads to familiar ways of being and the pseudo-family kindles old defenses and survival roles with concomitant unhealthy attitudes, thoughts, and feelings. The following is an example of a common scenario of an otherwise very efficient and competent treatment team of a substance-abuse program:

> When all went smoothly, the family hero of the team became bored by the predictability and reliability of her staff and looked for some minor but sensitive issue to stir emotions—possibly the productivity issue. The lost child became sick with worry and stayed home with a headache, thereby avoiding the painful issue of accountability, the mascot thought the whole issue a big joke and began making sexually inappropriate jokes, thereby offending the enabler, who in turn encouraged each staff member separately suggesting ways to smooth things over, or else. The "or else" was that the whole staff was to quit. This energized the hero enormously. She immediately went to the administration, telling them of her plight and promised, under penalty of expulsion from the agency, to convince the staff to reconsider and remain. Much pleading, promising, and negotiating ensued, and finally the staff agreed to stay on and, yes, they were going to try to increase productivity a bit. The hero returned to the administration still wiping her brow and informed them of her triumphant feat. Staff, also, was satisfied that the productivity issue was settled, and no one recognized that there was no issue to start with.

Such are the dynamics of collusion in a recreated family of origin in the workplace. Each role personification depends on the cooperation, indeed existence, of the other, and the whole works like a smoothly functioning machine.

SOLUTIONS

Laying blame on one person or condition is not helpful; but a recreated, dysfunctional system should be examined and treated much like an alcoholic family. The prevalence of denial in these systems does not lend itself to treatment from within and an objective outside source is usually necessary to confront the dysfunctional system. A consultant can diagnose the systemic "illness," identify symptoms, and proceed with treatment.

TECHNIQUES

Kern (1986) developed a model for working with ACOAs as professionals using Wegscheider's (1981) rules of the alcoholic family as guidelines. Their relevance and manifestations in dysfunctional organizations and their possible consequences for treatment agencies are the basis for consultations to agencies. As a consultant, I attempt to intervene in dysfunctional systems using techniques based on individual and family consultations and Kern's model (1986). Sculpting and psychodrama are useful approaches to identify individuals' perceptions of their position in the system. Using these techniques, secret ambitions, hidden hostilities, and motives become metaphors with surprising accuracy. An example of a sculpting exercise will illustrate this point.

> I was consulted by an agency that suffered from negative staff morale. In exploring problem areas, I found little willingness to communicate openly. I suggested that staff members and administrators pose for an agency portrait: however, they were to receive no help in posing and were requested to pose themselves until each was satisfied with the potential position in the group portrait. This became a difficult process. Before the posing for the portrait was completed, two staff members in particular became engaged in a lively discussion and attracted attention. A counselor had not appreciated having been placed with the rest of the staff by an administrator. It was later learned that this counselor had been promised job advancement after six months of employment, but had been bypassed for a promotion. The angered employee acted out nonverbally by insisting on positioning herself prominently, much to the chagrin of the administration. This sculpting experience did not alleviate all negative staff morale but it did expose one important conflict that could now be explored appropriately.

Sculpting can also be role played in terms of program needs or agency agendas and staff and administrative personnel can work on hypothetical issues or work out potential problems. These imaginary exercises often facilitate open communication without fear of negative consequences later. Role playing and psychodrama allow staff members (sometimes humorously) to become aware of impact on peers and provide the basis for constructive reenactment as models of change (see discussion under Supervision). Exploration of polarities within individuals and the system is usually helpful to get in touch with wider ranges of possibilities and to destroy rigid role patterns, labels, and assumptions (Perls, 1971, 1976). (Polarities as a technique will be discussed below.)

ACOA as Counselor

ACOAs often enter the field of counseling because they want to continue their child-hood functions in the role of the adult counselor (Lackie, 1983; Treadway, 1989). They may want to gain recognition for once-unacknowledged expertise or they may want to make a difference in areas where in their families of origin their efforts were in vain. Some therapists overtly want to be authoritative and directive. Others may want to share their own mistakes with clients so as to prevent them from experiencing similar pain (Ackerman, 1978; Lackie, 1983; Subby, 1987). An inherent problem with these motivations is that the therapist needs the full cooperation of the client to gain the pos-itive feedback desired. Considering the treatment populations, this becomes a frustrat-ing endeavor; the client is not often willing to change for the therapist in order to mirror an image of an all-powerful, master therapist. The client can easily fall into the trap of being the therapist's "bad parent" in not returning appreciation, recognition, and results for the therapist's efforts. Conversely, some clients become clingy and needy of the therapist's energy and time and feed into the therapist's narcissistic requirements to feel needed. This eventually consumes the therapist and leaves him or her feeling abused, and incompetent. If these things occur, the position of the "wronged child" within the family may be recreated.

ACOA versus Non-ACOA Counselors

The many different experiences and feelings with and about clients are usually shared by ACOA and non-ACOA staff members, each of whom has a different way of perceiving, interacting, and being with others, and all are based on their indi-vidual experiences in their respective families of origin. The combination of ACOA and non-ACOA counselors often creates a unique blend of problems. Opposing views on diagnosis and treatment of clients are presented and interesting dynamics emerge. ACOA and non-ACOA counselors recreate the relationship of the alcoholic family in relation to society—neighbors, friends, schools, employers. ACOA family members "guard" the secret of addiction from the outside world; consequently, the ACOA counselors become the "knowing insiders." Non-ACOA counselors become the "them," the uninformed "outsiders."

The topic of exclusivity creates interesting system dynamics. To non-ACOAs, it can appear that being an ACOA is the admission ticket to an elite organization that lays first claims to pain and features copyrighted recipes for becoming a whole human being in therapy. ACOAs deny that; they point to their attempt to include all dysfunctional families in partaking in their pain, engaging in survival-role adaptations, and having similar potential for recovery. For both ACOAs and non-ACOAs, this fruitless pursuit is a childlike attempt to assert their individuality in a sibling system that disallows uniqueness.

> A group of ACOA staff members reported on a case and commiserated with the client's feelings and experiences. They were having difficulties making a diagnosis of their own countertransference reactions. However, they wanted no input from the non-ACOAs. Obviously hurt by this apparent insensitivity, a non-ACOA therapist interrupted and explained that while she did not have the exact experience of being an ACOA, she did have problems, experiences, and feelings. After all, she continued, she felt she was an adult child of a "dysfunctional country." Laughter ensued and she was henceforth known as an ACDC and included in the diagnostic discussion.

Actually, ACOA and non-ACOA therapists are not mutually exclusive but mutually inclusive in their need to learn from each other. ACOAs can enlighten, instruct, and speak in support of their specific needs. Non-ACOA counselors may have worked without the knowledge of specific treatment concerns of the ACOAs, many of whom have struggled for years with painful issues in therapy. They can enrich the treatment repertoire of the experienced non-ACOA therapists who may be tempted to minimize the ACOA experience. Conversely, it is safe to assume that non-ACOA therapists also have had painful histories that sensitized them to the needs of others and allowed them to recognize their unique abilities to understand and reach out. Indeed, when the two groups meet and share openly mutually painful experiences, relationship problems, and addiction issues in a setting other than the workplace, their interactions take on a different flavor. The meeting becomes one of expanding awareness that each shares in the painful human condition, and that each has inherent potentials and limitations and the capacity to love and be loved, to respect and be respected. When ACOA and non-ACOA therapists share emotional experiences, it becomes apparent that the plight and struggles of the ACOAs are not very different from the sufferings of adult children of war, of concentration-camp survivors, of immigrants, of Hispanics, Blacks, and other minorities or of abusing or other dysfunctional families. The common denominator is always pain.

Supervision

Probably the most important ingredient for successful professional functioning of a therapist is good supervision (Corey, 1977; Haley, 1976; Mintz, 1987; Minuchin

& Fishman, 1981; Rogers, 1951; Whitaker, 1982). Given the particular professional and personal needs of the ACOA counselor, frequent, regular, ACOA-problem-specific, varied, and challenging supervision becomes imperative (Kern, 1986; Stanton & Todd, 1982). It is important that the supervisor is cognizant of ACOA issues, have an intimate working knowledge of alcoholic family dynamics, and be sufficiently objective to observe the emergence of old dysfunctional family patterns in the counseling relationship.

A supervisor must not only be alert to factual data presented by the supervisee, but also be sensitive to how the data are gathered, interpreted, and presented, and view this approach as an expression of the supervisee's inter- and intrapsychic process. The following is a list of potential treatment problems encountered by the ACOA therapist (although non-ACOA counselors are equally prone to these pitfalls).

1. Vicarious treatment of self through client.
2. Vicarious experiencing of emotions through the client.
3. Over-identification with the client and confluence with client's problems.
4. Over-directiveness, lack of emotional response-ability.
5. Rigid or lax boundaries.
6. Confusion over thinking, feeling, doing.
7. Catergorizing clients, misdiagnosing.
8. Recreation of family-of-origin dynamics within the context of the therapeutic relationship.
9. Inability to set limits for self and client.

Presenting supervision issues are as diverse as the supervisees and special ACOA needs must be handled sensitively, respectfully, and uniquely.

No particular agreement exists in the mental health field as to what kind of supervision is most beneficial. Some consider individual and/or group therapy a necessary adjunct to giving therapy and receiving supervision (Corey, 1976; Rogers, 1951; Whitaker, 1982). Others feel that personal therapy must precede supervision for the therapist to receive the most benefit from the supervisory experience (Nierenberg, 1972). Guerin and Fogarty (1972) consider a combination of supervision and therapeutic intervention most helpful (also see the discussion of personal development below). Whatever the orientation of the supervisor may be, the emotional and professional readiness of the supervisee must be considered. For instance, an ACOA counselor may have difficulty with trusting and be resistant to therapeutic interventions during supervision. The supervisor cannot violate the supervisee's boundaries and go beyond the parameters set by the supervisee's emotional barometer. An ACOA therapist with more advanced recovery may be more willing to risk vulnerability with another human being.

TYPE OF SUPERVISOR

The potential supervisor should be an experienced individual who has emerged from the above-described training experience and who can be open to new experiences with the supervisee, has a lively interest in the counselor personally and professionally, and is able to demonstrate genuineness, acceptance, empathy, and positive regard in the supervisory setting.

TYPE OF SUPERVISION

Supervision can take the form of individual, group, or peer supervision. In individual supervision, both the inter- and intrapsychic experiences are explored; in group settings, the group members must be willing to be both the client and the therapist, and the supervision leader becomes the mediator, facilitator, and source of reference. In peer supervision, such as the "professional cuddle groups" described by Whitaker (1982), the mental health professionals support each other and free-associate about the cases, but are ultimately individually responsible for the client and execution of treatment. There is no regression fostered or countertransference explored as there would be in a group supervision setting.

Techniques

Gestalt techniques are particularly useful in bringing problematic therapeutic interactions between client and clinician to the supervisee's attention. With the help of these techniques, "stuckness" by the therapist becomes figural and often brings to the counselor's awareness personal blocks that impede the therapeutic process. These approaches are most effective in helping the clinician gradually to identify and experience feelings toward and by the client rather than in terms of absolutes.

POLARITIES

One such approach and technique is to work with polarities. Polarities are the existence of one aspect of the self and its antithesis (Polster & Polster, 1973). Every human being moves between these polarities and the dominance of one to the exclusion of the other causes rigidified thinking, feeling, and behaving. These splits, the "top dog/underdog" syndrome (Perls, 1971, 1976), either cause conflict and ambivalence or motivate one to behave in one of the polarities at the expense of the other.

The ACOA counselor who considers the self to be strong and tough must be allowed to get in touch with the weak, dependent forces that most likely are hard for the counselor to experience. He or she, therefore, spends a lot of energy to keep these undesirable feelings in check. In the process, the counselor loses the freedom to be himself or herself, to own and appreciate all aspects of his or her personality.

When emphasizing and developing the weaker polarity in role play or when engaging the polarities in dialogue, the counselor can get in touch with the powerful feelings inherent in both and can then balance and integrate them. Both polarities need to become available to the individual for a fuller experience of the self.

CONFLUENCE

Many people have a tendency to become confluent with others, with ideas, with concepts, with work. This is often more pronounced with the ACOA counselor who has been confluent with a dysfunctional family for many years. Confluence is the inability to differentiate between the self and others; it is a means of reducing differences by making them like and thereby reducing the appreciation of self and otherness (Polster, 1973). This condition is also called enmeshment, fusion, or lack of boundaries. The ACOA counselor expresses this confluence—overidentification with the client and the client's problems, overidentification with work, knowing what the other person is thinking and feeling, and speaking for the client. This may represent a continuation of an ACOA therapist's childhood functioning, where the therapist did not have a separate identity but functioned as part of a dysfunctional whole.

The supervisor must undertake the difficult task of helping the supervisee keep a healthy separation from the client, and must be alert to signs of interdependency that may exist in the therapeutic alliance. To facilitate the process of individuation, the supervisor can ask such questions as: "What do *you* want?" "What do *you* feel?" "What are *you* doing?" This brings attention to confluent thinking and feeling, and helps to focus on the individual instead.

NEEDS VERSUS WANTS

This technique not only is supportive of professional development but helps on a personal level. ACOAs generally have difficulty identifying needs and differentiating between needs and wants. Basic survival "needs" are identified (food, shelter, safety). The expression of having a need beyond these basics is inaccurate and implies an expectation that someone or something will meet this need. When need becomes reidentified as "want," however, the speaker implies the active wish to pursue that which is wanted until satisfaction is assured.

Questions beginning with "how" and "what" make "wants" more easily identified. When individuals first get in touch with "wants," they are usually global and unattainable: "I want a happy family," "I want to be a different me." These wants can be made attainable by making them more specific: "What would a happy family be like?" or "What would it be like to be different?" "How could you make that happen?" An additional benefit of these exercises is the supervisee's realization that he or she can solve problems without assistance, and possesses self-support in addition to externally available support.

ROLE PLAY

Supervisees often benefit by role-playing the client when they have particular difficulties understanding where the client is or when they experience "stuckness" with the client (Mintz, 1987). These can be evidenced by lack of movement in therapy, emergence of more resistances, and an inability to make and maintain meaningful contact with the client.

> A counselor was patient, supportive and understanding of the client's intent to take care of himself. The client had been in a physically abusive relationship and wanted to learn to be kinder to himself. He began to cancel appointments and had several "no shows." The excuse given was that this was his way of doing what he needs to do when he wants to do it in order to take care of himself. The therapist's attempt to help the client with more constructive ways to do that met with even more cancellations.
>
> The supervisor had the therapist "be" the client. She tried to walk, talk, and think as though she were the client. In doing so, the therapist suddenly realized that she didn't feel supportive of the client at all, and that she was angry at the client's ruining her good productivity record at the agency.
>
> During the next session, the therapist became more active and concrete, and made a contract with the client, complete with consequences for breaking the contract. The client responded positively and energetically and confided that he really thought the therapist didn't care because she was too permissive.

This client-therapist interaction also demonstrates a polarity in process. The clinician had a need to be nice and understanding rather than to be attentive to her increasing anger about the client's lack of cooperation. She feared that the client might perceive her as confrontive and noncaring and, therefore, dislike her.

PERCEPTUAL-AWARENESS TRAINING

Supervision with a somewhat different focus is the raising of awareness of one's perceptions and simultaneously stimulating awareness of response differences in others to similar experiences or conditions. I have put an object in the middle of the room and asked the staff to attribute physical and emotional characteristics to it. Or the staff can allow the object to have an impact on them and report what it triggered cognitively and emotionally. This exercise powerfully exemplifies differences of perceptions and emotional effects of a particular experience. The therapist learns not "to know how you feel or think" or to "know what it's like for you," but rather gains an awareness and appreciation of differentness and otherness. Nonjudgmental response-ability in the therapist fosters responsibility in the client.

EDUCATION

It is also the responsibility of the supervisor to encourage the supervisees to pursue academic achievements by working toward an advanced degree. This would enable

ACOA clinicians to reach a wider target population for treatment and more ably to use their life experiences in the service of treating substance-abusing population and related issues, such as ACOAs and codependency. The pursuit of a degree can be an important developmental phase in the life of an ACOA counselor and deserves the help of the supervisor.

Training Issues

The training of aspiring substance-abuse therapists is a challenging and stimulating endeavor. Trainees are usually an enthusiastic and motivated group. In my experience as a trainer, the majority of substance-abuse counselors have been ACOAs or recovering substance abusers. Of interest is the sense of omnipotence many in this group bring to the training experience. They "know" that reality or behavior therapy is what works with substance abusers and "know" from personal experience what the life of an addict is like or how one is affected by one. They have the exact recipe (often their own recipe) for recovery: the client needs to trust and follow their explicit directions and guidance. The promised goal attainment is an enlightened life-style, with a minimum level of frustration. They know, because they have done it, and they have often chosen structured therapies because they seem to provide answers based on their own experience. Constructively confronting self-defeating behaviors, making choices, taking consequences, and practicing self-control and patience are part of the package that trainees often believe holds the key to successful treatment of substance abuse.

However, trainees are often surprised to learn that the amount of time spent on the teaching of actual counseling skills is minimal. Rather, the emphasis on teaching skills takes place indirectly through live demonstrations of problem identification and solving. Personal leadership styles are examined, old childhood roles explored, and present dysfunctional communication patterns identified. Counselors examine individual defense mechanisms as they surface through interaction with one another and through the use of various exercises. They have an opportunity to explore unfinished issues with their families of origin and often discover suprising motivations for entering the profession. Transferences and counttransferences make for rich therapeutic interventions and learning during training.

Group Issues

Initially, trainees learn to process their stylistic and personal differences in diads, triads, or larger group settings. They can become aware of perceptions, projections, confluences, and resistances in the relative safety of the training sessions where no formal evaluations take place and where each member is validated as an integral part of the total learning experience. Trust and cohesion develop quickly in an experiential group and trainees become sufficiently comfortable to drop their public personae, their "false faces," and to allow glimpses of their very "private selves." Trainees can allow themselves to become vulnerable and expose their insecurities, needs, and wants. It is here that confidentiality is stressed.

THE INNER CHILD

When group process is allowed to develop naturally, incongruencies and polarities of the individuals, the group, and ideas become fertile ground for personal and group therapeutic work. The shirt-and-tie-clad male may get in touch with "the scared little boy" within who uses clothes as his "armor." The shy female trainee becomes excited and wants to play a game of tag. The "cool cat," a seemingly independent adult, breaks down and cries because a group member reminds him of his father who abandoned him after many years of abuse. Exploration of the "child within" (Whitfield, 1987) is a powerful and necessary discovery for the trainee as individual and professional.

GUIDED IMAGERY

The need to be confrontative and reality based, tough rather than soft, dissipates quickly in this atmosphere and the trainees declare themselves ready to embark on a lengthy regressive fantasy. All are given permission to leave any time or do whatever is necessary to take care of themselves. The purpose of the fantasy is to get the participants in touch with forgotten experiences, "stuffed" feelings, needs, wants, and unfinished business, and to gain a new perspective on issues with which they have struggled for years. While the fantasy is somewhat directive, it allows each trainee the opportunity to free-associate, to explore in depth, or to skim over events at will.

I ask participants to relax and become comfortable. Then I guide them back into time through developmental milestones common to most people. These generalities are interspersed with specific suggestions if I have some knowledge of the people involved. The exercise regresses from the present throughout life back to the very earliest childhood experiences and feelings. The suggestions include social, familial, emotional, cognitive, sexual, and other biological experiences until the trainees appear fully in touch with their "inner child."

It is then suggested that the participants turn their focus slowly back to the "here and now," and without discussion of details of the experience, describe in adjectives what they felt like being a child. Many or most adjectives are negative. I write them in a column on the blackboard. The next column consists of a list of things they would have needed to feel better or differently as a child. How they feel as adults is listed in the third column and, last, they are asked what they would need as an adult to feel or to continue feeling whole. The columns are then compared and participants often discover that they do not feel very differently as adults from how they felt as children, and are amazed that they find similarities between the needs of the child and of the adult.

TRAINING OBJECTIVES

Trainees learn that not being "whole" can get in the way of giving effective treatment and that the confrontative approach to clients is not necessarily expressive of their total selves. The discovery of the projected public self versus the private self or "inner child" is a powerful realization, the exploration of which does not encourage an adaptation of one or the other; rather, it provides an opportunity to become familiar with and to synthesize and integrate opposites.

The "humanizing" exercises and processes serve the purpose of helping the potential therapist to get in touch with strengths and weaknesses, to raise awareness of existing behaviors, thoughts, and feeling patterns by becoming sensitive to needs, wants, defenses, and so on. Participants become aware of projecting their personal, unacceptable character attributes onto others and of how to reown important parts of their personalities. In order to be in contact with the client, the trainee must learn to be in touch with his or her own inherent creative capacities and risk using them in the therapeutic encounter. When teaching skills only, it is possible that the quest to achieve professional competence will become disruptive to healthy, integrated learning, particularly when the trainee wants to emulate an "admired" teacher (Sharaf & Levinson, 1969). Trainees must, therefore, develop their own independent views about the world, themselves, and others so that they will not be relegated to a shallow imitation of someone else and as a result be ineffective helpers.

It is my belief and goal in training substance-abuse counselors that one must acquire a strong sense of self and awareness of one's person. This is best learned through experience and feedback from significant others. Therapists cannot go beyond what they know to be true themselves; they must have a clear understanding of what belongs to themselves and to others, and they must be able to tolerate uncertainties and ambiguities in the process of personal exploration.

PERSONAL DEVELOPMENT

A psychotherapist must have a commitment to his or her own therapy to remain alive, spontaneous, creative, and integrated (Whitaker, 1982). In therapy, the counselor learns to differentiate the self from the other and becomes responsible for personal perceptions and interactions. When the therapist learns through self-knowledge that "my You acts on me as I act on it" (Buber, 1970), he or she can truly be present with the client with relative absence of distortions. Without it, the counselor can fall too easily into the trap of being the perpetual patient who vicariously seeks a cure through the client. Gravitz and Bowden (1984) have outlined a four-step program that can be sucessfully used by the ACOA counselor in therapy to deal with ACOA recovery issues.

Stage I.   Recognizing that substance addiction is the cause of chaos in the family and how this affects each family member;

Stage II.   "Coming out" and breaking the cycle of denial, which also entails the facing of latent, repressed feelings from childhood;

Stage III. Dealing with core issues (such as the "all or nothing" syndrome, habitual dissociation, or not recognizing feelings or equating feelings with behavior) and reducing them into smaller chunks that can be more easily managed;

Stage IV.   Limit and boundary setting between the client and others until the client begins to experience some freedom and awareness of personal rights.

After working through these stages, an ACOA can enter therapy with a generalist and explore existential issues common to all human beings.

SELF-HELP GROUPS

An important adjunct to therapy is the participation in self-help groups, Al-Anon, ACOA, or codependent groups that address the emotional needs of the ACOA counselor as a person. Criticism is often voiced about people becoming "group junkies" and is unjustly likened to other forms of addiction. Certainly not all self-help groups are well organized and functioning to model their purported healthful integration, but most are well intended and relatively successful in their pursuit to address addiction and coaddiction issues. Every person has the right to choose a form of therapy that he or she deems appropriate at a given time for whatever reason. Self-help groups and therapy are supportive and complementary and not exclusive of one another as is often assumed.

Many ACOAs have the need to belong to and identify with a group. A colleague explained to me, "We never had a family with whom we could identify; ACOA groups give us this respectable and noble identification." The need or want to be a part of a group can be attributed to the unmet needs of the individual in the family of origin. In the "group family," the person can experience acceptance, understanding, being needed, and giving. He or she can act up or out without the fear of expulsion from the family. The group member will learn that he or she is not really crazy but was raised in a "crazy-making" environment. The group member can learn, laugh, and weep with others, and each becomes instrumental in soothing the other's wounds.

The individual can learn what a real family feels like, and can dare to grow up and slowly to separate and differentiate from the family group as a whole and evolve to become his or her unique self. At this stage, the individual may seek out an individual therapist to further help in the journey of self-discovery. The family group continues to be available to the fledgeling as, most often, he or she is to the group. In this process, the individual can unravel painful experiences, thoughts, and feelings from the past, and, it is hoped, find more constructive ways of coping in the present to help live an integrated life-style. The becoming of the person of the ACOA therapist can be an exciting venture into the unknown.

BURNOUT

ACOA substance-abuse counselors are particularly prone to burnout in the practice of their chosen profession. Their lingering unresolved issues from their alcoholic families of origin energize many to overextend themselves to their clients, to overidentify with clients' presenting problems, and to become overinvolved in the process of therapy. Even if the ACOA substance-abuse counselor is personally involved in an active recovery process, the needs to care and to control remain active interferences in the therapeutic alliance until lingering family issues are resolved. In addition to sound supervision at the workplace, monthly attendance at AA, NA, Al-Anon, codependency, and ACOA groups becomes necessary for ACOA or non-ACOA addiction counselors to maintain the necessary perspective on their work (Vaillant, 1981; Treadway, 1989).

CONCLUSIONS

The study and the connection between the childhood role in an ACOA substance-abuse counselor's family of origin and the preference for more or less structured therapies is not necessarily generalizable to all ACOA substance-abuse counselors. It does support the hypothesis, however, that excessive and inappropriate parenting by a child and the need to retreat, act up, or manipulate for purposes of survival and to keep the family integrated in some manner can be precursors to entering the helping profession. Counselors with adapted childhood roles of the "hero" and "lost child" are particularly prone to practicing more structured therapies. They are accustomed to taking control or to functioning in isolation, and they can now gain covert recognition and purpose in the practice of administering therapy.

Individuals designing training programs for aspiring substance-abuse counselors must take the special needs of ACOAs and non-ACOAs into consideration. Curriculi must proffer opportunities for academic and personal development of the person of the therapist. ACOA and non-ACOA specific supervision of substance-abuse counselors is the responsibility of administration, and ideally an extension of the training philosophy. High on the list of priorities for ACOA counselors should be the active use of self-help groups in conjunction with in-depth therapy. Recommendations for the ACOA therapist also apply to the non-ACOA therapist, who, too, was very likely to have been cast into the caretaker's role prematurely. The development of the therapist as a whole person must be a priority for educators, administrators, and counselors, and is essential if the therapist is to help the client attain optimal benefits from therapy.

REFERENCES

Ackerman, R. (1978). *Children of alcoholics: A guidebook for educators, therapists, and parents.* Holmes Beach, FL: Learning Publications.

Ackerman, R. (1986a). Alcoholism in the family. In R. Ackerman (Ed.), *Growing the shadow: Children of alcoholics.* Pompano Beach, FL: Health Communications.

Ackerman, R. (1986b). *Children of alcoholics: A bibliography and resource guide.* Pompano Beach, FL: Health Communications, Inc.

Black, C. (1979). Children of alcoholics. *Alcohol Health and Research World, 4,* 23–27.

Black, C. (1986). Children of alcoholics. In R. Ackerman (Ed.), *Growing in the shadow: Children of alcoholics.* Pompano Beach, FL: Health Communications.

Buber, M. (1970). *I and tho.* (translation by Walter Kaufman) (p. 67). New York: Charles Scribner & Sons.

Cermack, T. (1986). Children of alcoholics. In: R. Ackerman (Ed.), *Growing in the shadow: Children of alcoholics.* Pompano Beach, FL: Health Communications.

Corey, G. (1976). *Theory and practice of counseling and psychotherapy.* Monterey, CA: Brooks/Cole Publishing Co.

Foster, W. (1976). The employed child of the alcoholic. *Labor Management Alcoholism Journal, 6*(1), 13–18.

Gade, E., & Goodman, R. E. (1975). *Staying sober: A guide for relapse prevention.* Independence, MO: Independence Press.

Gorski, T. & Miller, M. (1986). Therapeutic issues of adult children of alcoholics: A continuum of developmental stages. In R. Ackerman (Ed.), *Growing in the shadow: Children of alcoholics.* Pompano Beach, FL: Health Communications.

Gravitz, H. D. & Bowden, J. D. (1984). Therapeutic issues of adult children of alcoholics. *Alcohol Health and Research World, 8*(4), 25–37.

Gravitz, H. L. & Bowden, J. D. (1986). Therapeutic issues of adult children of alcoholics. In R. Ackerman (Ed.), *Growing in the shadow: Children of alcoholics.* Pompano Beach, FL: Health Communications.

Guerin, P., & Fogarty, T. F. (1972). The family therapist's own family. *International Journal of Psychiatry, 10,* 6–22.

Haley, J. (1976). *Problem-solving therapy.* New York: Harper & Row.

Harriman, S. G. (1987). Identification and evaluation of communicator style in adult children of alcoholics. Paper presented at the annual meeting of the Western Speech Communications Association, Salt Lake City.

Kern, J. C. (1986). Adult children of alcoholics as professionals in the alcoholism field. In R. Ackerman (Ed.), *Growing in the shadow: Children of alcoholics.* Pompano Beach, FL: Health Communications.

Lackie, B. (1983). The families of origin of social workers. *Clinical Social Work Journal, 11*(4), 309–322.

Laundergan, C., Flynn, D., Gaboury, J. (1986). An alcohol and drug counselor training program: Hazeldon Foundation's trainee characteristics and outcomes. *Journal of Drug Education, 16*(2), 167–179.

Lerner, R. (1986). Co-dependency: The survival of energy surrounded by confusion. In R. Ackerman (Ed.), *Growing in the shadow: Children of alcoholics.* Pompano Beach, FL: Health Communications.

Matzko, H. (1988). ACOA as substance abuse counselor: The influence of self-perceived dominant role in the family of origin on the selection of counseling approach. CAGS dissertation, Rhode Island College, Providence.

Miller, A. (1981). *The drama of the gifted child.* New York: Basic Books.

Miller, A. (1984). *For your own good.* New York: Farrar, Straus, Giroux.

Minuchin, S., & Fishman, H. C. (1981). *Family therapy techniques.* Cambridge, MA: Harvard University Press.

Mintz, E. (1987). The training of Gestalt therapists: A symposium. *Gestalt Journal, 10*(2), 73–106.

Murphy, J. P. (1984). Substance abuse and the family. *Journal of Specialists in Group Work, 9*(2), 106–112.

Naiditch, B. (1986). Why work with children of alcoholics? In R. Ackerman (Ed.), *Growing in the shadow: Children of alcoholics.* Pompano Beach, FL: Health Communications.

Nardi, P. M. (1981). Children of alcoholics: A role theoretical perspective. *Journal of Social Psychology, 115,* 237–245.

Nierenberg, M. A. (1972) Self-help first. *International Journal of Psychiatry, 10,* 34–41.

Paul, N. L. (1972). Critical evaluation: Changes? *International Journal of Psychiatry, 10,* 42–50.

Peck, M. S. (1978). *The road less traveled.* New York: Simon & Schuster.

Perls, F. S. (1971). *Gestalt therapy verbatim.* New York: Bantam Books.

Perls, F. (1976). *The Gestalt approaches and eye witness to therapy.* New York: Bantam Books.

Perls, F., Hefferline, R. F., & Goodman, R. (1977). *Gestalt therapy.* New York: Bantam Books.

Pilat, J. M., & Jones, J. W. (1984). Identification of children of alcoholics: Two empirical studies. *Alcohol Health and Research World, Winter,* 27–36.

Polster, E., & Polster, M. (1974). *Gestalt therapy integrated.* New York: Vintage Books.

Prewett, M. J., Spence, R., & Chaknis, M. (1981). Attribution of causality by children with alcoholic parents. *International Journal of Addiction, 16*(2), 367–370.

Qyreshi, M. Y., & Soat, D. N. (1976). Perception of self and significant others by alcoholics and non-alcoholics. *Journal of Clinical Psychology, 32*(1), 189–194.

Rogers, C. R. (1951). *Client-centered therapy.* Boston: Houghton Mifflin.

Rogers, C. R. (1961). *On becoming a person.* Boston: Houghton Mifflin.

Rohner, S. W. (1982). Alcoholism in the helping professions. *Alcohol Health and Research World, 3,* (3) 18–23.

Sharaf, M. R., & Levinson, D. J. (1969). The quest for omnipotence. The case of the psychiatric resident. Report of a study by the Center for Sociopsychological Research. Massachusetts Mental Health Center; Boston.

Smith, C. M. (1979). Overview of personality, behavior and parental alcoholism. *Currents in Alcoholism, 5,* 297–299.

Spensley, J., & Blacker, K. J. (1976). Feelings of the psychotherapist. *American Journal of Orthopsychiatry, 46*(3), 542–545.

Stanton, M. D., & Todd, T. C., et al. (1982). *The family therapy of drug abuse and addiction.* New York: Guilford Press.

Steinglass, R. (1987). *The alcoholic family.* New York: Basic Books.

Stephen, P. (1981). Pre- and post test measurements of self-concept of trainees in an alcohol and drug counseling program. *Journal of Alcohol and Drug Education, 27*(1), 78–81.

Subby, R. (1987). *Lost in the shuffle: The co-dependent reality.* Pompano Beach, FL: Health Communications.

Treadway, D. (1989). *Before it's too late: Working with substance abuse in the family* (pp. 192–201). New York: Norton.

Trice, H. M., & Eoman, P. M. (1979). *Spirits and demons at work: Alcohol and other drugs on the job.* New York: Cornell University.

Vaillant, G. E. (1981). Dangers in psychotherapy in the treatment of alcoholism. In M. H. Bean and N. E. Zinberg (Eds.), *Dynamics approaches to the understanding and treatment of alcoholism.* New York: Free Press.

Vaillant, G. E. (1988). The alcohol dependent and drug dependent person. In A. M. Nicvoli (Ed.), *The Harvard hand book of psychiatry* (pp. 700–713). Cambridge, MA: Belnap/Howard.

Wegscheider, S. (1976). *The family trap . . . No one escapes from a chemically dependent family.* Palo Alto, CA: Science & Behavior Books.

Whitaker, C. (1982). *From psyche to system.* New York: Guilford Press.

Whitfield, C. L. (1987). *Healing the child within.* Deerfield Beach, FL: Health Communications.

Woititz, J. (1986). Common characteristics of adult children of alcoholic families. In R. Ackerman (Ed.), *Growing in the shadow: Children of alcoholics.* Pompano Beach, FL: Health Communications.

Wood, B. I. (1984). Children of alcoholics: Patterns of dysfunction in adult life. Paper presented at the Annual Convention of the American Psychological Association, Toronto.

Woodside, M. (1986). Children of alcoholics. *Journal of School Health, 56*(10), 448–449.

PART IV

PUBLIC-POLICY PERSPECTIVES

13

The Growing Impact of the Children-of-Alcoholics Movement on Medicine: A Revolution in Our Midst

Robert L. DuPont, M.D.

John P. McGovern, M.D., Sc.D., LL.D.

Changes are taking place in contemporary American medicine in a threatening climate of tightening health-care financing and increasing dominance of procedure-based medicine at the expense of a more humanistic medical tradition. The discussion these days among physicians is more likely to be about these two topics than about potential for mutual-aid solutions to these troublesome medical problems. The third-party payer has emerged, after years of relatively silent and generally passive growth, as the newly dominant, and sometimes quite aggressive, force in the delivery of medical care. Third-party payers—insurance companies and employers—are also zeroing in on health-care costs and procedure-based medicine.

As we enter the 1990s, changes in the financing of medical care are altering the shape of medicine as profoundly as is the growth of procedure-based medicine. Although it is often confused with the increasingly scientific practice of medicine, procedure-based medicine is not the same thing as scientific medicine. For example, much new science has emerged in the past decade concerning the fundamental, biological basis of addiction, but this has not led to the development of any new treatment procedures.

The cognitive medical specialties which lack high-tech procedures, such as psychiatry and pediatrics, as well as most of internal medicine and family practice, are lagging behind other specialties, such as neurology, cardiology, and ophthalmology, that are increasingly procedure based. Today, the high-tech specialties attract the most and the best medical students and residents and provide the best incomes in medicine.

Even the most hostile critics of "managed care" and other efforts made by third-

313

party payers to contain health-care costs, and of increasingly technological med-icine, concede that these changes involve benefits as well as costs. These profound changes are still gathering force. They have become easily recognized by most phy-sicians, not as abstract ideas, but as powerful forces in the everyday practice of medicine.

While this discussion of health-care economics is no longer alien even to the most academically oriented physicians, there is a parallel concern on the intellectual front in contemporary medicine: How can medicine use the advances that are not derivative from laboratory science or high-technology development without becom-ing anti-intellectual or even antiscientific? This issue was explored by George Engel (1976) over a decade ago. The new developments in the prevention and treatment of chemical dependence are forcing medicine to confront new challenges on both the economic and the scientific front.

MEDICINE AND MUTUAL AID IN THE 1990S

This chapter identifies a change in medicine that comes from a different tradition, one that has broad impact on both medical research and medical practice. In many ways, this change in medicine is the antithesis of the better-known changes in financing and science. In fact, the strength of this change lies in the ways that it is dramatically different from the other two powerful forces changing medicine: it is free and it is the ultimate in low tech. This change, born in the field of chemical dependence mostly over the past decade, deals with individuals, families, and com-munities by focusing on life-styles—the ways we live and relate to each other. Most major health problems faced by modern medicine (including heart disease, cancer, and suicide, as well as AIDS and chemical dependence) have their roots in life-styles.

This new reality in medicine, which we see as a largely unrecognized revolution in our midst, is the emergence of "mutual aid," most often in the form of one of the 12-step programs, as a dominant force in contemporary American culture. In concert with other 12-step programs, one of the newest and perhaps the most rapidly growing of such programs, Children of Alcoholics (COA) Adult Children of Alcoholics (ACOA), is reshaping medical practice. Although the title of this chapter refers to the effect of this movement on medicine, it is apparent that these changes extend well beyond medicine to all the human-services professions. Today there are few American families that have not been touched by a 12-step program. Most Americans, nevertheless, including most physicians, have not yet grasped the immense power of this new force. Because these programs and the problems with which they deal are highly personal, most Americans fail to grasp the magnitude of the 12-step revolution because they relate only to their own experience, which many consider fairly unique.

The relatively unfamiliar term "mutual aid," rather than the more common "self-help" is used to refer to the 12-step programs. People with behavioral illnesses, such as alcohol and drug dependence, become aware fairly early in the evolution of the disease that something is wrong. This awareness is usually ambivalent and focuses not on the behavior itself but on its negative consequences. For example, developing alcoholics will notice that they have accidents or that their spouses argue with them when they have been drinking. They typically try to eliminate the "problems" without eliminating the feeling-driven behavior, the disease. They try to stop the accidents and the arguments without giving up their drinking. As the disease progresses, they try more and more futile self-help, self-control solutions to the problems caused by their drinking without facing that they have lost control and suffer from a serious disease.

When alcoholics go to an Alcoholics Anonymous (AA) meeting, they will be confronted with a new idea: The AA program's way of understanding and handling their drinking problem, which is defined as a disease. Recovery generally means giving up one's own way of handling the problem and using the time-tested approach of the 12-step program—that is part of what is meant in the first step in which one admits that one is powerless. When the term "self-help" is used, as it often is, to describe the 12-step programs, it usually refers to the fact that these are not professionally run treatment programs (e.g., there is no staff, no governmental licenses for the leaders of these programs, and no bills to be submitted for health-insurance reimbursement).

Twelve-step programs are not, however, self-help programs. A person who attends a meeting seeking help is part of a process of mutual aid. The treater and the treated are not easily distinguished. Helping others with the disease of alcoholism is a fundamental part of one's own recovery. Thus, mutual-aid programs are distinguished not only from professional health-care programs, but from truly self-help programs such as reading a self-help book to understand a behavioral disorder, such as a phobia or chemical dependence, and putting the principles into practice to overcome the disorder.

The mutual-aid movement presents medicine with a scientific breakthrough that meets the criteria for a scientific revolution as defined by Kuhn (1970). Although this movement did not come out of a laboratory and has not been widely debated in *Science* or the *New England Journal of Medicine*, it is as powerful as the earlier revolutions in preventive medicine, from cleaning up our drinking water to improving nutrition as ways to reduce infectious diseases.

Only recently in scientific medicine has it become clear that most of the life-style factors influencing health practices are related to personal choices, many of them driven by pleasure. Medicine has barely begun to understand the ways that family and community can be powerful promoters of or antidotes to the health problems caused by these life-style choices. The recent, impressive reduction in heart attacks in the United States through changes in smoking and eating behaviors—especially by middle-class, middle-aged men—is a good example of how behaviors or life-styles directly affect health.

The mutual-aid program for ACOAs builds on the foundations of AA and the first family-member mutual-aid program, Al-Anon. ACOA extended this by-now traditional approach to deal with the children of alcoholic parents, many of whom are adults. More recently, the mutual-aid approach has been extended to a newly recognized group in need: the roughly six million Americans under the age of 18 who still live with alcoholic parents. In reaching out to the children of chemically dependent parents, much new ground is broken for the mutual-aid movement, as one of the largest and most vulnerable segments of our population is involved. Most mutual-aid programs use the dedication and knowledge of people who are them-selves suffering from a dysfunctional problem. For example, Gamblers Anonymous and Overeaters Anonymous deal with people who suffer from compulsive gambling and compulsive eating respectively.

It has become increasingly clear in the past few years that all behavioral illnesses, of which these are representative, are family diseases. All family members invariably suffer as a result of the unhealthy behaviors of an afflicted family member. For example, it is not only the alcoholic or excessive gambler who suffers the conse-quences of his or her behavioral problems. Families are made dysfunctional, and even "crazy," by these out-of-control behavioral illnesses.

The characteristic reactions of families to behavioral illnesses are a combination of *enabling* (acting in ways that wittingly and unwittingly perpetuate the unhealthy behavior) and *denial* (acting as if the problem were not present). Family members caught up in enabling and denial can be called *codependent* (they are involved in and share the responsibility for the unhealthy behavior, primarily by focusing their lives on the sick or the bad behavior and by making their own self-esteem and well-being contingent on the behavior of the unhealthy family member). Both enabling and denial temporarily ease the discomfort of family members at the cost of long-term perpetuation of the unhealthy behavior. An older tradition in family therapy held that family members actually wanted, or even needed, the sick behavior to continue. While this idea no longer is in vogue, it contrasts dramatically with the more contemporary view that family enabling arises, not from the wish for the hurt-ful behavior to continue, but from a lack of understanding of these behavioral dis-eases and how best to cope with them.

The alternatives to enabling and denial are *intervention* (taking decisive action either to end the unhealthy behavior or to disengage from the life of the family member) and *recovery* (the process of personal and family healing, the cure for behavioral disorders). This new mutual-aid approach sees the entire family as suf-fering from the problem and as needing to work to overcome it. Neither the sufferer nor the family members are to blame for the disease; all are victims who can work together to overcome the disease they share. On the other hand, the new family mutual-aid movement makes clear that one must meet one's own needs, whether or not the affected family member achieves recovery. Making one's own happiness contingent on another person's behavior, even that of a beloved family member, is now understood to be a central part of the behavioral disease itself. Some mental health professionals propose that codependence be given the status of a diagnosed mental disorder. These five words are the core vocabulary of the mutual-aid movement: enabling, denial, codependence, intervention, and recovery (DuPont, 1984b).

The new mutual-aid movement extends beyond the realm of clinicians and into that of public policy. A key factor in the drug epidemic that began in the United States in the late 1960s was the strident claim that the use of drugs and alcohol is a personal matter and therefore not the appropriate concern of anyone except the users themselves. No more eloquent testimony exists to illustrate the folly of this assertion than the large and growing movement of the children of alcoholics and other drug abusers. Children who grow up in families made dysfunctional by chemical dependence are as much victims of chemical dependence as are the victims of drunk drivers. Chemical dependence and recovery are family matters. They leave no one in the family untouched.

During the past decade, one of the authors (R.L.D.) has worked to extend the mutual-aid concepts, including incorporating them directly into medical care in the treatment of anxiety disorders (Saylor, DuPont & Brouillard, 1989). This extension is a model for the use of these fundamental concepts in areas of medicine beyond chemical dependence, such as eating disorders and obsessive-compulsive disorder (DuPont, 1984a). This new model, using mutual aid in health care, has also been extended to nonmedical settings, including the college campus (DuPont, 1988).

The revolution in medical practice being brought about by mutual aid is not easy to see. It is, however, all around us. The millions of people who now participate in mutual-aid programs are potent, if quiet, evidence of this revolution. Most often, however, the revolution—or, as it is often called, the Program—is thought of as a private and somewhat exceptional activity. Few people, even those closest to the 12-step programs, have yet grasped the force of the process.

This chapter was written by clinicians for other clinicians. It is in the struggle of our patients with chemical-dependence problems, whether in themselves or in their family members, that we have come to the conclusion that the mutual-aid movement is a revolutionary process in our lifetimes. In academically oriented medicine, there is a powerful and generally positive tradition of physicians learning from the "literature" and from esteemed teachers and colleagues. Our journals and our professional meetings are major learning opportunities. Although it is seldom acknowledged, there is another powerful tradition of medical education: learning from our own patients. A doctor and a patient, working together, form a team with its principal goal being an improvement in the quality of the patient's life. The doctor brings much to this team, including knowledge and experience. What is less obvious is what the patient brings. It is now commonplace for a patient to read about a new development concerning his or her disease in the media and to alert the doctor to it. It is also common for a doctor to learn more about a disease because a patient does not get well, as expected, when the disease is treated in the doctor's usual way. When the doctor and patient have labored long and then the patient finds his or her own way to recovery, the patient often, in that process, educates the doctor.

What follows is a first-person account of the education of one of us (R.L.D.) by his chemically dependent patients:

Speaking personally, my own understanding of chemical dependence was taken from the best thinking in academic psychiatry when I was a medical student and resident in the early 1960s. I thought psychotherapy combined with a ten-day "detoxification" program was the treatment of choice for drug and alcohol problems. Surely, when the doctor told the patient that his or her drug or alcohol use was unwise and unhealthy, the patient would stop the sick behavior. Many times I failed to help my patients and still did not doubt my own understanding of the chemical-dependence problem my patient faced.

I learned in my medical training not to give up on even the most difficult patient because, in the end, the patient often will show the physician what is needed for recovery. As one of my professors, Elvin Semrad, said: "Remember that two heads are better than one. Neither the doctor nor the patient has all of the answers or all of the problems. When the doctor and the patient work together, they need each other to solve the patient's problems."

In the 1970s, my patients with alcohol or drug problems showed me a new way to get well: they joined AA or Narcotics Anonymous. They shared the joy of real recovery with me, and sometimes took me to meetings with them. In the process, they taught me about the disease of chemical dependence and how to overcome it. Later I got up the courage to go to meetings alone and learned even more about these mutual-aid programs. I bought my own copies of their *Big Books* and learned new ways to overcome a wide range of behavioral problems. I also became a better doctor because of that experience.

A colleague of ours described his own discovery of mutual aid:

When I first heard of AA in a medical setting, I was a psychiatric resident. Meetings took place in the chapel of our hospital on Tuesday nights, but the residents and fellows were never told about them. One evening when I was on duty I drifted into a meeting and heard something tantamount to a revolution in terms of my own thinking. Yet outside that room, I never heard any word spoken about those meetings. The attenders came and went without any comment from the high-powered scientific community we all prided ourselves on sharing. In fact, in those days in the early 1970s, there was an unwritten sign over the door of our prestigious hospital: "Alcoholics Not Wanted Here." It seemed to be generally agreed that alcoholics and drug addicts, unlike schizophrenics and depressives, were beyond our capacity to help. It is ironic, looking back at that time, that my assumption then was that these patients were simply too bad or too hopeless for help. Today it seems truer that we just did not know how to help them. The failure was ours, not theirs. Deepening the irony, the answer for these miserable human beings we spurned was right there in the chapel at those Tuesday night meetings. But because it was not "scientific," it did not register on us residents (Vaillant, 1980).

The mutual-aid revolution, like many of the great and truly democratic revolutions in human experience, was not led by one individual, but springs from the wisdom and experiences of millions of ordinary people. As such, it cannot be embarrassed by the foolishness of a particular guru or misled by some harebrained scheme. It is not dependent on the whim of a government program or a quirk in the tax laws. Ideas in the mutual-aid movement that help real people with real needs flourish and multiply. Those that do not help disappear. What persists is the distillation of the practical, experience-tested knowledge of millions of people.

SOME CENTRAL ELEMENTS OF MUTUAL AID AS IT RELATES TO MEDICINE

Community of Sufferers

A community is a group of people who share their lives on a day-in/day-out basis. One of the changes that has occurred in the late 20th century is the explosive increase in the alternative life-styles available in our society. The old village community, where families spent their lives in close association with other families who all knew each other over three or four generations, has been replaced in much of the world, with the United States leading the way, with urban communities in which people have known each other for a short time, often for only months, or at most a few years. Added to this weakened support network is the mind-bending diversity of human experiences. In the traditional village environment, the possible roles to be chosen from generation to generation were relatively few and reasonably stable over time.

Think for a minute about the impact of chemical dependence on the modern American community . People who are chemically dependent are isolated by the force of the stigma attending drug use and excessive alcohol use, and even more painfully by the failure of others to understand the difficulties they face. When one considers the family members of chemically dependent people, especially their children, one begins to understand the isolation in the modern urban community of people touched by addiction. How can children whose mothers or fathers are cocaine addicts or alcoholics tell their friends about their lives? If they try to describe their lives, their friends will not understand and may shun them altogether. What would "straight" parents of a first-grader think of the story of a friend's mother who was having an affair with cocaine? It is often helpful for children of an addicted parent to talk with professional therapists, but how much can therapists understand of the experience of such a child and what sort of real-life support can they offer?

Now think about the sense of community such children find at mutual-aid meetings during which other children share their experiences with chemical dependence. This participation in a 12-step meeting establishes a sense of "community" in an entirely new sense of the word: a community based on unique, powerful, and highly personal experiences. This is not the same sense of community that might have been provided by the old-style village community, simply because the experience of chemical dependence was either alien to the latter or stigmatized there. Thus the mutual-aid community can meet a deep, aching human need with a potency that a loving aunt or kindly grandparents cannot offer, not because they lack love, but because they lack knowledge of and experience with chemical dependence.

There is an important and profound insight that comes from experience of the ACOA movement. As modern life is increasingly characterized by a diversity of experiences, by an ever-widening range of choices, and by increasing mobility, the old strands that held human communities together are broken. With increases in time and economic pressure—the hurried-life syndrome—the intrusion of alcohol and drugs and the breakdown of the traditional nuclear family, how can people cope? Is the only answer the return to at least some aspects of traditional life-styles?

There are many changes in modern life-styles that pull us together in new ways, counterbalancing the now-isolating forces in our lives. Communication and air travel help us stay in touch over vast distances. As we have lost our sense of a "grounding" for our lives in a traditional village, the whole world is, through these high-technology connections, becoming one global village. While our increasingly diverse experiences make us less able to understand one another (how can a "normal" person hope to understand the relationship to food experienced by an anorexic or a bulimic?), we are able to form new connections based on highly specific experiences and needs. For example, programs for specific eating disorders and mutual-aid programs for people who have eating disorders help those afflicted with these illnesses to become part of working, caring, relevant communities.

Chemically dependent people may be part of a chemical-dependence community, usually through a mutual-aid group, but they may also be involved with other modern communities that share mutual interests, such as sports or music appreciation. Even the old-fashioned reunion is becoming popular again as people gather from all over the country, and even the world, to share family relationships. This modern community bonding is as new in the world as the drug epidemic or AIDS. At the center of these changes, which are called "market segmentation" in the economic sector, is the mutual-aid movement: a highly specific, open community providing intense forms of life-sustaining human contact in the midst of a bewildering environment of change, isolation, and personal diversity.

A growing body of scientific knowledge now exists about the special needs of children who grow up in alcoholic families (Earls et al., 1988; Putnam, 1987). This new information can be interpreted in various ways—such as casting a permanent shadow over the lives of COAs, or even to justify or excuse any problem these children might have. We prefer to view the solution differently. To us, the needs of children of chemically dependent parents are indisputable evidence that drug and alcohol problems are not injurious solely to those who use the alcohol or the drugs, but affect everyone in contact with chemically dependent people, especially the children in their homes. Children of chemically dependent parents are affected in many, often subtle, ways. Not all problems these children have are the result of growing up in a family dominated by chemical dependence. Having a parent with a drug or alcohol problem can be turned into an advantage, like any other handicap, through hard work. This is most likely to happen in a "community of sufferers"—a community that supports "tough love."

Wisdom of the Community

What are children of chemically dependent people likely to find at mutual-aid, 12-step meetings? They can find a shared sense of what is wrong and of what can be done about it. For example, one of the major concerns of a child of a chemically dependent parent is that if only the child were good enough or strong enough, the adult would not use drugs or alcohol. This problem cannot be solved, as human instinct suggests, by "trying harder." It can only be solved by "detaching with love." This wisdom of the mutual-aid programs is counterintuitive and is widely misunderstood in the straight society, where the standard of dealing with family problems is to try to help the suffering member overcome the problem or, failing that, simply to take over and "make it better."

Many examples of this sort of wisdom are directly available at mutual-aid meetings that are virtually unavailable elsewhere. For example, the idea that the parent is suffering from a "disease" and is not entirely responsible for the bad behavior from which the child suffers indirectly helps the child bear the pain of the chemical dependence without undermining the necessary loving relationship with the parent. This, like so much else of mutual-aid wisdom, is built on paradox. On the one hand, the addicted parent is the blameless victim of the disease; on the other hand, the parent's behavior is a major force in making the family dysfunctional. Recovery involves being able to see it, feel it, and live it both ways.

Closely related to this attitude toward addicted parents is the ability to make friends with other children who face similar problems and the realization that they are mostly good kids who are doing okay in their lives. Such friendships permit a positive identification that is not available in other settings, simply because other "okay" kids do not have chemically dependent parents. The meetings also let kids socialize with one another without the embarrassment they would feel with peers who do not have chemically dependent parents. Inviting a friend to one's home is quite different if that friend understands the uncertainty that goes with living in a family dominated by chemicals.

There are two positive outcomes that the parent can help the children reach as part of the process of family recovery. The first involves the biggest problem likely to be faced by children growing up in a family dominated by chemical dependence—the children's own use of drugs and alcohol as they go through their teenage years. The parent's addiction and the increased risk for chemical dependence faced by the children themselves give such children a compelling reason never, even once, to use drugs or alcohol. This increased risk for children of chemically dependent parents is often misunderstood by professionals as only a threat, which it is. This threat, because these are high-risk children for chemical dependence, can be turned into a lifesaving gift, if the children can understand and use it as such: a compelling reason not to use alcohol or drugs (DuPont, 1984b).

There is another, related positive outcome that chemically dependent parents can offer to their children: the motivation and opportunity to go to mutual-aid meetings, to use the wisdom and caring of the mutual-aid community. This caring community is not available to "normal" kids. Parents with chemical-dependence problems can go to meetings with older children and share directly in the process of recovery. Many parents have overcome their own problems with drug or alcohol because of the love and concern of their children. Many children have prevented or overcome their drug or alcohol problems because of their love for their parents, especially chemically dependent parents.

Spirituality

The secret weapon of the 12-step programs is their grounding in a personal relationship with a "Higher Power." This not only is the hardest part for most secular Americans to understand and accept about the 12-step programs, but it is also the major source of strength of these programs. When we first became involved with AA, we considered the spiritual aspect of the program an anachronism from AA's provincial, Midwestern origins. Today we know how wrong we were. Medicine needs to know more about how a foundation for one's life that reaches outside of one's own feelings is essential, not only to happiness, but also to health.

This spiritual grounding of the 12-step mutual-aid programs should not be confused with any particular religious orientation, even though for many 12-step followers their Higher Power is clearly and unembarrassingly part of a highly specific religious tradition. The Higher Power is approached by many routes, all of which are different ways to "know God." There is often one right way for a particular person, but there is not right way for all people. We have found it helpful in working with our patients to use the analogy of there being many roads to the single destination of serenity and peace. Many of our patients have difficulty with this spiritual aspect of mutual-aid programs when they first attend meetings. The tradition of reciting the Lord's Prayer at the end of meetings, for example, can be seen as a reflection of the Christian origins of many AA ideas. We have found that once people understand the principles of the 12-step way, they usually have little trouble incorporating any religious tradition into the process. Even agnostics or atheists do not find this aspect of the 12-step programs difficult to accept since they can identify the Higher Power in any way that works for them. One of our patients said that his Higher Power was his parole officer. Another patient considered his Higher Power to be "the community of all people." Yet another patient described the value of prayer in his life, which he discovered at the age of 32 as a result of going to Narcotics Anonymous meetings, this way: "For me, my waterbed is my 'Higher Power.' That's where I pray now and, funny as it sounds, it works for me."

Mutual-Aid Interface with Professional Healers

One of the more challenging aspects of the mutual-aid movement has been its relationship to professionals. After the founding in 1935 of AA, the first 12-step program, there were decades of uneasy relationships between the professionals and the program. One of the more aggravated controversies between the two approaches to the problem was the common attitude of doctors toward alcoholics: they prescribed either "willpower" or pills of various kinds. Both made the chemical dependence worse. In recent years, as the mutual-aid movement has gained strength and recognition, there has been a growing willingness to cooperate with professionals, including physicians. The many doctors who are AA members also have helped to educate other doctors about the message and power of AA. One of the two founders of AA, Dr. Bob, certainly offered a bridge for medicine to AA. The founding over a decade ago of the American Society of Addiction Medicine (ASAM), many original members of which were recovering alcoholics, provided another effective bridge between medicine and the 12-step programs.

There are still conflicts between the 12-step programs and health-care professionals. Too frequently, the professionals are seen as patronizing and ill-informed by the members of mutual-aid groups. On the other hand, the mutual-aid program members are seen as poorly educated about the latest in scientific medicine and hostile to the use of this knowledge for the betterment of chemically dependent people. Unfortunately, both points of view are often legitimate.

One fairly common, but painful, problem that can separate mutual aid and medical practice is the prescription of dependence-producing drugs by physicians. Such drugs—including barbiturates, stimulants, narcotic analgesics, and antianxiety medicines—either should not be prescribed at all for people with a history of chemical dependence, or only with great caution. Too few physicians understand this or take the trouble to establish whether or not a patient is chemically dependent. On the other hand, it is too common, even today, for AA and other mutual-aid-program members to condemn any use of a psychotropic medicine and to rely solely on the 12-step program, even when the addicted person suffers from a serious mental illness that may be partly underlying or compounding the chemical dependence. Classic examples are the marijuana-using schizophrenic whose Narcotic Anonymous meeting discourages his use of antipsychotic medicines that have no abuse potential at all. Another example is the manic-depressive whose use of antidepressants or lithium is decried as the use of mood-altering drugs at her AA meeting.

Another, often more difficult, problem is the use of antianxiety medicines, such as diazepam (Valium) or alprazolam (Xanax), for the treatment of chronic anxiety disorders such as panic disorder and generalized anxiety disorder. These illnesses are, like chemical dependence itself, increasingly seen as biological, often lifelong, disorders that can sometimes benefit from the use of medicines. Using willpower to overcome agoraphobia is as unlikely to be helpful as it is in overcoming chemical dependence. Nevertheless, that is precisely the advice given all too often by 12-step-program members who oppose all use of antipanic and antianxiety medicines. On the other side of the same coin, physicians who believe that chemically dependent people can use antianxiety medicines in the same way that nondependent patients use them can be a danger to their patients and, through the possibility of diverted drugs, to the entire community. The solution to this difficult problem requires a careful balancing of the risks and benefits of alternative treatments for the various anxiety disorders and recognition of the special needs of anxious patients who are chemically dependent (DuPont, 1986, 1989).

To achieve the full potential of the collaboration of the 12-step programs and medicine, it will be necessary for both groups to understand more about each other's point of view and to work together in more specific ways with specific clinical problems.

The recent emphasis on the problem of dual diagnosis, the coexistence of mental illness and addiction, offers another useful bridge for understanding between the 12-step programs and medicine. One benefit of new "dual-diagnosis" units in hospitals is the way in which they include 12-step meetings, on the unit and elsewhere, directly in the treatment experience. This not only introduces many patients to mutual aid, but it also introduces many physicians to 12-step meetings. The exposure of physicians to such meetings will encourage wider use of the 12-step principles in medicine, even beyond the problems of chemical dependence.

In our experience, it is often useful for doctors to attend 12-step meetings to help put the issue of the use of medicines by recovering chemically dependent people into perspective. It is also important that chemically dependent people who have benefited from medical care, including the use of medicines, speak up more openly at 12-step meetings. It will be useful for both groups to have more material appear in both the lay and professional media concerning these important, difficult, and shared issues.

Cautions About Mutual Aid

Not every recovering chemically dependent person needs or will accept a 12-step program, but most do need it and will accept it. It is important not to overstate the role of mutual aid or to create an oversimplistic conception of the highly varied and personal process of lifelong recovery.

We have two major concerns regarding the growing enthusiasm for the mutual-aid movement among health-care professionals. First, once health-care professionals understand the potency of the mutual-aid approach, there may be a tendency simply to walk away from a chemically dependent person with the admonition: "Go to meetings." This is not bad advice! But often it is not enough. It is even sadder when the agencies that fund drug- and alcohol-abuse treatment, both public and private, abdicate their responsibilities for the primary and the secondary effects of addiction by saying, "The only thing that works is AA, so why provide expensive treatment?" In a climate dominated by concerns for reducing health-care costs, it is too easy to fall for this attractive, but wrong, idea. Many successful 12-step-program members found their way to the program only when they became drug-free and were introduced to the program in a professionally run treatment program.

The second concern regarding the emerging enthusiasm for mutual aid is the tendency for mutual aid to deteriorate into either blaming someone else for one's distress or feeling sorry for oneself because of the disease. Both concerns indicate acute threats in dealing with COAs. It is vital that these children understand that they can use the support of the 12-step programs to learn what is wrong in their lives and what to do about it. Just as they are not able to make their parents "well," no matter how hard they try, so, too, their parents are not responsible for the children's suffering or their bad choices, no matter how sick the parents are or were. The responsibility for each person's behavior rests squarely, and unavoidably, with each person. It cannot be pushed off on anyone else even if an entire group wants to do just that.

It is all too easy to excuse failures and to lower one's sights by talking with others about one's handicaps. This is a common problem among mutual-aid groups that can be overcome only by a heavy dose of tough love. Al-Anon, and a growing number of COA groups, has gone beyond complaining and blaming to personal-recovery programs that really work.

IMPLICATIONS FOR MEDICAL EDUCATION

Medicine has lost a part of its soul under the pressure of cost containment and procedure-based care. The human touch leaves the encounter between doctor and patient when all the doctor sees of the patient are the results of high-tech tests. This dehumanization becomes worse when the doctor requires nothing more of a patient who is seeking relief from suffering than to submit to tests, to take medicine, or to undergo surgery. Equally deadly, for the interests of both doctors and patients, is the loss of the human and spiritual foundation to healing and recovery—loss that has become increasingly common in modern medicine.

One of the dramatic changes that our generation in medicine witnessed, and which we saw at close range, was the development of the first polio vaccine as a result of the culturing of the polio virus. Young doctors today can hardly imagine the fear that polio struck into the hearts of parents in the 1950s since the vaccines now taken for granted by parents, children, and physicians have virtually eliminated one of the most dreaded diseases of our childhood.

How ironic, and how educational, is the fear that has replaced that of polio for today's parents: the fear of chemical dependence for their adolescent children. Drugs have become the new "virus" for children and youth. Behavioral choices by teenagers include drug and alcohol abuse—two killers and maimers that are at least as cruel as the virus that was cultured for the first time 30 years ago by Drs. Enders, Weller, and Robbins. It seems unlikely that any brilliant and dedicated health researcher will find a vaccine for this disease. In fact, the change from the threat of infectious diseases to the threat of behavioral disorders is the central reality of the evolution of disease from the first decades to the last decades of the 20th century.

Modern medicine is discovering that in the last decade of the 20th century the major scourges of Americans are primarily caused, and prevented, by changes in behavior. That discovery opens the doors to the mutual-aid movement. Is there any doctor who has not told a patient who seems to be engaging in a high-risk behavior not to do it anymore? Such advice may make the doctor feel better, but is is unlikely to help the patient. Whatever the behavior—whether overeating, smoking, or using drugs or alcohol—it is unlikely that the doctor's admonition will produce the changes that the physician desires, even though they are unmistakably in the patient's interest. What is missing is what mutual aid uniquely can provide—a road map through the dangerous territory of behavior change and a community of guides, caring people who have been there themselves, to show the way.

Aesculapius, the Greek god of medicine, had two daughters: Panacea, the goddess of medicines, and Hygea, the goddess of healthy living, or what we now call lifestyle. Medicine in the 20th century has made much good use of the benefits that Panacea can provide. In the process, Hygea, the second daughter, once the mainstay of medical practice, has been neglected. If medicine is to prosper in the next decade, if patients are to continue to benefit from their work with physicians, then Hygea will have to be elevated once more to the role she had prior to the enshrining of Panacea as the great hope of medicine in this century. The mutual-aid movement offers both patients and doctors help in reestablishing this vital balance. Other human-services professionals, operating within the broad mandate of Aesculapius and prohibited by law from using the treasures of Panacea, can hardly be blamed if they are quicker than most physicians to grasp this important truth.

How can the 12-step concept be taught to medical students, residents, and doctors in both academic and clinical settings? We wish we could say that reading about it would do the job. Our own experience suggests that the best way is to learn with the heart first. The head will follow. That means going to meetings. It is surprising how education about mutual aid affects most physicians. They like the meetings and are impressed by the sincerity and power of the process of recovery. Once one has attended a few meetings, it becomes quite easy to refer patients, family, and friends to a 12-step program. One of the more informative books is *Getting Better: Inside Alcoholics Anonymous* by Nan Robertson (1988), a talented writer who is herself a recovering alcoholic.

As one of us (R.L.D.) observed:

> My own discovery of the 12-step program had a powerful effect on me and my practice that must have been like the effect on the professional life of my father-in-law, Dr. Wesley W. Spink, one of the pioneers in infectious diseases from the last generation, when, at the end of his residency training in Boston in the mid-1930s, he was introduced to antibiotics. Patients who had routinely died could now, almost as routinely, be saved. This revolutionary change in infectious diseases did not mean that everyone got well or that it was no longer important to learn about infectious diseases, but it surely did change the odds in the favor of a successful outcome for the patient-physician team. That is just what I have discovered about the 12-step programs: They are not quite the miracle that the early pioneers of the germ theory of infectious diseases dreamed of when they first conceptualized what was to become the antibiotic, but they surely are a big step forward—a revolution in medicine.

The story of mutual aid in medicine, however, does not end there. Many physicians are themselves impaired or recovering people who need to face their own problems with alcohol and other drugs. In addition, many people in the healing professions, including medicine, are COAs and one of the primary motivations in their career choice is their often-unrecognized, sometimes unconscious motivations to solve the problems of their own chemically dependent parents through their professional work (see Chapter 12). Such is the stuff of all human motivation, but it is best worked through to develop a more mature and realistic sense of self and one's own professional role. The COA program can, in this way, help healers begin to "heal themselves."

CONCLUSIONS

The mutual-aid revolution in medicine can extend the reach of both of the changes described earlier in this chapter: the push for more cost-effective health care and better use of procedure-based medical treatments. Mutual aid does this by bringing back the healing human touch and the spiritual foundation of medical practice. Rather than being antithetical to the other two changes, mutual aid can make them work better in the interests of both doctors and patients.

The mutual-aid movement was created in Akron, Ohio, when an unemployed salesman from New York gave a bottle of beer to an Ohio proctologist, on his way to the hospital to perform surgery, to stop the shakes from alcohol withdrawal. That was the last alcoholic drink taken by either man. These two self-styled drunks found that the only way they could remain sober was to help other drunks. The result was AA. Today the miracle they created, but could not have envisioned, offers American society its best hope of being able to end the drug-abuse epidemic. In the process, the mutual-aid revolution in our midst remains largely unrecognized. It offers new hope to medicine to find a way to rediscover some ancient values of helping people heal themselves and each other. In making use of this revolution, medicine will rediscover the partnership between patient and physician in which the patient is far more than simply a specimen to be subject to high-technology analysis. Patients are the partners of physicians in their own recovery. Not only is the partnership between the helper and the helped reestablished, but so, too, is the spiritual foundation to this partnership.

Today in medicine the average patient seeing the average physician has a better chance of benefiting from the visit than ever before. Doctors who want to help their patients get well have never had a better opportunity to achieve this goal than they do now. One reason for this improved performance is the explosive growth of scientific medicine. Another reason, far less appreciated by many physicians, is the equally explosive and more recent growth of the mutual-aid programs. This free, low-tech revolution promises to be medicine's major asset in its effort to promote healthy life-styles and to lower health-care costs, the key to medicine's future. When it comes to helping kids, COAs, and adults, ACOAs, who are living in "the shadow of the elephant in the living room" (as chemical dependence in the home is often called at mutual-aid meetings), then this new partnership has its finest hour.

The most urgent need now is to explore these new programs scientifically to identify the elements that work and the people for whom they do and do not work. It will be important in the future for both practitioners and researchers to become more involved in the mutual-aid movement so that the collaboration can be extended.

One of the more interesting aspects of these new developments is an understanding of the dependence of the individual on the family and the community. When it comes to behavior, it is easy for individuals to be misled by their own feelings into behaviors that not only are self-defeating, but often lethal. When behavior is brought out into the open, and discussed in families and communities, it is usually possible to find better ways of living; ways that are healthier and more productive. A problem remains, however, concerning the conflict between the desires of the individual and the desires of the community. When it comes to behaviors that are little understood, or even rejected, by the larger community, there is a real risk that the new community-based focus could impinge hostilely on individual choices. A balance needs to be struck with an active interplay between the individual and the group. Mutual-aid programs, using the 12-step tradition, have a long and instructive tradition of combining the wisdom of the community ("the Program") with an outspoken respect for the choices of the individual.

REFERENCES

DuPont, R. L. (1984a). Bulimia: A modern epidemic among adolescents. *Pediatric Annals, 13(12)*, 908–914.

DuPont, R. L. (1984b). *Getting tough on gateway drugs: A guide for the family.* Washington, DC: American Psychiatric Press.

DuPont, R. L. (1986). *Benzodiazepines: The social issues.* Rockville, MD: Institute for Behavior & Health.

DuPont, R. L. (1988). The counselor's dilemma: Treating chemical dependence at college. In T. M. Rivinus (Ed.), *Alcoholism/chemical dependency and the college student* (pp. 41–61). New York: Haworth Press.

DuPont, R. L. (1989). A practical approach to benzodiazepine discontinuation. *Journal of Clinical Psychopharmacology.*

Earls, F., Reich, W., Jung, K. G., & Cloninger, C. R. (1988). Psychopathology in children of alcoholic and antisocial parents. *Alcoholism: Clinical and Experimental Research, 12(4)*, 481– 487.

Engel, G. (1976). The need for a new medical model: A challenge for biomedicine. *Science, 196*, 129.

Kuhn, T. (1970). *The structure of scientific revolutions.* Chicago: University of Chicago Press.

Putnam, S. L. (1987). *Are children of alcoholics sicker than other children?: A study of illness experience and utilization behavior in a health maintenance organization.* Doctoral dissertation, Brown University.

Robertson, N. (1988). *Getting better: Inside Alcoholics Anonymous.* New York: William Morrow.

Saylor, K. E., DuPont, R. L., & Brouillard, M. (1989). Self-help treatment of anxiety disorders. In M. Roth, G. D. Burrows, & R. Noyes (Eds.), *Handbook of anxiety. Volume 4: The treatment of anxiety.* Amsterdam: Elsevier.

Vaillant, G. E. (1980). The doctor's dilemma. In G. E. Edwards & M. Graat (Eds.), alcoholism, treatment and transition. London: Croom Helm.

14

Policy, Issues, and Action: An Agenda for Children of Substance Abusers

Migs Woodside

INTRODUCTION

Public interest and research on children of alcoholics have increased steadily within the last few years. It is now time for legislators and public officials at all levels to articulate a public policy agenda to help reduce the pain, suffering and risk of alcoholism of the nation's 28 million children of alcoholics. It is crucial that the nation's leaders identify major concerns, develop an action agenda and implement public policies to make improvements in the lives of many. Development of a coherent public policy agenda in these and other areas is critical in alleviating and preventing the major social and public health problems of family substance abuse.

There are 28 million children of alcoholics (COAs) in this country, seven million of whom are under age 18. One out of every eight Americans knows the pain, fear, and loneliness caused by this family tragedy. One-eighth of all Americans experience the devastating effects of growing up with parents who drink too much. It is no wonder that COAs are more likely than others to have physical, emotional, and mental health problems and, because of their numbers, are readily found in all our educational, social service, health, and judicial systems (Woodside, 1988a). Yet, it is only within the past few years that public and professional attention has focused on this high-risk group. While local agencies, schools, health-care practitioners, and others are beginning to develop appropriate resources to meet their special needs, the development of a public-policy agenda lags very far behind.

According to former U.S. Surgeon General Julius Richmond, "The shaping of . . . policy involves three critical areas: the development of a knowledge base, the

330

development of political will and the development and implementation of public policy" (Richmond & Kotelchuck, 1983). At this point, information and knowledge about COAs is growing as a result of work by research scientists and clinicians. While many of the answers to questions of biogenetics are still unknown, an increasing number of investigations are under way. At this time, it is also clear that the public has an avid and ongoing interest in COA issues. Certainly, continued coverage by the media and the many popular articles and books stimulate this interest. However, what is lacking is the blueprint of a plan for public policy, including the identification of goals and social strategies to reach COAs and prevent future alcohol-related problems.

EDUCATIONAL MESSAGES

What To Tell the Public

There is a pressing need to educate the general public about the special risks and problems of family alcohol abuse. If informed, the public can be mobilized to serve as a resource for help. Given their numbers, everyone knows someone, whether a co-worker, classmate, team member, or relative, who is affected by a parent's drinking. All of us can play valuable roles by acting as supportive, nonjudgmental listeners, being good friends, learning about the issue, and finding out about local resources for assistance.

In developing educational messages, it is extremely important to ensure that they are crafted with care. Information must be scientifically accurate, simple, direct, and easy to understand. Quite likely, the feeling, tone, and content of messages will influence whether or not they are heard, accepted, or believed. When messages are painful or frightening, people turn away in despair.

Although problems exist, so do solutions, help, and hope. Everyone needs to know that parental alcoholism is a disease that children cannot cause, control, or cure; that alcoholic parents can and do recover; and that despite the parents' ability or inability to seek treatment, COAs are worthy of help for themselves.

To change attitudes and dispel the many myths about family alcoholism, messages must be repeated often and must encourage the members of the audience to examine their own beliefs. Recently, the Children of Alcoholics Foundation (of which the author is president) analyzed the results of a questionnaire given to over 800 schoolchildren in the fifth through eighth grades (Woodside, 1988b). The findings show that most children think alcoholism is a bad habit, that people drink because they do not care about themselves or because their children are "bad." Most youngsters believe that children can help alcoholic parents stop drinking, if they just try hard enough. Most youngsters do not know that COAs need help for themselves, whether or not parents are helped. Obviously, messages about the causes of family alcoholism must avoid any implications of blame and should be targeted to children as well as parents. The foundation's data show that most youngsters aged ten through 13 have already reached erroneous conclusions about family alcoholism. Without education and information, their attitudes will carry over into adulthood, leading to more stigma and distortion about this family disease.

What To Tell COAs

Since alcoholism runs in families and there is an inherited predisposition to the disease, it is imperative that COAs be given information about their risks. Many do not know they are more vulnerable than others. Many do not know they must be especially mindful of their own drinking practices. In fact, a 1986 survey conducted by the New York State Division of Alcoholism and Alcohol Abuse found that 16.6% of those who answered reported that one or both of their parents were alcoholic—but only 5% of them knew that COAs face a higher risk of alcoholism (Lillis, 1987). While it may be several years before research produces answers about degrees of vulnerability, COAs need to know, now, that they have a greater risk of alcoholism and alcohol-related problems.

Messages about levels of risk and individual vulnerabilities must always be phrased in the most positive terms. The concept that three out of four COAs will not become future alcoholics is far more palatable and easier to accept than messages that focus on the one child in four who does become alcoholic. The need to accentuate the positive cannot be overemphasized in educating a population that lives with so many negatives.

Because of denial and stigma, it is also difficult for many to accept or express the fact of a parent's alcoholism. For example, I heard one little boy tell his class how his dad had ordered him repeatedly to bring him a beer. Each time the youngster brought the can he found his dad asleep. Each time his father woke, he would yell at the child in fury because his beer was not on hand and would order the boy to get it. Again and again, the child reappeared with the beer, only to find his father asleep. This episode was repeated continuously over several hours, but still the child concluded, "Sure, my dad drinks a lot, but he's not an *alcoholic!*" In a similar instance, one large, athletic teenager, who resigned from the school football team in order to take care of his younger brothers and sisters, recalled the day the neighbors called him home from school so he could pick up his drunken mother, who had fallen in the street and was locked outside their house. Although the boy had attended a Student Assistance Program for almost a year, he was absolutely unable to express the fact his mother was an alcoholic. The truth was much too painful.

Youngsters need to know that they are not alone, that millions of others grow up in similar situations, and that help is available. Adolescents and adults need to hear that although a history of family alcoholism may indicate a higher risk for the disease, their own alcoholism is not inevitable. Messages should state that COAs, like all children, possess the ability both to control their own lives and to avoid drinking problems of their own. It is also important that messages targeted to the general public explain that no one—even those without a history of family alcoholism—is immune to alcohol-related problems.

Public Education Campaign

The Children of Alcoholics Foundation operates a referral line that responds to calls and letters from countless professionals, members of the public, and COAs. In the foundation's experience, the interest in and demand for education, information, materials, and help are steadily growing.

Professionals and the public contact the foundation for many reasons. Teachers write because they want to know how to help children in their classes. Physicians call because they need to know what to tell their patients. Therapists contact the foundation to find out how to set up programs, and letters flood in daily from research scientists, graduate students, libraries, and community agencies requesting information.

The Children of Alcoholics Foundation also receives calls every 15 minutes from individuals needing help for themselves. Some call to say they feel guilty and responsible and to express their relief at finding out that they are not alone. Some call to talk about their nightmares, to say they are depressed or suicidal, or to admit their worst fear—that they, too, will abuse alcohol or other drugs. Some callers confide that they are victims of abuse or incest. Others ask for help in locating a missing alcoholic parent. The role of the foundation is to listen. Often we are the first to hear their story. We also send free materials and suggest local resources for help.

A nationwide public-education campaign would help stimulate the already-present interest in this subject. It could give both the public and professionals added impetus to reach out and help those who grow up with parents who drink too much. Such a campaign would reinforce the messages that COAs are desperate to hear. For some, education and information may be enough. The knowledge that alcoholism is a disease and children are blameless brings tremendous relief. By reading or talking with others, some are able to come to terms with the effects of their parents' alcohol abuse on their own lives. Educational messages can also be the catalyst in encouraging other COAs to seek the help they need and deserve.

Raising public awareness about the problems, vulnerabilities, and opportunities to help COAs can improve the lives of millions. Public awareness is central to the advancement and sustenance of public policies affecting them, support for research, prevention, and treatment. A national public-education campaign could bring family alcoholism further out of the closet to be openly discussed and treated.

IDENTIFICATION OF INDIVIDUALS AT RISK

Screening Tests: Pros, Cons, and Precautions

As studies on the intergenerational transmission of alcoholism progress, the potential increases to identify those at risk of family alcoholism. Although no biological marker or specific DNA has yet been identified to predict future alcoholism, a range of factors are now being investigated. Currently, the first collaborative, multifactorial, multidisciplinary study of family alcoholism is being undertaken by a group of the nation's leading scientists. This study is the first to investigate the psychosocial, biological, and molecular underpinnings of family alcoholism within one framework. Most probably, study findings will yield many vital answers about levels of risk and why some COAs become alcoholic while others do not. In commenting on the application of research, Theodore Reich, professor of psychiatry and genetics at Washington University School of Medicine, wrote, "The possibility that persons at risk for alcoholism could be identified before they began drinking holds the exciting promise of true primary prevention" (Reich, 1988).

Three screening tests have already been developed and used to identify children from alcoholic families. These tests are based on environmental factors, using the child's perception that a parent drinks too much and that, in some way, the drinking interferes with the child's life. The tests, which contain from one to 30 questions, have been used to identify COAs in the health-care and school systems (DiCicco et al., 1984; Biek, 1981; Pilat & Jones, 1984).

While simple, accurate instruments for identifying high-risk individuals— whether based on biological or environmental indicators—could be invaluable in prevention efforts, the screening of populations also raises profound ethical and practical concerns. When alcoholic parents are in treatment, identification and labeling of their children as "COAs" can be a positive force. In a therapeutic setting, the COA label is part of a healing process in which alcoholism is understood to be a treatable disease. The label also helps youngsters understand their feelings and experiences and encourages them to participate in self-help or counseling groups. The COA label can help them account for their emotions. No longer do they need to feel isolated or that they are going crazy. At last they know their pain has a reason and a name.

However, in other nontherapeutic contexts, such as classroom or employment settings, labels may have potentially negative outcomes. For example, the administration of a screening test simply for the purpose of making a risk assessment could have a powerful effect on an individual's self-worth and self-esteem. A test to identify COAs as "high-risk" or "potentially alcoholic" could have devastating consequences. It could become a self-fulfilling prophecy in which people believe they are destined to become alcoholics. This sense of fatalism might well encourage them to abuse alcohol.

Likewise, labeling could adversely affect perceptions of COAs by their teachers, school counselors, peers, employers, and others. The COA label may lead others to form inappropriate levels of expectations about students' or employees' achievement or behavior.

In the event that screening tests or large-scale screening programs become factors in the workplace or the classroom, they must be accompanied by effective prevention and intervention programs for those identified as high risk (Blume, 1985). Screening programs need to contain the mechanism for individuals to refer themselves for help. Information should always be available about local referral sources, and supervisory personnel, teachers, and employers should be trained in referral techniques.

To ensure maximum confidentiality, an explicit policy statement should be provided to guide all those involved. Test results should be kept separate from school or employment records in compliance with the confidentiality required by law. Contact with parents and employers and any release of information should be limited to specific circumstances and prior permission for its release obtained from COAs or adult COAs.

As employers take a hard look at health-care costs and consideration is given to future hiring policies, it is important that the pros and cons of screening tests be carefully explored. Without careful study and proper precautions, a great deal of harm can be done to those in high-risk groups. To avoid the abridgement of individual rights and opportunities and still use the new knowledge scientists and clinicians provide, we must begin to formulate the responses and resources that will be needed in the future.

PARENTAL CONSENT

Helping Children Get Help

Denial is a hallmark of alcoholism (see also Chapters 4, 5, 9 & 10). Usually, alcoholic parents deny they have a problem; this denial is usually shared by the rest of the family. Although alcoholism rules their lives, it is also the family's unspoken secret. Many families do not know they are living with the disease until it reaches the most advanced stages. Even then, they are reluctant to discuss it with outsiders. Because of denial, it is very difficult to reach and help children whose parents drink too much. It is hard for sober parents to seek help for youngsters because asking for assistance connotes both a family problem and a family betrayal. It is even more difficult for children to obtain help for themselves for problems caused by their parents' drinking.

Even when COAs seek services, their way is often blocked. Throughout this country, children lack the clear legal right to obtain prevention and counseling services without their parents' permission. But how can youngsters confront parents with the awful truth that it is the parents' alcohol abuse that is ruining the child's life? How can youngsters bring the family secret out into the light? Realistically, they cannot. Often they are too terrified to talk about their own need for help. They are afraid they will be ridiculed, scorned, punished, or told to leave. Instead, they keep their suffering inside and the painful cycle of family alcoholism continues (see Chapters 7–10).

In addition, those who run programs designed to serve COAs are reluctant to provide help because of questions concerning program liabilities (see also Chapter 6). Many care providers are frightened that they will be confronted by a hostile parent. They are afraid of a parent's anger, of abuse to them or to the child, or of the possibility of legal actions. In practice, however, most alcoholic parents deny or hide their alcoholism and stay far away from those who would confront it. A report published by the National Institute on Alcohol Abuse and Alcoholism on the legal liabilities of care givers concluded that the risk "is minimal where intervention is professionally justified, is sought in good faith, and services are rendered with professional integrity" (McCabe, 1977). Nevertheless, many program providers remain unconvinced.

Helping Care Providers Give Help

Recognizing the formidable barriers to help for COAs, the Children of Alcoholics Foundation undertook a survey of state laws affecting access to counseling and prevention services by children of alcoholics and of other drug abusers (Children of Alcoholics Foundation, 1990). The survey found that most states have laws that govern whether and in what circumstances minors may consent to their own health care (i.e., for pregnancy, substance abuse, etc.).

Some states are restrictive, requiring parental consent for virtually all medical or health services that minors may want or need. Other states are more lenient, providing minors with varying degrees of autonomy. The survey also showed that most consent laws do not take into account the special needs of COAs. In fact, only six states have laws that permit preventive substance-abuse counseling for youngsters without parental consent. Of the six states, only New York has promulgated regulations that explicitly permit programs to help COAs without obtaining parental consent. The regulation also requires that alcoholism-counseling programs try repeatedly to obtain the children's permission to contact their parents. However, if a child feels such contact will be injurious, the counselor is still free to help the youngster. Family involvement in alcoholism and addiction counseling should be encouraged whenever possible, but because of family denial and the special problems that children of substance abusers face, states should adopt legislation or regulations that clearly permit minor children of alcoholics and drug abusers to receive help without parental consent.

CHILD ABUSE AND NEGLECT

The Legal Tangle

Public policies regarding prevention and intervention in cases of child abuse and neglect directly affect COAs. There is evidence that children from alcoholic homes are at increased risk of neglect as well as of physical and sexual abuse (Woodside, 1982). In 1988, Congress, acting on information provided by the Children of Alcoholics Foundation, mandated a study of the relationship between child abuse and familial alcoholism, and authorized grants to public and private agencies to prevent and treat alcohol-related child abuse and neglect (Child Abuse Prevention Act, 1988).

At the local level, states have adopted laws requiring professionals to report suspected instances of abuse and neglect to agencies responsible for timely investigation and intervention. However, until 1986, alcohol- and drug-treatment programs faced serious obstacles in reporting suspected child abuse because federal law and regulations required strict confidentiality of alcohol- and drug-abuse patient records (Department of Health, Education, and Welfare, 1978).

The conflict between the federal law, which guaranteed confidentiality to encourage alcoholics and drug abusers to enter treatment, and state laws on the reporting of child abuse led to tremendous confusion. In trying to apply the laws, service providers were unable to give patients the range of services needed. Since federal law supersedes state law, information about child abuse obtained from patients in substance-abuse programs could not be released without the signed consent of the parent in treatment, except in very restricted exceptions. Obviously, alcoholic or drug-addicted parents are unlikely to permit the reporting of their abuse or neglect of their child. Furthermore, child-abuse workers, in compliance with federal law, were unable to report substance abuse by patients they were treating for child abuse. The conflict in the laws left children in jeopardy, patients without needed treatment, and service providers in a legal quagmire.

However, one mechanism was set up to permit alcohol- and drug-abuse agencies to report child abuse and to permit child-abuse programs to report patients' substance abuse. The vehicle, termed a Qualified Service Agreement, was poorly understood and rarely used. It was not well publicized and little, if any, training was given care providers in how to use it.

In setting up a Qualified Service Agreement, the administrators of a substance-abuse program and of a child-abuse agency would negotiate and mutually agree to various conditions of reporting substance abuse and child abuse, as bound by the federal confidentiality law. A child-abuse agency would agree in writing to abide by federal confidentiality requirements as directed by a substance-abuse program and would adopt procedures necessary to protect any patient information it received.

The child-abuse agency would also agree to resist any judicial proceedings to obtain patient information, except as provided under federal regulations. Most administrators did not know how to negotiate or effect Qualified Service Agreements, and even when agreements were in force, most substance-abuse and child-abuse workers did not know how to use them.

In response to a national campaign spearheaded by the Legal Action Center, Congress in 1986 eliminated the need for Qualified Service Agreements as a vehicle to report child abuse. The federal confidentiality laws for alcohol- and drug-abuse-treatment programs were amended to state that they "do not apply to the reporting under State law of incidents of suspected child abuse and neglect to the appropriate State or local authorities" (Children's Justice and Assistance Act, 1986). Unfortunately, many service providers are unaware of the change in the law and still believe they are prohibited from reporting suspected child abuse (Harner, 1987).

It is important to note that, as in the past, the statute applies only to initial reports of child abuse or neglect and requires reporting only in cases where there is danger or harm to the child. To gain access to patient records for an investigation or to initiate or substantiate any criminal charges, child-abuse agencies must first obtain a court order.

Training for Providers

Despite the fact that substance-abuse-treatment programs frequently encounter child abuse and child-protection agencies frequently deal with child abuse resulting from parents' substance abuse, service providers often have little understanding of each other's fields. Substance-abuse professionals working with adults may be unaware of the need to ask questions relating to physical or sexual abuse, or may be unwilling to do so. In a survey of therapists, almost 40% felt that reporting of suspected abuse would harm their relationship with patients and almost one-half of the therapists claimed that they never reported abuse of any kind (Harner, 1987).

Similarly, child-abuse workers need to know about the disease of alcoholism and its impact on family life. All too often, child-protection workers, seeing food in the refrigerator, do not question the presence of empty alcoholic beverage containers. Because of stigma, denial, and the fact that they have not been trained to ask about or respond to substance-abuse issues, a child abuser's alcohol or drug problems are often left undetected or untreated and the abuse continues.

In 1987, the New Jersey State Department of Health and the Department of Human Services entered into a formal agreement that provides for a close working relationship between the Division on Alcoholism and the Division of Youth and Family Services (DYFS) (Waldman, 1988). A key component of the agreement provides for alcoholism-counseling training for at least one child-protection worker in each of the DYFS's 42 field offices throughout the state. Other aspects of the agreement include the development of joint working relationships with family court staff, joint training, and a statewide conference on issues of child welfare and alcohol and drug abuse. As of 1988, 75 DYFS staff members had already received training in alcoholism treatment, intervention, and case finding, and alcoholism counselors were functioning in each of the DYFS field offices (Fiorentino, 1988).

It is vital that *all* state and local government agencies take similar steps to ensure that resources for training are available and that training take place for substance-abuse and child-protection agencies and all the mental health, health-care, and other professionals who come into contact with substance-abusing families.

MANDATED TREATMENT

Keeping Families Together

In some states, the legal definitions of child neglect actually keep alcoholic parents from getting the treatment they need. In other cases, the law can lead to the unnecessary removal of their children. In many states, the abuse of alcohol or drugs by parents is *prima facie* evidence of child neglect. Parents are often deterred from entering treatment because an admission of their substance abuse is sufficient to bring about the removal of their child. Similarly, parents are also afraid to ask public agencies to provide temporary care for their children during the time they are enrolled in treatment programs. The law's tragic effect is that children of substance abusers are subject to permanent removal from their families as a result of their parents' efforts to recover from addiction. Instead of strengthening and keeping families together, the law serves to tear families apart.

To remedy this grossly unjust situation, the state of New York revised its statute to provide that a substance-abusing parent who is "voluntarily and regularly participating in a recognized rehabilitative program" will not automatically be considered guilty of child neglect (New York State Assembly, 1981). Indeed, state law has been changed to require that treatment be provided to substance-abusing parents before their children are permanently removed from their care. However, in most states, children continue to be split apart from substance-abusing parents and treatment is not mandated until after the child has been removed. Without question, states need to consider modifications to their laws on child neglect so that parents and their children have the right to remain together during recovery from parental substance abuse.

Parents' Treatment for Children's Problems

In response to their parents' alcohol or drug abuse, some children act out, become truant or delinquent, run away from home, or abuse alcohol or other drugs. To help these youngsters, and in recognition of the fact that it is their parents' behavior that is causing the child's poor behavior, New Jersey has set up juvenile family-crisis-intervention units (N.J.S.A. 2A:4A-76). In each county in the state, intervention units gather information, including evidence of alcoholism or drug dependency, and present recommendations for action to family courts. On the basis of these findings, "the court may require the juvenile, parent, guardian or family member contributing to the crisis to participate in appropriate programs and services" ((N.J.S.A. 2A:4A-86). Under this law, parents can be mandated to participate in treatment programs if their substance abuse adversely affects and causes behavior problems in their children. On the basis of New Jersey's example, other states should consider the enactment of similar legislation with regard to substance-abusing parents and delinquent children. Instead of judging the children, states should examine the family to determine whether it is the parent's alcohol or drug abuse that is causing the children's problems. Treatment of the parents could eradicate the real root of the problem and reduce the youngsters' delinquent behavior and potential for future involvement in the court system.

ETHICAL ISSUES

Prenatal Counseling

Research on the maternal abuse of alcohol and the damage caused the fetus has been widely documented in reports of the fetal alcohol syndrome (FAS) and fetal alcohol effects (FAE), and consideration is now being given to the ethical issues inherent in the abuse of alcohol by pregnant women. Although there is an extensive body of knowledge and laws concerning medical genetics and ethics, until recently, there has been little focus on the legal obligations of alcoholic mothers to their fetuses. Only minimal attention has been given to the legal obligations of those physicians who care for alcohol-abusing pregnant women. At present, it is unclear as to who is liable, and for what, when a child is born with FAS or FAE.

It is still too early to say whether these issues will evolve into major questions of public policy. However, given the current interest in genetics, the ability of scientists to map the genome, and the work under way to identify genetic markers for disease, these questions are likely to surface with regard to other diseases and to have implications for alcoholism and alcohol abuse (see Chapters 1 and 2).

In non-substance-abuse matters, courts have already been called upon to rule in cases where physicians failed to inform parents of an increased likelihood that a child would be born with birth defects, or they did not perform or interpret genetic tests properly. In such cases, referred to as "wrongful birth" claims, the courts have generally allowed some form of damages (Andrews, 1987). Because FAE and FAS can result in birth defects, it may be possible for parents who were not warned by a physician about the possible effects of alcohol consumption on the fetus to bring wrongful-birth claims. On the other hand, increased public awareness of the risks of FAS and FAE may limit the potential for such claims.

One example of public awareness may be the Anti-Drug Abuse Act of 1988, which required that as of October 1989 alcoholic beverage containers be labeled to read, in part: "GOVERNMENT WARNING: According to the Surgeon General, women should not drink alcoholic beverages during pregnancy because of the risk of birth defects . . ." (Anti-Drug Abuse Act, 1988). The use of the warning label, combined with other public-information efforts, may be sufficient for courts to conclude that parents themselves should be aware of the effects of alcohol use in pregnancy regardless of whether they receive such advice from their physicians.

Future Questions

Further questions for future consideration concern whether or not substance abuse by pregnant women can be considered child abuse. In 1985, a New York State court concluded that a prematurely born infant was a "neglected child" because the mother had abused alcohol during pregnancy (492 N.Y.S.2d 331). In California, following a court decision that the state's child-abuse law did not apply to the fetus of a heroin-abusing mother, the state legislature adopted a law requiring a parent to furnish necessary medical attention to a child and specified that "[a] child conceived but not yet born is to be deemed an existing person insofar as this section is concerned" (Cal. Penal Code, §270). Such decisions and statutes raise the possibility that pregnant women could be required to undergo treatment for alcohol or drug abuse to protect the unborn child from potential birth defects or other problems.

At present, interest in ethical issues is growing. While ethical issues are not yet subjects of conference agendas or topics of articles in the professional literature of the addiction field, the current public attention to "crack babies" may change this situation. It is likely that much of what will come to be established as guidelines or as the basis for legal action in addiction will be borrowed from other health-related fields. However, it is important that substance-abuse professionals, academicians, and public-policy planners be aware that these ethical issues exist. Eventually, they may have a high priority on our public-policy agenda.

CHILDREN OF SUBSTANCE ABUSERS

A Growing Population in Need

Children whose parents abuse mainly cocaine, heroin, or other drugs are starting to attract public attention. As a result of the appearance of crack, the increased availability of all drugs, and the widespread interest in the current drug epidemic, stories about children of substance abusers are often featured in the news. In comparison with COAs, less is known about children whose parents abuse other substances (see Chapter 2). There are few, if any, longitudinal studies of drug-addicted families or evidence of an inherited predisposition to addiction over generations. Drug abusers are a difficult population to identify and study, and even when they enter treatment programs, many do not remain. A further impediment to research is inherent in selecting a specific drug-addicted population for study. Today's drug abusers may be involved with cocaine or speed. By tomorrow, new designer drugs will be used in their place. The constant switching from one drug to another or the simultaneous use of several substances make it almost impossible for research scientists to draw solid conclusions or to replicate their findings. Furthermore, many drug abusers are separated from their families. An ability to locate addicted parents for study does not ensure access to their children. While research has already shown the damage caused newborn infants by maternal drug abuse, investigations of older children have been inconclusive (Deren, 1986).

Children of substance abusers are also burdened with substantial legal and ethical dilemmas unshared by COAs. In general, drug abuse involves unlawful behavior, including the purchase or sale of an illegal substance. Drugs have long been associated with criminality and their use considered by society as a moral weakness rather than an illness. These factors, combined with social stigma, make it extraordinarily difficult for children of substance abusers to ask for help. In fact, participation by a child in a program similar to those for COAs would be tacit admission of a parent's illegal activities. For such children entering treatment can result in severe penalties, including loss of parental income, a prison term for the addicted parent, and disintegration of the family. Few children want to place themselves or their parents in jeopardy (Morehouse, 1988). Children of substance abusers keep their shameful family secrets well hidden.

Another complex issue concerns children of drug users who have AIDS. These youngsters need information about their parents' condition and their own deep-seated fear of contracting the disease. While preliminary programming is being developed for children who themselves have AIDS, the issue of children of drug-abusing AIDS victims has thus far been ignored.

Interest in help for children of substance abusers is likely to increase, at least as long as the national spotlight shines on the latest "war on drugs." Some local, state, and national alcohol-related organizations have already amended their charters to incorporate in their mission the children of all substance abusers. For service providers, this is an especially appropriate action because many programs are already treating parents with dual addictions.

It may well be, however, that the complexity of the issues involved in services for children of substance abusers requires a major new effort for this population. The legal issues and AIDS issues alone are significant and warrant extensive consideration in the development of responses. It is doubtful that the handful of existing programs for COAs could assume this additional responsibility, although some are attempting to do so. In the development of its *Directory of National Resources for Children of Alcoholics*, the foundation found that most programs for COAs were relatively new and served fewer than 50 youngsters each year (Children of Alcoholics Foundation, 1986). Since most COAs are not receiving help, it is unrealistic to expect these programs to have the capacity to handle large numbers of additional children. Clearly, a significant increase in financial and personnel resources is needed in order for the current treatment methods for COAs to help children of substance abusers as well.

CONCLUSIONS

Interest in children of substance abusers has been growing steadily. While much of the focus is on problems caused by parental substance abuse and the need to develop adequate and appropriate responses, there has also been a carryover of interest into the public-policy arena. One outstanding example was the first Congressional Hearing on Children of Alcohol and Drug Abusers, chaired by Sen. Christopher J. Dodd in May 1987 (U.S. Senate, 1987). Other notable examples are the Child Abuse Prevention, Adoption and Family Services Act of 1988 (requiring study of child abuse and alcohol abuse) and the Anti-Drug Abuse Act of 1988 (providing funds for the development of school-based prevention programs for students who are COAs and requiring warning labels on alcoholic-beverage containers). But much more needs to be done. We have a long way to go before the development of our public-policy agenda nears the level of our existing knowledge base or comes close to society's awareness and interest. The issues are many, complex, and thorny. Some—such as mandated treatment, parental consent, and ethical considerations—are downright unpopular. However, if we are to reach our goals to help and bring hope to those who live with the tragedy of family substance abuse, we must also be ready to implement a public-policy agenda to bring about needed change.

We believe that substance abuse is treatable and beatable. We also believe that it is preventable. The development of public policy at this time can be a critical factor in alleviating the major social and public-health problem of family substance abuse for millions in this country.

REFERENCES

Andrews, L. B. (1987). *Medical genetics: A legal frontier* (pp. 138–139). Chicago: American Bar Foundation.

Anti-Drug Abuse Act of 1988. P.L. 100–690.

Biek, J. E. (1981). Screening test for adolescents adversely affected by a parental drinking problem. *Journal of Adolescent Health Care, 2,* 107–114.

Blume, S. B. (1985). *Report of the conference on prevention research* (pg. 7). New York: Children of Alcoholics Foundation.

Cal. Penal Code § 270 (West Supp. 1987).

Child Abuse Prevention, Adoption and Family Services Act of 1988. P.L. 100–294.

Children of Alcoholics Foundation (1986). *Directory of national resources for children of alcoholics.* New York: Children of Alcoholics Foundation.

Children of Alcoholics Foundation (1980). *Parental consent: Helping children of alcoholics get help.* Draft report. New York: Children of Alcoholics Foundation.

Children's Justice and Assistance Act of 1986. P.L. 99–401.

Department of Health, Education, and Welfare (1978). *Confidentiality of alcohol and drug abuse patient records and child abuse and neglect reporting: A joint policy statement, alcohol, drug abuse and mental health administration and national center on child abuse and neglect.* Washington, DC.

Deren, S. (1986). Children of substance abusers: A review of the literature. *Journal of Substance Abuse Treatment, 3,* 77–94.

DiCicco, L., Davis, R. B., & Orenstein, A. (1984). Identifying children of alcoholic parents from survey responses. *Journal of Alcohol and Drug Education, 30(1),* 1–17.

Fiorentino, N. (1988). Personal communication. Division of Alcoholism, Department of Health, State of New Jersey.

Harner, I.C. (1987). The alcoholism treatment client and domestic violence. *Alcohol Health and Research World, 12(3),* 150–160.

In the matter of Danielle Smith (1985). 492 N.Y.S.2d 331.

Lillis, R. P. (1987). *Comparison of COAs' and non-COAs' perceptions of risk and alcohol consumption.* Albany: New York State Division on Alcoholism and Alcohol Abuse.

McCabe, J. (1977). Children in need: Consent issues in treatment. *Alcohol Health and Research World, 2(1),* 1.

Morehouse, E. (1988). Personal communication.

N.J.S.A. 2A:4A-76.

N.J.S.A. 2A:4A-86.

New York State Assembly, Bill #6716-B, Cal. No. 733, 1981–1982 regular sessions, March 17, 1981.

Pilat, J. M., & Jones, J. W. (1984). Identification of children of alcoholics: Two empirical studies. *Alcohol Health and Research World, Winter* 1984–1985.

Reich, T. (1988). Biologic-marker studies in alcoholism. *New England Journal of Medicine, 318,* (3)181.

Richmond, J., & Kotelchuck, M. (1983). Political influences: Rethinking national health policy. In C.H. McGuire et al. (Eds.), *Medicine, dentistry, pharmacy, nursing, allied health, and public health* (pp. 386–404). San Francisco: Jossey-Bass.

U.S. Senate Hearing 100-333 (1987). Subcommittee on Children, Family, Drugs and Alcoholism.

Waldman, W., & Regan, R. (1988). *Affiliation agreement between the division of youth and family services and the division of alcoholism.* Trenton, NJ: State of New Jersey.

Woodside, M. (1982). *Children of alcoholics* (pp. 25–26). Albany: New York State Division on Alcoholism and Alcohol Abuse.

Woodside, M. (1988a). Children of alcoholics: Helping a vulnerable group. *Public Health Reports,* 103(6), 643–647.

Woodside, M. (1988b). What children believe about parents' alcohol abuse. *Alcoholism and Addiction,* 9 (2), 41–42.

15

The Effects of Psychoactive Substance Abuse on the Next Generation: The Epidemic View

Timothy M. Rivinus, M.D.

Human-made plagues, like war, have always involved some degree of human will-fulness and surrender of reason to emotion, the pursuit of pleasure, and greed (Freud, 1974/1920). We find ourselves struggling with new "enemies within." Freud confronted these notions in his essays on the pleasure versus the reality principle (Freud, 1974/1920) and in "Civilization and Its Discontents" (Freud, 1974/1930). Likewise, the existential philosophers (Barnes, 1959) have taught us that we are the children of the times in which we live.

It was a predictable irony that in 1990 the U.S. government would be committed to a "war on drugs" rather than to an effort to examine the psychological and social "enemies within." In fact, this war promises to be no less a failure than was the last war on drugs (there have been at least three such "wars" declared by previous administrations) or than the last major U.S. military effort in Southeast Asia. If there is no popular conviction that such wars should be waged, they are doomed to fail. It may be symptomatic of the naïve and combative way we Americans have of dealing with our problems by fighting "them" (and ourselves in the process) rather than by striving for peace within.

Vaillant (1988), in an essay on the nature of drug and alcohol problems, has said that "what should be understood is that drugs are no substitute for people." In the battle against addiction, a focus on drugs and not on people will have little effect in changing the nature of the problem. Just as napalm and dioxin did not "win" the war in Southeast Asia, "scientific" solutions will not bring us success in coun-tering today's alcohol/drug epidemic. Only by focusing on people will we be able to take the first steps toward at least a partial peace in that war.

William James (1911), in his essay on "The Moral Equivalent of War," suggested that to end the scourge of war, we will need to mobilize armies of the young to wage peace. In our efforts to minimize the use of alcohol and drugs, we must primarily educate our young people and try to prevent their exposure to the dangers of these substances. Equally important, we must also make very strong attempts to help those young people already exposed and traumatized. The addictions begin in the young and their incidence is increased for the children of substance-abusing parents (COSAPs), who not only are genetically susceptible, but have unconsciously realized that the only choices offered them were those taught by alcohol- or drug-related example, and who have learned the lessons of submission, rebellion, and fatalism provided by a substance-abusing environment during their formative years.

Our children have no more choices than we give them. If we expose them to the use of drugs or other maladaptive responses within an abusive system, they will slavishly replicate those roles in their own lives. Clinicians and researchers have noted that these are highly stereotyped roles (Wegscheider, 1981). They may provide a successful defense in a traumatic childhood and family system, but they often do not allow for functional adaptation either in life outside the family or later in adult life.

Without a clear definition of addiction, there can be little understanding of how an addiction process can influence a kinship or social system (see Chapters 5 and 6). The self-help movement and the medical profession have elucidated firm criteria for the diagnosis of addiction and how it operates within systems. No longer is there a wide tolerance for what constitutes the addiction process. Evidence of personal, physical, psychological, social, and spiritual deterioration; loss of control; and damaging effects on the self and others are essential components of the definition of addiction (Schaef, 1987; American Psychiatric Association, 1987, pp. 165–186).

Once addiction was defined as operating within social systems, the effects on other members of that system could be systematically studied. A review of these efforts is the core of chapters in this volume. What to call the heterogeneous presentations of children of chemically dependent families is an open question (see Chapters 5–9), and Jeanette Johnson and Stephanie Brown in this volume warn of the dangers of premature classification of COSAPS with diagnostic taxonomies that focus on pathological symptom profiles and do not include the individual's early development, place within a system, or current strengths and adaptive functioning.

Evidence that children of alcoholics (COAs), in particular, are a special group subject to traumatic circumstances first surfaced in the United States in the 19th-century literature of the Temperance Movement (Lender & Martin, 1982; Pleck, 1987). The temperance literature portrayed the plight of COSAPs, describing physical abuse, neglect, dissipation, infidelity, lack of financial support, and the absence of parents (see also Chapters 6 and 8). After Prohibition, a number of scientific studies of the particular risks of being a COA began to emerge. Current research includes a careful analysis of which factors may be more biologically determined and which may be toxicological, with regard both to exposure to drugs in utero and to the psychological and behavioral effects in later child development (see Chapters 1–3).

The genetic questions in the study of addiction are complicated. Although certain types of alcoholism apparently are inheritable (Goodwin, 1988), why are they not more completely inherited? Does the incomplete penetrance of an alcoholic gene (Blum et al., 1990) represent the complex interaction of nature and nurture (Chapters 1–3)? The biological effects of intoxicating chemicals on the prenatally developing human may be evident in their most extreme forms—the fetal alcohol syndrome (although it was overlooked for generations) and the toxic efforts of other abused substances (Chasnoff, 1989). However, regularly used, intoxicating chemicals may exert a *continuum* of prenatal damage or influence on a developing human that is less easy to detect clinically. Prenatal exposure to psychoactive chemicals affects prenatal growth, postnatal emotional reactivity, and vulnerability to psychological morbidity. Prenatal exposure may even predispose to the craving for and use of chemicals to deal with stresses later in life. The multiple variables involved in assessing the continuum of prenatal developmental toxicology will be a challenge for future research to untangle.

An understanding of the psychological issues of the child of the addicted parent will come from a careful assessment of the severity of the problem and the length of time that the child was exposed during childhood and adulthood to the distorted narcissism and personality disturbance of that parent (Beardslee, Son, & Vaillant, 1986; see also Chapter 7). The chronically progressive, yet fluctuating, behavior of the addicted person, and the tendency for society to characterize the addictions as incurable diseases, weaknesses, or unalterable character states, tends to relegate the addicted and those exposed to them to a leperlike status in our culture (see Chapters 5, 6, 8, 9, and 15). Yet the addictions and their effects on children are potentially arrestable or reversible, as the many therapists who work with them can attest (see, especially, Chapters 3, 7, and 9–14).

Many of the studies of the pathology of COAs have been done in high-risk populations, where personality and sociocultural difficulties have persisted over generations. These present challenges to the researcher, but more studies also need to be done of the offspring of less dysfunctional chemical-abusing families to ascertain the source of their strength and resilience (see further discussion in Chapters 3, 4, and 14). A question raised about COSAPs is, "Aren't the deleterious effects of being the child of chemically dependent parents (or parent) similar to those of being raised by other dysfunctional parents?" The answer suggested by the chapters in this volume is, "Yes, but with important differences." These differences include the "borderline" fluctuating and progressive nature of the parental addiction, the silence that surrounds it both within and outside of the family, and its propensity to recreate its image in the children and the children's children (Chapters 4–13). But differences notwithstanding, the chemically dependent families do provide a prototype for the weaknesses and strengths born of many types of dysfunctional family systems (see Chapter 3).

If we are to come to grips with the fact that COSAPs are our highest at-risk group for continuing the cycle of addiction in our society, then the kind of programs described in Chapter 9, the group outlined in Chapter 12, and the policies articulated in Chapter 14 might be good ways to work toward a peaceful settlement of our war on drugs. If we could address the drug epidemic in the same way that the country mobilized itself to come to terms with the Great Depression, we might set up a cadre of therapists to offer helping groups across the land as the moral equivalent of a peaceful army (James, 1911). Considered in these terms, the interventions described by authors Bianco and Wallace (Chapter 9), Treadway (Chapter 10), and Clark and Jette (Chapter 11) provide clinical maps, generically and specifically, for those interested in using family intervention and psychoeducational methods to promote early change in COSAPs.

Many therapists and counselors come to their work as a way of coming to terms with themselves, with their past, and with their own "enemy" within. A therapist's success, or lack of it, is often relative to whether the therapist has faced his or her past. Psychoanalysts, including Freud (1974/1914), recognized early that the prerequisite for performing useful psychoanalysis on others was one's self-analysis, and the tradition of introspection by teachers and healers goes back to prehistory (Frank, 1973). Many addiction counselors enter the field after having struggled with addiction themselves or because they grew up in chemically dependent families; Chapters 12 and 13 address the problems that can beset the healer.

FUTURE DIRECTIONS

More papers on children of parents dependent on chemicals other than alcohol are sorely needed. A chapter missing from this volume, we believe, is one that would cover the epidemic of very young children of chemically dependent parents, particularly the problems of children of cocaine-abusing mothers (although it is still too soon to discuss this topic definitively). Of those babies born infected with human immunodeficiency virus (HIV) crack babies represent just the tip of the iceberg (Chasnoff, 1989). HIV-infected babies are being born in geometrically increasing numbers in all U.S. cities and are the direct result of the epidemic of injectible substance addiction (Centers for Disease Control, 1989). This is the beginning of a wave of problems that will reach into the next generation and which already is of epidemic proportions.

Another chapter missing from this volume is a clinical discussion of work with very young COSAPs. More research on the effects of addicted parents on young children and how they are elaborated through action, language, and attachment is necessary. Further papers addressing the long-term aspects of the epidemic, particularly in special populations that long have been neglected by our society—including Native Americans, blacks, the poor, and, particularly, all children—will also be subjects of future collections. Native Americans and Eskimos have suffered for generations from the results of heavy alcohol use and its capacity to erode family life and parental nurture (Dorris, 1989; Kolata, 1989; Streissguth, 1988). Snyder (personal communication, May 1989) has pointed out that a treatise, with parallels to the Holocaust and other mass traumata, could be written about the group trauma for Native Americans and for the poor in our cities resulting from the impact of alcoholism and injectible opioids and smoked cocaine addiction on family life, on children, and on an entire culture (see also Chapter 14).

CONCLUSIONS

Drugs and alcohol offer a feeling of quick pleasure and escape from the major discontents of our time, and yet by their very nature have become a scourge of society (see also Chapter 13). Freud (1974/1930) was correct in suggesting that we are all discontented at a basic level and that some of us are more susceptible and discontented than others. In addition to their biological susceptibility COSAPs are often conditioned to adapt to early stressful or traumatic environments in ways that render them more susceptible and discontented. A life includes the right not to be traumatized, not to be exposed as children to agents that may cause us disease (e.g., addictive drugs and alcohol), to be loved and cared for, and to be allowed sufficient space, shelter, nurture, education, and health-promoting outlets for our drives to find pleasure and reduce pain. All children—and adults, as well—deserve to be allowed to grow physically and psychologically in a way that permits maximum positive personal growth and the development of respect for all sentient beings. This is the major social, medical, and political challenge of our day.

If there are 28 million Americans genetically susceptible to alcoholism alone (Woodside, 1988), if untold numbers of children have been exposed to the biologically and psychologically toxic effects of alcohol and other psychoactive chemicals, and if we continue to believe that there is only a "chemical" or biological solution to human dilemmas, then, indeed, we are facing a problem of immense proportions. This problem, fortunately, is being countered by a grass-roots movement toward enlightened self-help (Chapter 13) and public policy (Chapter 14) and by a growing body of data on and practice with COSAPs, and these advances offer us our best chance for victory in our struggle with the social and personal "enemies within."

REFERENCES

American Psychiatric Association. (1987). *Diagnostic and statistical manual of mental disorders* (3rd ed., rev.). Washington, DC: Author.

Barnes, H. (1959). *Humanistic existentialism* (pp. 1–22). Lincoln: University of Nebraska Press.

Beardslee, W. R., Son, L., & Vaillant, G. E. (1986). Exposure to parental alcoholism during childhood and outcome in adulthood: A perspective in longitudinal study. *British Journal of Psychiatry, 149*, 584–591.

Blum, K., Noble, E. P., Sheridan, P. J., Montgomery, A., Ritchie, T., Jagadeeswaran, P., Nogami, H., Briggs, A., & Cohn, J. B. (1990). Allelic association of human dopamine D_2 receptor gene in alcoholism. *Journal of the American Medical Association, 263*, (2055–2060).

Centers for Disease Control (1989). Update: Acquired immunodeficiency syndrome—United States 1981–1988. *MMWR, 38*, 229–236.

Chasnoff, I. J. (1989). Substance abuse: Pregnancy in the neonate. In M. Rathi (Ed.), *Current perinatology* (pp. 56–65). New York: Springer-Verlag.

Dorris, M. (1989). *The broken cord: A family's ongoing struggle with fetal alcohol syndrome.* New York: Harper & Row.

Frank, J. D. (1973). *Persuasion and healing: A comparative study of psychotherapy.* Baltimore, MD: Johns Hopkins University Press.

Freud, S. (1974/1930). Civilization and its discontents. In *The standard edition of the complete works of Sigmund Freud* (James Strachey, trans.; Vol. 21, pp. 57–146). London: Hogarth Press.

Freud, S. (1974/1920). Beyond the pleasure principle. In *The standard edition of the complete works of Sigmund Freud* (James Stachey, trans.; Vol. 18, pp. 1–64). London: Hogarth Press.

Freud, S. (1974/1914). On the history of the psycho-analytic movement. In *The standard edition of the complete works of Sigmund Freud* (James Strachey, trans.; Vol. XIV, pp. 1–66). London: Hogarth Press.

Goodwin, D. W. (1988). *Is alcoholism hereditary?* New York: Ballantine.

James, W. (1911). Moral equivalent of war. In *Memories and Essays* (pp. 265–296). London: Longmans, Green.

Kolata, G. (1989, July 18). A new toll of alcohol abuse: Indians' next generation. *New York Times*, A1, D24.

Lender, M. E., & Martin, J. K. (1982). *Drinking in America: A history.* New York: Free Press.

Miller, A. (1983). *For your own good: Hidden cruelty in childrearing and the roots of violence.* New York: Farrar, Strauss, Giraux.

Pleck, E. (1987). *Domestic tyranny* (pp. 401–68). New York: Oxford University Press.

Schaef, A. W. (1987). *When society becomes an addict.* San Francisco: Harper & Row.

Streissguth, A. P. (1988). A manual on adolescence and adults with fetal alcohol syndrome with special reference to American Indians. Washington, DC: Indian Health Service.

Vaillant, G. E. (1988). The alcohol- and drug-dependent person. In The new Harvard guide to psychiatry (pp. 700–713). Cambridge, MA: Belknap/Harvard.

Wegscheider, S. (1981). Another chance: Hope and health for the alcoholic family. Palo Alto, CA: Science & Behavior Books.

Woodside, M. (1988). Research on children of alcoholics: Past and future. British Journal of Addiction, 83, 785–792.

Name Index

*Subject Index**

*Please note that there are numerous terms used throughout the book to refer to "children of chemically dependent parents," including "adult children of alcoholics," "children of alcoholic parents," "children of addicts," and "children of substance-abusing parents."